Exploring
Christian Education

Exploring Christian Education

Editors:

A. Elwood Sanner • A. F. Harper

Writers:

Thomas Barnard • Chester O. Galloway
Ronald F. Gray • A. F. Harper
Don Hughes • K. S. Rice
A. Elwood Sanner • J. Ottis Sayes
F. Franklyn Wise

Distributed by
BAKER BOOK HOUSE
Grand Rapids, Michigan

Permission to quote from the following copyrighted versions of the Bible is acknowledged with appreciation:

Revised Standard Version of the Bible (RSV), copyrighted 1946 and 1952.

The New English Bible (NEB), © The Delegates of the Oxford University Press and the Syndics of the Cambridge University Press, 1961, 1970.

The Living Bible (TLB), copyright © 1971, Tyndale House Publishers, Wheaton, Ill.

New International Version of the New Testament (NIV), copyright © 1973 by New York Bible Society International.

Weymouth's New Testament in Modern English, by Richard Francis Weymouth. By special arrangements with James Clarke and Co., Ltd. By permission of Harper and Row Publishers, Inc.

The New Testament in Modern English, copyright © by J. B. Phillips, 1958. By permission of the Macmillan Co.

Contents

Preface

Exploring Christian Education was planned as a cooperative ministry. Nineteen professors of Christian education, denominational staff persons, field people, and others concerned with Christian education have been involved in the planning, writing, and editing. Most of these contributors came to their present positions from direct involvement in evangelical Christian education in the local church, either as ministers of Christian education or as pastors responsible for the educational work of their congregations.

The originating advisory committee included: Thomas O. Barnard, Harvey J. S. Blaney, Bennett Dudney, Robert Green, Don Hughes, Irving Laird, Lela London, Koy Phillips, Willis Snowbarger.

The writing responsibilities were as follows:

Chapter 1	A. Elwood Sanner
Chapter 2	J. Ottis Sayes
Chapter 3	Chester O. Galloway
Chapter 4	A. Elwood Sanner, A. F. Harper
Chapter 5	Ronald F. Gray
Chapter 6	F. Franklyn Wise
Chapter 7	Chester O. Galloway
Chapter 8	Chester O. Galloway, A. F. Harper
Chapters 9—12	F. Franklyn Wise
Chapter 13	J. Ottis Sayes, A. F. Harper
Chapter 14	J. Ottis Sayes
Chapter 15	Thomas O. Barnard, K. S. Rice
Chapter 16	J. Ottis Sayes, K. S. Rice
Chapter 17	K. S. Rice
Chapter 18	A. F. Harper
Chapter 19	Ronald F. Gray
Appendices	Don Hughes, A. F. Harper, Richard Spindle

Although nine writers contributed separate chapters, the plan from the beginning was to produce more than a symposium. We wanted a textbook with coherence and a point of view. To this end all of the writers read and critiqued the entire manuscript at various stages of development, offering suggestions to both authors and editors. In addition, the following Christian educators also read the final manuscript and made suggestions that have added unity and strength to the book: John W. Clark, Edward S. Mann, Neale McLain, Richard Lee Spindle, Wesley Tracy, Neil B. Wiseman.

Special thanks are due Dr. J. Fred Parker, book editor for Beacon Hill Press of Kansas City, who shepherded the project from inception to publication.

The first editorial responsibilities were carried by Dr. A. Elwood Sanner. He presided over plans for the book, writer assignments, and first draft revisions. At this point other responsibilities made it impossible for Dr. Sanner to continue with the work. The undersigned was asked to take over the editorial work and see the project through to publication. He must assume responsibility for some major reorganization of content, for changes made in the hope of achieving greater unity, and for the edited style in which the material appears.

All who have had any part in the work join in the prayer that the Holy Spirit may use this text for the furtherance of God's work in the lives of those who read it and who are guided by it in their ministries of Christian teaching.

—A. F. HARPER

PART I

Foundations of Christian Education

Preamble

Because Christian education is an interdisciplinary area, it looks in many directions for guidance. But because it is a discipline in its own right, it must formulate its own point of view as a basis for creating and using its objectives. Definitions, for clear self-identity, and objectives, for a clear sense of directions are, therefore, of prime importance.[1]

Christian education, one of the key ministries of the church, looks to the Bible, to theology, to Christian history, and to Christian experience for the *content* of its teaching. It has a heritage of Christian truth to receive, understand, and transmit. It is also responsible to nurture Christian faith in persons to whom it ministers. It is *Christian* education.

1. R. C. Miller, in Marvin J. Taylor, ed., *An Introduction to Christian Education* (Nashville: Abingdon Press, 1966), pp. 102-3, italics added.

But Christian education is also *education* and must reflect upon such questions as why and how it will go about its task. It requires a philosophy through which it will reach some working conclusions regarding its unique objectives and the procedures appropriate to achieve them.

The laws of learning are common to all fields of knowledge. Christian education therefore needs to master the psychology of learning in order to relate these important principles to its own teaching-learning tasks in promoting the Christian faith.

Moreover, the work of Christian education does not take place in a vacuum, nor, for that matter, exclusively within the walls of church buildings. All learners spend most of their time in a wider social context—in the home, the school, and society at large. Christian education, therefore, needs to have an understanding of these institutions and forces in order to work with them constructively when that is possible, or in order to help the learners cope with these factors when they are adverse.

Christian education is indeed an interdisciplinary area and "looks in many directions for guidance," even while it holds steadfastly to its unique message and methods as an agency of the Christian Church in carrying out the Great Commission.

CHAPTER 1

The Scope of Christian Education

Among American evangelicals, at least, Christian education is flourishing. The evidence for such a statement is manifold:

1. The construction of countless new church buildings regularly includes substantial facilities for the church school. In 1974, nearly 37 million people of all ages were enrolled in these schools in the U.S.A.

2. Such growth of educational activity in the church has produced a need for competent professional leadership and for qualified lay leaders as well.

3. In turn, this need has stimulated a greater academic interest in Christian education on the college and seminary campuses.[1]

4. Many—perhaps most—Christian denominations have engaged in prolonged and intensive study of the nature and purpose of Christian education and have recently developed, at enormous cost of effort and funds, new and comprehensive curricula. Christian schools and colleges have a renewed and growing sense of purpose; and they offer promise of continuing usefulness.[2]

---

1. Donald G. Bloesch, in *The Evangelical Renaissance* (Grand Rapids, Mich.: Wm. B. Eerdmans Publishing Co., 1973), gives a helpful description of the context in which evangelical Christian education seems to be flourishing. For a contrary view, from the more liberal wing of Protestantism, see Iris V. Cully, "What Killed Religious Education?" *Religion in Life*, Autumn, 1971 (Vol. XL, No. 3), pp. 404-11.

2. Cf. Arthur F. Holmes, "The Idea of a Christian College," *Christianity Today*, Vol. XIV, No. 22, July 31, 1970, pp. 974-76.

In surveying the scope of Christian education, we shall consider in this chapter the *what* and *why*. We shall look first at definitions in order to answer the question, What is Christian education? We shall then turn to a consideration of the purpose in order to answer the question, Why Christian education? In subsequent chapters, we shall take an overview of the entire program in order to answer the question, How is Christian education conducted?

I. What Is Christian Education?

A. The Need for Clarification

1. *The Purpose of Definitions*

Definitions clarify understanding, give direction to thought and action, and provide a common ground for mutuality, enabling persons to think together even amidst disagreement. Olive M. Winchester, a pioneer educator in the Church of the Nazarene, frequently advised, "When in a mental fog, attend to definitions." The alternative to such an effort is confusion and needless controversy.

2. *The Use of Definitions*

It may already be evident why definitions in Christian education are essential. Someone may have asked, e.g., What is the distinction between *Christian education* and *religious education?* Why do we use the term *Christian education* in this text? Other questions may arise: What makes education *Christian?* For that matter, what is education? Does the phrase *Christian education* mean education in the Christian faith, or does it mean education of any sort but from a Christian perspective? How will we know when Christian education has been successful?

It is at least probable that many such questions persist because the meaning of basic terms has so often been assumed, especially among evangelicals. The function of the definitions offered here will be to suggest answers to these and other questions. Furthermore, a serious attempt at definition will take us a long step toward understanding the purposes and objectives in Christian education.

B. Representative Definitions

The seriousness with which Christian educators view their task is to be seen in the numerous attempts to describe what Christian education is. Christians representing a variety of theological positions seek clarity of vision and purpose in the educational mission of the church. That mission is of urgent importance and must not be hindered by uncertainty of direction or vagueness of understanding.

Several representative definitions have been selected in order to depict the growing agreement as well as the continuing differences among those responsible for the description of Christian education.

1. *Presuppositions*

Definitions of Christian education normally presuppose or build upon some description of general education. Sound general educational practice is commonly regarded as valid for religious education also. It is crucial, however, to make a sharp distinction between goals of learning which are common to secular subject matter, and the values or philosophy which are implicit in the Christian faith. R. C. Miller has made this clear: "Christian educational theory must not be a footnote to secular discoveries. The goals and values of Christian education are derived from Christian theology and not from secular methodology."[3]

A significant part of the struggle in the search for a Christian education has been the necessity of disengaging it from any educational theory which has a world view incompatible with the Christian faith. The exclusively social goals of John Dewey's educational philosophy may be especially noted here.

Dewey (1859-1952) was an American philosopher with great influence on Western thought and education. A pragmatist (instrumentalist) in philosophy, Dewey developed a naturalistic world view thoroughly hostile to the Christian faith in its repudiation of all concepts of a supreme, supernatural Being.

W. Kent Gilbert has given us a useful definition of education in the broader sense which may be included here as a background for the definitions of Christian education to follow:

> Education, therefore, may be thought of as that process whereby the community seeks to assist the learner to assimilate, react to, integrate, and use those elements of its heritage which are most valued and relevant in such a way that he may grow in his own person and make the greatest contribution to the common good.[4]

2. *Interdenominational Statements*

The most widely circulated and probably the most influential statements have emerged from interdenominational studies sponsored by the International Council of Religious Education and later

---

3. R. C. Miller, *Education for Christian Living* (2nd ed.; Englewood Cliffs, N.J.: Prentice-Hall, Inc., 1963), p. 45.

4. W. Kent Gilbert, *As Christians Teach* (Philadelphia: Lutheran Church Press, 1963), p. 14.

by the various commissions of the Division of Christian Education of the National Council of Churches. An earlier and a later statement have been selected from these studies.

The *Study of Christian Education*, as reported by Paul H. Vieth, in 1947, produced a definition of Christian education which continues to command respect.

> Christian education is the process by which persons are confronted with and controlled by the Christian gospel. It involves the efforts of the Christian community to guide both young and adult persons toward an ever richer possession of the Christian heritage and a fuller participation in the life and work of the Christian fellowship. It is both individual and social in nature . . . It is concerned with the past, the present, and the future—with the past because it seeks to introduce persons to their religious heritage, with the present because it aims to make religion a vital force in every response to life, with the future because it cultivates creative experience leading to growth in wisdom and stature and in favor with God and man.[5]

A study document, *The Objectives of Christian Education*, was published in 1958 and contained the following description:

> Christian education is a means by which the church seeks to help persons respond to the Gospel (the message of God's redeeming love in Jesus Christ) and to grow in their understanding of its promises and their acceptance of its claims . . . Christian education is a life-long process by which persons are led to commitment to Jesus Christ, by helping them to understand and accept the Christian faith and its implications for time and eternity, and to an increasing understanding and more effective expression of Christian faith in relation to God and in all human relationships.[6]

3. *Statements by Prominent Scholars*

Each of these men is widely influential through his work as an educator and writer. Each represents a school of thought or point of view rather than a single denomination.

> *Lewis J. Sherrill:* [Christian education is] the attempt, ordinarily by members of the Christian community, to participate in and to guide the changes which take place in persons in their relationships with God, with the church, with other persons, with the physical world, and with oneself.[7]

---

5. Paul H. Vieth, *The Church and Christian Education* (St. Louis: Bethany Press, 1947), p. 52.

6. *The Objectives of Christian Education: A Study Document* (New York: National Council of the Churches of Christ in the U.S.A., 1958), p. 18.

7. Lewis J. Sherrill, *The Gift of Power* (New York: The Macmillan Co., 1955), p. 77.

L. Harold Dewolf: Christian education would then be described as the nurture of Christian commitment and character, in the Christian church, by the teaching of the true Word of God through the use of the Bible and catechisms or other church manuals, in constant relevance to life as experienced and including much group process.[8]

Randolph C. Miller: Christian education means telling the story of God's mighty acts in such a way that the listener participates in the dialogue and comes into an engagement with God in his daily life, and therefore sees the meaning of his life in a new way, and he is reborn daily with Christ as he lives in community as a Christian in the world.[9]

4. *Denominational Statements*

Many Christian churches have sponsored intensive studies of Christian education in preparation for the development of new curricula. Among these are the Lutheran Church of America and the United Church of Christ. Each group has given special thought to its definition of Christian education.

Lutheran Church of America: Christian education is a process in which persons are confronted and quickened and transformed by the Christian Gospel, and led into and nurtured within the church, the community which believes, lives, and proclaims the Gospel. In this process the learner becomes a willing and active participant.[10]

United Church of Christ: Christian education is the attempt "to introduce persons into the life and mission of the community of Christian faith."[11]

5. *Evangelical Statements*

Evangelicals have become increasingly aware of the need for improved understanding and articulation of the nature, aims, and philosophy of Christian education. J. Edward Hakes, editor of *An Introduction to Evangelical Christian Education,* has issued a call for a more scholarly approach to the study and work of Christian education on the part of evangelicals. According to Hakes, the problems to be solved within evangelical education in general include: (1) "the development of a comprehensive philosophy" ("Evangelicals have stopped short of spelling out fully their distinctive educational view-

---

8. L. Harold Dewolf, *Teaching Our Faith in God* (New York: Abingdon Press, 1963), p. 21.

9. R. C. Miller, in *Introduction to Christian Education,* Marvin Taylor, ed. (New York: Abingdon Press, 1966), p. 102.

10. Gilbert, *As Christians Teach,* pp. 153-54.

11. Roger L. Shinn, *The Educational Mission of Our Church* (Boston and Philadelphia: United Church Press, 1962), p. 20.

point"); (2) "creation of adequate aims and objectives"; (3) "wider acquaintance with learning theory"; (4) "preparation of professionals"; and (5) "training of lay personnel."[12]

Evangelicals who have attempted to formulate a definition or description of Christian education include C. B. Eavey and also a group of writers from the Church of God (Anderson, Ind.).

> *C. B. Eavey:* To understand Christian education, one must first gain a clear idea of the nature of education in general . . . Basically, education is a process of change undergone by human beings as they interact with their environment . . . One must have a clear idea . . . of the nature of religious education also . . . It is education which has for its purpose, first, the gaining of personal religious faith . . . and, second, the development of that faith . . . One must also have a correct conception of the nature of Christianity. Christian education has no existence in its own right . . . Christian faith and Christian education are inseparable; wherever the first exists, the second is found.[13]

> *T. Franklin Miller:* Whenever one surrenders to Christ in full commitment of his life and his nature partakes of the divine nature, there is a difference in the quality of his relationship to God; but prior to, during and forever following such a great decision, there must be the nurture and support of the Christian community.

> Education in the church concerns itself with the nurture of persons in all their relationships throughout the life-span.[14]

6. *A Roman Catholic Statement*

The Roman Catholic church has long been associated with a vast and intensive system of education. The following definition, by Redden and Ryan, is representative of a prevailing philosophy of education in that church:

> Education is the deliberate and systematic influence extended by the mature person upon the immature through instruction, discipline, and the harmonious development of all the powers of the human being, physical, social, intellectual, moral, aesthetic, and spiritual, according to their essential hierarchy, by and for their individual and social uses, and directed toward the union of the educand with the Creator as the final end.[15]

---

12. J. Edward Hakes, in Taylor, *Introduction,* pp. 325-26.
13. C. B. Eavey, *History of Christian Education* (Chicago: Moody Press, 1964), pp. 7-17, passim.
14. T. Franklin Miller, *et al., Basics for Teaching in the Church* (Anderson, Ind.: Warner Press, Inc., 1968), p. 17.
15. John D. Redden and Francis A. Ryan, *A Catholic Philosophy of Education,* rev. ed. (Milwaukee: Bruce Publishing Co., 1956), pp. 23-24.

7. An Emerging Consensus

It would appear that a commonality of convictions is developing with respect to the elements essential to an adequate definition of Christian education. Theological and philosophical differences obviously continue to exist, but a consensus is emerging and includes the following factors:

a. Christian education in the Church. Agreement seems virtually universal that the Church, conceived as the Body of Christ, *has* an educational ministry, and that this ministry undergirds and contributes to all other ministries of the Church. This is not to suggest that Christian educators harbor a latent inclination to dominate the other ministries—only that the Church seeks to effect change, and this is the process of education. Nothing the Church does can be isolated from the educational task. We may assert, with Dr. Shinn, "An effective Christian education program . . . needs to be planned in the light of the total mission of the church."[16]

b. The transmission of a heritage. The conviction is vigorous that Christian education must concern itself with the transmission of the essential Christian heritage of faith and life, i.e., of doctrine and ethics. That heritage is to be found first of all in the Scriptures and then also in Christian history and theology. The Christian gospel, and the Bible which conveys the "good news," are essentials in Christian education.

c. The significance of personal change. If Christian education was once either content-centered or experience-centered, it is no longer so. Education must involve a lively interaction of both. Most Christian educators insist that content *and* experience are essential to Christian nurture. The treasures of the Bible, e.g., must be made relevant and meaningful in the experience of the learner before constructive personal change will occur. It is agreed that without an internalization of the gospel message, Christian education is largely unsuccessful. Both biblical content and Christian experience are, therefore, indispensable to the educational task of the church.

d. The concept of service and mission. Another conviction in this emerging consensus is that Christian education should communicate a sense of stewardship as a philosophy of life. In all of his relationships the Christian disciple should be motivated by a desire to serve God and man; he is to be a redemptive, healing force in the church and in society at large.

---

16. Shinn, *Educational Mission*, p. 9.

C. Essentials for a Wesleyan Definition

Wesleyan evangelicals share with other Christians the conviction that Christian education is of crucial importance and join in the pursuit of excellence in the performance of the educational task. What are the essentials for a definition of Christian education compatible with the Arminian-Wesleyan persuasion?

1. Theological and Religious Presuppositions

Wesleyans are committed to the historic Christian faith, as expressed in the Nicene and Apostles' creeds, and to the key doctrines of the Protestant Reformation, such as justification by faith, the supremacy of the Scriptures, and the universal priesthood of believers. They sense a special calling, however, to stress the biblical teaching on original sin, prevenient grace, the new birth, Christian perfection, and the Spirit-filled life. It is their aim to walk in the Spirit, i.e., to exemplify the fruit of the Spirit, and to seek the glory of God and the redemption of man in a spirit of perfect love. All of these theological and religious factors are presupposed in a Wesleyan definition of Christian education.

2. Consistency in Purpose and Objectives

As we have already seen, our values and goals spring from Christian theology rather than from educational philosophy, which may be secular in nature. It should follow, then, that the purpose Wesleyan evangelicals desire to achieve in Christian education will be consistent with their theological position. It is hoped that the general purpose of Christian education and supporting goals proposed and discussed later in this chapter will give evidence of that consistency.

The relationship between theological position and educational purpose explains the fact, for example, that for Wesleyan evangelicals evangelism has a high priority among the objectives of Christian education.

3. Openness to Contemporary Discoveries

Historically, one of the characteristics of Wesleyan-Arminianism has been a spirit of charity and flexibility in dealing with Christians of contrasting theological viewpoints.[17] This spirit of generosity is not to be confused with the absence of convictions. It is rather the expression of the unique genius of Wesleyan thought—the conviction

---

17. See John Wesley's sermon "Catholic Christianity," *The Works of John Wesley* (Kansas City: Nazarene Publishing House, n.d., reprint of 1872 ed.), 5:492-504.

that perfect love should be the spring or motive of all the believer's attitudes and actions. It is possible to combine charity with commit-ment.

This spirit of openness enables the Wesleyan to be sympathetic, e.g., with the consensus that is emerging in the current study of Christian education. Without yielding "a hair's breadth" (Wesley) on basic convictions, the Wesleyan eagerly learns from all scholars, including those whose theological or philosophical position may differ from his own. The Wesleyan evangelical will be alert to contemporary discoveries in all fields and open to insights that may enrich the educational process. The need for such a spirit may be especially great in Christian education, because its roots draw nourishment from so many fields of learning.

D. Toward a Wesleyan Definition

The view held here is that Christian education is integral to the very life of the church; that the church, in its educational task, should seek to transmit the Christian gospel and do so in such a way as to induce evangelical change in all learners; and that these changes will include conversion, entire sanctification, personal growth, and the development of a sense of stewardship and mission as an enduring philosophy of life. We offer this definition:

> Christian education may, then, be defined as one of the essential ministries of the church *(ecclesia)*, by means of which the fellowship *(koinonia)* of believers seeks: (1) to prepare all learners to receive the power of the gospel in conversion and entire sanctification; (2) to inspire and lead them to experience personal growth in the Christian graces and in the knowledge of the truth as it is in Jesus; and (3) to assist them in preparing for and finding a place of productive service in the Body of Christ and in the world outside the Church.

II. WHY CHRISTIAN EDUCATION?

A. The Importance of Objectives

Objectives, purposes, and goals—terms often used interchangeably—are universally acknowledged to be indispensable in any educational process. An analysis of the nature and function of objectives will point up their importance.

1. *The Nature of Objectives*

What is an objective? An objective is a goal, a target. As R. C.

Miller puts it, "An objective is the point toward which an army is advancing."[18]

Objectives may vary in their nature or character. They may be *psychological, operational,* or *theological.*[19] That is, they may stress personal changes hoped for, or techniques by means of which Christian education is carried on, or the content of the curriculum. Objectives may be general or specific, i.e., they may attempt to state an overall, general policy, or they may articulate intermediate goals or steps by which a primary purpose is to be achieved.

A consensus seems to prevail that objectives should be neither content-centered nor experience-centered but should rather combine the two. Majority opinion also seems to favor the formulation of a single basic objective for Christian education in order to clarify overall policy. In order to be more specific, this broad statement would then be followed by a statement of intermediate or supporting goals.

2. *The Function of Objectives*

The importance of objectives is also to be seen in their functions. These include the following:

a. To set the direction of the educational task. "What are we trying to do?" is a question that we must answer. Directions are more important than conveyances, because directions determine destinations. Objectives in Christian education seek to answer the questions of direction. By definition, Christian education seeks to reach certain goals—to move in a certain direction.

b. To articulate the reason for existence. Religious communities may share common goals, as in the case of most Christian churches. Normally, however, each group senses a particular calling or mission. Its unique reason for existence will find expression in the educational objectives the group chooses to state.

c. To provide a framework for all participants. A basic objective may establish overall policy, and intermediate goals may offer more specific guidance, but there still remain the more detailed tasks of the educational process. These include the organization and administration of church schools, the planning and implementation of curricula, as well as the actual work of the Christian educator with activity programs or lesson plans and pupils. The formulation of

---

18. R. C. Miller, in Taylor, *Introduction,* p. 94.
19. See D. Campbell Wyckoff, *Theory and Design of Christian Education Curriculum* (Philadelphia: The Westminster Press, 1961), p. 59, where these terms are used and discussed.

comprehensive and satisfactory objectives insures the existence of a framework in which all educational participants may work cooperatively to achieve the selected goals.

d. To provide a basis for evaluation. We shall not know when we have succeeded unless it is clear what we are trying to do. Evaluation in Christian education awaits further development, but until objectives are clear, no educational process can be evaluated.

B. The Source of Objectives

Given the importance of educational objectives, an examination of their source (as an index to their character) would seem to be imperative. Such an examination has special import for Christian education, lest our teaching become merely a footnote to secular education and fail to draw its goals from the Christian faith.

Educational objectives spring from a variety of sources, but especially from "the learning theory and philosophy of education" espoused.[20] This fact has special relevance for the Christian, whose calling is to proclaim, teach, and practice the gospel.

In the early decades of this century, the Christian Church attempted to carry out its educational task in league with a philosophy of education that proved to be alien to the Christian faith. The renascence of biblical and theological studies, which came somewhat later, led to a sharp break with that philosophy and to a "search for a Christian education." On all sides now, the call is for church education to be *Christian* and not merely *religious.*[21] This means that, from the formulation of objectives and the preparation of the curriculum materials to the organization and administration of its programs, Christian education is to be governed by the gospel.

In the words of Kenneth O. Gangel, "It is essential that the church's education program should be pedagogically respectable. It is even more essential, however, that it be thoroughly Biblical."[22]

C. Statements of Objectives

1. *Interdenominational Documents*

During the past half century Protestant Christianity has given a

---

20. Benjamin S. Bloom, ed., *Taxonomy of Educational Objectives* (New York: David McKay, Inc., 1956), p. 25.

21. Kendig Brubaker Cully, *The Search for a Christian Education—Since 1940* (Philadelphia: The Westminster Press, 1965).

22. Kenneth O. Gangel, *Leadership for Church Education* (Chicago: Moody Press, 1970), pp. 19-20.

great deal of thought to the formulation of objectives for Christian education. This story has been told by several writers and should be perused by all students of the subject.[23]

a. The International Council of Religious Education. This interdenominational body adopted in 1930 a set of objectives formulated by Paul H. Vieth under the aegis of the Educational Commission of the Council. Modified in 1940 by the addition of an objective on the Christian family (No. 6), this statement has been published repeatedly with widespread influence:

1. Christian education seeks to foster in growing persons a consciousness of God as a reality in human experience, and a sense of personal relationship to him.

2. Christian education seeks to develop in growing persons such an understanding and appreciation of the personality, life, and teachings of Jesus as will lead to experience of him as Savior and Lord, loyalty to him and his cause, and will manifest itself in daily life and conduct.

3. Christian education seeks to foster in growing persons a progressive and continuous development of Christian character.

4. Christian education seeks to develop in growing persons the ability and disposition to participate in and contribute constructively to the building of a social order throughout the world, embodying the ideal of the Fatherhood of God and the brotherhood of man.

5. Christian education seeks to develop in growing persons the ability and disposition to participate in the organized society of Christians—the Church.

6. Christian education seeks to develop in growing persons an appreciation of the meaning and importance of the Christian family, and ability and disposition to participate in and contribute constructively to the life of this primary social group.

7. Christian education seeks to lead growing persons into a Christian interpretation of life and the universe; the ability to see in it God's purpose and plan; a life philosophy built on this interpretation.

8. Christian education seeks to effect in growing persons the assimilation of the best religious experience of the race, preeminently that recorded in the Bible, as effective guidance to present experience.[24]

During the quarter century following the publication of Vieth's

---

23. See C. B. Eavey, "Aims and Objectives of Christian Education," in J. Edward Hakes, ed., *An Introduction to Evangelical Christian Education* (Chicago: Moody Press, 1964).

24. Quoted in *The Objectives of Christian Education,* NCC, pp. 7-8.

statement, changes in the theological and educational climate prompted further in-depth study of Christian education, with resultant revisions in the objectives envisioned. In 1958, the Commission on General Christian Education of the National Council of Churches published the findings of a five-year study, conducted under the leadership of Lawrence C. Little. The committee formulated a single purpose supported by five goals or themes:

> The supreme purpose of Christian education is to enable persons to become aware of the seeking love of God as revealed in Jesus Christ and to respond in faith to this love in ways that will help them to grow as children of God, live in accordance with the will of God, and sustain a vital relationship to the Christian community.
>
> To achieve this purpose Christian education, under the guidance of the Holy Spirit, endeavors:
>
> To assist persons, at each stage of development, to realize the highest potentialities of the self as divinely created, to commit themselves to Christ, and to grow toward maturity as Christian persons;
>
> To help persons establish and maintain Christian relationships with their families, their churches, and with other individuals and groups taking responsible roles in society, and seeing in every human being an object of the love of God;
>
> To aid persons in gaining a better understanding and awareness of the natural world as God's creation and accept the responsibility for conserving its values and using them in the service of God and of mankind;
>
> To lead persons to an increasing understanding and appreciation of the Bible, whereby they may hear and obey the Word of God; to help them appreciate and use effectively other elements in the historic Christian heritage;
>
> To enable persons to discover and fulfill responsible roles in the Christian fellowship through faithful participation in the local and world mission of the church.[25]

The findings of a parallel committee, concerned with the development of objectives for youth, were published in the same year. The principal difference between the two statements seems to be that the human instrument is less obvious in the second document; also the second seeks to focus attention sharply on the divine-human encounter and its results in human life.

> The objective of Christian education is to help persons to be aware of God's self-disclosure and seeking love in Jesus Christ and to respond in faith and love—to the end that they may know who

---

25. *Ibid.*

they are and what their human situation means, grow as sons of God rooted in the Christian community, live in the Spirit of God in every relationship, fulfill their common discipleship in the world, and abide in the Christian hope.

The five general learning tasks are:

Listening with growing alertness to the gospel and responding to it in faith and love

Exploring the whole field of relationships in light of the gospel

Discovering meaning and value in the field of relationships in light of the gospel

Personally appropriating that meaning and value

Assuming personal and social responsibility in light of the gospel.[26]

b. The Cooperative Curriculum Project (CCP). Described as "probably the most important modern curriculum development," the CCP was a further expression of the ferment in the study of Christian education during the 1950s. Sixteen Protestant denominations, including several evangelical groups, founded the Project in 1960 "in order to formulate a curriculum design . . . that they might use within their denominational boards and agencies to plan a parish curriculum." Over 125 persons from these denominations were involved in the Project for a period of four years.[27]

Fundamental to the *Curriculum Plan,* which was the chief product of the Project, is the objective of the educational ministry of the church:

The objective for Christian education is that all persons be aware of God through his self-disclosure, especially his redeeming love as revealed in Jesus Christ, and that they respond in faith and love—to the end that they may know who they are and what their human situation means, grow as sons of God rooted in the Christian community, live in the Spirit of God in every relationship, fulfill their common discipleship in the world, and abide in the Christian hope.[28]

It will be noted that the foregoing objective is very similar to the

---

26. *The Objective of Christian Education for Senior High Young People* (New York: National Council of Churches in the U.S.A., 1958), pp. 14, 34. See Taylor, *Introduction,* pp. 102 ff., for a review of "The Issue" between the two committees.

27. See *The Church's Educational Ministry: A Curriculum Plan* (St. Louis: The Bethany Press, 1965). *A Design for Teaching-Learning* (St. Louis: The Bethany Press, 1967) is an abridged edition of the larger work. The Church of God (Anderson, Ind.) and the Church of the Nazarene were among the participating denominations, as was also the Southern Baptist Convention.

28. *Design for Teaching-Learning,* p. 8.

objective for senior high young people, quoted above. For all practical purposes, the two are identical. This would be expected because several of the same influential Christian educators served on both projects.

2. *Denominational Statements*

In connection with the renewed interest in Christian education, many denominations have reconstructed their curriculum materials and have reviewed and restated their objectives. Several useful summaries and analyses of these changes are available.[29] Two representative denominational statements have been chosen for inclusion here. Both are in the Wesleyan evangelical tradition.

a. The Church of the Nazarene. The church school is defined as a department of the local church, but the objectives of the church school may be thought of as representative of the denominational aims in all aspects of its educational ministry.

The objectives of the church school are:

> To teach the doctrines of Christianity and the standards of Christian behavior as revealed in the Bible, especially as interpreted by the "Articles of Faith" in the *Manual* of the Church of the Nazarene.
> To lay the foundation and begin the development of Christian character in young children.
> To seek the salvation of the unsaved and the entire sanctification of believers.
> To foster a progressive and continuous development of Christlike character, attitudes, and habits.
> To lead to the discovery of the Christian philosophy of life, and the biblical interpretation of the universe.
> To help the home become more effective in teaching the Christian faith.
> To influence strongly in favor of church membership and to train for service in the same.
> To reach the largest possible number of people for Christ and the church.
> These objectives are to be accomplished through devout and diligent study and teaching of the Word of God—the Bible—and through any other contributive agencies.[30]

b. The Church of God (Anderson, Ind.). The Church of God was 1 of

---

29. See Wyckoff, *Theory and Design*, pp. 72-76; Taylor, *Introduction*, pp. 98-102.

30. *Manual, Church of the Nazarene* (Kansas City: Nazarene Publishing House, 1976), Pars. 154-155.8. A. F. Harper has shown how these objectives may become operable in the curriculum of the Sunday school. See *The Nazarene Sunday School in the 70's* (Kansas City: Nazarene Publishing House, 1970), chaps. 4—9.

the 16 denominations associated with the CCP. This church has also been active in following through on the intentions and purposes of the Project, adapting it to their own doctrinal emphasis.

The following statement, similar in form to the general objective of the CCP, yet different at certain crucial points, expresses the educational aim of the Board of Christian Education of the Church of God:

> The objective of the church's educational ministry is that all persons be aware of God through all the ways he makes himself known, especially through his redeeming love as revealed in Christ Jesus,
> and that they respond in faith and love—
> to the end that as new persons in Christ
> they may know who they are and what their human situation means,
> grow as sons of God rooted in the Christian community,
> yield themselves to the Holy Spirit,
> live in obedience to the will of God in every relationship,
> fulfill their common discipleship and mission in the world,
> and abide in the Christian hope.[31]

3. *The Call to Evangelical Scholarship*

In recent years, evangelical churchmen have often noted and lamented that they have given too little serious and informed attention to the philosophy and objectives of Christian education. A call has gone out for them to remedy that situation.

Quoting Edward L. Hakes with approval, Kenneth O. Gangel warns: "Devoid of comprehensive statements of educational objectives, evangelical church education is in danger of being driven further and further into frantic activism."[32]

In response to this call to evangelical scholars, C. B. Eavey cites 2 Tim. 3:17—"that the man of God may be perfect, throughly furnished unto all good works"—as the basis for "a clear and definite aim for Christian education . . . sufficiently inclusive to comprehend within itself all other aims." In other words, "All that is done in Christian education has the one final aim of bringing those taught to perfection in godly life and character."[33]

A further suggestion of Gangel may also be highlighted: "To state it simply and biblically, the overwhelming and all-encompass-

---

31. T. Franklin Miller, *Basics for Teaching*, p. 40.
32. Gangel, *Leadership for Church Education*, p. 26.
33. C. B. Eavey, in Hakes, *Introduction*, pp. 61-62.

ing objective of the church is total Christian maturity for all its members."[34]

D. A Proposal: Toward an Objective for Christian Education

It should be clear, from the foregoing review, that the task of formulating objectives for Christian education is a formidable one. Universal agreement is virtually impossible. A final, ultimate statement is both undesirable and inconceivable. Nevertheless, because of the reasons already implied in our discussion of the importance, source, and history of objectives, the corporate attempt must be made.

The writers of this book, in consultation with approximately 40 leaders and educators in the Church of the Nazarene, propose a basic purpose or objective for Christian education.

This basic purpose is offered here in two forms: first, as a single, comprehensive statement; second, in the form of one objective, supported by seven goals or themes.

In a comprehensive statement the objective of Christian education, as representative Wesleyan evangelicals see it, is:

> *To confront developing persons with biblical truth and secular thought, including the church's history, polity, and doctrine . . .*
>
> *in order that they may respond fully to God's love as revealed in Jesus Christ, through the experiences of conversion and entire sanctification,*
>
> *and may progressively develop mature, Christlike, integrated characters, guided by consistent, practical Christian ethics,*
>
> *be strongly motivated in churchmanship,*
>
> *and be constantly sensitive to the Holy Spirit's leadership in all their social relationships and vocational pursuits,*
>
> *and work redemptively in a changing society as witnesses for Christ.*

The authors present the objective and supporting goals as follows:

> *The objective of Christian education, as these Wesleyan evangelicals see it, is to lead all men to a knowledge of God and to a full development of their powers, in order to help them live as children of*

---

34. Gangel, *Leadership for Christian Education,* p. 30. See also H. W. Byrne, *Christian Education for the Local Church* (Grand Rapids, Mich.: Zondervan Publishing House, 1963), pp. 23-24, for a useful contribution to this need.

God, members of the body of Christ, and redemptive citizens in society at large.

In order to achieve this objective, Christian education, in the power of the Spirit, seeks:

1. *To foster an understanding and experience of the gospel as the power of God unto salvation*

The central import of this goal is *evangelism.* The first and primary goal of Christian education is to assist in bringing all learners into a right relationship with the God who has revealed himself in Jesus Christ. The educational process and the crisis experiences of conversion and entire sanctification complement and support each other. In the words of H. H. Kalas, "Evangelism is particularly concerned with crisis moments of decision from which new life emerges . . . Christian education, which is interested in all of life, certainly should build toward these crises."[35]

The ministry of Christian education will not only prepare the learner to seek the Lord in the personal experiences of salvation but will also move at once to strengthen and sustain the new life through the work of Christian nurture, so that growth in grace will follow.

R. C. Miller sums it up well: "We must confront every learner with Jesus Christ, so that he will put his trust in God through Christ, and by the power of the Spirit live as Christ's disciple within the dynamic fellowship of a truly Christian church."[36]

2. *To encourage a progressive and continuous development of Christlike character, attitudes, and habits*

The essence of this important goal is *Christian maturation.* The New Testament makes it clear that personal growth in the Christian graces must characterize the life of the believer, if he is to please his Lord. The Apostle Paul reminds us that we are to move from childhood to manhood, "to the measure of the stature of the fulness of Christ; so that we may no longer be children" (Eph. 4:13-14, RSV). Moreover, if believers develop in Christ as they should, the whole

---

35. H. H. Kalas, in *Orientation in Religious Education,* P. H. Lotz, ed. (New York: Abingdon Press, 1950), p. 79.
36. R. C. Miller, *Education for Christian Living,* p. 54. Byrne also has a helpful word: "Evangelism is the chief work of the Sunday School. In fact Christian education cannot be Christian unless it is evangelistic. It is winning, keeping, building up in the faith all who are committed to our responsibility. To fail here is to fail in our primary reason for existence" (*Christian Education for the Local Church,* p. 24).

Body of Christ will grow in love and will function properly (vv. 15-16).

The importance of this goal can scarcely be exaggerated.

We believe that the grace of entire sanctification includes the impulse to grow in grace. However, this impulse must be consciously nurtured, and careful attention given to the requisites and processes of spiritual development and improvement in Christlikeness of character and personality. Without such purposeful endeavor one's witness may be impaired and the grace itself frustrated and ultimately lost.[37]

③ *To transmit the Christian heritage of faith and morals in relevant terms*

Several key words cluster about this significant goal: *instruction,* *appropriation,* and, in the best sense, *indoctrination.*

It is no longer true that religious educators look askance at instruction, i.e., the communication of "factual information . . . the telling of the story set forth in Scripture." Christians have a *"specific historical heritage"* which is their duty to understand, appropriate, and transmit to oncoming generations.[38] (See Ps. 78:1-8 for a moving biblical expression of the same conviction.)

Nor is it any longer true, if it ever was, that evangelicals believe instruction in biblical and doctrinal truths to be an end in itself. If learning is an activity by means of which constructive changes take place, instruction in the Christian faith should result in the personal appropriation of these truths. An internalization of the faith, on the part of the learner, must occur if instruction is to be meaningful.

LeBar reminds us that "Scripture is not intended to be an end in itself, but a means to the end of producing life. . . . Speaking or reading the Word is not necessarily communicating the Word. . . . We communicate the truth only when it penetrates the inner life of the receiver."[39]

We accept the New Testament admonition: "Put off your old nature which belongs to your former manner of life and is corrupt through deceitful lusts, and be renewed in the spirit of your minds, and put on the new nature, created after the likeness of God in true righteousness and holiness" (Eph. 4:22-24, RSV).

Properly defined, the term *indoctrination* sums up the import of

---

37. *Manual, Church of the Nazarene* (1976), par. 14.
38. Shinn, in Taylor, *Introduction,* p. 17.
39. Lois E. LeBar, *Focus on People in Church Education* (Westwood, N.J.: Fleming H. Revell Co., 1968), pp. 37-38.

the goal under review. To indoctrinate means "to instruct in the rudiments or principles of learning . . . to instruct (in) or imbue (with), as principles or doctrine."[40] In Christian education, we refer to the principles or doctrines of the Christian faith. The Christian educator can and should pursue this goal, all the while respecting the freedom and integrity of the learner.

④ *To foster a love for the Church as the Body of Christ and as the temple of the Holy Spirit*

The key concept conveyed by this goal is the development of *churchmanship*. It is a primary aim of Christian education not only to invite persons into the fellowship of believers (the ministry of evangelism) but also to incorporate them into the life of the church, to help them become "rooted in the Christian community."[41]

The achievement of this goal involves both *learning* and *doing*. Christian educators must teach what is important to know about the nature of the Church—its biblical basis, and its history to the present time; also the history, polity, and distinctive mission of the sponsoring denomination.

Christian educators must engage the learner in the characteristic acts by which Christians respond to God. It is important not only to learn the meaning of worship, but to worship meaningfully in the prayers, hymns, and sacraments of the church. It is important not only to become familiar with the polity of one's denomination, but also to have some fruitful experiences in cooperating with other believers in the activity of a local congregation.

But prior to and more basic than the suggested learning and doing should be the presence of a love for the Church which Christ founded and which the New Testament describes under the metaphors of the Bride of Christ (Rev. 21:2-3, 9), the Body of Christ (1 Cor. 12:4-31), and the temple of the Holy Spirit (Eph. 2:21-22). Such an affection cannot be *required*, but the pattern may be set, even in the very young, if in the Church *(ecclesia)* there is a fellowship *(koinonia)* of the Spirit.

⑤ *To encourage the full development of individual capacities for the achievement of personal growth, vocational competence, and social responsibility*

---

40. *Webster's New Collegiate Dictionary* (Springfield, Mass.: G. & C. Merriam Co., Publishers, 1956), p. 426.
41. *Design for Teaching-Learning*, p. 8. See footnote 27 above.

It is the intent of this goal to state that Christian education aims to assist in the development of the whole person; it is concerned with all Christian educational processes, whether in the home, the church school, or other educational institutions. Personal *competence,* in the areas noted, is a comprehensive but compelling goal of Christian education. It is the concern of Christians "to see men made whole in competence and conscience."

The chief thrust of goal No. 5 is to highlight the purposes of Christian higher education as integral to the task of the educational ministry of the church. The authors of this book believe it is an error to suppose that the Christian college should pursue goals basically different from those of the Christian home or the local church school. The curriculum of Christian education, according to Wyckoff, "cannot be conceived narrowly any more but must be thought of as broadly as to include its role as the church's agent in helping the person to reorient his total education, and *as broadly as to include the school of the church, the home, and even the college and university.*"[42]

Indeed, it was the confidence of those responsible for the Cooperative Curriculum Project that its proper use would "facilitate the construction of an overall design that defines a conscious linkage among the curricula *at all the institutional levels,* from the home through the seminary."[43]

A study of the philosophy of education undergirding evangelical Christian schools and colleges will reveal that they have a fresh awareness of their educational task and that they believe that task is compatible with their Christian commitment.

The educational ministry of the church includes the work of her institutions of higher learning. These institutions offer Christian youth unique opportunities to develop their individual capacities for the achievement of personal growth, vocational competence, and social responsibility.

6. *To foster the growth of a fellowship in the church and in the home through which all participants will discover the blessedness and healing of a redemptive community*

God has created man with a great need for fellowship with other persons. "Then the Lord God said, 'It is not good for the man to be alone; I will make him a helper suitable for him'" (Gen. 2:18, NASB). When God set in motion the forces which finally led to the

---

42. Wyckoff, *Theory and Design,* pp. 29-30. Italics added.
43. *Design for Teaching-Learning,* p. 6. Italics added.

coming of Christ, He began with Abraham and his family: "I will make of thee a great nation . . . and in thee shall all the families of the earth be blessed" (Gen. 12:2-3). It was therefore natural for his descendants to be called "the people of the God of Abraham" (Ps. 47:9).

This group concept of believers as the people of God also permeates the New Testament and is basic to the thought and possibility of fellowship: "But you are a chosen race, a royal priesthood, a holy nation, God's own people" (1 Pet. 2:9). We have already seen that one of the principal New Testament descriptions of the Church is "the body of Christ" (1 Cor. 12:4-31). "Now you are the body of Christ and individually members of it" (v. 27, RSV).

The New Testament word for "fellowship" *(koinonia)* connotes a variety of rich meanings, including: "association, communion, close relationship, generosity, fellow-feeling, participation, sharing," as well as "fellowship." Of the many uses of this term in the New Testament, perhaps none is more significant than in the benediction, "The grace of our Lord Jesus Christ, and the love of God, and the communion *[koinonia]* of the Holy Spirit be with you all" (2 Cor. 13:14). It is by means of our joint participation in the Holy Spirit that we enter into this fellowship in the church and in the home. Such fellowship has healing qualities and it brings a sense of blessedness.

The entire ministry of the church, including that of Christian education, must take responsibility for the cultivation of this fellowship, both in the church and in the home. It has been said that in looking for a good church school, parents might better examine the life of a congregation rather than its physical facilities. Roger Shinn has wisely observed: "A Church whose members bear one another's burdens and accept some responsibility for the world can overcome considerable ineptitude in education."[44]

Moreover, the church must sense anew its opportunities to strengthen and aid the family in its work of Christian nurture. Donald M. Joy writes: "The church must help keep alive the biblical and human vision of the significance of the family. The family is the institution in which persons are born and shaped, and in which human relationships find their highest meaning." It is possible, in the view of Dr. Joy, that the church, through its crowded weekly calendars

---

44. Shinn, in Taylor, *Introduction*, p. 13.

and its preoccupation with grouping and grading, may have sometimes damaged "the mystery of the fellowship of the church."[45]

We may close the discussion of this important goal of Christian education with Shinn's conclusion: "For both biblical and contemporary reasons, therefore, it makes sense to understand Christian education as the effort to introduce persons into the *life and mission* of the Christian *community*."[46]

⑦ *To encourage a sense of mission in the world as stewards of all we are and have*

The intent of this goal is to highlight such concepts as *service, stewardship, responsibility*—in a word, *mission*. If Christian believers are to live as "redemptive citizens in society at large," they need to have a sense of Christian purpose in their vocations, and a sense of stewardship for all aspects of life. Christian education, therefore, should seek to develop in all learners an eagerness to assume responsibility as members of society and to minister to the material and spiritual needs of their fellowmen.

One's *vocation* is literally his calling. It follows that daily work is one's response to God's call in his life and can be a sphere of Christian influence. A Christian witness can be given by deed and life as well as by word. Further, it is clear from the Scriptures that Christians have a responsibility for the health of society and for this planet. The followers of Jesus are to be salt and light (Matt. 5:13-14) —pervasive forces of flavor, preservation, illumination, and healing for the whole earth. Believers are to share in the sufferings of Christ for the redemption of the world. This is their *mission*.

III. SUMMARY

In this chapter we have considered the questions, What is Christian education? and, Why Christian education? In response to the first question, we have examined several definitions and have proposed still another to serve the purposes of this text.

In response to the second question, Why Christian education? we have analyzed objectives and have scrutinized several representative statements. In particular, the authors have proposed, in two forms, a statement of objectives for evangelical Christian educators,

45. Donald M. Joy, *Meaningful Learning in the Church* (Winona Lake, Ind.: Light and Life Press, 1969), pp. 121-23.
46. Shinn, in Taylor, *Introduction*, pp. 12-13. Italics added.

with special (though not exclusive) reference to those of the Wesleyan persuasion. It is our hope that these proposals will prompt further study and articulation of objectives in Christian education.

We turn next to consider biblical foundations, so significant and so critical in our task as educators in the Christian Church.

BIBLIOGRAPHY

Eavey, C. B., *History of Christian Education.* Chicago: Moody Press, 1964.

In his foreword Eavey explores the nature of education and of Christian education. He reminds us that whether such education is good or bad depends on "the ends sought, the content taught, and the quality of the teaching."

Gangel, Kenneth O., *Leadership for Church Education.* Chicago: Moody Press, 1970.

In chapter 1 the author bases his goals for Christian education firmly in Scripture and in the nature of the Church.

Joy, Donald M., *Meaningful Learning in the Church.* Winona Lake, Ind.: Light and Life Press, 1969.

Dr. Joy examines the purposes and procedures of Christian education from the perspective of an evangelical scholar.

Miller, R. C., *Education for Christian Living.* 2nd ed. Englewood Cliffs, N.J.: Prentice-Hall, Inc., 1963.

Dr. Miller is a recognized leader in the mid-century movement to restore the Bible and theology to central places in Christian education. In chapters 1 and 3 he states his position.

Wyckoff, D. Campbell, *Theory and Design of Christian Education Curriculum.* Philadelphia: The Westminster Press, 1961.

One of the few recent studies of curriculum for the church. In chapter 3 the author deals with the place of objectives in Christian education.

The Church's Educational Ministry: A Curriculum Plan. St. Louis: The Bethany Press, 1965. *A Design for Teaching-Learning.* St. Louis: The Bethany Press, 1967.

Probably the most thorough study available. An exhaustive analysis of the objective and scope of Protestant Christian education.

CHAPTER 2

The Biblical
Basis for
Christian Education

The nature, significance, and content of the Bible are important concerns of Christian education. To orthodox and conservative believers, the Bible is the Word of God; it communicates a valid revelation of God's will. The Bible inspires its readers because the men who wrote it were inspired by God. For this reason Paul indicates that the Scriptures are "profitable for doctrine, for reproof, for correction, for instruction in righteousness" (2 Tim. 3:16).

The Scripture provides Christian education with the foundation for its philosophy, the basis for its principles, and the content of its curriculum. In the Bible we also find clues to methodology and activity. It is appropriate, therefore, to explore the Old and New Testament heritage of our principles and practices in education.

I. OLD TESTAMENT HERITAGE

A. General Characteristics

Because Christianity has retained much of its Hebrew heritage, it may be characterized as a fulfilled Law of Moses, or "a transformed Judaism."[1]

---

1. Marvin J. Taylor (ed.), *Religious Education* (Nashville: Abingdon Press, 1960), p. 11.

1. *Education, a Primary Activity*

The Hebrew emphasis on training and instruction helped them to remain the "most persistent, resilient and irrepressible of peoples."[2] At times education became the sole means of perpetuating their way of life. This was especially true during the Babylonian Captivity, when there was no central place of worship; it was probably during this period that the synagogue was established to sustain faith. The Talmud proclaims, "If you would destroy the Jews, you must first destroy their teachers." Eby and Arrowood claim the Hebrews were the first to create a national ideal of character and a national system of education.[3] Among Jewish people today education continues to be a leading activity.

2. *All of Life Is Sacred*

This concept gave the Hebrews an integrated approach to life; there was no separation of the sacred from the secular. All truth is thus God's truth. The biblical doctrine of creation provided a careful balance between transcendence and immanence and thus delivered Israel from both fetishism and pantheism. The realm of nature and the realm of the mind were not viewed as alien to each other. Truth discovered and uncovered by man's rational processes is a part of God's self-disclosure through a general revelation.

When life is sacred, all activity is for the glory of God. Thus, education in all of its phases came under the sacred canopy. Jesus must have had this concept in mind when He said, "Men ought always to pray" (Luke 18:1). The conviction certainly is contained in the command to love God with the whole person (Deut. 6:5). Paul stresses the same idea when he writes, "Pray without ceasing" (1 Thess. 5:17), and "do all to the glory of God" (1 Cor. 10:31). In contrast, much of modern theology and contemporary education seems to have gone in the opposite direction, making all of life secular.

3. *Education Centered on God*

God is holy. He practices righteousness, and makes covenants with men who will maintain a relationship of faith to Him and obey His commandments.

In the New Testament Paul preached that "in him we live, and move, and have our being" (Acts 17:28). Because God is Spirit, He is not to be represented by any art form or image. No concrete object is

---

2. Frederick Eby and Charles F. Arrowood, *History and Philosophy of Education, Ancient and Medieval* (New York: Prentice-Hall, Inc., 1942), p. 108.

3. *Ibid.*, p. 132.

necessary to faith in His being. Eby asserts that this doctrine gave the Hebrews a good basis for developing conceptual thinking.[4]

God's dealings with men, and His intervention in their lives, were events to be told mouth to ear. Also there were obligations of Sabbath worship and stewardship responsibility. These were to be made known to the children. When the Hebrews failed to tell of God's work and His laws, they failed to educate properly. The Book of Judges shows the disastrous results of this failure: "And also all that generation were gathered unto their fathers: and there arose another generation after them, which knew not the Lord, nor yet the works which he had done for Israel" (Judg. 2:10).

4. *Education Was Practical*

"Learning by doing," now a popular phrase, was standard policy among the Hebrews. Every boy was taught a trade—to work with his hands. Agriculture and mechanical arts were a part of his training. Also the word of instruction was coordinated with visible and active participation. Very little education was of the spectator variety.

A study of the Hebrew family, the holy days, and the festivals reveals the emphasis upon practical outcomes. Everyday issues were discussed, including suitable and forbidden foods and other matters of health.

Conversation, imitation, and example were effective educational methods long before formal Jewish schools were established.

5. *Education Produced Results*

J. M. Price suggests three achievements in Hebrew education: (1) high ideals in religion and morals, (2) outstanding character, and (3) national greatness.[5] Three times the Hebrew system triumphed over the systems of other nations: in Egypt under Moses, in Judea under Solomon (1 Kings 4:30-31), and in Babylon under the exilic prophets (Dan. 1:20). But in all three there was the added dynamic of the unique presence of the Spirit of God.

Today we know more about Moses, Samuel, and David than is known about any of their non-Hebrew contemporaries. Also we recognize that, humanly speaking, Jesus was a product of the Jewish educational system. He was obedient to His parents and in His early years found favor with God and man (Luke 2:51-52).

---

4. *Ibid.,* p. 111.
5. J. M. Price, *et al., A Survey of Religious Education* (New York: The Ronald Press, 1959), p. 23.

B. The Hebrew Family

1. *Education Centered in the Home*

The family was the important place of educational activity, and the father was held responsible for training his children (Deut. 6:6-9). This role of the father is in sharp contrast to our current dependence upon the mother's influence to shape the lives of our children. In Hebrew education, however, mothers were not relieved from responsibility in family training. They actively taught their daughters domestic arts; also, children were urged to "hear the instruction of thy father, and forsake not the [teaching] of thy mother" (Prov. 1:8). Both Hebrews and Christians have had a high respect for women and have held them in high honor, ofttimes higher than in other societies. But the father's authority has been preserved. The current breakdown of the father's responsible place in the home may explain some of youth's difficulties in recognizing civil authority.

2. *Symbols Helped to Educate Children*

Devout Hebrews carefully avoided the use of images in their worship (Exod. 20:4). However, they made regular use of other visible symbols. They used a variety of phylacteries to remind them of walking in the Law and keeping the Commandments. These phylacteries were small receptacles containing verses of scripture; they were bound on the forehead and on the left arm during prayer.[6]

Passages of scripture were also attached to the doorposts of the home, as prescribed in Deut. 6:9; the containers were known as *mezuzah,* from the word "doorpost." Such symbols naturally aroused the curiosity of children and provided parents a teaching-learning situation.

3. *Dramatic Ceremonies Were Teaching Aids*

a. Family rites. The Hebrews attached religious significance to the rites of circumcision, purification, and weaning. They made these occasions times of religious worship and of remembering their covenant with God. The *bar mitzvah* recognized the boy as "a son of the Law," when he had completed his twelfth year. Thus the passage into manhood was observed as a religious privilege and responsibility. This may explain why Jesus expressed His independence and individuality at age 12 during His visit to the Temple (Luke 2:52).

---

6. *Beacon Bible Commentary* (10 Vols.; Kansas City: Beacon Hill Press of Kansas City, 1969), 1:537.

b. Community rites. When the Feasts of Passover, Pentecost, Tabernacles, and Day of Atonement were observed, families gave up some of their usual activities. Everyday foods were set aside for special diets. Houses and regular routines were deserted for tents or brush arbors to impress upon the mind and soul the wonder of God's action in Israel's history.

C. Holidays

All special events among the Hebrews had some emotional attachment in that they were either feasts or fasts; both joys and sorrows were celebrated. Israel proclaimed God as Lord of life, and all events, good or bad, were attributed to Him. Recurring season after season, their holidays dramatically reenacted Israel's history with scriptural recitations and other reminders. All five senses became involved as the whole man interacted with the festivals.

D. Places of Worship

In the Tabernacle and the Temple nothing was intended as an end in itself. Each part and appointment had functional and educational value. In order to gain the worship and educational values, attendance at these places was required. The Community of Covenant shared something important, for they gathered together as the *ecclesia* —"the church in the wilderness," as Stephen expressed it (Acts 7:38).

The first function of the synagogue was instruction in the Law. It is probable that the institution developed to fill a need during the time of exile and national difficulty in Babylon and Persia. More than one exile questioned, "How shall we sing the Lord's song in a strange land?" (Ps. 137:4). Far from the beloved homeland the synagogue became a place of community worship and helped Judah preserve her distinctive way of life in unfriendly circumstances.

With some later adaptations the synagogue became the most widespread of Jewish institutions. Educational innovations included instruction for women, the use of written documents as well as oral tradition, and changes in worship. Great literature was produced and preserved to assist in synagogue functions. Also through the synagogue the Hebrews gained deeper insight into the nature of the true God as present everywhere. Through synagogue worship and teaching they saw that the individual could have access to God and that each should assume personal responsibility for his own actions.

E. The Teacher in Israel

Although the scribe as a professional teacher may have made a late appearance in Israel, there were earlier professional teachers. In Jer. 18:18 we read ". . . the law [teaching] shall not perish from the priest, nor counsel from the wise, nor the word from the prophet." The priests, the wise men, and the prophets were all instrumental in molding the early life of Israel. By personal counsel and practical instruction they guided the faith and ideas of the Hebrews.

1. *The Priests*

Prior to the Exile the priests were guardians of the oracle, teachers of the people, judges, and directors of the sacrificial offerings (Deuteronomy 33). To translate this into modern terminology, one would say their tasks were to (1) preserve the sacred institutions, (2) teach the people how to live, and (3) lead them in their worship.

Teaching was to be a noble calling. No one could have a higher honor, but Malachi laments that the priests did not guard knowledge nor did instruction come from their mouths as messengers from the Lord (Mal. 2:6-7). Also in his day, Micah described their mercenary attitudes (3:11).

2. *The Wise Men (Sages)*

The sages were chiefly wise persons who ministered to individuals in Israel. The proverb became their most common literary characteristic. Influences of the sage are found in the riddle that Samson put to his wedding guests (Judg. 14:12-14). Also Joab seems to have benefited from the words of the wise woman of Tekoa (2 Sam. 14:1-22).

The influence of the sages reached its zenith in the words and sayings of Solomon whose advices were personal and practical. One of the aims of the wise man was to encourage a receptive mind on the part of the hearer (Prov. 10:8; 12:15). The sages encouraged their followers to fear the Lord, i.e., to reverence Him and to be loyal to Him (Prov. 3:5-6; 14:2). Character education also ranked high in the efforts of these teachers of wisdom (cf. Prov. 3:3-14).

3. *The Prophets*

Kent, in his extensive studies of the great teachers of Judaism, analyzes and enumerates the aims, activities, and methods of the prophets.[7]

---

7. Charles Foster Kent, *The Great Teachers of Judaism and Christianity* (New York: Eaton & Mains, 1911).

a. Aims. As probers of the conscience, the prophets' first aim was to point out and counteract the evils of the day. No one was excluded from their denunciations, and often the rulers of Israel were targets of their attacks.

To get men to act justly and love mercy, as expressed by Micah (6:8), was another aim. Righteous acts and loving deeds were to abound among the people. To do less than this would not please God. The prophets wanted to make God's character known to men and to impress upon them that God expected His will to be done on earth.

b. Methods. An internal and divine compulsion led the prophets to respond to external conditions in a variety of ways. They gave didactic names to their children (Isa. 8:3-4; Hos. 1:3-9). Sometimes they delivered impassioned addresses, illustrated by vivid object lessons: Elijah tore his garments; Jeremiah wore a yoke upon his neck; Isaiah walked barefoot through the streets; Ezekiel cut his hair and weighed the clippings. The prophets trained disciples and left an inspired literary legacy. Their written words still speak to the social, moral, and spiritual ills of our society.[8]

4. *The Scribes and Rabbis*

Jeremiah 8:8 is the first reference to the scribes found in the Old Testament. In Jeremiah's time, the fall of Judah and the destruction of the Temple called for a preservation of the written and oral traditions of Israel. In performing these functions the scribes were not only copyists, but they also became editors and interpreters of the Law. They became extremely important during and following the Babylonian exile, because they were able to transform the Jews into a people who loved the Scriptures.

Ezra, as a scribe, read and interpreted the Law. His ministry in Jerusalem after the Exile stands out not only as an example of effective teaching but also as a means of producing revival (Nehemiah 8).

By the time of Jesus many of the scribes had achieved distinction and were given the title Rabbi, or "my Master." Thus, the disciples of Jesus bestowed upon Him this honored title.

The teaching methods of the scribes included public discussion, questions and answers, memorization, exact verbal reproduction of the teacher's words, stories, oral laws, precepts, proverbs, epigrams, parables, beatitudes, and allegories. Kent concludes that the failure of

---

8. See R. B. Y. Scott, *The Relevance of the Prophets*, rev. ed. (New York: The Macmillan Co., 1968).

the scribes was due not to their methods but rather to their interpretation of the Scriptures.[9]

It may be said in summary that the teachers of Judaism produced great results, but too many of them in New Testament times failed to see the fulfilment of their teachings in Jesus Christ.

II. New Testament Heritage

A. Influence of the Old Testament

One needs only to check the number of Old Testament references found in the New Testament to see that from its inception Christianity was influenced by Hebrew education. Nevertheless, God revealed to the writer of Hebrews that "they without us" were not to be brought to perfection (Heb. 11:40). Jesus Christ is the Author and Finisher of our faith (Heb. 12:2); He is the Perfecter of that which we have been taught through the Scriptures (Eph. 3:14-21; Heb. 12:20-21).

B. Jesus as a Teacher

1. *His Emphasis on Teaching*

Because Jesus is the embodiment of Christian teaching, He serves as our best Example for teaching and education. He was a teacher—a designation which He acknowledged (John 13:13, RSV), and by which others identified Him (John 3:2). Entire books have been written to describe Jesus as a teacher and to set forth the emphasis He placed upon teaching.[10]

2. *His Aims*

Although Jesus' primary aim was to bring life to men (John 10:10), He communicated the abundant quality of that life through teaching. His message included a clearer concept of God, deliverance from pain, freedom from false and paralyzing fears, victory over temptation, effective citizenship in the kingdom of God, and training in discipleship.[11]

---

9. Kent, *Great Teachers,* p. 96.

10. Claude C. Jones, *The Teaching Methods of the Master* (St. Louis: The Bethany Press, 1957); Norman Perrin, *Rediscovering the Teaching of Jesus* (New York: Harper and Row, 1967); J. M. Price, *Jesus, the Teacher,* rev. ed. (Nashville: Broadman Press, 1960); Willard H. Taylor, *And He Taught Them, Saying* . . . (Kansas City: Beacon Hill-Press of Kansas City, 1968).

11. Kent, *Great Teachers,* pp. 7-48.

3. *His Methods and Principles*

Direct teaching was a deliberate choice of a method by Jesus inasmuch as He did not commit His message to writing. He emphasized the truths that men already knew, and stressed what had been written in the Scriptures. He inscribed these teachings upon the hearts of men, and the Holy Spirit was sent to bring them to conscious reality (John 14:26). That He was successful in communicating His message is verified by the fact that we have recorded in the Gospels so many of His sayings.

Jesus employed good educational principles. As we see in the parable of the talents (Matt. 25:14-30), He recognized the possibilities in each individual and challenged him to fulfill every God-given potentiality. Jesus began where His learners were and proceeded into the unknown by way of the known. This procedure is clearly illustrated in His conversation with Nicodemus (John 3:1-12). He bound His followers to himself with a personal trust and relationship not only because of His friendship but because He taught with a self-authenticating authority. His approach was simple and direct, appealing to the whole person, but He especially directed His command to the wills of men.

The parable became Jesus' most characteristic form of teaching, but He also used other methods, such as lecture, question and answer, object lessons, and projects. Although He used the customary learning techniques, His teaching was unique and exceedingly effective. Those who heard Him "were astonished at his doctrine: for he taught them as one having authority" (Matt. 7:28-29).

C. The Teaching of Paul

The life and ministry of the Apostle Paul gives strong support for religious education. He was a "Hebrew of the Hebrews," extremely zealous for his heritage (Phil. 3:5); and he had been well schooled at the feet of Gamaliel (Acts 22:3). In his ministry, teaching supplemented his preaching (Acts 15:35). Paul used discussion, argumentation, and persuasion in Thessalonica, Athens, Corinth, and Ephesus (Acts 17:2, 17; 18:4; 19:8). He called himself a teacher as well as an apostle (2 Tim. 1:11) and designated his work as teaching (1 Cor. 4:17). In his church administration Paul recognized teachers as one of the distinct groups of Christian leaders (1 Cor. 12:8; Eph. 4:11).

D. Nameless New Testament Teachers

A host of unnamed New Testament Christians "devoted themselves to the apostles' teaching and fellowship" (Acts 2:42, RSV) and to faithful teaching in the Temple and at home (Acts 5:42). Through this ministry of teaching and preaching, the Church increased.

III. EDUCATIONAL PRINCIPLES IN THE BIBLE

A. Biblical Purpose

The purpose to communicate biblical truth is set forth as a motif in 2 Tim. 3:16: "All scripture is given by inspiration of God, and is profitable for doctrine, for reproof, for correction, for instruction in righteousness." Bible truth is to be taught and learned. The Scriptures are therefore central in Christian teaching. Gaebelein identifies the Bible as the heart of the curriculum of Christian education.[12] For the evangelical, the Bible is central to all moral and religious truth; the truths of the Bible must therefore undergird and penetrate the whole of Christian education.

B. Commands to Teach

God commands us to teach. This ministry is spelled out clearly in both the Old Testament and in the New.

> And these words, which I command thee this day, shall be in thine heart. And thou shalt teach them diligently unto thy children, and shalt talk of them when thou sittest in thine house, and when thou walkest by the way, and when thou liest down, and when thou risest up. And thou shalt bind them for a sign upon thine hand, and they shall be as frontlets between thine eyes. And thou shalt write them upon the posts of thy house, and on thy gates *(Deut. 6:6-9)*.
>
> Then the eleven disciples went away into Galilee, into a mountain where Jesus had appointed them. And when they saw him, they worshipped him: but some doubted. And Jesus came and spake unto them, saying, All power is given unto me in heaven and in earth. Go ye therefore, and teach all nations, baptizing them in the name of the Father, and of the Son, and of the Holy Ghost: teaching them to observe all things whatsoever I have commanded you: and, lo, I am with you alway, even unto the end of the world. Amen *(Matt. 28:16-20)*.

---

12. Frank E. Gaebelein, in J. Edward Hakes (ed.), *An Introduction to Evangelical Christian Education* (Chicago: Moody Press, 1964), p. 47.

C. Teaching Is God's Action

A command is enhanced when the commander himself puts it into action. Job writes:

> Behold, God is exalted in his power; who is a teacher like him? *(Job 36:22, RSV).*

An example of this activity is seen in Exodus 35:34 where God put into Bezaleel's heart the wisdom to perform his task in building the Tabernacle.

Paul reminds us that "the grace of God . . . hath appeared to all men, teaching us" to deny ungodliness and worldly pleasures (Titus 2:11-12). This is a compelling insight, because it means that God gives enabling grace through the educational process.

Faithful parents, teachers, and church leaders work together to release God's grace in the lives of persons under their care. Perhaps, as Wesner Fallaw writes, "we do not evoke (God's grace) . . . for it is always there, a free gift—but we do invoke it."[13] Paul indicates that in this ministry we are "workers together with God"; he beseeches us not to frustrate that grace (2 Cor. 6:1).

He further recognizes this teaching responsibility given to the Church when he tells Timothy, "The things that thou hast heard of me among many witnesses, the same commit thou to faithful men, who shall be able to teach others also" (2 Tim. 2:2).

D. Biblical Principles of Learning

1. *Early Training*

Psychology has emphasized that we are profoundly impressed by those things which we learn early in life. The Hebrews were early advocates of this principle. One of their wise men wrote, "Train up a child in the way he should go; and when he is old, he will not depart from it" (Prov. 22:6). Jesus supported this concept when He blessed the children (Mark 10:13-16). And Paul recognized the effect of early teaching when he wrote to Timothy, "From a child thou hast known the holy scriptures, which are able to make thee wise unto salvation through faith which is in Christ Jesus" (2 Tim. 3:15).

2. *Teaching and Learning in a Free Atmosphere*

The Psalmist implies that both teaching and learning should be uncoerced. In his recognition that God teaches and guides, he ad-

---

13. Wesner Fallaw, *Church Education for Tomorrow* (Philadelphia: Westminster Press, 1960), p. 30.

monished Israel not to be "as the horse or as the mule, which have no understanding: whose mouth must be held in with bit and bridle" (Ps. 32:9). This principle means that the pupil learns best when he is ready and when he has the most favorable environment for response. However, the Psalmist also indicates responsibility on the part of the learner; he is exhorted not to take the attitude of a stubborn mule. His frame of mind is important to learning. Paul stresses the truth that when our spirits are open to Christ, we grasp spiritual truth most readily. To understand spiritual things we must have the mind of Christ (1 Cor. 2:9-16).

3. Methods and Means

Biblical methods and means of education include: (1) repetition, "precept upon precept; line upon line" (Isa. 28:10); (2) warning, "beware lest thou forget the Lord" (Deut. 6:12); (3) object lessons (Judg. 8:16); (4) systematizing or organizing blocks of information. In Eccles. 12:9 we read, "He . . . taught the people . . . and sought out, and set in order many proverbs"; (5) In Neh. 8:8 we find Ezra reciting and reading with interpretation: "So they read in the book of the law of God distinctly, and gave the sense, and caused them to understand the reading."

4. Understandable Language

It is clear, from Paul's experience with the Corinthian church, that he preferred plain, understandable language to either ecstatic utterance or high-sounding rhetoric. The parables of Jesus, as well as His teaching in general, are examples of clear and effective communication.

5. Moral Content

a. Respect for authority and law. Wisdom begins with the fear of the Lord (Prov. 9:10). Jesus instructed His followers to teach His commandments—all that "I have commanded you" (Matt. 28:20). Paul testifies that a knowledge of the law is prerequisite to a conviction of sin (Rom. 7:7).

b. The necessity of the negative. The question often arises, Should the educational approach be positive or negative? Most educators prefer a positive approach; and in this they have biblical support. The gospel is positive in its appeal. Jesus proclaims, "I am come that they might have life, and that they might have it more abundantly" (John 10:10). But the Scriptures also employ negatives easily and freely. Life has a way of presenting choices to which one must respond by avoiding evil. An early command to Adam and Eve was, "Thou shalt not" (Gen. 2:17). The Ten Commandments certainly support the importance of clear-cut negatives in moral teaching.

Good Christian education uses both negatives and positives. Paul placed the positive and negative factors together in his admonition "Study to shew thyself approved unto God, a workman that needeth not to be ashamed" (2 Tim. 2:15). In writing to Titus, he linked "denying ungodliness and worldly lusts" with the command to "live soberly, righteously, and godly" (2:12). Peter describes the Christian virtues of faith, knowledge, temperance, patience, godliness, brotherly kindness, and charity as attainable through a positive partaking of the divine nature. But this occurs only after one has "escaped the corruption that is in the world through lust" (2 Pet. 1:2-7).

6. *Qualified Personnel and Media*

The personnel of religious education, according to the Bible, would certainly include parents (Deut. 6:1-2) and priests (Lev. 10:8, 11). The writers of the Bible also respected the wisdom of the mature; and they believed that men could learn from history if they would. In the story of Job, Bildad exhorts his friend, "Enquire, I pray thee, of the former age, and prepare thyself to search of the fathers" (Job 8:8). In the New Testament we find a special teaching ministry listed along with other designated Christian leadership roles; "God hath set some in the church . . . apostles . . . prophets . . . teachers" (1 Cor. 12:28).

"Learn from nature" and "observe natural phenomena" are popular phrases in contemporary education. Elements of these concepts are also seen in the Bible. The Psalmist reflected upon the nature of man as he observed the heavens (Psalm 8). Job understood that the beasts and the earth could be sources of education (Job 12:7-8). Jesus suggested that His disciples learn from the lilies of the field and from the birds of the air (Matt. 6:25-30).

7. *Motivation and Inspiration*

Teaching is one of the gifts of God to men; He also gives the inspiration to teach. Ezra, we are told, set his heart to study the law of the Lord, to practice, and to teach it (Ezra 7:10). Dedication to teaching must carry one through even rejection by his pupils. When the Israelites rejected both God and the sons of Samuel as their leaders, Samuel thought they had made a mistake. But in spite of this feeling he was determined to help them: "God forbid that I should sin against the Lord in ceasing to pray for you: but I will teach you the good and the right way" (1 Sam. 12:23). Faithful, patient, prayerful teaching are needed when one's followers make wrong decisions.

8. Conversion and Instruction

In Christian education when one discusses the remedy for a sinful heart and life, he must confront the question of crisis conversion as well as Christian nurture. The mutual relationships of teaching and conversion are seen clearly in Ps. 51:13, "Then will I teach transgressors thy ways; and sinners shall be converted unto thee." In Matt. 28:20 Jesus commands us, "Go ye therefore, and teach [make disciples] . . . teaching them to observe all things whatsoever I have commanded you." Paul declares, "Faith cometh by hearing, and hearing by the word of God" (Rom. 10:17). Sinners are awakened by the Word of God when it is faithfully taught or preached.

9. Involvement of the Whole Person

If Christian education is to follow the biblical ideal, it must include the education of the whole person. The cry of the Psalmist is, "Teach me thy way, O Lord; I will walk in thy truth: unite my heart to fear thy name" (Ps. 86:11).

Jesus indicated that the essence of righteousness is to love God with the whole person and to love one's neighbor as himself (Mark 12:30-31). The Wesleyan doctrine of God's prevenient grace recognizes this principle of the wholeness of man. We understand that grace affects the whole personality rather than only the will as in strict Calvinism.[14] The Bible does not recognize a compartmentalized life. One cannot send his mind to school, his soul to church, and his body to the gym. It is the whole spirit, soul, and body that are to be sanctified and preserved blameless (1 Thess. 5:23).

10. A Sure Hope for the Future

The future hope of biblical education is seen in the promise of Isa. 2:3 that the day will come when all nations will come to the Lord's house and ask to be taught. Whether Hebrew or Christian, such a hope will be realized in the new Israel of redeemed people who faithfully respond to the divine call.

As long as the present order exists, there will be a need for religious and moral education. Its popularity rises and falls from generation to generation, but the current "quality of life" emphasis

---

14. H. Orton Wiley, *Christian Theology*, 3 vols. (Kansas City: Nazarene Publishing House, 1941), 1:352-57.

associated with ecology could turn to the realm of the spirit. David Seeley predicts that the day may come when the installation of "antipolluting mechanisms in people" will be more important than "installing them in furnaces."[15] Men must have moral and spiritual guidance if they are to develop spiritual strength.

IV. SUMMARY

The Bible is the Word of God; it is the Foundation and final Authority for the goals and content of Christian education. In it the Christian finds his heritage from the past and his hope for the future. He discovers that he is a part of a great teaching tradition. The Hebrews used instruction effectively to perpetuate their faith and their way of life—they taught through the parents, the priests, the wise men, the prophets, the Temple, and the synagogue. Jesus himself was the Master Teacher, His disciples spread the Good News through preaching and teaching.

God honors such teaching with His grace. Biblical principles of education challenge us to perform our teaching tasks with total commitment. We cannot rest content until all men come to know Jesus Christ whom to know is life eternal. To love Him, to be like Him, to serve Him, is the fulfillment of Christian education.

BIBLIOGRAPHY

Barclay, William. *Educational Ideals in the Ancient World.* Grand Rapids, Mich.: Baker Book House, 1974 reprint.
In chapter 1 Barclay discusses education among the Jews, and in chapter 6 he explores the role of the child in the Early Church.

Eavey, C. B. *History of Christian Education.* Chicago: Moody Press, 1964. Pp. 19-100.
In one chapter Eavey seeks to identify principles of education found among early peoples. He devotes a chapter each to Jewish education and to early Christian educational practices.

Grassi, Joseph A. *The Teacher in the Primitive Church and the Teacher Today.* Santa Clara, Calif.: University of Santa Clara Press, 1973.
Three of the main sections deal with teaching models in the first century, Jesus the Teacher, and the teacher in the Early Church.

---

15. David S. Seeley, "Moral Fiber and All That," *Saturday Review,* 53, no. 29 (July 18, 1970): 56.

Person, Peter P. *An Introduction to Christian Education.* Grand Rapids, Mich.: Baker Book House, 1962. Pp. 15-40.

The author contrasts religious education among the Hebrews with the religious teaching among other ancient peoples—the Chinese, Hindus, and Persians. In a second chapter he explores the nature and mission of the New Testament Church.

Price, J. M. *Jesus the Teacher.* Revised edition. Nashville: The Broadman Press, 1960.

A classic treatment of Jesus' ministry as a teacher.

Sherrill, Lewis Joseph. *The Rise of Christian Education.* New York: Macmillan, 1944.

One of the best sources for the history of early Christian education. Chapters 2—3 treat education among the Hebrews. Chapters 4—6 explore Christian education in New Testament times.

CHAPTER 3

The Historical Development of Christian Education

I. Introduction

Asking *why* may tend to shed some light on the *what* of Christian education through the centuries. Why did people do what they did? What were the needs that prompted educational attempts? How well did the programs reach the objectives they sought? In attempting to answer these questions, we often find parallels to present problems.

This exploration should make us aware of some recurring cycles. Each successive era of the church exposes new needs. God's people respond with new educational objectives and content. These call for new and more appropriate methods.

This chapter should also show us some constants in Christian education. The church's educational task from generation to generation must always witness to who God is and to what His plan of salvation involves. It must also declare the biblical doctrine of man and the unity of the family of God.

Other educative functions show more conflicts than constants. These tensions appear in the following areas:

the church—conservator of heritage or catalyst of change
the church—organism or organization
emphasis—revelation or reason

dependence—nurture or nature

educating—for membership or in membership.

The heart of the educative task centers in its teachers. Throughout history the participants remain rather constant: parents, other persons in the home, clerical, professional, and lay volunteers. However, the role and the degree of responsibility varies from period to period.

Historical perspective should allow greater objectivity in viewing issues currently before us. We can see how others have wrestled with issues and solved the problems. Or it becomes clear how they failed to nurture persons being attracted to the Christian faith or growing up in it. Reading of the successes and failures of others should provide guidelines by which we can avoid their mistakes and build on their successes. Looking carefully at our beginnings and tracing them to the present should provide perspective for the future. From this exploration of history, our objectives should become clearer, our anticipations more realistic, our curriculum more adequate, and our successes surer.

In chapter 2 we looked at the biblical foundations of Jewish education, at Jesus as the Teacher, and at the practices of Paul. In this chapter we follow with Christian education in the church after the death of Jesus. The divisions follow major shifts in educational ventures. These shifts reflect changed cultural settings and religiosocial needs of the Christian community. As Marvin Taylor says:

> Religion and education are inevitable companions of each other; for wherever any religion exists as a living, vital experience, its adherents wish to guarantee its perpetuation. Education is the means most often utilized for initiating both the mature convert and the young into the practices and beliefs of the religious fellowship. This goal is partially—even though indirectly—reached as the community practices its religion; for the act of worship, the observance of ethical norms, and the like are themselves educational in significance for both participant and observer.[1]

II. The Early Church (A.D. 50-325)

A. The Setting

In Antioch, where the followers of Jesus were first called Christians,

---

1. Marvin J. Taylor, ed., *Religious Education: A Comprehensive Survey* (Nashville: Abingdon Press, 1960), p. 11.

we have the earliest occurrence of the divinely appointed gift and position of teaching by persons other than the apostles. There Barnabas and Saul for "a whole year . . . assembled themselves with the church and taught much people" (Acts 11:26). A little further on we read, "Now there were in the church that was at Antioch certain prophets and teachers; as Barnabas, and Simeon . . . and Lucius of Cyrene, and Manaen" (Acts 13:1). From this same congregation the first men were selected, separated, and sent as missionaries to the Gentiles (Acts 13:2-3). Teaching was an appropriate complement to proclamation of the gospel for the purpose of evangelism and training.

J. D. Murch writes:

> The great commission was at once an educational challenge and program. It is most commonly interpreted as a missionary pronouncement. It is that, but it is more. The word "teach" is undoubtedly the most prominent in the passage. They were to *teach*— Christian education is the process by which Christ's purpose is to be accomplished. They were to *go* teaching—Christian education is to be democratic and cosmopolitan. They were to teach *baptizing*—Christian education is to secure open submission to Christ. They were to teach men *to do all things commanded*—Christian education is to include the sum total of Christ's commandments concerning man's duty both to God and to man, and is to secure Christian action.[2]

Paul, in his speech to the people of Jerusalem, reminded them that he had been a student of Gamaliel, educated "according to the strict manner of the law of our fathers" (Acts 22:3, RSV). But Paul was not typical of the Christians of his day. During the apostolic era, there were no formal schools for Christian education. Many of the early Christians were uneducated men and women.

Today, we might be tempted to label theirs an oral society. The Grecian emphasis upon mass education had waned; the dispersion of the Jews had so scattered them that many of their communities were without the services of synagogue education; and the Romans evidenced no great concern for the education of the masses.

1. *Geographic Spread*

But during this period several things happened as the Christian Church moved out of the Jewish milieu. There was a geographic widening as the Church sought to take Christ to the dispersed Jews.

---

2. James DeForest Murch, *Christian Education and the Local Church*, rev. ed. (Cincinnati: Standard Publishing Co., 1958), p. 30.

There was also a search for leadership. While Christ was on earth, His followers sought no other authority. When He left, He named no one person as leader. The Eleven led in group counsel, at times with one disciple dominant and at other times another. However, when the disciples began to be killed or to die, the sources of authority became less clear. At the same time, evangelistic inroads upon the Gentiles had begun. Therefore, the distance from Jesus increased geographically and psychologically as the years passed.

2. Linguistic and Social Communication

No longer did Christian Jews talk only to Jews. By this time Jews were talking to Greeks, Greeks to Greeks, Greeks to Romans, Romans to Greeks, and Romans to Jews. This tended to develop an uncertainty in communications both linguistically and culturally.

In Hellenic thought, reason was the key approach to authority. The mind of man was most important. He arrived at truth through *reason*. The Christian viewed the source of truth from an entirely different vantage point. He found truth through *revelation* from God. A third approach to truth was the mystical emphasis of the Gnostics who stressed the revelation of *experience* as the way for man to know reality. These differences in basic assumptions made communication difficult.

3. Political and Philosophic Pluralism

In addition to complications of communication caused by intellectual approaches, there was a confusion of political philosophies. The Roman world was still dominant, but its form of government was shifting. The old Roman concept of a republic was fading. In its place men were accepting an empire governed by the emperor and his subordinates. The state was beginning to deify itself; they were saying, "God is Roma." In contrast, the Christians felt their citizenship belonged primarily to the kingdom of God. To ignore moral questions in government as did the Romans was anathema to the Christians.

Pluralism in politics, religion, education, philosophy, and culture made the task of Christian education difficult because Christianity had to develop its own identity. New needs had to be identified and met. Confrontation on so many fronts caused Christian leaders to adapt their faith, culture, and education to the world. This seemed necessary in order to communicate with that world. Latourette writes: "Since it has its birth, its first triumphs, and its initial chief stronghold in the Graeco-Roman world, Christianity was profoundly moulded by it. In organization and in thought it conformed in part to it."[3]

B. Needs and Objectives

Anticipating the Lord's imminent return in their lifetime, early Christians saw little need for intellectual development. However, in contrast to the low moral standards of the day, they sought moral training from Christ's teachings, thus endeavoring to keep themselves pure, in readiness for the new Kingdom. The very disfavor with which the Christian religion was regarded served to draw the Christians closer together. In this close-knit society their meager schooling took place. Their characteristic concern for another world further isolated them from much of the social and educational emphasis of their day.[4]

1. *Instruction of Converts and Children*

After the second century began, the rapid spread of Christianity made new needs apparent. Pagans who had been converted needed instruction in their newfound faith. It also seemed wise to consider seriously the education of children who had been born into Christian homes. Because these people had never heard the story of Jesus from the lips of those who followed Him on earth, they needed Christian instruction to enable them to understand, accept, and perpetuate the faith of their parents.

2. *Preservation of Heritage*

Although many adult Christians probably still expected the speedy return of Jesus, there was an increasing desire to know more of His teachings than they had picked up by word of mouth. There was an increasing demand to preserve in writing the teachings of Jesus and His disciples. It was also necessary to correct unauthentic additions to the growing collections of manuscripts about Jesus. Even in the first century, Luke indicated that his Gospel was designed as a corrective to false and incomplete information circulating at that early time.

C. Curriculum and Personnel

Paul implies that the emphasis of Jewish education was carried over into the Early Church. A major concern of his was that the instruc-

---

3. Kenneth Scott Latourette, *A History of Christianity* (New York: Harper and Brothers, 1953), p. 20.

4. C. B. Eavey, *History of Christian Education* (Chicago: Moody Press, 1964), p. 86.

tion be totally in the ideas of the Christian culture. Fathers were to rear their children "in the nurture and admonition of *the Lord*" (Eph. 6:4). This teaching was to be accompanied by love, kindness, mutual respect, and disciplined moral conduct. Most instruction was informal. The Christians shared their witness, insight, and memory of Jesus' teaching spontaneously in their homes and in fellowship with other believers.

However, as the Church spread into Gentile communities and became further removed from the days of the apostles, it seemed necessary to set up training classes to prepare both Jewish and pagan converts for church membership; also to require a period of probation to assure the permanence of the faith of new converts. During this probationary period they were enrolled in semiformal classes. These classes were designed to acquaint the new converts with the biblical backgrounds of the Christian faith and with the moral and ethical standards of the Christian life; here they also learned the doctrinal and liturgical practices of the Christian fellowship and worship.

1. *Curriculum*

There may have been as many as five or more ways in which Christian teaching was conducted in the Early Church:

(1) interpretation of the Hebrew Scriptures,
(2) sharing of the gospel apart from preaching,
(3) public confession of personal faith (both as a creed and as personal experience),
(4) instruction concerning the life and teachings of Jesus, and
(5) teaching of ethical and moral conduct.[5]

This pattern evolved from the synagogue school model. These new Christians were called catechumens, and the classes were known as catechumenal schools. Instruction was given to interested adults and to children in accordance with their probationary status between conversion and church membership. The three-stage progression from the "kneebenders" to "listeners" to the "elect" was reflected in the curriculum, in participation in worship, and in involvement in the corporate life of the community of believers. The curriculum of the catechumenal schools was designed to provide everything necessary to support the student's salvation: here he found moral and

5. Lewis J. Sherrill, *The Rise of Christian Education* (New York: The Macmillan Co., 1944), cf. pp. 142-53 for a thorough development of these types of teaching activities.

religious instruction, the study and memorization of scripture, elementary psalmody, also liturgical and doctrinal teachings.[6]

2. *Curriculum Materials*

The curriculum resources for these schools included: laboriously prepared, handwritten copies of the Old Testament, the Gospels, the letters of the disciples, the *Didache,* and *The Shepherd of Hermas.* The *Didache* was an attempt to provide a collection of the fundamental beliefs of the Christian faith together with suggestions for instruction. Thus it provided both content and methodology. It apparently was patterned somewhat after the manual of instructions for the teacher of the Jewish proselytes.

3. *Teachers*

The teaching office gradually changed from those recognized as having the charismatic anointing for teaching to those who were the elected officers (bishops, presbyters, and deacons).[7] As the church increased in size and administrative structure, the primary responsibility for teaching seemed to pass gradually from the bishops to the presbyters, then to the deacons and finally to minor clerics trained for the ministry of teaching.[8]

The Christian teachers employed essentially the same methods found in the synagogue schools. They stressed accurate memorization, question and answer sessions, and discussion accompanied by the exhortation and lecture of the instructor. Active participation in the life of the community of faith provided what might today be called direct, purposeful experience. There was also much informal day-by-day learning of Christian ethics in the crucible of life.

4. *Varied Patterns to Meet Varied Needs*

Because the Church cannot be treated as a static organ either in time or place, we must consider other emphases in her educational life. Time and sociopolitical tolerance allowed the beginnings of associations of Christian bands. These associations tended to develop influence centers such as those at Rome, Alexandria, and Ephesus. The Christians were no longer small groups of insignificant people. The Church was establishing herself, not just in remote villages, but in the centers of learning. In these centers she had to withstand intellectual attack as well as religious resistance.

---

6. *Ibid.,* ch. 6.
7. *Ibid.,* chs. 6-7.
8. *Ibid.*

Educated people who were being won to the faith wanted to reconcile Christianity to philosophy, to science, and to their society. Out of these needs the catechetical school, a pilot project of higher education, was established at Alexandria under the successive leadership of Pantaenus, Clement, and Origen. This attempt foreshadowed the schools of religion and the campus ministries of today. Christian scholars deliberately located adjacent to the libraries and schools of Alexandria to counteract the influence of the pagan schools. They offered instruction in higher education for Christians who were to become future leaders of the church.

There were also ways in which pagans and Christians intermingled in higher education. Ulich notes:

> In all likelihood, pagan youth studied at the famous catechetical schools of Alexandria, Antiochia, Edessa, and others, though these schools were originally established for the catechumens eager to receive instruction in the new doctrine. On the other hand, Christians studied at the famous pagan universities of Alexandria, Pergamon, and especially Athens.[9]

The contention of these leaders of Christian higher education was that God was the Author of all truth and all knowledge. As followers of God and seekers after knowledge, they felt compelled to be interested in truth no matter where it was found. For this reason, the basic curriculum included both the materials then current in university instruction and the resources common to the catechumenal schools.

The method of instruction in Alexandria took a turn to the question and answer approach in Socratic fashion. This inductive approach was designed to enable the Christian both to defend and to communicate his faith. The questions were such that a principle was revealed in question form and the student's attempts to find adequate answers led him to a confrontation with God. The method also helped to foster appropriate dialog with the intellectual leaders of that day.

A different question-answer approach was used by the teachers in a similar school at Antioch in Pisidia to achieve a different objective. They followed the Platonic method, emphasizing the ability to move from the general to the particular in a more deductive approach to learning. Their approach permitted them to raise a question, then to provide a thoroughly developed and carefully

---

9. Robert Ulich, *A History of Religious Education* (New York: New York University Press, 1968), p. 46.

stated response as a conclusion or creed. The result was a much greater dependence upon credal Christianity and a more uniform belief (dogma) and behavior pattern. Whether for good or for ill, the pattern of the Church tended to follow the implicit educational philosophy of this northern school.

D. Evaluation of Results

How well did Christians accomplish their objectives? The following results may be noted here. First, the Early Church sought for identity. They had been foreigners racially, ideologically, geographically, and religiously. But by the close of this period they had influenced the entire Roman world through evangelism, faith, and nurture.

1. *A New Identity*

Without question, the new settings, new needs, and new approaches to Christian education resulted in new trends in the Church. Out of the modes of nurture a new plant arose. Instead of the relationship model of early Christians, we find an organizational, formal, and credal community developing. Replacing the informal family instruction, there developed a more formalized preparation for church membership. A new law replaced the Jewish law—a law governing the sacraments and priestly functions. The church became institutionalized. Ulich states the cause-effect relationship as follows:

> When the ancient Church became more and more immersed in the complicated society of late Antiquity, it could no longer educate its youth for the *"parousia,"* the new coming Christ, but had to prepare it also for participation and even leadership in the secular community. As a consequence, the separatists had to yield ground to the conciliatory minds.[10]

2. *A New Status*

Second, through efforts to buttress their faith, the early Christians became evangelistically aggressive against the attacks of their enemies. As a result, Christianity became recognized in 325 when Constantine came into power. He gave the Christian religion his personal support and moved toward the church-state synthesis of a later period. How well they lived that faith and witnessed to their world is attested to as follows:

> On the whole, the Christians helped each other and even their enemies; they cherished hospitality and charity, celebrated their festivals in a mood of gratitude, and, living in the Hellenistic

---

10. *Ibid.,* p. 46.

world with its sublime sense of symbolic beauty, developed rituals not only for the purpose of regulating their daily lives, but also for giving rare and elevated form to the rare and elevating experiences connected with their religion.[11]

Finally, they sought to bring man into right relationship with God. At every period during these years there were Christians who were completely committed and deeply spiritual. But there were also those who chose to live as voting members only, without the sacrifice or the satisfaction of deep experience. Ulich summarizes this era succinctly:

> All this—teaching as a divinely ordained mission and not merely as an educational enterprise; the knowing of God's nearness; the moral commandments; the *imitatio Christi* in a spirit of love, forgiveness, and sacrifice; and the urge for ritual expression —all this would have created the desire for strong and hierarchical organization, even if there had not been the threat of persecution during the first four centuries. So strong became this capacity for organization, constantly reinforced by the central consciousness of a divine mission, that under Constantine the Great (323-337) the Christian Church became recognized by the state because it offered the best guarantee of order in a general confusion of ideas and political forces. It continued in this role even when, after the end of the fourth century, more and more provinces of the Roman empire succumbed to foreign invaders.[12]

III. THE WESTERN CHURCH (CA. A.D. 325-529)

The period between the recognition of the church by the Roman Empire and the fall of that empire has carried different designations. We have identified this period simply as "The Western Church."

A. Needs and Objectives

1. *Instruction of Members*

During the second and third centuries no major educational innovations appeared in the church. But when Christianity became recognized by the Roman Empire, many were baptized into the faith without personal commitment to its ideals or precepts. Since these masses of people were unchanged in faith or conduct, new needs suddenly confronted the church. In addition to providing education designed to lead toward membership, the church had to assume the task of educating its own members in the faith. Persons already in

---

11. *Ibid.,* p. 51.
12. *Ibid.*

the church needed instruction in doctrine, training in church cere-monials, and teaching in ethical conduct.

2. *Instruction for Leaders*

To meet these burgeoning needs, bishops' schools were gradual-ly developed in every bishopric to train young men for the priest-hood or to instruct further the clergy of the area. Soon clerical promotion in the church was enhanced by the applicant's having received such an education.

Gradually the life and functions of the priests in each area were subjected to standardized regulations. These more uniform standards resulted from decisions of the various councils, from the canonization of Scripture, and from the general agreement on the major creeds of the Christian faith. This trend soon led to the establishment of stan-dards for the bishops' schools, bringing a much greater uniformity to Christian education throughout the empire.

B. Education and Educators

The third, fourth, and fifth centuries witnessed the church seeking corporate identity in credal conformity. But the Church, as the Body of Christ, found that many of its members viewed the Body different-ly. Along with these doctrinal differences there were also organiza-tional differences. Several groups claimed catholicity for themselves while denying it to others. Gradually, however, the church at Rome assumed dominance. Eventually, the schism between western and eastern groups was complete, and the Roman Catholic church reached its eminence. When the seat of the Roman government was moved to Constantinople, the church at Rome began to loom ever more important politically and ecclesiastically.

1. *Augustine*

Perhaps the most powerful educational and theological figure of this era was Aurelius Augustine (354-430). Latourette has said, "No other single Christian thinker after Paul was to influence so pro-foundly the Christianity of Western European peoples."[13] Augustine's vision of the greatness of God and the goodness of His grace empha-sizing the sinfulness of man carried wide influence among church thinkers. He was careful to distinguish between knowledge *about* God and knowledge *of* God. Augustine maintained that God can be known only through faith. And this faith, for him, was not merely a matter of propositional beliefs. Rather, faith was the means by which

---

13. Latourette, *History of Christianity*, p. 174.

man finds participation in the divine nature, finds an immediate acquaintance with God.

Other concepts of Augustine which were to exert greater influence later included his doctrine of original sin, the predestination of man, the irresistible grace of God, the perseverance of the saints, and the necessity of both baptism and the Lord's Supper for salvation to be complete.

2. Unconverted "Christians"

As mentioned above, the support of Constantine caused throngs to be baptized as Christians. But they were children of God chiefly because the emperor said they were. This new brand of Christian required that the teacher assume the task of nurturing them in the faith more than of confronting them with requirements for membership in the Church.

Also, with the church becoming an avenue to political position, Christian education became a route to influence in the earthly kingdom instead of an avenue to a place in the eternal Kingdom. The decline in true spiritual life caused many to feel the only way to escape the pollution of this world was through withdrawal. Such escape was glorified by many who were influenced by the mystery cults; they held that asceticism was necessary to move into the presence of God.

C. Evaluation

During the period of the Western church education became much more formal in content, organization, and method. Its purpose was altered radically to achieve new objectives. One must make a value judgment concerning these new objectives. As an evangelistic instrument, Christian education was woefully weak. However, as a socializing force, it must be deemed effective. As a vehicle for training leadership, it became a major route to ecclesiastical and political prominence. Ulich summarizes the accomplishments of the first two eras of the church as follows:

> The development of Christianity during the first five centuries of its existence offers us one of the most amazing spectacles in the history of mankind. From the "carpenter of Nazareth," derided, tortured, and finally crucified by the Roman soldiers at the demand of the leaders of his own people, there comes a message more persuasive than the great schools of philosophy and more revolutionary in its impact on individual and social life than any revolution in the Western world. Its periods of persecution

are at the same time its periods of flowering, while its periods of peace often coincide with its decay. Like the religion of the Jews it grows through suffering.[14]

IV. THE MIDDLE AGES (CA. A.D. 529-1350)

Many historians have named the fall of the Roman Empire (A.D. 476) as the beginning of the Middle Ages. Others have dated its beginning with Charlemagne in the ninth century. For our purposes the Middle Ages may be understood better by going back far enough to review developing situations that affected Christian life in the West.

The traditional date of the founding of the Benedictine rule (A.D. 529) by Benedict of Nursia denotes a marked change in educational attempts. His rule and model for life dominated western monasticism for most of the Middle Ages. The Benedictine order shaped the reform of the Frankish church and paved the way for the conversion of England and Germany. Its practice of preserving and reproducing early manuscripts required literacy of the monks; it kept literature and learning alive in an age when most of the church placed minimal value upon them. Although the Benedictine contribution was considerable, Ulich notes its limitation as follows:

> However great the merits of these monks in transmitting ancient and patristic literature to later generations, they did not advance the frontiers of Christian knowledge. They and the secular clergy, trained by them or in the growing cathedral schools, reveal sometimes a profound and touching simplicity; but their main ambition was to save and teach a unique body of wisdom they considered so great, profound, and superior to their own knowledge, that any attempt to add or to change would have been considered frivolity.[15]

A. Needs and Objectives

In A.D. 529, all pagan schools were suppressed by the edict of Justinian, leaving no elementary education for the masses. Two years later, the Council of Toledo in Spain instructed that boys who wished to enter the ministry be put under the supervision of the Bishop for preparatory schooling. This action led to the development of village schools where, at seven or eight years of age, boys were given elementary education to prepare them for their ministerial training. Soon these schools were unable to accept all who wanted to learn.

---

14. Ulich, *History of Religious Education*, p. 49.
15. *Ibid.*, p. 58.

Thus these parish schools developed in the villages to serve essentially the same purposes as bishops' schools served in the cities.

1. *Purity Versus Power*

Individual concern for purity of life gave way to a frequent concern for power or position. The state church became an avenue to secular influence. Thus the challenge to the church to withstand annihilation from without was superceded by the challenge to prevent dilution and corruption from within.

2. *Monastic Schools*

In 529, the year of Justinian's edict, Benedict fled from Rome's corruption and established a monastery in southern Italy. His ideas of monasticism, summed up in the vows of poverty, chastity, and obedience, seemed to have little bearing on education. However, Benedict prescribed for his followers seven hours of manual labor and two hours of reading and meditation daily. This meant that if the young men who joined the order were to obey the rule, they must first be taught to read and write. Thus the monastic school was born. Its specific purpose was to teach novitiates elementary education.

A further educational contribution arose from the monastic insistence upon meditation. This discipline required the preservation and copying of religious literature designed for educational, devotional, ethical, and supervisory purposes.

The popularity of the Benedictine order encouraged others to seek asceticism as an escape from the corruption of social life during the demise of the Roman Empire. As political power lost its grip on the populace, the hand of the church moved in to take control. But in the turmoil and upheaval attending the changes, education seemed to be of minor concern. The influence of earlier forms tended to wane, and no dynamic substitutes emerged to fill the educational void.

3. *New Objectives*

New objectives for Christian education in this period can be inferred from the educational forms. First, there seemed to be a trend away from educating all believers. Education was designed more for the cleric or for the monastic than for the masses. The church was concerned to provide a priesthood of the clergy rather than to encourage a priesthood of all believers.

A second related purpose seemed to be that education was for leadership in the body rather than for sharing. Instead of educating for commitment, there was now evidence of educating for control and conformity. Salvation through belief in Christ was understood as being mediated only through the church.

In general, the purposes of education during the Middle Ages were to prepare men for service to God, to the church, and to their fellowmen. Knowledge was considered important only as it related to God and to the way of salvation.

B. Curriculum and Personnel

By the time of the Middle Ages the curriculum resources for Christian education were rich and varied. The materials of the Early Church were still available. In addition, the writings of the church fathers, the records of the councils, the formulation of creeds, and the contributions of earlier educators and theologians were at the disposal of teachers in the medieval period.

At this time secular writings were held in disrepute by church leaders, therefore classical materials were not readily available.

1. *Knowledge by Revelation*

Out of the understanding that knowing God and knowing oneself is a matter of revelation, comes an awareness that one must guard this revelation carefully. It must be kept sacred, yet it must be prevented from becoming so esoteric that people cannot understand it. Many of the priests taught the possibility of knowledge by revelation. But by implication they restricted this revelation to persons who sought it through the ministry of a priest.

2. *Knowledge for Vocation*

In actual practice, Christian education became largely church vocational training. Monastic schools taught monks what they needed to know to carry out their vows, and prepared novitiates for future service. Because of the need of manuscripts for literary activities, the monastery became publishing house, library, and center of literary activity.

3. *Cleric and Lay Teachers*

During the later Middle Ages, largely through the influence of Thomas Aquinas, study apart from theology was quelled. Faith took preeminence, and reason followed along chiefly to explain what faith had already acclaimed.

However, in the twelfth century the place of reason in other fields received a new emphasis. New schools arose around mendicant teachers. As these teachers became more popular, they tended to settle in a hospitable city, and students formed a guild to learn what they could from them. These schoolmen became great promoters of education. However, many of them did not have the blessing of the church even though they were quite faithful to her doctrines. The problem was that their method of inquiry did not blend happily with the approach taken by the scholastics who were at that time the educational elite of the Roman church.

4. *Universities and Specialized Schools*

The earliest universities were not founded; they developed without planning in the tenth to the twelfth centuries as new and deepening needs became apparent. Professor Cannon writes:

> The university was a distinctly medieval creation. . . . In *structure* the universities resembled the trade guilds. As a matter of fact they were the tradeguild of teachers. As a worker remained an apprentice or journeyman until he was admitted into full membership in his guild, so a pupil remained a student until he was licensed by his university as a master. . . . A master was nothing more or less than a qualified teacher of the arts.[16]

As man sought to provide answers to the hunger for learning, more and more people turned to the universities for direction. More and more the universities were looked to for training in law, medicine, theology, the arts, or university teaching. These universities became marketplaces of ideas as excited travelers came from all parts of the known world. Through these travelers new information, ideas, and theories filtered back from the far-flung civilizations.

Prior to and concurrent with the rise of the universities, we find a growing trend to specialized education such as the guild schools for vocational training, the burgher schools for business and practical arts, parish schools for religious and elementary instruction, and cathedral schools for the liberal arts. This specialization in the schools engendered dialog which fanned the fires of learning.

5. *Curriculum Resources*

Icons, relics, the great festivals and days of the local saints gave rise to processions, religious plays, and other activities. These provided reminders of man's responsibilities to God as well as to

---

16. William R. Cannon, *History of Christianity in the Middle Ages* (New York: Abingdon Press, 1960), pp. 282-83.

others. The development of the *trivium* and the *quadrivium* as the Seven Liberal Arts provided both organization and content to much of religious instruction during this era.[17]

6. *The Priest as Teacher*

The priest of the Middle Ages was considered a channel through whom the supernatural could impinge upon the natural order. It was he who could show how tradition was really an explication of Scripture. His sermons on the saints of an earlier day were designed to show God incarnating himself anew in the flesh of man in order to communicate more effectively with man.

7. *Methods of Education*

The curriculum of the Middle Ages was not so much interested in passing on information as it was in bringing the learner to understand that human information had its limits. Information could only open up man to see the demands of the supernatural—demands for obedience, faith, and self-renouncement. Education emphasized that revelation was complete. What man needed was a right relationship with Christ through the church. Memorizing and systematizing became the educational methods for such a task. The monastic order was an excellent place for promoting this concept because the disciplined physical life presumably enhanced spiritual development. And finally, scholasticism added discipline of the mental life in order to sharpen the mind to perceive the divine revelation when given in the language of God.

Although scholasticism attempted to support Christian creeds by reasoned arguments, it failed to save the church from decay. Because scholasticism involved primarily the scholar rather than the man on the street, it often caused as much doubt as faith. Ulich, however, reminds us that

> the scholastics enriched the Christian teaching of the time through the acceptance of Greek psychology and science. And through founding great centers of learning . . . they took learning and theological education out of the narrow walls of monasteries where there was little chance for further development.[18]

---

17. The *trivium* and *quadrivium* were the liberal arts of the middle ages. The *trivium* included grammar, rhetoric, and logic. The four fields in the *quadrivium* were arithmetic, music, geometry, and astronomy.

18. Ulich, *History of Religious Education*, p. 71.

C. Evaluation

1. *Schools*

The Middle Ages lacked centralized political power and thus gave opportunity for ecclesiastical power—but it was power without adequate educational foundation. The overlapping and often conflicting educational programs seemed to be ineffective at best. Mysticism disciplined the mental life for the sake of the spiritual. This contrasted with the monastic schools where ascetic influence emphasized the discipline of social life for the sake of the spiritual. The work of the cathedral schools, the beginning of the burgher schools, the inception of the universities and specialized schools seems to indicate a rampant pluralism. However, these ages spawned some of the brilliant minds of history: Anselm, Abelard, Aquinas, Peter Lombard, and Albertus Magnus among them.

2. *Objectives*

It is difficult to ascertain specific values and faults because of the interplay of pluralistic forces. But let us review the apparent educational objectives. These included (1) an educational program for leadership more than for the masses, (2) a program emphasizing obedience and agreement rather than divergence in thought or action, (3) a program of education for nobles and clerics rather than for common laborers, and (4) a program designed to bring all men under the dictates of the church as the representative of God on earth. We must admit that these objectives were reached to a great extent.

3. *Doctrines*

When looking from a Protestant perspective, we can only conclude that Christian education in the Middle Ages was inadequate and distorted. It did not continue to seek the objectives of the Early Church. In terms of evangelistic impact, the educational institutions fell short; for affecting the ethical life of the world, they held little power. Even in preserving the Christian heritage, these centuries saw little evidence of the Early Church emphasis on purity, the Greek emphasis upon intellect, or the Roman regard for justice.

However, during the last three centuries of the Middle Ages both the learning of the past and the knowledge existing beyond Europe were rediscovered to a much greater extent than ever before.

V. Reform, Renewal, and Discovery
(A.D. 1350-1750)

A. The Setting

The decay and corruption of the Middle Ages bottomed out about the time scholasticism was beginning to flourish. Because of her corruption, the church was losing control over the intellectual life of her people. Those who could read the Scripture became aware of the chasm between biblical ethics and those of the clergy. Scholasticism had brought in Greek philosophy and psychology and had thus reawakened scientific inquiry. The Crusaders brought back ideas, practices, and theories which demanded consideration. Humanists were finding a following.

Fourteenth- and fifteenth-century Europe in some ways might well be considered a counterpart of the present day. The Middle Ages had set the stage for the rebirth of classical writings and classical ideals (the Enlightenment). The rediscovery and acceptance of man as a rational being had set in motion a chain of events even as the rediscovery and acceptance were themselves links in that chain.

1. *Geographic and Scientific Discovery*

There was also a new awakening to the physical world. The age of exploration had arrived, and the impact of other civilizations was being felt across Europe. The hunger for new products increased trade. Again, exploration expressed itself in the search for new lands. The theory that man would drop off the edge of the earth if he went too far was being tested rather freely.

As new products were imported, man began to look to ways of improving what he had. Perhaps the most notable development for Christian education was the invention of moveable type. This meant that entire large print blocks did not have to be carved new for each job. Instead, a font of letters could be carved individually and placed in whatever order the message required; then the press table could be disassembled and the letters used repeatedly. Thus a whole new world of educational tools was made available.

2. *Political and Social Reform*

Politically, the fifteenth century witnessed many emerging nations. The vast Roman Empire was scarcely remembered, and the one politically stabilizing influence was the Roman church.

Socially, the resurgence of city life was fostered by trade and by the beginnings of factory work through guilds and crafts. But disease, lack of sanitation, and inadequate government typified the traumas of this age and called for renewal, reform, and discovery.

3. *Spiritual Renewal*

Spiritually, a paradox existed. The evangelistic force of the Christian witness had spread throughout the known world. But coupled with this spiritual vitality there was such an ethical degradation of the clergy and of the religious life of the masses that one almost blasphemes to call it Christian. Despicable cancers threatened the life of the body of Christ: church taxes, sale of indulgences, worship of saints, graft, open sin of church leaders, and lack of concern for social and spiritual ills.

4. *Educational Leaders*

Into this kind of a world were born three men who were to influence the next age in a marked way. Desiderius Erasmus (1466-1536) was a lover of the church, but he also loved the Bible. He insisted that the most exalted aim of the church was to obtain a knowledge of the pure and simple Christianity of the Bible. To gain this knowledge, he felt it necessary to go beyond the Latin scriptures to the Greek manuscripts. In doing this, he produced the first critical edition of the Greek text of the New Testament. For this act and for daring to question the ruling hierarchy, he incurred the wrath of the church.

Another figure entering this scene was Martin Luther, a German monk (1483-1546). From a study of the Scriptures, Luther felt compelled to challenge the practices of the church, especially the dispensing of grace by which one could purchase his own salvation and pay for his practice of sin. Both he and Erasmus called for purging the church of nonbiblical and contrabiblical beliefs and practices. Luther was excommunicated, but this did not dissuade him from his avowed purpose. He persisted in providing the Word of God in the German language so that his people could study its precepts and obey its commands.

A contemporary of Erasmus and Luther was a soldier, Ignatius Loyola (1495-1556). A hospital illness provided him opportunity to review life and its claims. After pondering the plight of the Catholic church, he felt God would have him give up his military career and establish a band which could begin to purify the life of the church. He organized his new order on a military format, demanding complete obedience of every follower. This Society of Jesus (the Jesuits) was destined to become one of the most powerful reform movements ever to influence the Catholic church. Its model of religious education has helped to determine the course of the Catholic church to this day.

B. Needs and Objectives

From the early pluralism the pendulum had swung to an unnatural and often forced unity during the Middle Ages. Now the seeds of individualism had sprouted again. The emphasis upon faith had been so great that it had almost denied reason. Now men dared to challenge the church's right to place life in a mold of abject obedience that excluded reasonable living. The challenge confronted sharply the church's doctrine of man. Was he so utterly sinful that he could not cooperate in his own salvation? If so, how could he, through indulgences, assure his salvation?

1. *Representative Needs*

These questions pointed up some of the needs for Christian education. Luther contended for the priesthood of all believers, which made it necessary that the Word of God be available in the language of the people. A further need was that the people be literate in order to fulfill their priestly responsibilities.

Luther's concept of the priesthood of all believers was not in the direction of extreme individualism or of anarchy in spiritual affairs. On the contrary, it was a contention that each believer was an intercessor for others. It was a cry to return to the true unity of the Church as a body of believers. Here was a mediating position between the dictatorship of the church and a rising tide of individualism.

Luther also called for a new emphasis upon the doctrine of grace in contrast to salvation by good deeds. God alone could and did provide grace sufficient for salvation through faith.

2. *Objectives of Lutheranism*

Luther insisted upon schools. He wrote:

> We must certainly have men to administer God's Word and sacraments and to do pastoral work among the people. But where shall we get them if we let our schools decline and do not replace them with others that are Christian?[19]

In addition to the objectives of compulsory universal education

---

19. From Kendig Brubaker Cully, *Basic Writings in Christian Education* (Philadelphia: The Westminster Press, 1960), p. 147.

for both sexes and of providing God's Word in man's language, Luther stressed the writing and using of music. He also insisted upon family religious instruction and the preparation of devotional literature. To provide the foundations necessary for man's understanding of his relationship with God, Luther sought to develop basic theology through simple catechisms using Scripture as the primary base for the concepts and for much of the wording.

After his excommunication, Luther was forced to seek a further objective: developing an organizational structure for the new bands of Protestants who chose to follow him instead of the pope.

3. Jesuit Objectives

In the Society of Jesus the objectives were similar to those of Luther in many areas. Loyola stressed education—but the extent of a person's education was determined by his leadership position. Loyola planned an educational program scaled to the needs of the person as he rose in the levels of leadership. He felt that if leaders were well educated and disciplined, the masses would be obedient and need no education.

Loyola also stressed personal repentance and faith, but he did not release the individual from unquestioned obedience to the church represented in the authority of his immediate superior. The godly, disciplined, obedient soldier was Loyola's means for purging the church and for evangelizing the world. At least in part, Jesuit education was a Counter-Reformation move designed to win back territory and persons lost to the Reformers.

C. Curriculum and Personnel

1. Emphases of Education

We have already implied that the Word of God took a new central position in the educational nurture of the church, whether Protestant or Catholic. In addition, there was a new sense of freedom to use classical and modern secular resources to enable the Christian to be a good citizen of his state. But among the Reformers, especially Luther insisted that the Bible be the only Guide for determining the worth or danger of a particular scholarly contribution. His use of catechisms, family devotional material, hymnody, and celebrations of faith and hope established new directions for the Christian education of the future.

The new awareness of man stimulated the beginning science of psychology and encouraged research into educational philosophy and methodology.

2. *Influential Educators*

We have already mentioned Erasmus, Luther, and Loyola. Melanchthon can hardly be overrated for his contributions of structure, content, and motivation to theological education. Calvin and Zwingli must be considered primarily for their theological and church polity innovations.

Johann Amos Comenius (1592-1670) was another of the outstanding educational reformers of this era. He stressed equality and his aim was to make all men Christlike. Comenius suggested shifting a dominant role of education to the school under teachers chosen for their scholarship and love of children. He stressed the importance of sense experience, imagination, learning by doing, purposeful practice, and reasoning more than rote memory. He also stressed developmental readiness to learn. Education was to be viewed as anticipation of the future rather than acceptance of the past. He emphasized the value of great teachers and excellent resources.

Supporting these views, Comenius provided a model textbook incorporating illustrations, motivation through anticipation, step-by-step procedures, movement from the general to the particular, and language adapted to the age levels. His text has been seldom surpassed to this day.

Now for the first time in the history of the church, the state was charged with making universal education available and required for all children of the state.

D. Evaluation

When comparing the results of education to the objectives during the Reformation period, one recognizes evident success. Education became more widespread than at any prior time in the history of western Europe. The public-school system gained a stronger foothold and thus contributed to the beginning of the age of science. Knowledge began to increase in almost geometric expansion. The emphasis upon the study of man and the recognition of his capabilities contributed to social and cultural expansion as well as to growth in the sciences.

The education of these four centuries encouraged individualism, the scientific method, and a student-centered approach to teaching. It placed responsibility for education more upon the family and society than upon the individual. The primacy of the Bible and justification by faith were stressed which gave rise to more widespread preaching and teaching. Leaders also insisted upon personal and family Bible study.

However, the education of the period was not an unmixed blessing, as Gutek so cogently points out:

> While both the lower and the upper classes were to be educated, they were to receive different kinds of education. A vernacular, basic elementary education was suited for the lower classes so that they might read, write and know their particular religious creeds. The upper classes, destined to rule, were to receive a classical humanist secondary education designed to prepare them for higher education, the professions and positions of authority in the church and the state.[20]

The Jesuit educational system has persevered until today. It placed great emphasis upon content and upon discipline, and influenced the Spanish philosophy of education to become authority-centered. The responsibility for education rested more upon the individual than upon society as a whole.

Ulich summarizes the period as follows:

> If we look at the character and role of religious education during the Reformation and the Counter Reformation, one fact cannot be doubted. The conflicts of the period forced upon the leaders of the time a thorough reexamination of the premises and conditions of the Christian upbringing of youth. Always the shock of revolution impels the policy makers to ask themselves what they want to achieve in the long run, and how they can direct the minds of the younger generation into desirable channels. The progressive will have to formulate the new so that it can root, and the conservative the old so that it can stay alive.[21]

Kinlock says this period taught us that education is inadequate without religion as the controlling element; that it must be based upon Holy Scripture; and that home, school, and church must unite in total education if the child is to live aright.[22]

VI. THE MODERN ERA (A.D. 1750—   )

A. The Setting

The combined impact of Renaissance and Reformation introduced an

---

20. Gerald L. Gutek, *A History of the Western Educational Experience* (New York: Random House, 1972), p. 136.

21. Ulich, *History of Religious Education*, p. 141.

22. T. F. Kinlock, *Pioneers of Religious Education* (Freeport, N.Y.: Books for Libraries Press, 1939), p. 32.

era of activism throughout Europe. With the development of science came a consequent introduction of industrialism. This reshuffled the political power structure of Europe. New boundaries were drawn and an increased nationalism developed. Through the recent centuries this trend has become ever more conspicuous and complex. The population of the whole world is more and more concentrating in huge cities.

1. *Industrialization*

With greater emphasis upon mass production came a new demand for labor that decimated the ranks of apprentices in the skilled trades. Machines were constructed to take over much of the manual labor market. Education lost much of its appeal because now a man could earn a living in the factory or the mine without having to know how to read or write. Factory locations gave rise to the massing of people into multi-family dwellings which caused greater sanitation problems and increased crime. The courts of law were archaic, and jurisprudence was not equipped to protect the rights of the individual.

2. *Spiritual Pluralism*

The church, too, failed to keep up with new economic and social developments. The old forms of worship and education were too formal to cope with the new demands placed upon them. Man, with his increased capacity, seemed to have less dependence upon God. Societal and moral standards became inconsistent. As people moved from place to place, they found conflicting mores and cultural patterns. Individualism became more prevalent.

B. Needs and Objectives

1. *Needs*

In this kaleidoscopic setting many needs became apparent. Among them we note:

> Recognizing the worth and dignity of every man
> Awakening to the increasing social ills of the times
> Balancing an appreciation for man with reverence for God
> Providing true Christian education as well as public education and church worship
> Providing leadership for understanding and promoting Christian education
> Bringing theological understandings to bear upon present life

Supporting and strengthening missionary outreach

Controlling both physical and moral pollution

2. *Objectives*

Out of these needs many objectives have developed:

A return to specific spiritual instruction

The training of teachers and other leaders for Christian nurture

Providing a viable organizational structure for the churches, flexible enough to cope with rapid change

Providing Scriptures in the new idioms of the day

Finding a functional spiritual substitute for homes threatened with collapse

Separating evangelism from acculturation, missionary work from political influence, and indigenous church organization from inflexible international polity

C. Curriculum and Personnel

1. *Curricular Emphases*

This era has seen great curricular change in resources and printed materials. Everywhere one goes in the Western world, religious literature abounds.

There has also been a corresponding change in organizational structure for educational purposes. The Moravian movement with its group loyalty emphasized interpersonal needs. Count Zinzendorf (1700-1750) with his Bible study approach influenced the small-group emphasis that has lasted in some form to the present day. The Sunday school movement was founded in 1780 by Robert Raikes of Gloucester, England. We have seen the founding of youth action groups, the development of the vacation Bible schools, the fostering of parochial schools and weekday religious education. All of these are changes in the structures for Christian education.

2. *Personnel*

The personnel for Christian education are still found in the home, the church, and the school. However, we find a return to an emphasis upon lay leadership initiative and responsibility for Christian education. This has been true both within denominational structures and in interdenominational cooperative movements.

Along with lay responsibility has come an extensive impact by the educational philosophers. Rousseau (1712-78) stressed a "back to nature" move. He insisted first on negative learning in order to guard the mind against vice and error. Later he would teach the principles of virtue and truth. He also insisted that the child's life situation and the process of his experience should furnish the means of his education. The child should not be forced into a theological commitment until he is old enough to understand fully.

Pestalozzi (1746-1827) stressed the grading of curriculum and methods to the developmental level of the child, and the use of the inductive method of teaching. Sense impression and the use of objects and experiences formed essential elements of Pestalozzi's teaching. One of his greatest contributions was the arrangement of textbooks in progressive complexity and coherence of the materials, starting with the simplest elements and moving toward complete comprehension of the entire subject.

Herbart (1776-1841) stressed the development of moral character in Christian education with a balanced emphasis upon the individual and society. For him ethics is the major test of education. His five formal steps have influenced education to this day. These steps are:

    Preparation
    Presentation
    Association
    Generalization
    Application—with a balance among them.

Wisdom and judgment are far more important than the mere acquisition of facts.

John Locke, Horace Bushnell, and John Dewey affected religious instruction greatly in the United States with the philosophy of the neutral (if not morally good) nature of the child. This view placed primary responsibility upon the environment for shaping the child's religious awareness and commitment.

Robert Raikes (1735-1811) was one of the most important figures in the field of Christian education. His significance lay not only in founding the Sunday school movement but also in advertising, promoting, and supporting it until it could succeed on its own.

John Wesley (1703-91) envisioned the value that the Sunday school movement had for the church. He was concerned that the Sunday school become an adjunct to his class meetings to provide the necessary prelude to conversion and the essential follow-up for nurture and growth in grace. Through the influence of Wesley and others the Sunday school was adapted by the church to serve spiritual ends rather than purely secular goals. Through the years it has been the single most important structure of Christian education in this present era.

Until recent years, the Sunday school faced the dubious distinction of being an auxiliary to the church—self-staffed, self-supported, and self-controlled by the laity. By and large, it has not been the *church* educating its own or reaching the lost. Even as late as the middle of this century Paul Vieth warned:

> This independence of the Sunday school from the church has tended to persist. It has stood in the way of the Sunday school's own highest achievement. . . . If Christian education is to achieve its highest purposes, it must be an expression of the entire life and work of the church and must eventuate in leading its pupils into the membership and work of the church.[23]

3. *Curricular Agencies*

The 19th and 20th centuries have witnessed a multiplication of religious activities designed to promote Christian education. These include: church-related colleges, foreign missions organizations, interdenominational Sunday school associations, youth movements, parochial schools, singing schools, vacation Bible schools, weekday religious education, summer camps and conferences, leadership and teacher training emphases, and multiple-staff professional ministries for the local church. No period in history has seen so many programs brought into being for the purpose of evangelism and Christian nurture. Most of these developments in local church ministries have sprung up since the turn of the 20th century. (See chapters 13, 14, and 18.)

D. Evaluation

1. *Complexity*

In modern times as in every prior era, the church has struggled between being an agent for change and an agent for the faithful transmission of its heritage and culture. There has been a necessary and appropriate tension between educating to preserve the past and to prepare for the future; between seeking to know through revelation and to know through reason; between teaching to be accepting and to be discriminating; between emphasizing growth of the mem-

---

23. Paul H. Vieth, ed., *The Church and Christian Education* (St. Louis: The Bethany Press, 1947), p. 27.

bers and growth of the organization. Such diversity makes objective judgment difficult. Also we are too close to these events to evaluate them accurately.

2. *Expansiveness*

The Christian Church during the modern era has taken its gospel and its educational programs to the far corners of the earth. As a result the Judeo-Christian ethic has formed major bases for international justice and for accepted moral standards. It has undergirded most of the Western world's public school curriculum. Latourette writes of the recent past: "The Gospel was having effects far outside the circles of those who bore the Christian name. It was by no means dominant but it was more widely potent than at the beginning of the century."[24]

3. *Shortcomings*

While the church has made this impact around the world, it has waxed and waned in its impact in the United States. Dr. Kennedy has cited some of the failures:

> The new programs generally failed to halt the disturbing movement away from the church-dominated culture to which Americans had grown accustomed. Critics continued to claim that new forms for church life and nurture were needed. . . . Christian educators are searching history to understand effective forms of education in other periods when somewhat similar conditions existed, and to gain deeper grasp of how and by what forces the present forms emerged. For the great axles of society are turning more rapidly, and Christian education in America cannot long postpone major changes. In varying degrees churches of other lands face the same problems.[25]

As in every century, the church is only one generation from extinction. As with every period of history, we must conclude that this era has seen magnificent successes and miserable failures. The church has gained in organizational strength. It has become much more democratic and interested in the individual. It has sustained severe and appropriate criticism and has now begun to look at itself through research, reexamination, and reevaluation. Out of this process we agree with Harvey's estimate of our failures. He reminds critics of the church that "by blurring fine but important distinctions

---

24. Latourette, *History of Christianity*, p. 1451.

25. William Bean Kennedy: "Christian Education Through History" in *An Introduction to Christian Education*, Marvin J. Taylor, ed. (Nashville: Abingdon Press, 1966), p. 30.

. . . abstractions tempt us to look for wholesale answers to what are, in fact, retail questions."[26]

VII. THE FUTURE ERA

A. Its Heritage

When one is standing on the brow of a ridge, it is difficult to determine whether the crest is just a rampart or the continental divide. Just so it is impossible to determine whether we are on the threshold of a new era or in the midst of the current one. We are a part of our past and it is a part of us. Latourette speaks vividly of our heritage:

> Across the centuries Christianity has been the means of reducing more languages to writing than have all other factors combined. It has created more schools, more theories of education, and more systems than has any other one force. More than any other power in history it has impelled men to fight suffering, whether that suffering has come from disease, war, or natural disasters. It has built thousands of hospitals, inspired the emergence of nursing and medical professions, and furthered movements for public health and the relief and prevention of famine.[27]

B. Its Potential

The future appears both bright and bleak. Renewed emphasis upon the following factors makes the future look promising.

The priesthood of believers

Unity of effort

Tolerance of cultures and expressions of faith

The authority of the Bible

The central work of the Holy Spirit as the revealing Teacher

Assuming responsibility to teach *for* membership as well as *in* membership

Greater individualization and diversity in curriculum materials

More effective methods of instruction

Variation in practices and activities

Careful research leading to more effective evaluation and accountability

---

26. Van A. Harvey, *The Historian and the Believer* (New York: The Macmillan Co., 1966), p. 247.

27. Latourette, *History of Christianity*, p. 1473.

All of these are encouraging, but conversely, Western history has never known a period when there was more antagonism to the Judeo-Christian moral standards and ethical codes than now. Pluralism and growing secularism have expressed themselves in license and permissiveness. Irresponsibility and hedonistic attitudes prevail to the point that there is a serious eroding of authority of every kind. There are few continuing, much less fixed or absolute moral standards. The doctrines of God and of man are undergoing reevaluation and attack. The credibility of a Christian ethic is low because of disparity between creed and practice.

C. Its Task

What then of the future? We have some needs and some objectives. The objectives, more than at any other time in history, need to be articulated in specific detail, yet more coordinated in direction. Randolph Crump Miller says educators today

> must be competent in educational psychology, developmental psychology, the sociology of learning, and many other scientific disciplines. But these studies, important as they are for insight and method, do not provide the goals, establish the truth, or describe the person we are to educate. For this we must turn to the theology of the church.[28]

The Church must not fear to continue its role as conservator of a heritage. Indoctrination and tradition are wholesome concepts when that indoctrination and that tradition are Christ in His-story. As in previous times the Church must find a way to speak to the whole man—not only to the mind but to his emotionality, in his physical activity, and in his social need. As we find ways to do this, man in his loneliness will turn to the church of love.

Because of complexities of scheduling, retreat living will require Christian emphasis. Specialists and resource consultants in Christian education, in Bible, and in theology will be used more in areas of their specialization. Both mass teaching and individualized instruction will be improved and employed. Central communication media will become more important. Functional substitutes for traditional programs will continue to arise.

The process of Christian growth will be stressed more than before through rewarding developments in value education, decision-

---

28. Randolph Crump Miller, *Education for Christian Living*, 2nd ed. (Englewood Cliffs, N.J.: Prentice-Hall, Inc., 1963), p. 38.

making skills, and accountability teaching. The church's members will discover and develop new ways to serve the Body of Christ and to seek the unsaved. Again, Dr. Miller identifies some of the directions he sees:

> In the future, then, we may move away from the typical schoolroom approach for some purposes and stay within it for others. We may have careful analysis of subject matter as a discipline in itself, and we may have experiments with life on the parkway. We may find that Bible quizzes are fun, but discover at the same time that there is nitroglycerine in the Bible story that may blow up traditional ways of doing things. We may preach from time to time on the Good News and we may scold and prophesy and promise, but we will also enter into relationships with the preached-at on a level of discussion and criticism. We may analyze religious language so that we know what language game we are playing, and then use any language game that promises to communicate. We may work for conversion and commitment and seek to evoke insights like our own, and then be happy as the learner makes his own decisions which are not like ours.[29]

The Church must continue to be an agent of change and an agent for the transmission of its faith. It is a redemptive community. Its task of reconciliation and atonement, evangelism and nurture, worship and witness are intertwined inextricably. It will continue to encounter crises. Those crises will bring conflict, and that conflict will offer choice.

The hope of the future is for the Church to recognize that Christian education is not an adjunct or an activity. It is the Church teaching—teaching all of its life through all of its life. Its educational nurture will insist that the Church reflect Christ for whom it is the Body and that it reflect man for whom it exists.

We believe in the priesthood of all believers. That priestly function involves each individual's direct access to God—but it involves more. It implies that each individual has responsibility to every other human to speak in behalf of God, to intercede with God on behalf of that person, and to call to unity and service in the will of God. The commission for the future is still, "go . . . teaching."

---

29. Randolph Crump Miller, "Predicaments and Pointers in Religious Education," *Colloquy* (November, 1972).

BIBLIOGRAPHY

Cully, Kendig Brubaker. *Basic Writings in Christian Education*. Philadelphia: The Westminster Press, 1960.

An excellent piece of research, presenting influential educators through their own writings. Invaluable as support data to personalize the reading or teaching of the history of Christian education by referring to translations of primary source material.

Latourette, Kenneth Scott. *A History of Christianity*. New York: Harper and Brothers, 1953.

A doctrinal history, pointing up major issues affecting content, methodology, and personnel of Christian education. It is exceptionally thorough.

Petry, Ray C., ed. *A History of Christianity: Readings in the History of the Early and Medieval Church*. Englewood Cliffs, N.J.: Prentice-Hall, Inc., 1962.

Excerpts from the writings of those who influenced the history of the church to the time of the Reformation. It is rich, cohesive, and progressive. A flavor of tradition and advance can be gained from reading his essays and translations of primary source material.

Sherrill, Lewis J. *The Rise of Christian Education*. New York: The Macmillan Co., 1944.

Still one of the best histories of Christian education of the Early Church. He provides background for the beginning of Christian education and follows its development to the Reformation.

Ulich, Robert. *A History of Religious Education*. New York: New York University Press, 1968.

This book will rank alongside Sherrill's for excellence. Its more inclusive scope, however, makes it an even better source for the total span of Christian education.

CHAPTER 4

The Theological and Philosophical Bases of Christian Education

In Part I, "Foundations of Christian Education," we are exploring the principal factors upon which Christian education builds. These are the important disciplines that influence the character and function of Christian teaching. In this chapter we are to consider how Christian education builds upon theology and philosophy. After examining the nature and function of these disciplines, we shall attempt to describe what is meant by an evangelical philosophy of Christian education, then take some steps toward the development of such a philosophy.

I. Influence of Theology

We have already seen in chapter 1 how our theology governs the objectives and content of our educational ministry. Christian education is not simply a reflection of secular education. Our aims are to be determined by our Christian faith. Likewise, the content of Christian education is under the control of Christian doctrine.

A. Theology in Christian education

1. *Definition*

In this chapter several terms are used interchangeably: *theology, doctrine,* and *faith*—faith in the substantive sense: "the faith that God has once for all entrusted to the saints" (Jude 3, NIV). In the words of Jaroslav Pelikan: "What the church of Jesus Christ believes, teaches, and confesses, on the basis of the word of God—this is Christian doctrine."[1] What the Church *believes* refers to its devotional literature and practices; what it *teaches* refers to its proclamation of the biblical message; and what the Church *confesses* refers to the use of its creeds and dogmas.[2]

Theology may be thought of as encompassing a broader field than doctrine; sometimes the term is used to include all areas related to Christian ministry. Also the term *faith* may involve the act and life of trust as well as the body of what Christians believe. For present purposes, however, these terms will be thought of as interchangeable and used in the sense that Pelikan defines *doctrine*—"what the church of Jesus Christ believes, teaches, and confesses, on the basis of the word of God."

2. *Influence*

Theology influences Christian education in the following areas:

a. Formulation of definitions. It was seen earlier that "Christian educational theory must not be a footnote to secular discoveries"; the values of Christian education spring from "Christian theology and not from secular methodology." Typical definitions include such language as: "Christian education is a means by which the church seeks to help persons respond to the gospel (the message of God's redeeming love in Jesus Christ)."

The descriptive definition of Christian education offered in chapter 1 is imbued with biblical and theological truth:

> The view held here is that Christian education is integral to the very constitution of the church; that the church, in its educational task, should seek to transmit the Christian gospel and do so in such a way as to induce evangelical change in all learners; and that these changes will include conversion, entire sanctification, personal growth, and the development of a sense of mission as an enduring philosophy of life.

---

1. Jaroslav Pelikan, *The Christian Tradition.* "The Emergence of the Catholic Tradition" (Chicago: The University of Chicago Press, 1971), 1:1.
2. *Ibid.*, pp. 4-5.

It is evident from these references that Christian doctrine has a penetrating influence on the formulation of definitions and descriptions of what Christian education is. Theology affects the very constitution of Christian education, at least, as such education is conceived by evangelicals.

b. Development of objectives and goals. The objective and supporting goals, offered by this text in chapter 1, clearly have their source in our biblical faith, as that faith has been interpreted theologically by the historic Christian Church. An examination of the "single, comprehensive statement" (p. 27) will reveal references to the nature of God, the mission of Christ, the work of the Holy Spirit, the capacities and needs of man, the Church, and the Christian life. A further analysis of the "objective and supporting goals" (pp. 27-33) will disclose similar theological concepts and terms. The objectives of Christian education are rooted in Christian faith and doctrine.

c. Content of instruction. The content of education—if it is to be Christian—must include Christian doctrine. We assert that "Christian education, one of the key ministries of the church, looks to the Bible, to theology, and to Christian history for the content of its teaching. . . . Christian education has a heritage of Christian truth to receive, to understand, and to transmit."

Further, one of the supporting goals suggested by this text in chapter 1 is "to transmit the Christian heritage of faith and morals in relevant terms."

This position is affirmed by Butler: "Theology certainly has a place in the content of teaching in the Church. *Primarily,* the content of written curriculum and classroom teaching in the church school should be biblical, theological, and historical."[3]

Butler observes that several important truths follow from this fact. It is essential that curriculum writers and classroom teachers put the doctrine of the church into language that students of all ages can understand. At the same time they must be careful not to corrupt or mutilate the doctrine. Further, the function of theology, especially in the Christian education of young people and adults, is not to provide learners with pat and easy answers to all questions. Rather, it enables them to share in the fellowship of the church on an intellectual as well as on emotional and volitional levels. "If the community

---

3. J. Donald Butler, *Religious Education: The Foundations and Practice of Nurture* (New York: Harper and Row, Publishers, 1962), p. 128. Italics added.

of Faith feels the Faith and acts the Faith, it must certainly also think the Faith."[4] Truth is to Christian love what fuel is to the fire.

d. Ministry of Christian nurture. It is sometimes supposed that theology is not relevant to the Christian life. Butler has a helpful word on this point also. He suggests that a continuity exists between theology and nurture; that theology is "the Church thinking the Faith" and nurture is "the Church communicating the Faith."[5] These are companion activities and processes; both are vitally rooted in the faith.

In the creeds of the Church, in the classic works of theology, and in the contemporary statements of belief,[6] the Church has been thinking the faith, but always with a view to strengthening believers. Thus Christian doctrine points to God and to the Christian life even though God and life are more than doctrine. Doctrine is of critical importance to the disciple in the development and practice of his beliefs.

II. INFLUENCE OF PHILOSOPHY

The influence of philosophy in Christian education is not as obvious as is the impact of theology. Nevertheless, philosophy renders valuable service to the Christian Church, including its educational ministry; the contribution of hard, clear thinking is foundational and pervasive in every area of human experience.

A. Definition

The word *philosophy* literally means the love of wisdom. It has been described as an unusually persistent effort to think clearly. Brightman writes: "Philosophy may be defined as the attempt to think truly about human experience as a whole; or to make our whole experience intelligible."[7]

Any person, then, who is deeply concerned to know and accept the truth, reflects the spirit of philosophy. He who examines all observable facts or ideas carefully to see how they fit into the rest of his experience, uses the method of philosophy.

---

4. *Ibid.,* p. 130.
5. *Ibid.,* pp. 131-32.
6. See, for example, the Articles of Faith in the *Manual: Church of the Nazarene,* and comparable statements in the Discipline of the Free Methodist Church, the United Methodist Church, and other Christian denominations.
7. Edgar Sheffield Brightman, *An Introduction to Philosophy* (New York: Henry Holt and Co., 1940), p. 4.

B. Relationships

1. *Christian Education and Philosophy*

Christian education must be concerned with philosophy because to seek to know the truths about God and man and to communicate those truths to others is the business of Christian educators.

2. *Philosophy and Theology*

There is a close tie between philosophy and theology because theology also is concerned with all the truths that relate to God and to man. How then do philosophy and theology differ? Butler affirms, "Philosophy derives its nature and structure from the categories of the human mind. . . . By contrast theology derives its structure and consequently its nature from the events of revelation and the literature of revelation, the Bible."[8] The philosopher becomes a theologian when he recognizes revelation as a source from which truth and meaning may be gained. The theologian becomes a philosopher when he employs in his theology all that he otherwise knows about the world. He is a philosopher also when he applies the principles of clear thinking to his interpretation of God's revelation found in the Bible and in nature.

Some of the fundamental areas of historic concern to philosophers are also the central concerns of theologians—and therefore of Christian educators. Among the most fundamental questions raised by the human mind are: What is the nature of reality (metaphysics)? How do I know something to be true (epistemology)? What is the nature and source of value (axiology)?

The Christian in philosophy renders a major service to Christian education as he develops a metaphysics, an epistemology, and an axiology that are "adequate for the biblical understanding of the nature of God, the world, man, and sin."[9]

C. Schools of Philosophy

We have seen in chapter 1 that an important objective of Christian education is "to lead to the discovery of the Christian philosophy of life, and the biblical interpretation of the universe." The history of philosophy includes a half dozen schools of thought that impinge upon Christian education today. Each one has something worthwhile

---

8. Butler, *Religious Education,* p. 125.
9. Albert E. Bailey, "Philosophies of Education and Religious Education," in *Religious Education: A Comprehensive Survey,* Marvin J. Taylor, ed. (New York: Abingdon Press, 1960), p. 33.

to say about our world. If there were not some abiding core of truth in these systems of thought, it is inconceivable that they would continue to commend themselves to thoughtful persons.

On the other hand, each of these systems seems to fall short in accounting for some facts of life revealed to us in the Scriptures and widely recognized by thoughtful persons.

How shall we explain the fact that every school of philosophy has some true insight to offer, and yet no system wins the assent of all thoughtful persons?

Perhaps one answer is that our universe contains so much variety that no human mind can put it all together under one system. Our Christian faith itself includes truths that seem to us to be in tension; for example, the sovereignty of God and the freedom of man, or the unity of God and the plurality of the Trinity. Perhaps the best that human thought can achieve is an eclectic philosophy that recognizes facts wherever they appear and seeks to frame a system of thought that does justice to the facts as we perceive them.

A Christian philosophy of life and a Christian evaluation of systems of philosophy must rest upon two premises: (1) a complete openness to truth, and (2) a basic theistic faith judgment about the nature of the universe.

(1) Of our openness to truth, Ferré writes:

> No philosopher may compromise one whit with truth, nor may a Christian. . . . If choice has to be made between Christian faith and integrity of truth, the Christian philosopher, to be authentic, must choose truth. Such truth pertains to three realms: (1) willingness to face fact, (2) readiness to use reason with maximum competence and scrupulous care no matter where it leads, and (3) openness to the fullest circle of context that can provide maximum meaningfulness to all experience and the fullest possible explanatory adequacy.[10]

(2) Every system of thought rests on one or more controlling premises. The validity and reasonableness of every secondary position in the system depends on its own obvious factuality and also upon its being consistent in view of the major premise. A Christian philosophy accepts as true any fact that maintains itself when we apply the three criteria under "openness to truth." The thoughtful Christian must then relate this acknowledged fact to his controlling

---

10. Nels F. S. Ferré, *A Theology for Christian Education* (Philadelphia: The Westminster Press, 1967), pp. 88-89.

principles so that his whole system becomes as consistent and as meaningful as possible.

The controlling premise of Christian philosophy is a faith in God as revealed to us in Jesus Christ. One of the clearest Arminian thinkers of the 20th century was Dr. James B. Chapman. In speaking to college students, he said, You won't go far wrong in finding your way through conflicting philosophies if you start with the following premises, and evaluate every position in the light of them: *(a)* Behind the universe there is a personal intelligence whom we call God. *(b)* God loves man and desires his highest welfare; Jesus teaches us to call God "Father." *(c)* God wants to make himself and His will known to us. Such a framework of meaning

> is implicitly a metaphysics following from a dominant faith judgment. Such a metaphysics is implicit in its central organizing event, which affords its central presupposition and its overall perspective. The Christian perspective becomes the all-controlling point of reference, the all-transforming angle of vision, the all-transvaluating faith judgment, the all-organizing context of meaning, the all-pervasive element in every analysis with which it is concerned.[11]

The thoughtful Christian educator, therefore, looks at every school of philosophy to discover (1) what facets of truth are there reflected, and (2) how this philosophical position agrees with or contradicts a biblical metaphysics.

1. *Naturalism*

Naturalism is basically a metaphysics. It accepts the viewpoint that the world of physical nature is all there is to reality. The ancient Greek philosophers sought for the ultimate substance of the universe in earth, air, fire, and water. Today, naturalists find the ultimate source of life and the final meaning of human existence in the physical world with its laws of action and reaction.

The appeal of contemporary naturalism lies in its close affinity with the scientific method. In order to validate truth, science today relies on verifiable experiments observed through sense experiences. The Christian accepts this scientific method as a valid test of truth in the world of sense experience. He rejects, however, the naturalist's position that a valid test for sense experience is the only valid test for all experience.

Naturalism is weakest in its failure to adequately account for

---

11. *Ibid.*, p. 89.

mind and its place in the universe. To Christian thought it seems more reasonable to believe that intelligent planning explains the physical universe than to hold to the opposite view that nonthinking matter could account for the presence of intelligent beings.

The Christian believes that "in the beginning God [an intelligent Being] created the heaven and the earth" (Gen. 1:1). Revelation affirms it, and Christian reason finds it a more meaningful explanation than naturalism.

2. Idealism

Idealism is almost the exact opposite of naturalism. Where naturalism finds its ultimate explanations of reality, of knowledge, and of value in the material world, idealism finds these explanations in mind or ideas—hence the term *idealism.*

The problem of epistemology is basic in all idealistic philosophies. How can we know the material world around us? How, indeed, can we know anything? Berkeley (1685-1753) wrestled with this issue and reached the conclusion that mind is the most fundamental reality in our knowledge. We may doubt the reality of even the physical world, but we cannot doubt that we are doubting. It is the mind that knows; also, what the mind knows is known in the form of ideas. The idealist reasons that like can know only like. The mind can grasp only something that is like mind.

From its theory of knowledge, idealism moves to a view of ultimate reality and to a theory of value. If only mind can be known, only mind is ultimately real and therefore of supreme value.

There is much in idealism that supports the concerns of Christian education. Man's mind is what makes him higher than the animals. Improving his ideas is basic to making him a better man. When one commits himself to become a Christian and follow Christ, he commits himself to shape his life by the ideas that make up the mind of Christ. Paul appeals to Christians everywhere, "Let this mind be in you, which was also in Christ Jesus" (Phil. 2:5).

Ideas are important—highly important—but they are not all that is important. Idealism in the first place falls short as a full Christian philosophy of life because it fails to do justice to the created physical world. The teaching of Jesus does not deny material existence. Physical realities are genuine facts to be reckoned with. What Jesus teaches is that we can be at home in our physical environment because God is in control of it. He says, "Therefore do not be anxious, saying 'What shall we eat?' or 'What shall we drink?' or 'What shall we wear?' . . . your heavenly Father knows that you need them all.

But seek first his kingdom and his righteousness, and all these things shall be yours as well" (Matt. 6:31-33, RSV).

Idealism also singles out mind as of supreme importance. In doing so it neglects the roles of feeling and of choice in the formation of personality. The biblical view of man, in contrast, makes an appropriate place for the affective side of life. Jesus said, "Let not your heart be troubled" (John 14:1); "Be not afraid" (John 6:20); "Ask . . . that your joy may be full" (John 16:24).

The Bible also recognizes the roles of volition and action. Paul declares, "It is God which worketh in you both to will and to do of his good pleasure" (Phil. 2:13). Jesus says, "If any man will do his [God's] will, he shall know of the doctrine, whether it be of God" (John 7:17).

Ferré sums up the case for idealism thus:

> Idealism has . . . a main contribution to make to philosophy. . . . All sub-idealistic philosophies, so to speak, are immediately discounted as partial and distorted. We can have more than idealism in philosophy, but not less. . . . It is only when idealism makes its own truth ultimate and exclusive that it becomes false . . . and inadequate.[12]

3. *Personalism*

Personalism is a form of idealism that holds ultimate reality and ultimate values to be personal. This view is quite in agreement with our Christian doctrine of a personal God. It is also in accord with Jesus' emphasis upon the high value of human persons. When the Pharisees put a religious institution above human need, Jesus declared, "The sabbath was made for man, and not man for the sabbath" (Mark 2:27). When considering the spiritual worth of a child, Jesus uses strong language. "Whoever receives one such child in my name receives me; but whoever causes one of these little ones who believe in me to sin, it would be better for him to have a great millstone fastened round his neck and to be drowned in the depth of the sea" (Matt. 18:5-6, RSV).

In a philosophy class at a state university, a student presented the views of personalism. The professor's put-down was a grunt, followed by two words: "Methodist theology!" The professor may have thus unwittingly acknowledged the high correlation between personalistic metaphysics and the biblical doctrines of God and man.

---

12. *Ibid.*, p. 63.

4. *Pragmatism*

Pragmatism has been called "a rebel child of idealism." In some forms, it could also be accurately described as a first cousin to naturalism. John Dewey preferred to call his pragmatic views empirical naturalism.

Pragmatism is chiefly an American philosophy. It says the way to test the truth of ideas is to see how they work out in practical experience; what works is true, what fails to work is false.

As a way of testing procedures in Christian education, pragmatism has much to offer. We do well to stop and evaluate the materials we use and the methods we employ. The whole movement of educational testing is a pragmatic approach that seeks to find out if what we are doing is bringing the results we desire.

But there are also dangers in the pragmatic emphasis. Pragmatism has been closely allied with empiricism. If we are not careful, we construct our tests exclusively in terms of what can be known through sense experience. Ferré[13] points out that the physical world seems most real to us, the social environment is next real, and God often seems the least real—and of least practical importance. But Christian thought reverses the order of these values. We must, therefore, avoid applying the pragmatic tests in areas where they are least useful. Faith in God and selfless service to our fellowman seem not to pay off in the short run. If, therefore, we are to accept pragmatic tests, we must ask, Will the idea work in the long run? and, Is the plan workable in view of God's promises?

5. *Existentialism*

Existentialism is more a mood than a system of philosophy. It places emphasis upon the importance of the present, the *existential moment*. Christian faith does not deny the importance of our present experience. However, a Christian view of life bids us evaluate the present in the light of God's care in past experiences and in view of His promises for the future—both here and hereafter. For Christian education, existentialism's emphasis upon the supreme importance of the present moment is more an error to be corrected than a guideline to be used to see life clearly and to see it whole.

A second focus is that existentialism views knowledge more for decision than for information. Such a view is a needed corrective in our age. Too often in pure science, knowledge for the sake of knowl-

---

13. *Ibid.*, p. 71.

edge is viewed as of supreme value. We have already noted idealism's emphasis upon a rationalism that excludes feeling and choice. Such a view contradicts the biblical emphasis upon God's concern for the whole person. At this point existentialism furnishes a needed corrective to an extreme intellectualism.

When, however, we accept existentialism as a full-orbed philosophy, we endanger knowledge as well as Christian faith. If the existentialist rejects logic and science, he endangers the whole educational enterprise. Christian education needs more than accurate data and clear thinking, but we cannot get along with less. Christian education calls for decision, but Christian decisions must be based on accurate knowledge and a rational understanding of the results of our choices.

D. Toward a Christian Philosophy

A valid view of the world must make a place for facts. The empirical world given through sense experiences is an undeniable datum to be accounted for. Christian thought holds that this world was created by God as a home for man. These views of creation and of Christian responsibility for the earth are premises of Christian faith based on confidence in revelations of Scripture. Because man is a rational creature, he is under compulsion to find meaning in his existence.

A Christian philosophy seeks to recognize the realities of empirical facts, of meanings, and of faith. It seeks to assess the importance of each and to discover how each is related to the others.

Christian philosophy must employ reason as a basic tool for meaning. God created man as a reasoning person. The mind cannot accept contradictory meanings and remain satisfied. We must accept the principle of coherence as a guide to truth, or we cannot find meaning in our experience. But when reason has taken us as far as it can in finding meaning to life, it falls short unless we find some help beyond ourselves. Every philosophy that omits a loving Creator fails to account for the meaning that Christians find in life. Any acceptable philosophy must account for the values discovered by those who commit themsleves in faith to God, the Father.

III. A Survey of Recent Trends

It will be helpful at this point to review the major streams of thought within the church that have helped to shape Christian education as we find it today.

As Kendig B. Cully has shown,[14] Christians have been in search, during much of this century, for a philosophy of Christian education. For decades prior to 1940, students of religious education (evangelical circles excepted) were indoctrinated with a theological liberalism which had a philosophical rather than a biblical basis. The influence of John Dewey and progressive education was strong. Educators such as George A. Coe and Harrison Elliott devoted their energies to the support of religious education within the context of theological liberalism.

As a proponent of the liberalist viewpoint, Harrison Elliott had raised the question in 1940, "Can religious education be Christian?"[15] and had replied in the affirmative.

However, in 1948, H. Shelton Smith shattered the foundations of the "liberalist continuum," at least in its older form, by his epochal work, *Faith and Nurture.*[16] Smith gathered up the emerging movements in biblical theology and called for a reexamination of liberal Christian nurture. He asserted that Christian nurture should find its basis in the biblical and historical roots of the Christian Church rather than in secular positions.

In tracing the search for a Christian education since 1940, Cully describes eight streams of thought including those associated with Harry C. Munro (a moderate liberal), Lewis J. Sherrill, Randolph Crump Miller, D. Campbell Wyckoff, and J. Donald Butler (all appreciative, albeit critical, of the "new orthodoxy"), Lois E. LeBar and Frank E. Gaebelein (neo-evangelicals), Jacques Maritain (Roman Catholic), and A. Victor Murray (a moderate British liberal.) Each of these authors and movements represents a unique response to the challenge articulated by Elliott and Smith. Each has been influential in Christian educational circles. Several have been heavily involved in the development of new curricula for the major denominations.

The watershed issue, separating the discredited liberal *religious* education from the emerging *Christian* education was, and continues to be, the extent to which the biblical, historical, and theological

---

14. Kendig B. Cully, *The Search for a Christian Education* Since 1940 (Philadelphia: The Westminster Press, 1965).

15. Harrison S. Elliot, *Can Religious Education Be Christian?* (New York: The Macmillan Co., 1940).

16. H. Shelton Smith, *Faith and Nurture* (New York: Charles Scribner's Sons, 1948).

roots of the Christian faith are allowed to nourish the educational ministry of the church.

This core issue centers about the following pairs of contrasting terms: process versus content, existential versus historical, relevant and personal versus biblical and theological. Those on the theological left tend to identify with process, existentialism, and relevancy. Those on the theological right tend to identify with content, with the historical, biblical, and theological emphases. More educators, however, including evangelicals, desire to unite these pairs, blending process and content, the existential and historical, in order to make the biblical and theological elements of the Christian faith relevant and personal.[17]

Differences, of course, remain among Christian educators. However, it is a source of gratification to those who are committed to the historic Christian faith to know that the search for a Christian education has led away from secular philosophies, to the biblical and theological wellsprings which have fed the Christian faith for so many centuries. In the words of Kendig B. Cully, "There has been for some years a joyful celebration of theology's rightful return to the religious education arena."[18]

IV. COMPONENTS FOR A THEOLOGY OF CHRISTIAN EDUCATION

It was suggested at the outset of this chapter that possibly the principal contribution theology and philosophy can make to our cause is to assist in the formulation of a viable view of Christian education.

A. What Are the Ultimate Principles?

The following quotation may serve as a succinct summary and preview:

> A Christian philosophy of education accepts and builds upon the Christian revelation as the true word of God . . . upon the bib-

---

17. See, e.g., Kenneth O. Gangel, *Leadership for Christian Education*, pp. 37-38, and Lois E. LeBar, *Focus on People in Church Education* (Westwood, N.J.: Fleming H. Revell Co., 1968), ch. 2.

18. Kendig B. Cully, *A Search for Christian Education*, p. 160. For accounts that parallel Cully's, see "Theology and Christian Education" by James Blair Miller in the *Westminster Dictionary of Christian Education*, pp. 665-68, and Wayne R. Rood, *Understanding Christian Education*, pp. 170-78.

lical views of God and man, man's possibilities for good or evil, and man's need of a Saviour.[19]

The ultimates that affect educational practice among us are our Christian beliefs. We shall first see what these beliefs are, and then examine what bearing they have on our educational practice. A viable theology for Christian education, espoused and offered here, may be described as Christian, Protestant, and Wesleyan.

1. *A Theology That Is Christian*

The theology implicit in the Apostles' Creed is Christian and evangelical in the classical sense.

I believe in God the Father, Almighty, Maker of heaven and earth.

Natural theology can provide a reasoned defense of theism, a defense encouraged by the Scriptures (1 Pet. 3:15) and so is not to be scorned. However, the biblical account begins with the announcement that God is and that He is the Creator and Sustainer of all things. The early Christians thus taught that the God of redemption and the God of creation are one and the same. We believe that "this is my Father's world."

And in Jesus Christ, His only Son, our Lord.

The Christian Scriptures clearly teach that the Almighty God has revealed himself in the Son, the Eternal Word who became flesh in Jesus of Nazareth (John 1:1, 14). The disciples of Jesus at first saw Him as Rabbi, but later as Messiah and Lord, then finally as the Son of God (Heb. 1:1-4).

His birth among men was unique: *conceived by the Holy Ghost, born of the Virgin Mary.* His deity and sinlessness were thus assured. His life and death were historical, redemptive, and vicarious: *suffered under Pontius Pilate, was crucified, dead, and buried.* In affirming that *He descended into hell* (hades, realm of the dead), the Church declared its faith that the death of Jesus was real and that between His death and resurrection, He carried a message to those already dead (1 Pet. 3:18-19; 4:6).

The assertion *The third day He arose again from the dead* embodies the cornerstone of the Christian faith, for He was "designated Son of God in power according to the Spirit of holiness by his resurrection from the dead" (Rom. 1:4, RSV). The hope of mankind for the life to

---

19. J. William Jones, "A Philosophy of Education for Christian Educators," an unpublished paper presented to the faculty of Northwest Nazarene College, 1969. See Appendix IV for a complete statement of the philosophy of Christian education upon which the Church of the Nazarene bases its curriculum.

come rests upon the validity of this statement. "For as in Adam all die, so also in Christ shall all be made alive" (1 Cor. 15:22, RSV). The fact that *He ascended into heaven, and sitteth at the right hand of God the Father Almighty* assures us that He lives forever and intercedes with the Father for His Church.

The Church looks not alone to the past, but also with hope to the future, for *from thence He shall come to judge the quick and the dead.* The doctrine of a real Second Coming is a cardinal element in the historic Christian faith.

I believe in the Holy Ghost. The great majority of Christians believe that God is triune in essential being and that He has revealed himself in history as Father, Son, and Holy Spirit (John 14:26; 15:26). It is important also to see that the believer's present experience of God is trinitarian, for it is through the name and merit of Christ that we have access in the power of the Spirit to the Father (Eph. 2:18).

The holy catholic (universal) *Church.* The Church—an assembly of called-out ones—is the Body of Christ, and believers are members severally of it (1 Cor. 12:27). If Christ founded the Church (Matt. 16:18) and gave himself in sacrifice for its holiness (Eph. 5:25-26), how can His disciples fail to love the Church and support it?

The immeasurable love of the Father, finding expression in the self-giving of the Son, makes possible *the communion of saints* and *the forgiveness of sins,* by the power of the Spirit. Believers are called out of the world to form the Church *(ecclesia),* in order to enjoy the fellowship *(koinonia)* of the Spirit among the disciples, who are members of the Church Militant (on earth) and the Church Triumphant (in heaven).

The "theology of hope" is in reality nothing new, because the New Testament teaches, and the Christian Church has always proclaimed, *the resurrection of the body, and the life everlasting.* This present, frail body is sown "a natural body," but at the time of the *parousia,* it is raised a "spiritual body" (1 Cor. 15:44). Many details of the end time remain unclear or unknown, but nothing is more certain than that finally we shall be forever with the Lord (1 Thess. 4:17).

To all this the forgiven, Spirit-filled believer may gladly say, *Amen.*

It is quite true that the Apostles' Creed can be recited in a perfunctory manner. But this is true of any religious exercise, including prayer. It should be noted that each of the principal paragraphs of the creed begins not with the statement "I believe *that,*" but rather,

"I believe *in*." To make this hallowed confession of faith is to give a testimony of personal commitment to God.

2. *A Theology That Is Protestant*

We owe an enormous debt to the Reformers of the 16th century and to their precursors, such as John Huss and John Wycliffe. Martin Luther, Philipp Melanchthon, Ulrich Zwingli, John Calvin, and others were men of great learning and piety. The harsh things they had to say concerning the medieval Roman church were no more severe than the criticism of men like Erasmus, who did not leave the institutional church.

In its original usage, the word *Protestant* was not essentially a negative term. Those who chose to break with the Roman Catholic church wished to "protest," in the sense of proclaim, their beliefs. These convictions included: the supremacy of the Scriptures, justification by faith alone, and the universal priesthood of believers.

a. The supremacy of the Scriptures. In the Roman Catholic view, the Church has given the world both dogma (tradition) and Scripture, therefore the two are coordinate or equal and both subordinate to the Church. In the Protestant view, both the Church and its teaching stand under the judgment of the divine Word, communicated through the Bible.

In this view, God has revealed himself through His people Israel and in His Son, Jesus Christ. Inspired by the Holy Spirit, the prophets and the apostles received and transmitted this revelation in what we know as the Old and New Testaments. Revelation is, therefore, first of all *personal*, because God has spoken by the prophets and by His Son (Heb. 1:1-2). Revelation is also *propositional*, because the statements of the Bible convey the divine Word. We are confronted in the Scriptures with revealed truth. Inspired men (2 Pet. 1:21) produced an inspired literature (2 Tim. 3:16-17). The divine Word brought the Church into being and stands in judgment over it. All standards of doctrine and ethics are to be measured by the Word.

b. Justification by faith alone. This doctrine was one of the pillars of the Reformation in all its major segments: Lutheran, Reformed, and Anglican. The watchword of the Reformers was: "By grace alone; through faith alone; to God alone be the glory."

The Reformers, of course did not originate this doctrine but rediscovered it in the Bible and removed from it the encrustations of the centuries. In the words of Paul, "Therefore being justified by faith, we have peace with God through our Lord Jesus Christ" (Rom.

5:1). The Epistles of Paul to the Galatians and to the Romans expand powerfully on this theme.

But Paul was at pains to show that Abraham was justified by faith, centuries before the Law was given (Gen. 15:6), and that David bore witness to the forgiveness of sins (Ps. 32:1-2). Thus, although the Gospels proclaim this truth (John 3:16), the message of justification by faith did not begin even with the Christian era.

Two groups become uneasy upon hearing this doctrine announced: Roman Catholics, who believe in justification by works as well as by faith; and some Protestants, who fear the doctrine will discourage good works. To the Catholic view Eph. 2:8 comes as a sharp rejoinder: "For by grace are ye saved through faith." The fears of the second group may be allayed by remembering that it was Paul himself who wrote to the Galatians: "The only thing that counts is faith expressing itself through love" (NIV), or, as the King James Version has it, "faith which worketh by love" (Gal. 5:6).

It is true that we are justified by faith alone, but this grace does not stand alone; it either produces good works or it atrophies and dies (Jas. 2:20). But let the word never be diminished: *the righteousness which is of God by faith will set you free!*

c. The universal priesthood of believers. Martin Luther gave this doctrine special stress, but it is fundamental to all Protestantism. The full implication of this teaching, however, is often missed. Every Christian is indeed his own priest, "but what is most important is that every Christian is a priest to others . . . This common priesthood . . . binds the church together . . . and liberates it from subjection to hierarchical authority."[20]

The hedges against rampant individualism are the unity of the Church, and the awesome responsibility that the Church has to guard the purity of its preaching, teaching, and sacramental ministry.

Jesus meant exactly what He said in giving the keys of the Kingdom to Peter and the other disciples (Matt. 16:19), and from them on to us: we may open and close the doors of the Kingdom. There is a sense in which there is no salvation outside the Church. If men who know Christ, and are thus part of the Church, fail to proclaim Christ, there is no salvation for those outside. "How shall they hear without a preacher?" (Rom. 10:14).

But the role of the Church, though important, is only instrumen-

---

20. Justo L. Gonzalez, *A History of Christian Thought* (Nashville: Abingdon Press, 1975), 3:53-56.

tal. The Scripture declares, "There is one God, and one mediator between God and man, the man Christ Jesus" (1 Tim. 2:5). Thus, all men have direct access to God through Christ, in the power of the Spirit.

3. *A Theology That Is Wesleyan*

The theology for Christian education espoused in this text is representative of one stream of thought in the contemporary movement described earlier as neo-evangelical. The new evangelicalism embraces a variety of theological emphases including: classic orthodoxy (Lutheran and Reformed), Anglican thought, Pietism, Arminianism, Keswickianism, Fundamentalism, and others. All of these groups, however, communicate well through such publications as *Christianity Today* and such organizations as the National Association of Evangelicals. The Wesleyan bodies have association through the Christian Holiness Association.

The following exposition of key Wesleyan-Arminian positions is designed to strengthen evangelical understanding, particularly of the doctrines related to salvation.

Just as the Protestant Reformation revived such biblical truths as justification by faith, so the evangelical revival of the 18th century, under the principal leadership of the Wesleys, revived and clarified the biblical emphasis upon sanctification and related issues. The Wesleys as well as the Reformers, brought to expression movements of thought and experience long surging in the church. As George C. Cell has observed, John Wesley's contribution was "an original and unique synthesis of the Protestant ethic of grace with the Catholic ethic of holiness."[21]

a. John Calvin, following Augustine, had taught an absolute predestination, a limited atonement, and an effectual (irresistible) grace. Basic to this system was a doctrine of total depravity that offered no hope of recovery except through unconditional election and effectual grace.

James Arminius (1560-1609) and the Remonstrants of Holland resisted Calvin's views on predestination. Although defeated and banished by the Synod of Dort (1618-19), they set loose in the world the concept of universal, prevenient grace, the teaching that all men may be saved if they will.

Arminianism specially influenced the Anglican Church in

---

21. George C. Cell, *The Rediscovery of John Wesley,* quoted in George A. Turner, *The More Excellent Way* (Winona Lake, Ind.: Light and Life Press, 1952), p. 16.

nearby England, and one of her sons, John Wesley. Through him and his Methodist societies, the concept of an unlimited atonement and universal prevenient grace has affected the Christian world.

John Wesley believed in original sin and total depravity as seriously as any Calvinist. He writes, "Is man by nature filled with all manner of evil? . . . Is he wholly fallen? Is his soul totally corrupted? . . . Allow this and you are so far a Christian. Deny it, and you are but an Heathen still."[22] But Wesley also believed and preached that a universal, prevenient grace (preceding salvation) has quickened every man, enabling all to hear the Savior's voice and, if they will, to repent and believe. "For allowing that all the souls of men are dead in sin by *nature,* this excuses none, seeing there is no man that is in a state of mere nature . . . But this is not natural: It is more properly termed, *preventing* [prevenient] grace. Every man has a greater or less measure of this, which waiteth not for the call of man."[23]

A true Arminian affirms the doctrine of original sin but holds equally to a saving grace freely available to all men.

b. Christian assurance. John Wesley was not the first, of course, to teach the doctrine of the witness of the Spirit.[24] It was a group of Moravian Brethren missionaries, heirs of Pietism, who first convicted Wesley of his inner poverty and need of assurance. Nevertheless, Wesley's own experience sparked the great spiritual awakening of 18th-century England:

> In the evening I went very unwillingly to a society in Aldersgate Street, where one was reading Luther's preface to the *Epistle to the Romans.* About a quarter before nine, while he was describing the change which God works in the heart through faith in Christ, I felt my heart strangely warmed. I felt I did trust in Christ, Christ alone for salvation; and an assurance was given me that He had taken away *my* sins, even *mine,* and saved *me* from the law of sin and death.[25]

In subsequent years, through a long lifetime and an incredible ministry throughout the British Isles, Wesley developed and refined his understanding of Christian assurance in sermons, letters, and the debates and discussions of the business meetings of his Methodist societies. This teaching has served to revive the biblical emphasis

---

22. Robert W. Burtner and Robert E. Chiles, eds., *A Compend of Wesley's Theology* (Nashville: Abingdon Press, 1954), p. 131.

23. *Ibid.,* p. 148.

24. Gonzalez, *History of Christian Thought,* 3:139-40, et passim.

25. Burtner and Chiles, *Compend of Wesley's Theology,* pp. 101-2.

upon assurance (Rom. 8:16, e.g.) and is one part of the legacy the Wesleys have given to the Christian world.

> *Blessed assurance, Jesus is mine!*
> *Oh, what a foretaste of glory divine!*

   c. Entire sanctification. John Wesley pursued relentlessly, it seemed, the ideal of Christian holiness and found entire sanctification to be a provision of God's grace—later than justification, but earlier than death. Wesley and his cohorts therefore preached a second work of grace, which he called Christian perfection (a perfection in love or motive). He believed their people were raised up chiefly to propagate this message. "The Methodists maintained the doctrine of free, full, present justification . . . and of entire sanctification, both of heart and life; being as tenacious of inward holiness as any Mystic; and of outward, as any Pharisee."[26]

   Wesley's own theology of sanctification included a dual stress— sanctification as gradual and as instantaneous. As the emphasis by the church upon a crisis experience waned, especially in America, various groups emerged during the 19th century to promote Christian holiness, as Wesley had taught it, and as they had experienced it. Several of these groups have grown and flourished in the 20th century and have joined moral forces in the Christian Holiness Association. The largest of these denominations are the Church of God (Anderson, Ind.), the Church of the Nazarene, the Free Methodist Church, and the Wesleyan Church. The theology of the Salvation Army and of several conferences of Friends is also strongly Wesleyan.

   These groups believe and teach that there is not only a birth of the Spirit, but also a baptism of the Spirit; not only a forgiveness of committed sins, but also a cleansing from inherited sin or depravity.[27] They find this truth in the Scriptures. Quite naturally and without evident thought of doctrinal teaching, the Psalmist prayed, "Hide thy face from my sins, and blot out all my iniquities. Create in me a clean heart, O God; and renew a right spirit within me" (Ps. 51: 9-10).

   A weak view of the nature of sin weakens the seriousness with which sin is regarded. In terms of daily life, if no deliverance from sin is possible, the practice of sinning soon ceases to cause concern

---

   26. John Wesley, Sermon, "On God's Vineyard," *Works*, 7:204, quoted in George A. Turner, *The Vision Which Transforms* (Kansas City: Beacon Hill Press, 1964), p. 217.
   27. For a thorough treatment of these positions, see H. Orton Wiley, *Christian Theology* (Kansas City: Beacon Hill Press, 1952), 2:440-517.

This century has seen a revival of interest in the biblical doctrine of sanctification. The darksome aspect of human behavior has pointed up the need for the work of God's grace *within* man as well as *on behalf of* man. The late W. E. Sangster, for example, described this work of God's grace in the following winsome words:

> There is an experience of God the Holy Spirit, available for all who will seek it with importunity, which imparts spiritual power far above the level enjoyed by the average Christian; which inspires a caring Godlike love different in kind and degree from the affections of normal nature; which communicates to the eager soul the penetrating power of holiness.[28]

d. Christian tolerance. To speak of Christian tolerance as a doctrine is not to think of it in the sense of an article of faith so much as the expression of a spirit. Wesleyans, loyal to their Arminian heritage, hope that this attitude will characterize their relationship with believers who differ from them on doctrinal issues. The following ideal of one denomination will serve as an example: "Recognizing that the right and privilege of persons to church membership rest upon the fact of their being regenerate, we would require only such avowals of belief as are essential to Christian experience."[29] Immediately following this position are 8 brief statements (summarizing the longer 15 Articles of Faith) which are deemed "to be sufficient."

Surprisingly, perhaps, such a sentiment has a long and distinguished ancestry in Arminian and Wesleyan history. Heick, for example, observes that early Arminianism in Holland and in Great Britain advocated a "tolerance and mutual recognition on the basis of a distinction between fundamentals and nonfundamentals."[30] Among those he cites as examples are George Calixtus, a 17th-century German Lutheran, Richard Baxter (d. 1691), and Edward Stillingfleet (d. 1699). It is said that Baxter's motto was: "In essentials, unity; in non-essentials, liberty; in everything, charity."[31]

Representative of this Christian tolerance is a sermon John Wesley preached and published, entitled "Catholic Spirit." In it he says, "Is thine heart right, as my heart is with thine heart? . . . If it be, give me thy hand." Wesley teaches in this sermon, "A man of catho-

---

28. W. E. Sangster, *The Path to Perfection* (New York: Abingdon-Cokesbury Press, 1943), p. 8.

29. *Manual, Church of the Nazarene,* 1976 (Kansas City: Nazarene Publishing House, 1976), p. 32.

30. Otto W. Heick, *A History of Christian Thought* (Philadelphia: Fortress Press, 1966), 2:48.

31. *Ibid.,* p. 84.

lic spirit is one who . . . gives his hand to all those whose heart is right with his heart."[32]

Closer to our time, Phineas F. Bresee, a leading founder of the Church of the Nazarene, bequeathed to his people, shortly before his death, the following persuasion:

> On the great fundamentals we are all agreed. Pertaining to things not essential to salvation, we have liberty. To attempt to emphasize that which is not essential to salvation and thus divide forces, would be a crime. An unwillingness for others to enjoy the liberty that we enjoy in reference to doctrines not vital to salvation, is bigotry, from which the spirit of holiness withdraws itself.[33]

It should be evident that for those holding these sentiments, the distinction has already been made between the fundamentals and nonfundamentals. There is an unqualified commitment to all doctrines regarded as "essential to salvation." Also, it is hoped that Christian tolerance is an expression of the perfect love Wesleyans trust will characterize even their theological work.

B. Theological Principles and Educational Practice

Randolph Crump Miller writes:

> Christian education is concerned with the relevance of Christian revealed truth. Theology, which is the *truth-about-God-in-relation-to-man,* is the determining factor in the development of a philosophy of education, of techniques to be used, of goals to be attained, and of the nature of the learners to be taught.[34]

How does a theology that is Christian, Protestant, and Wesleyan affect educational practice among those committed to that theology? The following positions appear to be essential.

1. *The Uniqueness of the Bible*

At this point Wesleyans agree with all evangelicals. The uniqueness of the Bible is summarized well by Bernard Ramm:

> *The Bible is binding upon the Christian because it is a part of the organism of divine revelation* . . . The content of the Bible is given by

---

32. Sermon XXXIV, "Catholic Spirit," *Wesley's Standard Sermons,* Edward H. Sugden, ed. (London: Epworth Press, 1951), 2:126-46.

33. E. A. Girvin, *Phineas F. Bresee: A Prince in Israel* (Kansas City: Pentecostal Nazarene Publishing House, 1916), p. 452.

34. Randolph Crump Miller, *Education for Christian Living,* 2nd ed. (Englewood Cliffs, N.J.: Prentice Hall, Inc., 1963), p. 5.

the double action of special revelation and divine inspiration and therefore it is for the Christian the revealed word of God.[35]

To be sure, every responsible effort must be made to see that the Scriptures are "rightly divided" (2 Tim. 2:15). Sound principles of hermeneutics are essential.

> *But that which is educed from the Scriptures by reliance upon the teaching ministry of the Holy Spirit and upon the soundest principles of Biblical interpretation will be taken by the Christian as the authoritative truth of revelation for the guidance of his own soul.*[36]

The whole sweep of the Christian faith—from the doctrines of God, man, and nature, to the doctrines of sin and salvation, the Church, ethics, and the Christian life, on to the truths concerning the end time—all spring finally from the Bible. If we accept the biblical point of view, we shall see all of these truths in a light quite different from that shed by secular sources.

It will, therefore, be an educational aim of the church not only to help all learners to gain a knowledge of the Bible, but also to seek the cultivation of the biblical point of view and the development of the biblical mind, the mind that was in Christ (Phil. 2:5). This must be the aim of all educational agencies of the evangelical church, not only the local church school, but all other schools as well.

2. The Worthiness of the Christian Church

We have already examined the historic Christian affirmation of *the holy catholic* (universal) *Church*, the Church which Christ founded (Matt. 16:18) and for which He gave himself in love (Eph. 5:25).

Through its long history, the visible church has sometimes been unworthy of its Lord. When that occurs, divine judgment falls, but powers of cleansing and renewal are also released. The gates of hell have never prevailed against the Church (Matt. 16:18).

The implications of these truths for Christian education are at least twofold: (1) the teaching of the church in any generation is under the influence of the centuries of Christian thought preceding; (2) one of the aims of Christian education will be to draw all learners into the fellowship of the church, to train them in churchmanship, and to bind them to the church with cords of love and loyalty.

The place of churchmanship has already been discussed in chap-

---

35. Bernard Ramm, *The Pattern of Religious Authority* (Grand Rapids, Mich.: Wm. B. Eerdmans Publishing Co., 1957), p. 38.

36. *Ibid.*, p. 40.

ter 1. The history of Christian thought, however, calls for additional comment.

It is sometimes supposed that each generation of believers can and should begin anew with a fresh interpretation of the Scriptures and the faith that they convey. In the words of Cotton Mather, "The Lord hath more light yet to break forth out of his Holy Word." This light we should welcome. It is also true, however, that the Spirit of truth has been at work through the centuries in the minds of thoughtful believers, as they have wrestled with the thorny issues of the faith. To quote Bernard Ramm again:

> If Christ has founded a Church and given it His word, if the Holy Spirit is the Teacher of the faithful; if the Church is the "house of God . . . the pillar and ground of the truth" (I Tim. 3:15); *then every generation of Christian theologians must be prepared to take seriously the history of theology* (broadly interpreted to include symbols, councils, theologians, treatises) *as possessing manifestations of the teaching ministry of the Holy Spirit.*[37]

Practically speaking, this means that all Christian educators should check the content of their teaching against the historic Christian doctrines, such as the doctrines of the Trinity, original sin, the atonement, and salvation. Further, as young disciples are inspired to catch a vision of the vast throng of believers "marching to Zion," through the ages, a sense of awe and respect touches them and strengthens their commitment.

3. *The Seriousness of Sin and the Primacy of Salvation*

The overarching human problem is sin. Its effects are far-reaching and powerful. The work of redemption through Jesus Christ is salvation from sin. "Thou shalt call his name Jesus: for he shall save his people from their sins" (Matt. 1:21). Moreover, the central purpose of the Scriptures is to make us "wise unto salvation" (2 Tim. 3:15).

The Epistle to the Romans, the leading doctrinal treatise of the New Testament, is evidence for the validity of the foregoing assertions. After announcing the theme of the Epistle—the righteousness which is of God by faith (1:16-17)—the apostle launches into a prolonged description of man's fall from grace to idolatry, with its subsequent corruption in the sensual and antisocial vices (1:18-32). He pursues the subject further in a consideration of the barrenness and darkness of the merely moral man who has the law but has rejected

---

37. *Ibid.*, p. 57.

its precepts. Paul concludes that "all the world" has "become guilty before God" (3:19). Only after this extended discourse on man's need does the apostle go on to describe the remedy in the gospel.

Such an analysis of the reality and ugliness of original sin has long been an offense to the natural mind. Liberal religious education, with its tendencies to deny original sin and to discount sinning, gave short shrift to the doctrine of conversion. Indeed, according to this view, a child should grow up never knowing himself to be other than a Christian.[38]

Christian education, drawing on its biblical and theological roots, acknowledges the reality and ugliness of sin and seeks to prepare all learners to experience the reality and beauty of salvation. As stated in chapter 1, the first goal, in the pursuit of the objective of Christian education, should be evangelism.[39]

4. *The Importance of Moral Guidance*

Churches committed to the heritage of Christian holiness usually require of their adherents a high standard of personal and social ethics. These standards have often taken the form of rules or guidelines for behavior. The purpose of such rules is to offer guidance for the moral life of the believer and to express a consensus as an aid to the unity of the church. Legalism, the doctrine of salvation by works, was never the intent.

---

38. A teaching associated with the thought of Horace Bushnell. One may disagree with Bushnell on this point without depreciating his genius or the lasting significance of his life and work.

39. Richard S. Taylor suggests, in an unpublished essay, that the doctrine of original sin bears on educational theory in the following ways:

(1) It brings a new dimension to the understanding of human behavior. No longer is one puzzled or surprised at the irrationality of man.

(2) The doctrine gives insight into the stubborn impediments to learning and to the growing process.

(3) The fact of depravity imposes limits on the educational process in achieving maturity and inner fitness.

(4) The doctrine of original sin requires that at the heart of educational theory there be a counter-balancing doctrine of sanctification.

(5) Acknowledgment of this doctrine will shape educational methods:

(a) Conversion and heart cleansing become essential elements in personal change toward Christlikeness.

(b) Discipline becomes an integral and logical necessity, as a means of combatting natural obstinacy and moral weakness.

(c) There must be maximum exposure to the good, the beautiful, and the true, with minimum exposure to the evil, ugly, and false.

(d) Because of the incalculable strength of the downward pull in fallen human nature, the Christian educator will include a large measure of dependence on prayer in his total methodology.

The Bible offers ample evidence that the church needs to provide wise moral instruction for its people. The decalogue of the Old Testament (Exod. 20:3-17) and the Sermon on the Mount of the New Testament (Matthew 5—7) come to mind at once. Paul, in his Epistles, consistently discussed Christian doctrine and then Christian ethics. The Epistle to the Ephesians, e.g., is equally divided between the two: chapters 1—3 dealing with Christian doctrine, chapters 4—6 with Christian ethics.

An interesting commentary on the importance of moral guidance in the church is to be found in Acts 16:1-5. Paul and Silas, after the Jerusalem conference, revisited the churches of Galatia and delivered to them "the rules decided upon by the apostles and elders in Jerusalem, and told them to obey these rules" (v. 4, TEV). The prophets and apostles believed strongly in the importance of moral guidance for the people of God.

The implications of this factor for Christian education are obvious. Both by precept in the curriculum and by example in the life of the teacher or leader, Christian educators should seek to promote standards of Christian behavior. When this is done attractively and constructively, the beauty of the Christian life stands out in sharp contrast to the moral decay of the times and is self-authenticating.

5. The Sacredness of Human Personality

That man is of infinite value to God is clear from biblical teachings:

a. Man was created in the image of God (Gen. 1:26-27). This doctrine means that man is capable of fellowship with God and that his true destiny is fulfilled when in godliness he is like his Creator.

b. Man is the special object of God's love and care, first in *redemption* and then in *providence.* The wonder of the gospel is that "God sent forth his Son" (Gal. 4:4), in order to deliver man from the burden and penalty of his sin. But this is only the beginning: "He that spared not his own Son, but delivered him up for us all, how shall he not with him also freely give us all things?" (Rom. 8:32). God's providential care will follow those who love Him all the days of their lives (Rom. 8:28).

c. Man's ultimate destiny is complete personal fulfillment, both individually and socially, in a new heavens and earth. The hope of man is essentially eschatological, i.e., associated with the end time and the life to come.

Swift to its close ebbs out life's little day.
Earth's joys grow dim; its glories pass away.

The finest achievements of man soon crumble to dust. Our only real and lasting hope is in Him who has promised "everlasting life" to those who believe in Him (John 3:16). By the inspiration of the Holy Spirit, Paul has recorded for all time the sublimity of this Christian hope. "The Spirit itself beareth witness with our spirit, that we are the children of God: and if children, then heirs; heirs of God, and joint-heirs with Christ; if so be that we suffer with him, that we may be also glorified together" (Rom. 8:16-17).

The nobility, dignity, and grandeur of man are clearly evident from these teachings of the Bible. "What is man?" God has "made him a little lower than the angels" and has "crowned him with glory and honor" (Ps. 8:4-5).

It should be no surprise, therefore, that in the societies influenced by the Christian faith, life is precious and sacred. Both abortion, at the outset of life, and euthanasia, at its close, are frowned upon. Ignorance, sickness, discrimination, injustice, oppression, brutality, and distress of every sort become enemies of society when the gospel leavens the whole.

Let the Christian educator draw the inevitable conclusions. By the grace of God, he will have compassion and concern for all learners of every age and station of life. He will love them equally and well. He will toil, in every educational endeavor, to help them find the highest possible fulfillment as persons and as disciples of the Lord.

Summary

It has been our concern in this chapter to see how Christian theology and the Christian in philosophy provide for Christian education a solid foundation in faith and reason. It is imperative that the Christian educator discover the biblical, theological, and historical wellsprings which nourish the faith he seeks to transmit through the educational ministry of the church. If he misses these resources, his work will be shallow and his own interests will wane and die. Enriched by the glory of the Christian faith, revealed in the Scriptures and interpreted by the historic Christian Church, the Christian educator will find he has a message that he will never tire of communicating. It will be his lasting joy and reward to see that message transform the lives of young and old, as, through his efforts, Christ is formed in them (Gal. 4:19).

BIBLIOGRAPHY

Ferré, Nels F. S. *A Theology for Christian Education.* Philadelphia: The Westminster Press, 1967.

Chapters 6—9 provide an excellent discussion of philosophy and the major philosophical schools as they relate to the objectives of Christian education.

Little, Sara. *The Role of the Bible in Contemporary Christian Education.* Richmond, Va.: John Knox Press, 1961.

The author sees the role of the Bible in a place of increasing importance in Christian education. In chapter 2 she reviews the theological influences of the mid 20th century that moved Christian education from an extreme dependence on social science to a firmer foundation in biblical theology.

———. "Theology and Religious Education" in *Foundations for Christian Education in an Era of Change,* Marvin J. Taylor, ed. Nashville: Abingdon Press, 1976.

Dr. Little here explores the subject from the current pluralism of both theology and education in the last quarter of the 20th century.

Richards, Lawrence O. *A Theology of Christian Education.* Grand Rapids: Zondervan Publishing House, 1975.

In Part 1 the author discusses theological considerations. His theology may be called a theology of love. He sees the goals of Christian education as coming (1) to know one another as persons, (2) to care for one another deeply, (3) to share in one another's lives.

Schreyer, George M. *Christian Education in Theological Focus.* Philadelphia: The Christian Education Press, 1962.

Dr. Schreyer stresses the need for theological content as the core of Christian education.

Smith, H. Shelton. *Faith and Nurture.* New York: Charles Scribner's Sons, 1948.

The landmark work that challenged Christian education to modify its early 20th-century rootage in an extreme liberal position and to move back into a closer dependence on biblical theology.

Wiley, H. Orton. *Christian Theology.* Kansas City: Beacon Hill Press, 1952.

The best comprehensive treatment of Arminian-Wesleyan theology in which the authors of this text find their theological foundations. Volume 2, chapter 29 deals with Christian perfection.

CHAPTER 5

The Psychological Bases of Christian Education

I. PSYCHOLOGY AND CHRISTIAN EDUCATION

The field of psychology has earned high respect in recent decades. Therefore discussion of education would be incomplete apart from references to established principles of human growth and development.

These findings have evolved from the two major dimensions of psychology—clinical and experimental. As instruments for psychological measurement have become more precise, gains have been made in understanding human development and learning. Greater skills in the use of statistical measurement and computer capabilities signal continued advances in the field of general education.

Christian education, however, is education of a specific kind. In Christian education we recognize divine revelation as the source of what is to be learned. We also recognize that God's revelation of himself is the most important way that we learn about Him. But also we are especially concerned for individual persons. Therefore, if Christian education is to be taken seriously, consideration must be given to the findings of developmental and learning psychology.

Only as the issues are faithfully explored and Christian education is articulated within the framework of established psychological findings will the Christian message be communicated effectively and made most relevant to the needs of the persons to whom we minister.

A. Psychology Defined

> Psychology was first considered to be the study of the soul, then the study of the mind, next the study of consciousness, and lastly the study of behavior. It has been said that psychology first lost its soul, then lost its mind, finally lost consciousness. Psychology now is commonly defined as the study of the behavior of living organisms; it is sometimes described as the science of behavior.[1]

The goal of psychology is to observe, understand, and influence behavior. For the purposes of this text the use of the term will be restricted to human behavior. Many Christians will perhaps resent the implication of controlling human beings. Such a feeling is understandable, but in this context it is unwarranted. Few social scientists seek to make other persons faceless pawns or mechanical robots controlled by psychological operators. But they know that human beings cannot live together successfully without control—both external and internal. All human beings are externally controlled to some degree. The Sunday school class is dismissed when the bell rings to signal the end of the period. Someone decided what time the class should end and the method by which its end would be signalled. How could a Sunday school or any other social group function if such control was missing?

Man is also controlled by inner states. When his hunger drive is aroused, he seeks food. When he is full, an inner control inhibits further food consumption. Basic life needs exert controlling influences over us. These include the need for water, air, sleep, relief of bowel and bladder tension, pain, and sex expression.

Persons have many psychological needs to which Christian educators must pay close attention: the need to be loved, to love someone else, to belong to a group, to engage in meaningful activity, to learn. Honest attempts to meet these needs relieve the burdens of the less fortunate, fill Sunday school classrooms, and increase church membership.

Because emotional needs influence human behavior, tears of joy

---

1. Harry F. Harlow, James L. McGaugh, Richard F. Thompson, *Psychology* (San Francisco: Albion Publishing Co., 1971), p. 2.

and sorrow flow, shouts of glee erupt, groans of anguish rack the body, and words of love soothe the crying child.

Psychologists can help the Christian educator. They help us understand human behavior so that we can assist man in learning to control himself individually and in groups. As persons respond to such Christian education, each one achieves maximum fulfillment of his God-given potential with a minimum of interruption and anxiety.

B. Psychology and Theology

Just as was done in the previous chapter with philosophy and theology, for clear thinking, it is necessary to distinguish between the legitimate contributions that psychology and theology make to Christian education. Both are deeply concerned with man and his nature as will be discussed in detail in a later section. Theological views are based on God's revelation and the biblical record. Psychological views, like philosophical ones, are based on man's efforts at explanation.

Zeigler writes:

> Psychology has no tools for investigating the nature of God, the reality of guilt from God's view, the nature of faith from the view of the one in whom faith is placed, and therefore cannot properly speak on these matters. But all matters having to do with a person's perception of, evaluating of, having feelings about, and initiating action with regard to these same realities are proper subjects for the psychologist.[2]

Psychology studies man objectively, mainly from the perspective of his interaction with the environment; there is little emphasis upon moral evaluation of his responses. Theology, on the other hand, describes man in terms of his moral relationships to God and to other persons. Miller points out:

> Contemporary scientific psychologies are by and large empirically rather than theologically oriented. . . . We can conclude only that a Christian view of man cannot ignore the findings of empirical psychology, but that it should be critical of the faith assumptions of any psychology. Christian education will use the findings of empirical psychology to elucidate the gospel, but never to replace the gospel.[3]

---

2. Jesse H. Ziegler, in *Religious Education: A Comprehensive Survey,* Marvin J. Taylor, ed. (Nashville: Abingdon Press, 1960), p. 34.
3. Donald E. Miller in *An Introduction to Christian Education,* Marvin J. Taylor, ed. (Nashville: Abingdon Press, 1966), pp. 50-51.

Theology provides Christian education with the content of its curriculum and reminds us of revelation as a way of learning. Psychology offers principles for effective teaching and learning.

C. Science and Faith

Psychology, like other sciences, is earthbound. It has no tools for reaching into the spiritual dimensions of man. It deals with the body and the mind; its tools of investigation are limited to electronic devices, introspective reports, and subjective observations. Psychology, therefore, cannot hope to appraise the reaches of faith. The psychologist should also recognize that every fact in the realm of science has a faith assumption—that even his own scientific findings rest on a faith in the scientific method.

Our Christian faith, however, cannot be proved by scientific methods. God must be in the midst of every human experience of Christian faith, but God is beyond empirical knowledge. Nevertheless facts of experience can alter one's faith. Thus man's encounter with God involves both faith and observable behavior. Yet through faith, knowledge of God is possible. Through such knowledge faith in God is increased. Moses reminds us of such spiritual certainty when he writes: "Seek the Lord your God, and you will find him, if you search after him with all your heart and with all your soul" (Deut. 4:29, RSV). John also points us to the Source of Christian certainty: "No man hath seen God at any time; the only begotten Son . . . he hath declared him" (John 1:18).

Science can give man no direct knowledge of God; it can only provide facts upon which to ground faith. The results of psychological research into the nature of man and his behavior will not disclose any facts contrary to God's revealed truth. Truth is truth wherever it is found. Also truth discovered in one realm will not contradict truth in another. Any seeming contradiction is the result of mistaken data or mistaken interpretations that the researcher makes about his discoveries. When the psychologist turns from collecting experimental data to interpreting his data as it affects man's relationship to God, he is no longer acting as a research scientist but as a theologian. Christian educators do not deny any results of careful psychological research; but we question any of their conclusions that may seem to contradict biblical truth and Christian principles.

Psychology depends as much on the scientific method to extend its knowledge as theology depends on a clear understanding of revelation. The two disciplines are simply working in different realms—

and Christian education needs the contributions of both. Both disciplines make their distinctive contributions to understanding man—how he behaves, how he learns, how he can find the highest values, and how he can grow in his spiritual life. At this point Dean Bertha Munro's statement is pertinent; Christian education must combine "the best in education with the best in religion."[4]

II. THE NATURE OF MAN

Basic to any discussion of psychology are underlying assumptions about man. Allport underscores not only the fact of such assumptions but also their influence.

> Theories of learning (like much else in psychology) rest on the investigator's conception of the nature of man. In other words, every learning theorist is a philosopher, though he may not know it. To put the matter more concretely, psychologists who investigate (and theorize about) learning start with some preconceived view of the nature of human motivation.[5]

Because all theorists work from assumptions, we need not be ashamed of our Christian approach to psychology. Intellectual honesty, of course, requires us to state forthrightly our assumptions and the rationale for our position. Jaarsma has commented:

> A theory is always subject to an experimenter's point of view or reference of thought. There is no such thing as "let the facts lead where they will." Facts as isolated events are meaningless. The experimenter relates the facts into a meaningful relationship. But he always does this in the framework of his world and life view. Hence, the importance of how we as Christians view learning. The Christian considers the experimental data and techniques, but he does this as a Christian. As a Christian he hears the voice of God, verbally in the Scriptures, and providentially in history, in nature, and in conscience and culture.[6]

A. Man's Relationship to Environment

A primary question concerning man's nature must be, Is he master of his environment or is he victim of it?

Our response to such questions is crucial. If the response is that man is essentially a product of his environment, then Christians

---

4. Bertha Munro, *The Years Teach* (Kansas City: Beacon Hill Press of Kansas City, 1970), p. 48.
5. Gordon W. Allport, *Patterns and Growth in Personality* (New York: Holt, Rinehart and Winston, 1961), p. 84.
6. Cornelius Jaarsma in *An Introduction to Evangelical Christian Education*, J. Edward Hakes, ed. (Chicago: Moody Press, 1964), pp. 77-78.

tacitly subscribe to a view that places responsibility for man's actions outside himself; he is not morally accountable. How can one hold to a theology of moral responsibility and at the same time accept a view that allows a mechanistic control of all of man's responses?

We must have biblical answers to the following questions—and our answers must be consistent with the established truths of psychology.

Does the environment totally control man?

What role has the Holy Spirit in influencing man's behavior?

B. The Christian Perspectives

Christian writers have approached the nature of man and human development in different ways. Brief summaries of some of these are appropriate before proceeding with our own analysis.

1. *Development as Encounter*

Ziegler,[7] who admits to a strong bias toward Freud's psychoanalytic theory, integrates his thinking around the idea of encounter. This encounter is defined as confrontation which occurs and must be resolved among the various systems of the personality as postulated by Freud. Ziegler describes the original encounter as occurring in the baby or growing child. The child is dominated by untamed, pleasure-seeking drives without regard to whether such goals are morally right or wrong. Freud calls these drives for pleasure *id* functions.

In order for the child to choose an appropriate Christian behavior to satisfy his *id* functions, a development must occur. Ziegler sees this development growing out of the encounter between the most primitive part of the personality, the *id,* and the child's physical and social environment. Out of this necessity to choose, and out of the decision-making itself, the conscious intellect *(ego)* is produced.

"A second major encounter resulting in personality formation is the encounter of the drives of the *id* with the demands of the culture."[8] *Id* functions are characterized by impulsive attempts to get immediate satisfaction, e.g., sexual gratification. To many of these attempts Christian culture says no. This "no-saying" of culture then becomes internalized in the child's conscious and unconscious mind. Freud calls this internalized, negative monitor of one's behavior the *superego.* When the *superego* generates guilt feelings, it is described as

---

7. Zeigler, in *Religious Education,* p. 35.
8. *Ibid.,* p. 37.

conscience. When the *superego* gives the individual feelings of approval for his behavior, it is called the *ego-ideal*. Many of these positive feelings result from ideas the individual has internalized from peers and social institutions, such as the church and school.

Ziegler suggests that one's meeting with God as ultimate reality can be part of either of these two major encounters. In other words, God can be met through encounter with the objective physical world or through encounter with the world of culture and people. Such a view is consistent with our belief that God reveals himself in nature and through the people of God.

Ziegler, however, goes on to emphasize that God is not limited to these two avenues of personality development. He suggests a third as his unique contribution. When the *id* encounters God directly, another part of the personality is developed, the spirit. "Just as part of the culture is internalized so that a person has the controls always with him, so in the encounter with God there is an internalization of the object."[9] Thus God becomes internalized with the person as spirit. The spirit as the representative of ultimate moral right gives the person a sense of destiny, a home base, and a courage to be and to do. The task of Christian education, as Ziegler sees it, is twofold: (1) to capitalize on the usual encounters of persons with the objective world and with culture in order to promote the development of Christian habit patterns *(ego)* and also Christian conscience *(superego)* and (2) to promote the direct encounter of persons with God, thus developing the spirit.

2. Development as Self-involvement

Jaarsma's discussion[10] of human development explores the historic philosophical debate, Is man a whole inseparable unit, or is his nature twofold? Conservative theology has usually supported the dual nature of man, but Jaarsma rejects the tendency to separate man into discrete elements of mind and body. He argues that the view is unscriptural as well as unsound in the light of evidence from the behavioral sciences.

When psychology and sociology describe man as a functioning whole, writers are usually thinking in biological terms. Jaarsma, however, is unwilling to limit man's unity to this one dimension. He suggests that a Christian view of man must stress his inseparable wholeness—both body and mind. But man also has a godlike quality,

---

9. *Ibid.*, p. 39.
10. Cornelius Jaarsma in *Introduction to Christian Education*, pp. 72-75.

the image of God, which he received at his creation and which sets him distinctly apart from plant and animal life. This godlikeness, the ego or the "I," infuses the mental and physical dimensions of a person's life. The objective of personal development is self-fulfillment, the realization of godlikeness in every dimension and function of life.

Heredity furnishes man his physical and mental equipment; environment provides him opportunity to fulfill his potentialities. But heredity and environment are inadequate to account completely for human development. Early in life the self or ego takes over the making of the person. Thus, "heredity, environment, and the self function as an integrated whole in the organic unity of the person. . . . In part we are born, in part we are made, and in part we make ourselves."[11]

These two views of human development illustrate the primary shades of difference among Christian perspectives. They also illuminate the main issues between Christian and secular views. Both theories underscore the basic importance of considering the nature of man. With this background let us seek a better understanding of man's nature through a relatively simple structure relating hereditary and environmental forces.[12]

C. Heredity and Environment

The relative roles and impacts of heredity and environment are described by some psychologists as *active, passive,* or *interactive.* Hereditary influences are internal in man and environmental influences are external to the person. When one speaks of man being *active,* he is describing the dominance of the internal, hereditary forces over the external, environmental influences. Insofar as the environmental forces dominate the hereditary factors, man is regarded as *passive.* *Interactive* theories hold that man's nature and personality are shaped by the interplay between the hereditary and environmental forces.

1. Man as Active

For many centuries the emphasis was on the power of heredity to determine one's social position and the quality of his personality. Family background was the crucial factor. Having "good blood" or

---

11. *Ibid.,* p. 74.
12. Morris L. Bigge and Maurice P. Hunt, *Psychological Foundations of Education,* 2nd ed. (New York: Harper and Row, Publishers, 1968), p. 58.

being from "good stock" determined one's destiny. The lines of royalty and inherited monarchies were probably built on this belief.

Emphasis on the internal forces has taken various forms and has influenced thinking in many areas. When this active concept stresses biological drives or instincts, the emphasis of educational philosophy is weighted heavily in favor of the body, such as stamping habits in the neural pathways. When emphasis is on mental foundations, education tries to help individuals control the body by exercising the power of their minds; for example, if one knows the right thing to do, he will do it.

2. *Man as Passive*

According to this view environment determines man's personality. An early form of this theory was John Locke's *tabula rasa* concept—a baby is a blank tablet; give him planned experiences and he will become anything that the planner desires. This theory did not even ask whether the child has prerequisite potential to become what was planned for him.

In more recent history the emphasis on environmental forces has paralleled the growth of psychology as a science. Many findings of research on animal behavior, when applied to the human realm, result in this passive view of man. The influence of this environmental deterministic thinking is responsible for many of the current efforts at social reform through environmental change. The popularity of environmentalism may well be a pragmatic expedient; certainly it makes good sense for educational planning. Man can do something about his environment, but he can do little to affect his heredity.

3. *Man as Interactive*

It should be evident by now that there are varying degrees in the active or passive views of man. The truth probably lies somewhere between the two extremes and incorporates elements of both. Therefore, let us consider the terms *active* and *passive* as opposite directions on a continuum. In this view the combined middle ground could be called *interactive.*

This position suggests not a mere mixture of alternating hereditary and environmental forces but a confrontation of these forces competing for dominance and contributing in varying degrees to the outcome. This view is similar to the concept of coming to terms with the environment. It is illustrated when a person walks into a room where the temperature is 90°. His inherited drive to be comfortable moves him to turn on the air-conditioner. The environment influences him but he in turn acts upon the environment.

An interactive view of man best explains all of the facts while remaining open to new options. It also offers the Christian maximum flexibility in relating faith and knowledge as he seeks to engage in a meaningful dialogue with man's psychological understandings.

Interaction can best explain the operation of hereditary and environmental factors in producing uniqueness in individuals. Neither factor is constant in its impact for any two persons—not even for identical twins. Also each twin, from his own vantage point, perceives the family unit differently. The action of these divergent forces tends to develop differences rather than similarities. The uniqueness that results from this interaction may be construed as comprising the self. As these forces impinge on the individual, and as he interacts with them, the self emerges. He becomes a differentiated individual.

The emerging person develops capability for self-direction through the capacity called *will*. A test of maturity is the ultimate degree of independence from hereditary and environmental forces which the self attains in setting the direction of one's life. Maturity is, in part, becoming responsible for one's decisions and actions. While influenced by environment, he is not a victim of it. Rather, he increasingly masters the hereditary and environmental influences that impinge upon him, making the most of their assets and coping with their limitations.

This interactive view also makes psychological room for the operation of God through the Holy Spirit in the formation of the human spirit. If selfhood is influenced by the interaction of heredity, environment, and self-direction, who is to say that the Spirit of God cannot involve himself directly in this process of life building? Thus we are not limited to Jaarsma's hereditary concept, nor to Ziegler's environmental thesis. We can encompass the values of both views. Interaction also provides a possible basis for explaining the existence and operation of sin in unregenerate man. Similarly, the theory makes room for a psychological understanding of the cleansing action of the Holy Spirit, and of the continuing irreversible after-effects of sin, such as physical and mental illnesses.

4. Man as Moral Being

A vital issue involved in the heredity-environment debate concerns the moral nature of man. Is he inherently good, bad, or neither? The traditional Christian answer that man is born naturally bad, depraved because of Adam's fall, has been widely accepted for many centuries. However, in the 18th century Rousseau, a French philosopher, popularized naturalistic humanism—the idea that man is intrinsically good when not corrupted by his environment. The debate on this issue has been heated, even in Christian circles.

a. Secular perspective. Today in the behavioral sciences the concept of inherent depravity has lost much of its overt support, except in orthodox Christian circles. Because of the difficulty of scientific verification and the popularity of environmental rather than hereditary influence, the debate over original sin is largely overlooked in secular circles. However, Carl Jung is one psychologist who discusses the subject.

The popular secular view today is that man's nature is morally neutral. For such a view, inherent badness or goodness is incongruous with the current emphasis on external or environmental forces.

b. Christian perspective. In Christian circles the issue is also frequently overlooked, but in a different way. Too often in conservative theology the tendency has been to accept the theory of depravity, but in practice to operate from the premise of goodness in dealing with individuals. An unfortunate compartmentalization of theological pessimism and psychological optimism can easily result from fuzzy thinking. Such contradictions are dangerous to a coherent and convincing evangelical witness. The tension must be recognized and dealt with.

c. Human depravity. A pervasive optimism concerning the progress of the race has been devastating to the concept of universal depravity. The problem is accentuated by two factors: (1) confusion over interpretations of depravity, and (2) a resultant difficulty in explaining obviously good behavior in individuals who claim no Christian faith. These two factors have made it difficult to deal with the moral nature of man as either entirely and inherently good or entirely and inherently bad. However, for Christian educators to settle for the unbiblical expediency of a morally neutral human nature, as defined in secular circles, is unnecessary. For us, depravity is a factor in man's nature. Our principles of Christian education must take account of this element.

In the broad context of life, depravity should be viewed as affecting every aspect of human personality without necessarily manifesting itself in every human act. Total depravity has a dual connotation. (1) It means that all of man's personality is tainted by original sin. (2) It also means that because of inherited sin man, apart from grace, is totally deprived of fellowship with God, individually and racially. Any good or compassionate acts by unregenerate persons are not indicative of restored fellowship with God. They are the result of God's prevenient grace working in the race to restrain the tendencies of sinful man and to save the world from destroying itself.

5. *Summary*

Nothing is more central to an authentic psychology and a sound Christian education than a clear view of the nature of man. Without a distinctly Christian stance at this point little but confusion can be expected in additional developments of psychological foundations of Christian education. The foregoing discussion suggests that an interactive view of the nature of man is our best option. It provides Christian education with a framework both for meaningful communication with today's psychological thinking without identifying solely with any one view. It also leaves room for embracing other Christian perspectives.

Man is born into the world totally bereft of fellowship with God. He is powerless in his own capacities to initiate overtures of restoration with God.

He is born with hereditary factors that shape his intelligence, his physical appearance, and his temperament. His environment, physical and social, is a strong factor in molding his behavior and view of the world. Both factors provide limitations and opportunities for him to grow and develop as they interact during his life.

During the prenatal period hereditary forces are almost the only factors shaping man and setting his limitations. As one grows, develops, and matures, the environment assumes greater importance; also environment is most amenable to being consciously structured. This ability to change persons through structuring their environment makes formal education possible.

The rigidity of one's environmental situation decreases with growth and development. Older children are better able to alter their environment and to control their interaction with it. As they mature and learn, they acquire skills to interact with the environment.

Also, maturation results in the differentiation of the self. The clearer the self becomes defined, the more potent the will becomes. This freedom to choose gives Christian education its greatest opportunity. The gospel of Christ clearly offers man assurance. He is not locked into nor need be victimized by hereditary and environmental factors. With God's grace available through the Holy Spirit, men can become their full, real selves as they interact with God. He is a present reality in every internal and external situation.

III. Principles of Growth and Development

Some basic concepts of human growth and development are essential to a full understanding of the implications of psychology for Christian education. Upon these concepts the whole structure of age grouping and graded curriculum rests. If these principles are understood, the whole spectrum of individual differences and group similarities can be correctly interpreted.

A. Individual Differences

Every individual is different because of two commonly recognized factors and their interaction—biological inheritance and social environment. Everyone has a different set of genes and chromosomes, except identical children who are the result of the fertilized ovum breaking apart in the early stages of growth. All children, except identical twins, even though born to the same parents, receive different combinations of genes and chromosomes. Thus they have different appearances, different interactive patterns with their physical and social environment, and different intellectual potentialities.

Added to the more obvious hereditary differences are variations of maturational rate and skill readiness. Each individual matures at his own rate; he comes to his own level of readiness to learn a new skill in his own unique manner. Some children mature rapidly; others more slowly. Such maturation is usually not smoothly progressive; it tends to be uneven, spurting ahead at a rapid rate, leveling off at a plateau, and later regressing or advancing to new levels. The general trend, however, is a movement toward maturity. Even the different parts of the body and brain mature at different rates. In the first year the cerebellum and cerebrum gain 300 percent in weight, but the cerebral cortex will not become mature until adolescence.

B. Principles Guiding Growth and Development

Although every person is unique, each normal human being goes through life's stages in a similar pattern. Dependable principles characterize growth and development from the moment of conception until maturity is reached. Because childhood is the period of most rapid change, psychologists have studied this age-group more intensively than the others. But adults change also. The chief difference is that their physiological and mental changes are slower, involve social and emotional dimensions more extensively, and are less dramatic to the casual observer. For adults these changes are nonetheless important, and they are being studied today more intensively than ever before.

Harlow suggests five principles of human growth and development that help to explain individual differences.[13]

1. All human beings grow continuously without interruption, provided a safe, nourishing environment is available to them.

2. While growth is uneven and is characterized by periods of slow growth alternating with rapid growth, the process proceeds in an orderly sequence.

3. More complex and life-controlling structures, such as the brain and heart, develop before the less essential elements, e.g., toenails of the fetus. Also, internal organs such as the glands develop before the fingers and fingernails. In motor skills, learning moves from global and undifferentiated movements to very specific, highly articulated motions; e.g., the flailing of the baby's arm will later become the basic motion in pitching a baseball.

4. There seem to be periods when certain stimuli have profound effects upon development but at other times do not have such effects. If an expectant mother ingests harmful drugs early in her pregnancy, the fetus will be more severely damaged than if the same drugs are taken later in the pregnancy.

5. The various parts and systems of the body develop at different rates.

C. The Norm View of Development

From the work of psychologists like Arnold Gesell, who studied large numbers of children in his Child Study Clinic at Yale, have come some levels of performance which can be expected from normally developing children at various ages. Jean Piaget has done similar work specifically on the intellectual stages of development. In relation to our active-interactive-passive structure, such normal develop-

---

13. Harlow, *Psychology,* pp. 19 ff.

ment viewed as an outgrowth of inner, hereditary forces tends to be active.

Norms are useful in planning curriculums and in testing children who seem to have developmental problems. However, the norms should not create despair in parents and teachers when a particular child does not seem to fit. There is considerable latitude in the time table for different skills. For example, it is normal for a child to learn to walk anytime between 10 and 14 months.

D. The Organismic View of Development

Today, students of human development take an organismic view. They recognize that various elements of growth tend to move along together and to interact with environment. Therefore although the above discussion focused sharply on the physical aspects, Christian educators know that emotional, social, and intellectual development tends to proceed in similar patterns.

A detailed knowledge of these areas of growth and development is not needed by Christian educators. However, a clear awareness of the facts and their interrelationships helps us to understand the persons with whom we work. Such an awareness helps to know what kind of behavior to expect from different age-groups; it enables us not to overexpect from younger pupils. These levels of development are also basic to the differences between the curriculums planned for preschool children and those prepared for older pupils. A combination of the organismic and norm views provides the Christian educator with the soundest approach to understanding children.

IV. THEORIES OF LEARNING

We turn now to a brief historical survey of learning theories. The assumptions discussed earlier about the nature of man are often clearly reflected in these theories.

A. Influential Remnants

Two nonexperimental psychologies of learning prominent prior to the 20th century continue to influence education today. These theories are known as *mental discipline* and *natural unfoldment*. Both views favor an active role for man in relation to his environment. This view is consonant with the prevailing hereditary emphasis of earlier centuries. Explanation must be brief but greater detail is available from other sources in the bibliography.

1. *Mental Discipline*

The mental discipline psychology views learning as training the mind through rigorous exercise. Like developing muscles in the gymnasium, such mental powers as reason, imagination, memory, will, and thought are similarly cultivated. Mental discipline, with philosophical roots in classical humanism going back to Plato's idealism, stresses the study of the classics as best suited for developing the intellect. The modern great books emphasis by Robert Hutchins and Mortimer Adler follows this reasoning.

Mental discipline tends to see man as morally neutral but also as an active agent in relation to his environment. The emphasis is on the inherent powers and self-discipline rather than on any specific external learning materials.

Branches of Christian idealism, stressing an active will in overcoming an inherently bad human nature, fit into what is known as *faculty psychology*, which also underscores the cultivation of distinct mental powers. An underlying expectation is that development of a strong faculty in one area will automatically mean effective transfer of that power to other situations. However, it was precisely at this point that early research challenged the validity of faculty psychology. Experiments demonstrated that training for specific tasks in one sphere of life (e.g., neatness, or memory) did not necessarily carry over into other areas.

In spite of much discrediting of this preexperimental theory of learning by researchers, it still influences current general education and religious education in particular. Wisdom suggests that we hold on to principles that are valid but recognize elements that have been proved psychologically untrue. Memorization of Bible verses, for example, unquestionably does have value but not for the purpose of cultivating a faculty of memory.

2. *Natural Unfoldment*

The natural unfoldment theory views learning as the active growth and development of the individual without external aid. In fact, the assumption of inherent goodness means that this natural process of development is supremely desirable and should be guarded from contamination by the environment. Thus a natural environment for learning is favored over a structured one. Pupils' interests should decide the content and sequence of learning experiences.

This view holds that planning by adults on the basis of what they feel pupils should know in order to fulfill societal expectations is bad education.

In the light of modern educational research, which emphasizes the influence of environment, natural unfoldment has lost much of its appeal to educators. Nevertheless, in some quarters pleas can still be heard to let nature set the pace for learning. Furthermore, while wars, prejudice, and pollution have tarnished the concept of an inherent goodness, there is still a strong optimism about man and his future on the part of those who hold to the natural unfoldment concept.

B. Associationism Theories

Modern stimulus-response associationism comprises one of the two principal families of learning theory today.

Association theories view man as essentially passive in relation to his external environment. This concept has its historical foundation in the *tabula rasa* theory of John Locke; man is at birth a blank slate to be written on by external forces. Thus the emphasis was placed on the physical senses, as opposed to mental faculties, as a means of learning. Learning consisted of establishing connections, or associations, within the person. If the association was mental, it was due to the similarity of the material, as in Herbart's apperception theory discussed below. If association was based on the nervous system, it resulted from the passage of the nervous impulses over the synapses, as in Thorndike's connectionism. Skinner's interpretation of associationism contends that the appropriate response will more likely follow a stimulus if an adequate and immediate reward (reinforcement) is given. His theory illustrates clearly the principle of conditioning which presently dominates associationism.

1. *Herbart's Apperception*

Apperception is a preexperimental theory of learning, a forerunner of modern associationism. J. F. Herbart was the foremost advocate of this early theory which emphasized the association of ideas. He defined apperception as the "attentive consciousness . . . by which one apprehends the meaning of a situation."[14] All new facts coalesce with their proper associations and restructure one's percep-

---

14. William Clark Trow, *Educational Psychology*, 2nd ed. (Cambridge, Mass.: Houghton Mifflin Co., 1950), pp. 376-77.

tion of that subject area. When a new fact is learned, it will be associated with others that have been learned.

Herbart's theory has generally receded in acceptance because of the current trend to experimental research. Nevertheless, it still persists in serious educational dialogue wherever there is an emphasis on the interrelatedness of mental ideas rather than solely physical relationships.

2. *Thorndike's Connectionism*

E. L. Thorndike's connectionism[15] represents the first of the scientific theories of learning. His work led the assault on the pre-experimental theories of the 19th century. To his credit Thorndike's work still stands as a monument to a comprehensive, detailed account of learning.

Successive associationist theories rely on some modification of Thorndike's explanation of learning; all accept as basic the establishment of neural connections based on stimulus-response patterns. The simple responses to an environmental stimulus become the building blocks for the explanation of complex behavior. The strengthening of these bonds depends largely on their continued use and on getting satisfaction from the response. The more an association of a given stimulus and response (S-R bond) is repeated and rewarded, the more securely the behavior is learned.

3. *Skinner's Operant Conditioning*

In any survey of stimulus-response theories of learning some attention should be given to the most widely known current systematic theory—B. F. Skinner's operant conditioning.[16] Skinner stresses the stimulus that follows a reinforced (rewarded) response. Rather than the S-R pattern this is more like an R-S sequence.

Through carefully rewarding desired actions and repeating stimuli, Skinner has successfully modified the behavior of animals to the extent that he has taught pigeons to play Ping-Pong. Skinner and other behaviorists believe human learning can be fully accounted for and controlled in the same way; human learning is simply a more complex procedure.

The deterministic nature of this narrow cause-and-effect view of learning is obvious. The Christian educator can accept the demon-

---

15. Ann Neal, *Theories of Psychology* (Cambridge, Mass.: Schenkman Publishing Co., Inc., 1969), pp. 81-90.
16. *Ibid.,* pp. 171-76.

strated facts of stimulus-response learning without agreeing to total determinism. We know that learning occurs with repetition, that we learn better when we are rewarded for our efforts, and that changes in the nervous system are related to changes in human behavior. We may agree that some learning can be explained on this basis, but at the same time we must point out the failure of behaviorism to account adequately for much of the whole marvelous process of human development. Complete determinism is seen as a fatal limitation even by many secular students of education. This limitation has given rise to the other major family of learning theories to which we now turn.

C. Cognitive and Field Theories

The cognitive theories of learning have their foundation in gestalt psychology, developed and formally stated first in Germany. *Gestalt* is a German word without an exact English equivalent, but generally meaning an organized pattern or configuration. This view of psychology was established in North America in the 1920s and 1930s largely as a result of the many scholars who had visited the great German universities. Challenging the prevailing connectionist view, gestalt psychology forced some modification of Thorndike's theory. However, full resolution of these differing views has not taken place, and they continue as two distinct families of learning theory.

A major cornerstone of cognitive-field theory is that the whole is greater than the sum of its parts. This wholistic view contrasts with the atomistic emphasis of the associationists. Rather than stressing a collection of numerous small parts of learning (S-R bonds), the cognitive theorist focuses on perceiving the organized whole in learning. To the gestaltist *the perception of reality* is more important to learning than the reality itself.

These theories thus define truth as the degree to which the perception agrees with the thing seen. For these reasons cognitive theories are identified with relativism. An illustration of the gestaltist theory is the tendency of the mind to perceive motion instead of separate stimuli (the phi-phenomenon). The flashing arrows on an electric sign are perceived as moving; in reality the light bulbs are progressively lighted and turned off.

Cognitive theories deal with the subjective psychological reality, rather than trying to discover objective reality. What is experienced by the individual is real and important to him. Purpose and insight play a key role.

When viewed from the active or passive perspective, gestalt theory would be placed more on the active side of the continuum. Probably most cognitive theorists would prefer the interactive label because man's perception is influenced by both internal and external factors. Also these influences operate in an interactive rather than in an alternating fashion.

In the educative process, gestaltists stress the wholeness of the learning experience. If education is to be most effective, the curriculum, the environment, the teacher, and the pupil with his total personality must be considered. Christian educators find much in this position to support Jesus' emphasis upon the wholeness of persons. When we are at our best, we are deeply conscious of the physical, mental, emotional, and spiritual needs of our pupils.

D. Eclecticism

While there has been no emergent synthesis of the two major families of learning theory—stimulus-response and cognitive—and while remnants of past theories still influence the present, there are certain common elements which can be found. In fact, most introductory textbooks in educational psychology tend to treat the subject in this way rather than favor one systematic view over another. This process of borrowing from various viewpoints is known as eclecticism and is frequently used when reconciliation of divergent views is difficult. An eclectic approach usually overrides theoretical differences and emphasizes practical applications. Hilgard underscores the potential dangers of both systemization and eclecticism when he says: "Science ought to be systematic, not eclectic, but a premature systematic position is likely to be dogmatic and bigoted just as an enduring eclecticism is likely to be superficial and opportunistic."[17]

Christian educators in the Cooperative Curriculum Project agreed that no present theory of learning is adequate to serve Christian education. They are on record as follows:

> Various theories of learning have been advanced to interpret the accumulating research data related to the whys and wherefores of human changing. But as yet there is still no one generally accepted theory of learning capable of satisfying all the necessary

17. Ernest R. Hilgard and Gordon H. Bower, *Theories of Learning,* 3rd ed. (New York: Appleton-Century-Crofts, 1966), p. 13.

considerations introduced by the evidence. There are, however, many practical views about the learning process which are widely supported by most learning theorists.[18]

V. DEFINITIONS OF LEARNING

Thus far we have been concerned with learning theories, without defining learning itself. We shall look first at some representative definitions by psychologists who view it from their academic discipline; second, some concepts of learning as seen by the educator who has a Christian perspective.

A. Learning Defined by the Psychologist

Few psychologists would be in total agreement on a single definition of learning. Many, however, would agree that learning involves: (1) a change in behavior; (2) the stabilizing of the change; and (3) the active participation of the learner.

Logan defines learning as "a relatively permanent process resulting from practice and reflected in a change in performance."[19] According to Harlow, "Learning involves those relatively permanent changes in behavior that result from practice or actively attending to the environment."[20]

In this context *behavior* is broadly defined and includes cognitive functions, motor responses, and emotional feelings. Change would not necessarily include a dramatic shift in any or all of these areas, nor would it be always observable. Any slight modification would indicate that learning had taken place.

B. Learning Related to Christian Education

Christian educators usually will not disagree with the above definitions. They will, however, want to inject a religious element which is not considered by the scientific psychologist.

1. *Jaarsma's Independent Self*

Jaarsma puts the concept of selfhood into his Christian definition. Learning is "the self-active process of a person exploring reality perceptively for meaning, and thus coming to grips with truth that

---

18. *The Church's Educational Ministry: A Curriculum Plan* (St. Louis: The Bethany Press, 1965), p. 25.

19. Frank A. Logan, *Fundamentals of Learning and Motivation* (Dubuque, Ia.: Wm. C. Brown and Co., Publishers, 1970), p. 2.

20. Harlow, p. 19.

forms him as a son of God to mature self-fulfillment."[21] He goes on to explain: "A person learns by being involved in a challenging situation that is meaningful and purposeful and calls forth ideas and concepts that disclose truth to channel behavior as self-expression and self-fulfillment."[22] Jaarsma's description of learning involves eight overlapping facets put together in the following way: (1) Felt needs (2) generate direction for (3) exploration in an external situation. If the exploratory process is perceptive, (4) goals emerge, (5) new meanings of ideas and concepts are understood, and (6) truth is uncovered which results in (7) channeling or forming behavior leading to (8) creative expression.[23]

2. Boehlke's Creation-engagement

Boehlke tries to fit psychological insights into a theological framework. He describes the learner as "an active, intelligent, responsible but sinful self to be understood through observation, self-perceptions, the quality of his relationships, and revelation."[24] Boehlke pictures the learner at the center of concentric circles. The innermost circle is the ego, the self; the outermost, the church and God. Thus Christian education concerns itself with the engagement of persons within their field of multi-relationships. Out of these engagements, God creates new values within the person.

Boehlke's theory of Christian learning is described as "creation-engagement." "Creation encompasses the full scope of God's participation . . . engagement includes such meanings as interaction, encounter, commitment, and naturally accepted responsibilities."[25] He asserts that "the concerns of Christian nurture are learned as God creates new selves through the engagement of persons with their field of relationships."[26]

Boehlke proposes that "the context of learning is the church . . . through which the learner engages his personal and nonpersonal field of relationships."[27] For him,

> The dynamics of learning are operative as the learner is existentially motivated to engage and to restructure his field of

---

21. Jaarsma in *Introduction to Christian Education,* pp. 76-77.
22. *Ibid.,* p. 84.
23. *Ibid.,* pp. 80-84.
24. Robert R. Boehlke, *Theories of Learning in Christian Education* (Philadelphia. Westminster Press, 1962), pp. 187-95.
25. *Ibid.,* p. 187.
26. *Ibid.,* p. 188.
27. *Ibid.,* p. 193.

relationships, and as these perceptual processes are utilized by the Holy Spirit to bring about encounter and response to Jesus Christ.[28]

Boehlke acknowledges his indebtedness to gestalt theory without embracing it as his foundation for Christian education. Because of its emphasis on interaction, the encompassing flexibility of structure, and its compatibility with Christian thought, cognitive-field theory is often appealing to Christian educators.

C. The Learning Process

What constitutes the learning process? When does the pupil learn? What is our role as Christian educators in this process? These questions are basic and provide an appropriate theme with which to conclude this chapter.

Obviously the teaching-learning experience is effective for the learner to the degree that the educator understands the learning process and is able to structure the experience in accordance with sound principles. Learning cannot be imposed; it must evolve out of the nature of the learner and the material to be learned. Christian educators cannot afford to ignore sound psychological principles; neither can we rely entirely on psychology. We are dealing in the spiritual realm. The human spirit is fully accessible only to the Holy Spirit. When we have exhausted our skills and understanding, we have the assurance that the Holy Spirit's work continues. He is the One who leads into all truth.

Cronbach[29] describes seven essential aspects of learning which teachers and Christian educators should incorporate into their teaching-learning experiences as they aid the efforts of the learners.

1. *Goal.* The goal of the learner is some consequence which he wishes to attain.
2. *Readiness.* A person's readiness consists of the sum-total of response-patterns and abilities he possesses at any given time.
3. *Situation.* The situation consists of all objects, persons, and symbols in the learner's environment.
4. *Interpretation.* Interpretation is a process of directing attention to parts of a situation, relating them to past experiences, and predicting what can be expected to happen if various responses are made.

---

28. *Ibid.,* p. 195.
29. Lee J. Cronbach, *Educational Psychology* (New York: Harcourt, Brace and Co., 1954), pp. 49-51.

5. *Response.* A response is an action or some internal change that prepares the person for action.

6. *Consequence: confirmation or contradiction.* Some events that follow the response are regarded by the learner as the consequences of the response.

7. *Reaction to thwarting.* Thwarting occurs when the person fails to attain his goals. If his first try is not confirmed, he may make a new interpretation and adapt his response.

Cronbach sums up his discussion by saying,

> Once the teacher is fully aware of these seven aspects of the learning process, he is equipped to examine and plan educational experiences. To alter behavior, the teacher provides experiences which permit the pupil to select appropriate goals, which are suited to his readiness, which permit him to learn important sorts of interpretations, and so on. If any of these conditions is not satisfied, the pupil will learn undesirable responses.

VI. SUMMARY

From the previous discussion, it will be clear that the learning process is complicated; the psychological bases for Christian education are complex. Psychologists are still trying to discover more specific ways to increase the effectivenss of the teaching-learning situation. While no one theory or definition of learning encompasses all the factors involved, the basic elements of several of the theories may be combined into an eclectic system with effective results. This process of borrowing applicable strategies from various points of view is frequently used in other disciplines when reconciliation of divergent views is difficult.

As Christian educators we recognize that we are involved in trying to educate fallen man who lives most of his life in a sinful environment. We must therefore make room in our theory and practice for the work of the Holy Spirit. We recognize that our pupils' motivations for learning are different, their readinesses divergent; but their potentialities in Christ are promising. We labor to structure the learning environment with full confidence that human nature can be changed by the power of God working through Christian nurture. Man is not an unredeemable victim of his past nor merely the reflection of his environment. Through the power of Christ man has the resources to become his full self.

BIBLIOGRAPHY

Bigge, Morris L., and Hunt, Maurice P. *Psychological Foundations of Education,* 2nd ed. New York: Harper and Row, Publishers, 1968.

A representative educational psychology textbook based on a systematic cognitive-field approach and utilizing the active-interactive-passive framework.

Boehlke, Robert R. *Theories of Learning in Christian Education.* Philadelphia: The Westminster Press, 1962.

Examines representative theories of learning from the Christian perspective and explores the theological foundations for learning. Outlines a creation-engagement view of learning that includes divine participation and an active thrust of the whole person as he learns.

Cronbach, Lee J. *Educational Psychology,* 2nd ed. New York: Harcourt, Brace & World, Inc., 1963.

A popular educational psychology textbook representing an eclectic view.

Hilgard, Ernest R., and Bower, Gordon H. *Theories of Learning,* 4th ed. New York: Appleton-Century-Crofts, 1975.

A highly regarded treatise which includes separate chapters giving a systematic treatment of each specific theory within the two major families of learning theory.

Jaarsma, Cornelius. *Human Development, Learning and Teaching.* Grand Rapids: Wm. B. Eerdmans Publishing Co., 1961.

A textbook amplifying the author's Christian view of development as self-involvement.

Theories of Learning and Instruction, ed. Ernest R. Hilgard. Chicago: The National Society for the Study of Education, 1964.

One of the fine series of NSSE Yearbooks. Contains a collection of writings by prominent persons representing various views in learning theory.

Ziegler, Jesse H. *Psychology and the Teaching Church.* New York: Abingdon Press, 1962.

Chapter 4, "Psychological Development as a Factor in Religious Readiness," seeks to show how levels of human development relate to Christian life and growth.

CHAPTER 6

The Sociological
Bases of
Christian Education

Man is by nature a social being. To understand him and his behavior, one must consider the individual living in his societal environment. We must also look at the institutions that man fashions to preserve and perpetuate his cultural values.

Christian education cannot escape the influence of these forces in human development because Christian education is both a product of change and an agent for change in man's institutions. Any adequate study of the field must include some analysis of the sociological bases of religion and of learning.

I. THE NATURE OF SOCIETY

Society has become the subject of intensive study in this century. To help us understand its nature and influence, we may view it as a complex of interdependent systems. From this perspective society may be understood by looking at its educational programs, its religious life, its political structures, its family patterns, and its economic systems. It may be described in terms of its subgroups such as the scientific community, government leaders, Japanese Americans, the "Bible belt," the rich, the middle class, and the poor.

Society may also be described as a collection of persons who in interaction constitute an ongoing social system. These persons may interact in small, highly specialized groups, such as prayer cells in a local church. On the other hand they may be a part of larger groups that function through complex organizations such as national political parties or religious denominations. Whether groups are large or small, the individual's behavior is influenced by the group's expectations.

A. Society and Culture

Culture is the total accumulation of familial, racial, national, and social experience. It is transmitted from one generation to another through the institutions of society. Our culture includes language and forms of social behavior. It involves knowledge of history and political structures, and the social expectations implied in good citizenship.

Society thus becomes both the locale and a shaper of the individual's behavior. It creates and preserves, by its financial and emotional support, the institutions necessary to the transmission and inculcation of its ideals and values. It fashions behavior by rewarding and punishing conduct. Society passes formal laws which reflect group experience in complex living. Such laws are designed so that the individual can be protected, his personal freedom defined, and his welfare, safety, and health secured.

B. Social Change

Society is basically conservative and slow to change. By its very nature and structure it tends to be static. On the other hand the surface is constantly changing. Riots, insurrection, and revolution force immediate cultural shifts. These disorders often result from continued frustration with society's reluctance to change by the orderly processes of legislation and administrative decision.

II. RELIGION IN SOCIETY

Religion is a significant factor in most societies. Even in Russia where religion is denounced, her political system appeals to the dynamics of religion in her citizens.

A. Religion Reinforces Social Values

In general, religion espouses and advocates conformity to the laws of society. Both from a sense of duty to God and from a desire for well-being, religious leaders normally call for obedience to law. This may be, in part, a kind of instinct for self-preservation because the church along with other social institutions suffers from war and civil disturbance.

The Christian sanction of marriage and the sacredness of the home illustrates further how religion reinforces social values. If the family should decline as a viable institution, both society and the Christian faith would be threatened.

B. Religion Meets Basic Human Needs

Christian teaching offers answers to man's basic needs and in this way assists society.

1. *Standards of Sexual Behavior*

Society legalizes marriage and thus attempts to control it. The church is not insensitive to human sexuality but views its uninhibited expression as a threat both to the individual and to society.

Christian teaching raises stern warnings against disregard of responsibilities in marriage, aberrations of sexual activity, and the consequences of immorality. It provides for the legitimate satisfaction of normal sex desires through marriage, and for effective avenues of sublimation through humanitarian service in schools, orphanages, hospitals, and religious orders.

2. *The Experience of Death*

Societies differ widely in their views of death. In general, the less complex social groups accept death as inevitable. Some tribes in New Guinea, for example, eliminate older people through the practice of cannibalism. More complex societies tend to develop greater sensitivity and consequently develop more complex religious rituals to assist the bereaved.

People in our more sophisticated culture usually find death devastating. In order to cope with its irreversibility and its apparent uselessness, we must find ways to adjust psychologically to this "last enemy" of man. Religious faith—especially the Christian faith, with its message of the resurrection, and its ministry of comfort and fellowship—helps society to handle this sobering reality.

3. *The Importance of Health*

Religion supports the laws that promote good health. Its condemnation of drugs, alcohol, tobacco, gluttony, and sexual promiscuity—as well as its promotion of the disciplined life—contributes to the physical and spiritual health of society. Before the advent of public hospitals and medical clinics, it was the Christian Church that established such institutions.

Analysts of modern society have become increasingly concerned with the increase of mental illness and psychosomatic disorders. Guilt is a major factor in these problems. A sense of loneliness and uselessness augment the tendency to withdrawal. The Christian emphasis upon the forgiveness of God, His love, and His personal concern for all men is a message that society needs in order to maintain mental health at a desirable level.

4. Social Strata and Mobility

The population explosion and rising affluence tend to solidify social class boundaries. At the same time our mass media incite the aspirations of lower social classes to share in the abundance of material goods, services, and comforts. Riots and demonstrations by minority groups are sometimes symptoms of these aspirations.

The Christian view of life assists society by warning that affluence often detracts from spiritual growth. The church also helps by encouraging persons of the lower socioeconomic levels to move out of their restrictions—especially through education. Church colleges, at considerable sacrifice, offer an education in a morally stimulating climate in order to help young people improve their lot in life, while strengthening their spiritual values.

5. Conflict Between Groups

A complex society tends to generate conflicts, especially between the people in power and those who feel oppressed by that power. Unmet needs heighten the frustration and hostility of these groups. The teachings of loyalty and Christian love help society to cope with this problem by encouraging its members to be good citizens.

Unfortunately, institutionalized religion has too often been identified with an oppressive power structure or has been insensitive to the conflicts and deprivations associated with it. Prophets, however, invariably arise in the church to denounce such lethargy and blindness and to secure a greater degree of social concern among religious groups.

Whenever the power structure debases the human dignity of minority groups, Christians support peaceful change through law and order. At times when laws seem to be immoral, some Christian leaders advocate civil disobedience. Although some individuals, clearly identified with institutionalized religion, have thus advocated and practiced disruptive tactics, the mainstream of Christianity has adopted a policy of working within the structure of society for justice and equality. Because of this preponderance of supporters for law and order, the church does act as a counterbalance to disruption and makes possible a calmer climate for society.

6. Suffering and Loneliness

Human suffering, whether due to poverty, misfortune, physical deformity, or cruelty, is prevalent in society. Without some assistance such pain can become intolerable. We have today programs of psychological counseling, recreation, and membership in a variety of social groups. These are helpful but they do not provide fully satisfying answers to these issues. Christian faith may not be the only source of help, but it is an important one. The biblical message of faith and personal worth provides inner strength. The message of God's love, expressed concretely in ministries for the aged, helps people cope with the loneliness of an impersonal, youth-oriented society.

7. Moral and Natural Evils

All societies must deal with the problem of deviant moral behavior. Each society establishes its own limits of acceptable conduct and devises its distinctive methods of punishment to secure conformity. Whatever form these pressures have taken, one function of religion has been to sanction and support society's actions.

In addition, people in all societies must deal with the catastrophes inflicted upon them by the uncontrollable forces of nature; there are floods, earthquakes, droughts, and epidemics. In our affluent, technical societies, a great deal of therapy and medical service is available. But beyond these psychological and physical aids religion must help people caught in misfortune to adjust to their problems. Christian teaching provides supportive care by its message of faith in God and the promise of His grace.

C. Religion Canalizes Social Expectations

The term *canalizing* refers to the process by which a culture, through reward and punishment, shapes its children into an accepted pattern. The folkways followed, the religion practiced, the family structure demonstrated, and the civil organization established, all contribute to this process. The child becomes a product of the culture and the society of which he is a part. At any given moment of his life, he is conforming or reacting to this canalization.

In this setting, especially in view of the increasing secular trends of Western civilization, religion has a special function. The church is concerned with the moral education of the young. Christians seek to inject the commandments of God into this process. By its insistence that man must accept God's authority and achieve God's expectations, the church performs a unique function for man. Christian education teaches man to accept the lordship of Christ and to live by God's value system.

III. SOCIAL FACTORS INFLUENCING RELIGION

Not only does religion affect and assist society through its teachings and activities; in turn, the church is influenced by society. Periods of social crisis, such as war and overpopulation, put pressures on Christian thinking and cause changes in the beliefs and values. For example, current pressures for improved communication have influenced the Roman Catholic church to celebrate the Mass in the vernacular. The tendency in modern society toward specialization has also changed the church. It is not surprising to find that Christian education has increasingly become the responsibility of specialists—the minister of Christian education, the youth pastor, and the director of children's ministries.

A. Factors Modifying Religion's Appeal

1. Social Change

Social change often reduces the appeal of the ritual and belief system of the church. The preciseness of scientific discovery stands in sharp contrast to the more mystical appeal of religion. One function of faith is to explain the unknown. Therefore, because the area of unexplained phenomena is constantly shrinking, religion seems to become less needful.

Expanding frontiers of knowledge, mass media of communication, space exploration, density of urban population, and a shorter work week all tend to raise new questions for our Christian value system. Especially is this true when ritual and ethical demands reflect a simplistic, agrarian society that contrasts sharply with our urban, industrial life. In the minds of many persons, Christian values and prohibitions do not seem to fit the changing times.

2. The Younger Generation

As society's proportion of age-groups shifts toward the younger generation, institutional religion seems to lose its appeal. Part of this loss of faith among youth may be attributed to the tendency of adults to accept the social status quo with its inequities and problems. Youth are quick to question the sincerity of religious adults whom they perceive to be insensitive and unconcerned in the areas of life where human values are involved.

Youth also forces language changes upon a culture. Currently the phrases "I dig you," "cool it," "soul music," and "hang-ups" are popular. At the same time, religious terms are undergoing change. Youth often replaces the "Thees" and "Thous," used in addressing God, with the more direct "You."

It seems normal for youth to find traditional creedal phraseology less communicative, the rituals less significant, and the belief system less viable than they are for their parents. The rapid social changes of the mid 20th century have tended to make the traditional religious belief system even less acceptable to the current younger generation.

One of the major tasks of Christian education is to communicate the essential beliefs and practices of the Church so effectively that they shape the next generation as fully as they have formed our lives. There is encouragement for us of the current decade in the religion of young people. The extent and power of the "Jesus revolution" was awesome.[1] This religious awakening, as all revival movements, promises better things for society and for the Christian Church.

3. *Institutional Perpetuity*

As the appeal of a belief and value system decreases, society becomes more critical of the supporting religious institution. Such institutions react defensively, as individuals do, when they are even dimly aware that criticism leveled at them has some basis in fact.

All institutions must, of course, be concerned about continued existence if they are to perform their essential functions. Institutionalized religion must not, however, become so preoccupied with its self-preservation as to be insensitive to the changes and consequent needs of society. To do so is to become irrelevant and to lose the loyalty of many persons. When people in the society itself become disillusioned at this point, they become church dropouts and seek to identify with other, more responsive groups.

Criticism of institutional religion may sometimes be accurate.

---

1. *Time* Magazine, June 21, 1971, pp. 56-63.

It may, however, reflect only the individual's rationalization for change. Or, it may be an expression of his personal refusal to accept and live by Christian values.

Critics do not always assess fairly the efforts of the church to alleviate human needs: the drunkard converted, the family recruited to Christ, the groceries provided for senior citizens, and the day-care center operated. These ministries may not be dramatic but they are effective.

Today the appeal of institutional religion to many persons in the church and outside of it seems directly related to its effectiveness as an agent for change. When the church is perceived by society as impotent in making an impact on social problems, it loses its effectiveness and appeal. On the other hand, as religion is able to elicit the loyalty and support of society, it can be an agent of change. We may be too close to the contemporary scene to evaluate fairly the present effectiveness of religion. Some observers suspect that during the current period the church has become less influential in coping with the problems of society. It is encouraging, however, that others believe the church has exercised significant influence in effecting constructive social change and they view the future with cautious optimism.[2]

In the effort to increase their influence, some denominations have followed the ecumenical road. They have merged their institutional structures in order to speak for larger segments of society. They have lowered administrative costs and hoped for increased income so that more money would be available to influence the power structures of society.

Others follow the avenue of activism. Financial support is solicited on behalf of minority groups who engage in revolutionary and sometimes violent activities. Calls to protest meetings, marches, or civil disobedience are issued on the basis of ethical and moral imperatives. Violence is sometimes condoned and practiced.

Conservative evangelicals rely heavily on evangelism as their agency for change. Through mass evangelism and personal witnessing the churches seek to change both persons and society. The Billy Graham Crusades are successful in part because of organized effort, concerted prayer, and effective use of the media of mass communica-

---

2. K. S. Latourette, *Christianity Through the Ages* (New York: Harper and Row, 1965), p. 308, et passim; Timothy L. Smith, *Revivalism and Social Reform* (New York: Abingdon Press, 1957).

tion. Prophetic voices are also calling evangelicals to combine a more dynamic social concern with their zeal for evangelism.[3]

4. *Power Structure Identification*

The power structures of society are those agencies where policy decisions are made that bring about social changes. Sometimes these power structures—big industries, political parties, and civil decision-makers—are thought of as oppressing the poor. When the church is perceived as supporting the powerful in their oppression of these minority groups, the influence of religious institutions wanes.

Such identification with the power structure of society may or may not be accurate, but the effect on popular attitudes is the same. Religious institutions are seen as hypocritical and inconsistent in their witness. Both the groups that feel oppressed and the people who sympathize with them become alienated from the church.

B. Factors Affecting Individual Choices

Sociological factors not only affect the strength of religion in the community; they also influence individuals in their choice of religious affiliation. The bases for such choices are often more subtle than the answers usually given. The assumed reasons are religious experience, doctrinal compatibility, and the quality of fellowship. Less obvious are the psychological appeals of worship forms, and the whole psychological, social, and emotional climate of the group. Buried here one also often finds academic and economic factors.

1. *Personal Needs and Preferences*

Each individual has emotional and psychological needs. Several of these can be met only by identification with groups. Almost every person identifies with several groups at one time. Each affiliation is maintained to meet a special need—vocational, social, instructional, or religious. A college teacher, for example, may belong to a university seminar, a service club, a professional educational group, and his church. At the same time he will be developing deeper relationships with his family and friends.

People join and support the church that meets their needs. When an individual becomes actively involved, it is because he sees the church and his own activity in it as satisfying. Whenever enthusiasm for the program and activities of a church wanes, it has lost its

---

3. Sherwood Wirt, *The Social Conscience of the Evangelical* (New York: Harper and Row, 1968); Carl F. H. Henry, *Aspects of Christian Social Ethics* (Grand Rapids, Mich.: Wm. B. Eerdmans Publishing Co., 1964).

ability to meet the needs of that part of its constituency. Such a church should study its program carefully seeking to involve its less active members in the evaluation, so that its service may once again meet the needs and preferences of those members.

Tragically, some churches try to regain losses by becoming more tolerant of activities and life-styles that they had previously excluded. Such a lowering of standards is likely to cause further losses by increasing the confusion of the faithful and raising doubts about the integrity of the church.

2. Socioeconomic Status

The socioeconomic class to which one belongs is often a factor in one's choice of a denomination. Ritualistic, liturgical churches seem to appeal more to the wealthier, professional classes. The church with an informal service that appeals to the emotions, flourishes among blue-collar workers. Evidences of these appeals are also seen in the type of church architecture that is chosen by the churches in the different socioeconomic levels. Further indications of these preferences show up in the tensions that develop when members of a religious group begin to shift from one social class to another.

3. Nationality Differences

Although people of many different nationalities can be found in all denominations, nationality types seem to predominate in certain traditions. For example, Germanic groups predominate among the Lutherans; Dutch among the Reformed; Scottish among the Presbyterians; and English among the Anglicans. Other denominations reflect their national origins in such names as the Greek, Russian, and Serbian Orthodox churches. Newer denominations which are largely of American origin appeal to no particular nationality.

4. Social Mobility

One of the distinctive features of American society is its mobility. It is easier for a person in our society than in many other cultures to move from one social stratum to another. Several factors facilitate this movement: higher educational levels, acquisition of wealth, election to political office, and marriage into a higher level.

Social mobility has a parallel in geographical movement. People move from rural areas into the cities, and the urbanites move to the suburbs. Only a small percentage of Americans do not change communities at least once in a lifetime.

This mobility has three effects on religious life. *First,* as we have seen, when one changes social class, he may find the previous church identification less satisfying or totally unacceptable. He then seeks for a new religious group.

Second, one may wish to retain the value system to which he is committed but finds the churches in his new community hold different views. The rural person tends to be conservative, slow to change. The urban-oriented member is likely to be less sympathetic and to be less open to the needs of others; he is impatient with methods and customs that are rooted in a rural tradition.

Third, geographic mobility often results in the breaking of ties with the church. It is easy for socially and geographically relocated persons to allow their allegience to the church to lapse. To be sure, evangelical persons with high personal Christian loyalties are less likely to be lost to the church than are the merely nominal Christians. But even in evangelical churches there are high losses. Some churches reduce these losses by encouraging pastors of moving members to alert pastors in the new location of the arrival of these persons.

5. *Internalization of Beliefs*

Religious loyalty is directly proportional to the degree to which the Christian belief system is internalized by the believer. Internalization is the process by which the spiritual and ethical implications of a person's beliefs become his operational values. Many people profess to believe in God but their assent is only on the intellectual level. It does not affect their behavior. On the other hand, some persons conform to the rules of the church because of external pressure, while their real values are different. When such persons are freed from this social pressure, they behave according to their real values. For example, when a young person goes to college, or when an adult goes on vacation, if he follows a different standard of behavior, he has been conforming at home.

The strength of one's allegiance to Christian faith is in direct proportion to the degree that he has accepted that faith and made its values operational in his life. If he holds those values lightly or merely conforms to them, he will eventually find a group whose beliefs are more congruent with his own.

6. *Social Roles and Expectations*

For some people, the choice of a church is influenced by their professional roles. A lawyer or physician may choose one denomination over another because of its compatibility with his profession.

In some cases such identification is a political asset. The politician knows that religiousness will get him votes. We should not, of course, infer that all professional people who go to church attend for selfish reasons. Neither is it fair to belittle a head of state whose religious activities are frequent and conspicuous. God judges the heart of a man. However, the social expectations of such a job may reinforce his involvement in religion and may affect the particular type of church he chooses.

IV. THE RELIGIOUS EDUCATIONAL ROLES
OF INSTITUTIONS

All major institutions of society perform some Christian educational functions. The role may be either direct or indirect, and the specific involvement differs with the nature of the institution. Nevertheless, the family, the church, the school, and the government all have potentials for Christian education.

A. The Family

1. *The Primary Agency*

The family is the primary religious educational agent. God has given a very clear commandment to parents to teach religious values to their children.

> These words which I command you this day shall be upon your heart; and you shall teach them diligently to your children, and shall talk of them when you sit in your house, and when you walk by the way, and when you lie down, and when you rise. And you shall bind them as a sign upon your hand, and they shall be as frontlets between your eyes. And you shall write them on the doorposts of your house and on your gates *(Deut. 6:6-9, RSV)*.

This divine requirement is based squarely on the realities of family life. The family has the first and most influential contact with the child. It is the family that provides the care, security, and nurture for him all the years of his childhood.

Not only does the family provide for the physical well-being of the child, but it also fashions his self-concept.[4] From the child's perceptions of the family's acceptance and esteem for him, he develops his attitudes about himself. If he feels rejected and inadequate, he

---

4. See James C. Dobson, "Strategies for Esteem," *Hide or Seek* (Old Tappan, N.J.: Fleming H. Revell Co., 1974), pp. 47-138.

forms a self-concept of being inadequate or unloved. Children who have negative self-perceptions often become antisocial, inconsiderate, and unloving adults. This concept and life-style may make it difficult for one to respond to God's call because it is difficult for him to believe that God loves him.

On the other hand, when the family provides a warm, loving, environment, the child develops a picture of himself as an adequate, accepted person. He is more likely to become an adult who finds it easy to love God and others, because he feels no compulsion to prove his worthiness to them. In the light of these facts, Jesus' admonition to "love thy neighbour as thyself" becomes an axiom of personality development. The ability to accept God and others is directly influenced by one's self-concept.

The family also gives the child his first sense of moral values. Each time a parent punishes the child for a violation of parental codes, or rewards him for compliance, he is building into the child's life foundations for a conscience. The content of conscience varies from social group to social group, but the capacity to feel guilt and approval is universal. Based on this inherent human capacity, we fashion the Christian conscience by what we teach. This training is inescapable and one of the most important tasks the family group undertakes. The family whose moral and ethical code is clearly seen in consistent parental training and example will develop a more sensitive conscience in their children than one whose code is obscured by inconsistent example and training.

Through the process of identification, the child unconsciously adopts the values of his family. Until he comes to adolescence, his beliefs show a strong similarity to those of his parents. During the adolescent search for identity, young people examine these values carefully. Some reject them. Others modify them while retaining their basic structure. But whether in conformity, in modification, or in revolt, young people receive their values initially from their parents.

The last area in which the family demonstrates its primary educational influence is in personal growth. As parents respond to the child's attempts to gain approval, they are teaching the child how to influence others. If parents are influenced by threats and temper tantrums, the child learns that force is an effective means of imposing his will on others. When parents respond to the child's feigned affection and do not impose a promised punishment, they are teaching him to use flattery in achieving his goals. It is important for the child to learn that obedience is the surest avenue of securing parental approval.

All of these factors underline the significant responsibility that the family has in Christian education. From earliest childhood all of the interactions of the parents and the family are increasing or decreasing the probability that children will become vital Christians. Any program of formal Christian education that fails to give a high priority to family training will surely miss the mark and will be displeasing to God.

2. *The Basic Educational Influence*

Recent research in the area of mental development is discovering how early family influences affect a child's intelligence. Mothers who talk to their babies, who interact with them, who respond to their curiosity, increase the intellectual development of their children. Verbal and cultural deprivation retard intellectual growth. In contrast, the success of the children's television program "Sesame Street" illustrates how important visual and auditory stimulation are to childhood development. The child learns his vocabulary and much of his cultural heritage and social expectancies at home.

3. *Implications for Christian Education*

The family carries the primary responsibility for a child's Christian nurture and for his ultimate spiritual destiny. Although it is impossible to predict whether a child will accept or reject Christ, it should be clear that the family, especially the influence of the parents, will either encourage or discourage his becoming a Christian.

a. Important child-rearing practices. Parents who wish to assist their children will try to fulfill the following principles:

(1) *They will demonstrate impartiality to all their children.* The lives of Jacob and Esau tell the tragic consequences of parental discord and partiality (Gen. 25:19—28:9). For best results, parental love and acceptance of each child must be equal.

(2) *They will practice consistent discipline.* What is taboo today will not be permitted tomorrow with the same child or with another child of corresponding age. Dobson writes: "Respectful and responsible children result from families where the proper combination of *love* and *discipline* is present. Both these ingredients must be applied in the necessary quantities."[5]

---

5. James C. Dobson, *Dare to Discipline* (Wheaton, Ill.: Tyndale House Publishers, 1970), p. 21.

(3) *They will themselves be exemplary Christians.* Their lives before the children will be living examples of what Christians should be and do.

(4) *They will admit to human fallibility.* Parents who cannot admit to making mistakes or who cannot acknowledge inability to answer a problem restrict the ability of their children to admire and believe them. Especially is it damaging when parents try to maintain this facade of infallibility under the guise of Christianity.

(5) *They will accept their child's individuality.* Too often parents try to mold children into their own unfulfilled wishes. Often in a sincere desire to help the child avoid the pitfalls of life, they do not allow his individuality to develop.

Parents who accept each child as a unique person and allow him to fulfill his personality in God's kingdom, lessen the likelihood of driving him away from God. As one parent said when masculine hair styles were changing: "Son, I do not approve of your long hair, but I do want you to know that wherever you are, and whatever you do, in this house you are loved."

b. Pitfalls to avoid. Parents who wish to help their children in the Christian way will avoid some pitfalls also.

(1) *They will avoid developing an extreme sense of guilt in their children.* Young people often have a difficult time believing that God forgives them because their sense of guilt has been exaggerated by censorious parents.

(2) *They will avoid comparing siblings.* It is easy for parents to hold up the conforming, capable child as an example for the less capable to copy; it is easy, but devastating to children.

(3) *They will not be harshly authoritarian.* Christian parents will not abdicate their responsibility to establish rules for the family to live by. But they will avoid stern authoritarian attitudes and insensitivity to the feelings of children. A harsh attitude often drives children away from God and the church.

(4) *They will not express disappointment at the child's sex.* Boys will not be reared as the girls their mothers wanted. Nor will girls be encouraged to become tomboys because their fathers wished for sons.

B. The Church

1. Special Interest Groups

The church extends the Christian teaching of the family by providing small, special-interest groups according to age or life function. Within these groups there are opportunities for learning social behavior and ethical values that cannot be found in non-Christian social groups. In the church the Christian faith and Christian values are central. Through discussion and other group endeavors, new dimensions and implications of that value system are discovered. Members learn the limits and responsibilities of personal rights in a Christian context. They learn the value of Christian love in all of life's relationships. A serious effort is made to help pupils transfer these skills and understandings to real-life situations outside the church.

2. Special Family Ministries

The church helps the family in its Christian education task by providing for the nurture of parents. Their spiritual resources and Christian understandings must be renewed and enlarged. Sermons on Mother's Day and Father's Day help the home to function in a Christian manner. By thus helping parents to become more Christlike, the church contributes to the fulfillment of their role as models. They become better examples of the way Christians are to live.

The church also provides curriculum materials for Christian education in the home. Family worship aids are available.[6] Cradle Roll materials help parents of young children to understand their task. Sunday school teaching materials have maximum value when parents follow carefully the sections prepared for use in the home.

From its experience of history, the church brings the wisdom of the past to bear upon today's situation. In these insights families can find guidance for meeting their problems.

The church also provides a basis for identity in a complex, impersonal society. Persons deprived of identity with a group feel alone and isolated. The church enables both individuals and families to maintain a sense of personal worth in an impersonal society. Together Christians can exert a moral force against social evils. Through the church they can feel together that they are doing something constructive in the face of otherwise unsolvable problems.

In the church, marriage becomes more than an approved, legal, sexual relationship. By solemnizing the marriage ceremony, the church points to the religious expectations for the family, including the wide range of educational functions in the home.

Guides to family life published by the church set marriage in

---

6. *Table Talk,* published by Beacon Hill Press of Kansas City, is a quarterly guide for family worship where there are children at home. The daily devotions are based on the weekly Bible studies of the Aldersgate Graded Curriculum for the Sunday school.

the Christian context.[7] This spiritual dimension is generally missing from other psychological and sociological books designed to help the family.

Pastoral counseling offers assistance where husband and wife find it difficult to make the adjustments necessary for a harmonious home. When death invades the family, the pastor is there to minister to the bereaved. Young couples, through the Sunday school and young adult programs, can share their family problems and find guidance in Christian child-rearing.

Special observances, such as Children's Day, highlight the Christian regard for the family. Also many congregations plan family retreats, family nights, and weeks of family emphasis, in order to strengthen the family's influence and to help the home achieve its purposes in God's plan of Christian nurture.

3. *Specific Educational Services*

The church further assists the family by providing special educational programs beyond the normal Sunday activities. Among these are day-care centers, nurseries, kindergartens, and Christian day schools. In a Christian atmosphere the children learn not only basic cultural and social skills but the Christian perspective as well. Many churches are finding these programs effective instruments of outreach as well as avenues of service to the community. Mucci reports:

> During a three-year period at least 16 new families were reached and are presently attending. Two families were converted and joined the church. These families have helped reach six other families. At least 60 new members were gained for the Sunday school through the weekday kindergarten. The Sunday school grew from an average attendance of 105 to 220. Church membership doubled and contributions increased by 300 percent.[8]

C. Public Education

1. *Indirect Involvement*

In the early history of American education and until the middle of the 20th century, the public school made a direct Christian educa-

---

7. The current titles are *Between Christian Parent and Child*, by Kenneth O. and Elizabeth Gangel (Grand Rapids, Mich.: Baker Book House, 1974); and *The Christian Family*, by Larry Christenson (Minneapolis: Bethany Fellowship, 1974).

8. Dallas D. Mucci, *Weekday Nursery and Kindergarten Schools* (Kansas City: Beacon Hill Press of Kansas City, 1966), p. 19.

tional impact. In recent years, however, a growing secularism and an increased emphasis upon the separation of church and state have blunted this direct thrust. Two significant decisions of the United States Supreme Court illustrate this blunting process. In the 1948 McCollum case, the court decreed that sectarian religious instruction could not be carried on in public school buildings. Many school boards have carried this decision beyond its intent and have refused to allow churches even to rent school buildings on Sunday.

The other landmark was the 1962 New York decision in which the Court held that requiring children to learn and repeat a prayer prescribed by the state was unconstitutional. Again many school boards have gone beyond the court ruling and have banned every kind of prayer in the classroom. The Court has not ruled out voluntary participation by pupils in a devotional period, if the Scripture lesson and the form of prayer are not imposed on the pupils. (For a further discussion of various court rulings see chapter 14 under "Weekday Christian Education.")

A few school systems, especially in Kentucky, specifically try to teach the moral and spiritual values that are inherent in the public school curriculum. No sectarian point of view is espoused, but the obligations of good character, citizenship, and concern for others are stressed as the curriculum affords opportunity. In some states, high school courses explore the Bible from a literary, objective point of view. The law does not prohibit presentation of religious viewpoints for the purpose of comparison.

One of the most direct contributions of the public school is the opportunity it provides for children from Christian homes to develop their skills in Christian living. As they associate with youth from non-Christian homes, they can learn how to be truly Christian and how to witness for Christ. Obviously, such skills presuppose a family and church education that teaches the children and youth how to transfer their learning from the sheltered climate of the home and church to the broader arena of life.

2. Tangential Programs

On the elementary and secondary levels, some Christian educational programs operate in connection with the public schools. For many years released time, dismissed time, and shared time programs have supplemented the curriculum of the public school. Usually these programs are conducted in churches near the school building, and they are interdenominational or interfaith projects. Specific Bible teaching and basic religious beliefs are the core of the curriculum.

Religious assemblies and baccalaureate services are conducted by public schools on the grounds that religion is a part of our culture and should be an element in good education.

In some places Youth for Christ and similar groups organize and conduct Bible clubs in the school building at lunch periods or other free times. Attendance is voluntary, and of course these programs are possible only where the school authorities give their permission for the clubs to function.

On the college and university levels, courses in religion, broadly defined, are flourishing. Denominations sometimes provide residence halls near college and university campuses where they conduct worship services for their students and offer courses in Bible and religion. Many denominations support campus ministers who serve as spiritual leaders for students. Campus Crusade for Christ and Inter-Varsity Christian Fellowship engage in active witnessing to college and university students.[9] Except for the courses offered by the state-supported institutions, all of these programs exist with the permission but without the financial support of the college or university.

D. The Government

The United States Constitution requires the separation of church and state. Some have interpreted this position to mean that the state must have no involvement in a religious ministry to any of its citizens. Theoretically, this is the view of the government; practically, however, the action is different. The government feels a responsibility to provide spiritual guidance for some of its functions and for some of its personnel. The Senate designates a clergyman to be its chaplain and to open its sessions with prayer. Chaplains are provided for the various branches of the armed services and for veterans' hospitals.

Perhaps the greatest role of the government in religion is to establish and maintain an orderly society in which freedom of worship and protection of worshippers are guaranteed. The whole Christian educational enterprise advances more efficiently in such a peaceful climate. Anarchy and lawlessness undermine it.

---

9. See chapter 19 for a fuller explanation of these ministries related to public education.

V. Current Sociological Challenges

From the foregoing discussion, we can see several challenges to Christian education. Changing social patterns may continue to intensify some of these problems in the foreseeable future. Indeed, the forces of social change may confront us with other urgent issues not now foreseen on the horizon. However, all of the following issues persist and should be considered in planning for successful Christian education in the last decades of the 20th century.

A. Indifference Versus Intensification of Interest

Some social forces discourage religious allegiance. The widening variety of life-styles, increases in leisure time, and advances in scientific knowledge seem to weaken religious commitment. Christian education must find ways to encourage the growth of religious interest in persons who live in this kind of society. Clearly defined goals and a program based on personal and societal needs can aid this process. Also there is encouragement for us in the laws of action and reaction. As vice and immorality seem to increase, religious commitment and activity normally increase also.

B. Direct Versus Indirect Involvement

The social problems that challenge Christian ministry today are unusually complex; they do not yield easily to simple solutions. They involve not only faulty laws but also attitudes, emotions, and customs of people. Should Christian education leaders become directly involved in social activism, such as protest marches and sit-ins? Or should the approach be more indirect? Will mass evangelism, visitation, and Christian education achieve the same ends in the same length of time? Every concerned Christian must face the issue and reach a decision for himself.

C. Institutional Versus Personal Ministry

Another challenge which the church of today faces is to avoid letting its ministry shift from saving individuals to promoting institutions. Christian educational outreach programs ideally serve both interests, but it is easy to allow the rewards of institutional growth to subvert the basic Christian calling—to serve men.

D. Internalization Versus Legalism

As the tempo of social change increases and the differences between rural and urban life-styles become sharper, Christian education must play a more decisive role. It is easy for those who resist change to adopt a legalistic approach to Christian living. It is equally easy for those who welcome change to become spiritually proud of their pragmatic intellectualism.

Christian education must seek additional ways to help persons on both sides to understand basic Christian beliefs, and to accept Christian values. As these goals are achieved, Christians will be genuinely committed to Christ even in the midst of a changing society.

E. Recruitment Versus Communication

Christian education must focus on the communication of the gospel message so that it not only brings salvation to lives but also nurtures and sustains them. Christian behavior must spring from an inner knowledge of God's joy and grace. Recruitment should be the result of communication. To reverse the order is an error. We are inclined to invite a neighbor to come to church to hear the gospel. Should we be sharing the gospel message in such a way that our neighbors will want to find and join the church?

F. Adaptation Versus Continuity

Effective Christian education demands that we confront persons with the gospel at the point of their needs. Curriculums may need to be revised, methods evaluated and changed. At the same time the essential Christian message must be retained intact and transmitted without loss of content or meaning. The planners of Christian educational strategies must discover the limits of change-tolerance their constituencies will allow and then devise programs that will communicate the unchangeable truth through workable methods.

BIBLIOGRAPHY

Demerath, N. J. *Religion in Social Context.* New York: Random House, 1969.

This volume analyzes the sociological components of the religious movement. Religion is used in its broadest meaning.

Hill, M. *Sociology of Religion.* New York: Basic Books, 1973.

This book evaluates the literature on several key issues in the sociology of religion and provides a comprehensive bibliography of that literature.

Nottingham, E. K. *Religion: A Sociological View.* New York: Random House, 1971.

Three aspects of this book are interesting. In chapter 4 the author discusses religion and human stress; chapter 5 discusses religion and human meaning. The appendix explores theoretical approaches to research in the sociology of religion.

Schaeffer, Francis A. *The Church at the End of the Twentieth Century.* London: The Norfolk Press, 1970.

A respected evangelical Christian describes the sociological milieu in which the church finds itself in our times.

Whitley, O. R. *Religious Behavior.* Englewood Cliffs, N.J.: Prentice-Hall, Inc., 1964.

The author brings together aspects of the dialogue between religion and sociology about the church, the religious revival, the problems of the suburb, and religious denominations in an organizational society. One chapter discusses the role of the Protestant minister.

PART II

Curriculum
in
Christian Education

Preamble

As we move into the next six chapters, the reader is likely to find himself on more familiar ground than in some of the foundation areas. Here we encounter experiences familiar to the Sunday school teacher, youth leader, and pastor in their week-by-week ministries in the local church. But effective work in these ministries depends every Sunday on a grasp of the principles derived from one or more of the foundation areas. That is why they are important.

Christian education is not child's play. Our task is to help men and women, teens, and children to a living faith in Christ—and then to help them grow to full Christian maturity. Providing effective curriculum for this enterprise is an exhausting discipline. Somewhere in the process we must present to the learner all that God has revealed of himself to us in Scripture, in nature, and in the history of the Church. And mere presentation is not enough. We must present these supremely important truths in ways that move the learner to accept them as God's will for himself, and to make them the guidelines for his life-style.

To be this kind of teachers in the church, we must everlastingly seek to be Christian motivators. We follow in the spirit of Paul who cries, "We are ambassadors for Christ, God making his appeal through us. We beseech you on behalf of Christ, be reconciled to God" (2 Cor. 5:20, RSV). We follow in the succession of Peter in his plea for Christian nurture, "Grow in the grace and knowledge of our Lord and Savior Jesus Christ" (2 Pet. 3:18, RSV).

If in this ministry we are to be "a workman who has no need to be ashamed, rightly handling the word of truth" (2 Tim. 3:15, RSV), we must know the persons to whom we minister. We must know the potential and the limitations of preschool children. We must know how to challenge elementary children and guide eager teens. We must sense the deep needs of uncertain young adults, the pressures of middle years, and the changing roles of the aging.

Our term "curriculum" comes from the Latin *currere*—a road, or a path. In Christian education it is the path along which we seek to guide the follower in the footsteps of Jesus until he reaches the homeland of God.

To a better understanding of these important elements of that pathway we turn our attention in this section to "Curriculum in Christian Education."

CHAPTER 7

Principles of Curriculum Development

I. Concepts of Curriculum

A generation ago, George H. Betts made a statement that is as fresh and accurate now as it was then:

> No problem confronting the church today more concerns thoughtful leaders than that of the curricula for its schools. This problem has recently taken on new significance from a realization of the very literal truth contained in von Humboldt's dictum that *what you would have in the life of a people you must first put into its schools.*[1]

Curriculum may be conceived in a very narrow or in a very broad sense. It may denote (1) just the printed Bible lesson, the passage to be studied; (2) the printed materials prepared for the lesson, plus the appropriate resource materials; (3) all of the lesson materials, resources, and activities that relate to the objectives, or (4) the total experience of the learner. We have chosen the third as best suiting our purposes for a discussion of curriculum development.

Basic elements in every learning experience must include someone who needs to learn (the learner), something that can be learned (the content), and some way of accomplishing the learning (the

---

1. George Herbert Betts, *The Curriculum of Religious Education* (New York: Abingdon Press, 1924), p. 25.

method, or activity). Since interpersonal relations are involved in most learning, the list should also include a guide (a teacher) to facilitate learning.

A. Foundations Determine Concepts

A person's concept of curriculum is affected by his philosophy of education, his theological tenets, his psychological and sociological understandings, and his historical heritage. From these foundations one must determine whether education is to be viewed primarily as transmissive, as creative, or as a synthesis of the two. Today the learner is generally viewed as both active and interactive in his learning. His background influences his perception of a stimulus. He is active in choosing the response appropriate to him. He is active also in his motivation for assimilating and integrating each response into his total behavior.

B. Definition of Curriculum

Curriculum must be an outgrowth of these foundation systems. Curriculum design must, in turn, direct the establishment and program of the agencies for education. The following definition of Christian education seems to meet the foundation requirements of evangelical Christians. Some variant form of it has been adopted by many Protestant Christian education groups:

> Christian education is that ministry of the church which provides the educational undergirding for the church's entire ministry of worship, witness, and work. In this Design, Christian education is construed as related to all opportunities offered to persons primarily for the purpose of education in the Christian faith and for the Christian mission.[2]

Curriculum may therefore be seen as the planned educational program of the entire church for the development of its constituents. As a fellowship of faith the congregation is encountered by the gospel of Christ and responds in faith and love.

C. Components of Curriculum Design

The participants in the Cooperative Curriculum Project[3] (CCP)

---

2. *The Church's Educational Ministry: A Curriculum Plan* (St. Louis: The Bethany Press, 1966), p. 3.

3. The CCP was a cooperative project undertaken by 16 denominations to explore jointly curriculum development and to formulate a curriculum design upon which they could then build their individual denominational structures. See chapter 1, p. 34; also footnote 27.

defined five components in their curriculum design: objective, scope, context, learning tasks, and organizing principle.

These five components are interdependent and interactive with one another. For example, each component must be seen in the light of the objective in order that it may facilitate progress toward the objective. Also, learning tasks must be in harmony with the objective; they must be congenial to the context; they must be appropriate to the learner in his situation; and they must give promise of dealing dynamically with scope.[4]

The *objective* is synonymous with the aim or purpose of the total design. *Scope* implies the total area that should be explored. *Context* is the setting in which Christian education is attempted. The *learning tasks* are the activities consciously pursued by the learner in order to acquire what he wants to know. The *organizing principle* describes the way the various components of the design are related to one another.

D. Campbell Wyckoff, one of the professional advisors to CCP, has been explicit in distinguishing between curriculum, curriculum theory, curriculum design, curriculum content, and curriculum materials. A detailed review of these definitions would be helpful to one wishing professional information regarding curriculum planning.[5]

For our discussion here, Wyckoff's summation of what is involved in an adequate concept of Christian education is apropos.

The context of Christian education is seen as the worshipping, witnessing, working community of persons in Christ. The scope of Christian education is the whole field of relationships in the light of the gospel. The purpose of Christian education is awareness of revelation and the gospel, and response in faith and love. The process of Christian education is participation in the life and work of the community of persons in Christ. The design of Christian education consists of sequences of activities and experiences by which the learning tasks may be effectively undertaken by individuals and groups.[6]

A working concept of the curriculum of Christian education must include concern for a *home* that is truly Christian and a *church* that is the concerned body of Christ at work in and for the community. It calls for a *program* that is genuinely educational, with sound *instructional materials* and adequate resources. It needs adequate *buildings* and *equipment* and requires an informed and dedicated *administration.*

---

4. *The Church's Educational Ministry*, p. 4.
5. D. Campbell Wyckoff, *Theory and Design of Christian Education Curriculum* (Philadelphia: The Westminster Press, 1961). See pp. 83 ff.
6. *Ibid.*, p. 79.

II. CONCERNS OF CURRICULUM

A. Inclusiveness

Curriculum is the directing and implementing program of Christian education—including all content and experiences through which God is revealed, and the grace of God's presence is encountered. Curriculum should eventuate in salvation. Conversion should lead to nurture through the curriculum. The life of the church itself is a vital part of the curriculum because it is the context in which Christian learning occurs.

The concern for inclusiveness, therefore, relates to people, to agencies, and to content. Curriculum should provide for persons just entering the community of believers as well as for those who are longtime members of that community. An inclusive curriculum should also provide for and relate to every agency of the church that has an educational task to perform. It should provide means and materials for nurture in every aspect of living which can be fostered in the Christian faith.

B. Theological Integrity

Theology serves the dual functions of providing subject matter to be taught and supplying a frame of reference for the curriculum design.

At the point of design, one must decide whether the task of Christian education is primarily to teach facts or to encourage human response in the divine encounter. Inculcation of facts tends to imply behavioristic curriculum planning. Stress upon human decision in the divine encounter emphasizes the free will of the learner. If free choice and glad response is our goal, we must provide more than a stimulus-response kind of learning. Insight learning as described in chapter 5 allows for the divine impingement of the Holy Spirit upon the mind and therefore upon the learning of man. This view of learning does not deny that some things are learned by conditioning; there is an appropriate place for stimulus-response learning in Christian education. But there is more—much more. The creation engagement concept of learning posited by Robert Boehlke[7] treats at length these theological issues of revelation, the doctrine of man, and the doctrine of the Holy Spirit in relation to Christian learning.

In explaining his "Gospel-centered Curriculum," Schreyer emphasizes the need for a theological base:

---

7. Robert R. Boehlke, *Theories of Learning in Christian Education* (Philadelphia: The Westminster Press, 1963), pp. 181-201.

To place the curriculum in a theological setting is to furnish the curriculum with a revelatory background and a theological direction which support a communication between God and man. Interpreting the curriculum in a theological focus does not mean that the curriculum becomes completely a content of theology; it means that all content materials and activities used are revelatory in nature, that they are conducive to and permit a flow-through of God and his Christian truth in a communication to persons who respond.[8]

Further, according to Schreyer, curriculum has a threefold purpose which is theological in nature:

. . . that of assisting in making God real to man, of creating a theological directive-atmosphere so natural that the materials and methods find the climate sufficient to create a Godward outreach, and of awakening man through the Christian gospel to his need for a response to God.[9]

C. Educational Integrity

Beyond these theological questions, the curriculum must seek educational integrity in accounting for how one learns, when he learns, where he learns, what he learns, and, to some extent, why he learns.

The question of *who* learns leads to consideration of individuality, relationships, and grouping of pupils.

The issue of *how* one learns requires curriculum planners to take into account all of the established principles of learning theory— behavior modification, insight, problem-solving behavior, communication theory, and group dynamics.

The question of *when* one learns concerns a whole catalog of factors: homogeneous grouping, grading, organization for learning, developmental psychology, fragmented time periods with spaced review versus total immersion, application of learning, recognition, recall, and savings available in relearning.

Where one learns requires consideration of facilities, equipment, atmosphere, and activities.

What one learns involves curriculum planners in consideration of total resources, specially contrived curriculum materials, relationships, nonverbal communications, and imitation of behavior.

The issue of *why* one learns involves motivation, needs, insight, inspiration, revelation, and objectives.

---

8. George M. Schreyer, *Christian Education in Theological Focus* (Philadelphia: The Christian Education Press, 1962), p. 148.

9. *Ibid.*, p. 151.

To achieve educational integrity, curriculum planners must allow flexibility. Provision must be made for formal and informal learning, individual and group learning, central and peripheral learning, first exposure and reinforcement learning. Planners must balance tradition and innovation, boldness and carefulness, the long range and the immediate, the ultimate and the instrumental. Educational integrity must deal with the immortal man in his life as he lives it.

D. Individual Application

Curriculum must consider the learner as interactive with his environment. Learning implies change. The concern of curriculum, then, is what kinds of changes are possible and desirable. Curriculum must minister to the individual in the light of his past experience, his present need and interest, his maturity and aptitude, and his physical and social environment. Planners must realize that intersecting with the experience of the learner is more essential than mere logical continuity of subject matter. In the words of Donald Joy:

> Learning requires that the path of a student's interest is brought to *intersect* with a given idea, concept, or body of information. . . . What we teach must first be set on a collision course such that it intersects with the awareness and interest of the person who needs to learn. . . . Once the learner has intersected with the gold mine route leading to the rewarding concept, he needs help to *investigate* and work the rich conceptual field. . . . He will probe, explore, unmask, and synthesize his findings in the act of discovery. . . . When the learner has intersected with learning and has proceeded to investigate the resources available to him, his third obligation in meaningful learning is to infer—to draw inferences from his findings, which he can apply to real life. . . . Once inferences have been made and implications defined, it then remains for the learner to *implement* those understandings in actual practice.[10]

1. *Appropriate Content*

From the earliest records of religious education, subject matter for instruction has been a consistent concern of those who planned curricula. One obvious change desired in the learner is the increase of his knowledge. Curriculum planners must therefore include information that is to be imparted to the learner.

What do we want the student to know at a specific age? Or

---

10. Donald M. Joy, *Meaningful Learning in the Church* (Winona Lake, Ind.: Light and Life Press, 1969), pp. 142-45.

perhaps more important, what should he know at specific crisis points that may be somewhat distinct from chronological aging? These crisis points include salvation, baptism, church membership, accepting a leadership position in the church, and ordination for full-time ministry. What we teach is appropriate if it deals with revealed truth and if it meets some need of the learner at his own level of development.

In Christian education there is a knowledge that cannot be taught—it comes only through immediate experience. God's revelation of himself to man is not a knowledge *about* God; it is a knowledge *of* Him. Yet what we teach about the character of God and the responsibility of man can open the doors for God's revelation of himself. The skills and the building blocks of learning that lead from the known to the unknown are helpful in leading us from mere response into purposive behavior.

2. *Attitude Formation*

The learner's incorporation of appropriate attitudes must be a concern to the curriculum builder. Much of life is spent in interpersonal relations. One does not live to himself. As someone has put it, "The world is inhabited chiefly by other people." Communications involve feeling levels as much as they involve knowledge. Feelings are therefore important in interpersonal relationships.

Society largely determines what attitudes are valued and what are disvalued. But the New Testament is our Guideline to moral and ethical standards. We firmly believe that they come from God. The learner must therefore be led to an acceptance of those standards. Further, he must be enabled to internalize them so that they will find expression in Christlike behavior.

The earliest social attitudes are internalized from parents or other persons who are significant in the life of the learner. Further values are learned and accepted as a person encounters them beyond the family circle. Alfred Adler includes the development of unique personal attitudes as part of the individual's style of life.[11] Since attitudes are developed as a result of learning, the curriculum must include experiences contrived or chosen to cultivate and reinforce them.

The learning of attitudes and emotions is called *affective learning*. It may come through imitation, through psychological incorporation,

---

11. Alfred Adler, *The Practice and Theory of Individual Psychology* (New York: Harcourt, Brace and World, 1927), p. 10.

or as a result of positive reinforcement of behavior. Also, existing attitudes, motives, and emotions influence the way a pupil perceives new facts and responds to them. A curriculum that is truly Christian must allow for and foster the formation of true values as revealed by God through His Word. Christ implied that the inward motive which prompted the act is as important as the outward act itself (Luke 11:39). One of the concerns of curriculum must, therefore, be the formation of right attitudes and holy motives which find fruition in appropriate choices for proper conduct.

3. *Decision-making Skill Development*

"Training of the will" was at one time a major emphasis in character education. Today there is widespread agreement that we need to educate Christians to exercise responsible moral judgment. The possibility of alternative courses of action and the anticipation of possible consequences makes possible free human choices. Such decisions are based primarily upon the goals of the person in the act of deciding. But in addition, (1) the information he has at his disposal; (2) his perception of the situation in which he finds himself; and (3) his attitudes and needs of the moment all contribute to his decision.

Either anticipation of reward or fear of negative consequences has a major bearing upon the choice among alternative actions. Also the willingness to invest personal time and energy often depends on whether one has had a share in the choice that is made. Consequently, training in the art of bringing all relevant data into consideration before making a decision should find a place in the curriculum design.

4. *Appropriate Behavior Change*

We are interested in the behavior of the person. If one of our aims in Christian education is to enable the learner to become more Christlike, then his behavior should be patterned after the behavior of Christ.

Behavior is caused. However, the cause involves more than response to a given stimulus or even to a whole set of stimuli. Behavior is the result of the knowledge, attitudes, motivations, needs, and goals of the individual in his engagement with his environment. Much of one's behavior follows his decisions. Behavior is thus designed to implement goals, to avoid conflict, or to expedite social concerns. We must recognize this complex nature of behavior and deal with it.

The curriculum should include opportunities and activities that promote desired behavior. We must reinforce the learner's sense of achievement and his acceptance by God and by the group of which he is a part. But Christian education is more than manipulation of stimuli to obtain specific behavioral responses.

We see that there is an interrelationship among needs, motives, attitudes, knowledge, volition, and behavior. The individual does not act in accordance with only one need or motive at any given time. Rather, he responds as a whole person in every instance. And for the Christian every response must be in accordance with his value structure. Curriculum planning should enable him to keep those values gospel-centered.

We have implied that our curriculum is consciously planned and guided experience directed toward the fulfillment of specific purposes of Christian education. We may, therefore, accept the assumptions that greater knowledge and holier attitudes will lead to more valid decisions and thus to more acceptable behavior. All are part of the concerns of Christian education curriculum. We must include the increase of knowledge, the cultivation of attitudes, the development of decision-making skills, and the modification of behavior.

E. Relationships

A concern for relationships is a recognition of the importance of the individual in his interpersonal contacts. Dialogue, so essential in Christian education, implies a sense of personal worth and personal dignity. It also implies effective communication; and such communication implies a union that results in community. Roger Shinn writes:

> Because Christianity is the life of a community, its educational ministry is the work of that community. Its aim is not the promotion of the community but the reconciling mission to which the community is called. Hence Christian education may be described as the effort "to introduce persons into the life and mission of the community of Christian faith." This conception of Christian education, I suggest, is consistent both with the biblical understanding of the church and with the findings of recent educational psychology about the learning process.[12]

A realization of community requires a sense of the heritage of that community as well as a sense of its cohesive nature. Christian

---

12. Roger L. Shinn, in *An Introduction to Christian Education,* ed. Marvin J. Taylor (Nashville: Abingdon Press, 1966), p. 11.

education curriculum must be designed to perpetuate the essential elements of that heritage. It must interpret the heritage as well as current Christian elements. It must also seek to modify cultural elements that militate against the Christian community. Sherrill writes:

> *Koinonia* is community. But *koinonia* is a kind of community which transcends ordinary human community in that God is present and participant in the community. For the connotation of *koinonia* is that the *Spirit of God is forthgoing into, and present in, every relationship within the community.* . . . Thus *koinonia* is by its nature a community intimately indwelt by the Spirit.[13]

Wyckoff also stresses this concern for community in planning the curriculum design. For him, the context for Christian education must be the church.

> The worshiping, witnessing, working community of persons in Christ may be said to be the definitive locale of Christian education and its curriculum, since without the dynamic reality of the community of faith, Christian meaning cannot be communicated. . . . The communication of the faith, then, requires an active, believing community that is reaching out from itself as an instrument of God's evangelization of the world. Education in the Christian faith cannot be carried on outside this context.[14]

F. Practicality and Workability

The design for curriculum must be practical and workable. Our objectives must be attainable. Early education must be simple, and simplicity should also characterize organizational design, educational staffing, and the statement of objectives.

The curriculum must be economical in terms of leadership, time, effort, and cost. However, economy should not be made synonymous with reduced outlay of time, effort, or finance. The greater outlay may be the more economical in terms of long-range learning.

Another aspect of economy must be a balance between curriculum and other activities. Is so much time and effort expended in education that the church neglects its fellowship, witness, worship, or other Christian work?

The curriculum design must be functional in nature. It must lead naturally into an effective educational ministry in the church.

G. Viability and Accountability

Education must be for a purpose. It must be direct and individual. It

---

13. Sherrill, *Gift of Power*, p. 50.
14. Wyckoff, *Theory and Design*, pp. 116-17.

must be experiential. It must be linked with life and provide a critique of life. The curriculum design must also be concerned with enlargement of the church so that it becomes ever more comprehensive and evangelistic. It must provide training for perpetuation of the faith from one generation to another. It must have eternity in its purpose, and it must build in means by which each of these concerns may be evaluated.

To provide most effectively for viability and accountability, the design must be in accordance with a stated purpose which will provide direction, enlargement, and evaluation for the total plan. Wyckoff writes:

> A sound situation in Christian education maintains priority for the objective, with the curriculum serving it, and administration serving curriculum. A radically unsound situation exists where curriculum is designed to serve administrative ends or where the objective is cut to fit the assumptions of a particular curriculum.[15]

III. Objectives in Curriculum

A. The Nature of Objectives

Two questions dominate the concern for Christian education curriculum: What kind of person do we hope to see ultimately develop through this curriculum? and, What kind of person is the learner involved at any given point in the educational process? It is from primary concern for the individual and where he is going that objectives are determined.

Paul Vieth has defined the objective as "A statement of a result consciously accepted as a desired outcome of a given process."[16] In reference to Christian education, he writes:

> Education objectives are statements of desired outcomes to be achieved through the process of education. Their function is to set a mark in advance. They constitute the goal for which education exists—the *raison d'etre* for its being. Objectives are to education what the architectural drawing is to the builder ... With a goal in view, proper activities may be selected for reaching that goal,

---

15. D. Campbell Wyckoff, "Curriculum," in Kendig Brubaker Cully, ed., *The Westminster Dictionary of Christian Education* (Philadelphia: The Westminster Press, 1963), p. 171.

16. Paul H. Vieth, *Objectives in Religious Education* (New York: Red Label Reprints, 1930), p. 18.

each in its proper sequence, and their success measured by the criterion of the results achieved toward the building of a house.[17]

The major task of Christian education is to enable each person to experience his greatest potential in Christ. Paul phrased it, "That the man of God may be perfect, throughly furnished unto all good works" (2 Tim. 3:17). A curriculum, therefore, should be designed to deal with facts acquired through reason or revelation. James Smart emphasizes the theological nature of our teaching task:

> We teach so that through our teaching God may work in the hearts of those whom we teach to make of them disciples wholly committed to his gospel, with an understanding of it, and with a personal faith that will enable them to bear convincing witness to it in word and action in the midst of an unbelieving world. We teach young children and youths and adults that by the grace of God they may grow up into the full life and faith of His Church, and may find their life's fulfillment in being members of the very body of Christ and sharers in this mission.[18]

B. Comprehensive Objectives

Appropriate objectives must be comprehensive. Reason and revelation must be recognized as the bases upon which one builds a Christian philosophy of life. Appreciations and attitudes must be developed that are appropriate to the age and development of the learner. Application of factual content in developing skills of Christian living and communication must evolve out of the understandings, appreciations, attitudes, and motives of the individual. This process is made possible by establishing a curriculum that is built to achieve one overarching objective or several interrelated objectives.[19]

Each denomination is responsible to relate the objectives of its educational program to the objectives for the total church. At all times there should be a logical and experiential relationship between curricular objectives and institutional purposes. A good example of this relationship can be seen in the "Southern Baptist Design Elements," in which the two basic objectives are defined as follows:

---

17. *Ibid.,* p. 19.

18. James D. Smart, *The Teaching Ministry of the Church* (Philadelphia: The Westminster Press, 1954), p. 107.

19. Part One of *The Church's Educational Ministry* and Stephenson's *Why the Church Teaches* offer good descriptions and statements of a single overarching objective. Vieth's *Objectives in Christian Education* explains several interrelated general objectives for Christian education. See bibliography.

1. *Church*

   The objective of a church, composed of baptized believers who share a personal commitment to Jesus Christ as Saviour and Lord, is to be through the power of the Holy Spirit a redemptive body in Christ, growing toward Christian maturity through worship, witness, education, and ministry, proclaiming the gospel to the whole world, and applying Christian principles to man and society that God's purposes may be achieved.

2. *Educational*

   To help persons become aware of God as revealed in Jesus Christ, respond to him in a personal commitment of faith, strive to follow him in the full meaning of discipleship, relate effectively to his church and its mission in the world, live in conscious recognition of the guidance and power of the Holy Spirit, and grow toward Christian maturity.[20]

In summary, the framework for establishing objectives toward which education must move is the redemptive encounter and creative-engagement of man with his God. Objectives must account for the theological tenets of the church. They must foster faith and worship, witness and outreach, fellowship, and Christian citizenship. The focus of objectives must always be the learner. They must reflect an awareness of him in his total experience, address him at his point of need, and evoke in him a response and involvement in his own education.

C. Specific Objectives

We have said that each denomination is responsible to point the direction of its curriculum plan through a statement of general objectives. But beyond such an overall statement of objective each group responsible for curriculum development must provide specific short-range objectives. These are usually objectives for units of study. A further division establishes one or more specific objectives for each immediate activity or session. They will be subordinate or specific aspects of the larger whole toward which they point. Vieth has indicated the interrelatedness between these types of objectives:

> Such division into comprehensive and specific is justifiable only from the standpoint of practicable usability—never from the standpoint of assuming to accept one type in preference to the

---

20. Howard P. Colson and Raymond M. Rigdon, *Understanding Your Church's Curriculum* (Nashville: Broadman Press, 1969), p. 156.

other. Unless the two types of objectives serve as complements one to the other, we do not have a satisfactory statement of educational goals.[21]

D. Characteristics of Objectives

1. *Clarity*

The cry for clarity of objectives cannot go unheeded without danger to the educational process. It is commonly agreed that much of the failure of educational enterprise has been because the goals have not been clearly seen or sharply defined. Objectives should be stated singly and in as simple terms as possible.

2. *Inclusiveness*

Objectives must be as inclusive and as complete as necessary to accomplish the goal intended. It is only as the specific objectives are outlined and arranged in a logical, progressive order, and evaluated, that gaps are noted in the plans. When gaps are filled in, the learning activities can take on completeness and allow for continued development. Some educators contend that when objectives are fully and finally stated and understood by the learner, most of the task of teaching-learning has been completed.

3. *Cohesiveness*

Objectives can hardly be complete if they are not cohesive. There should be the probability of easy transition from one specific objective to the next until the general objective has been attained. Interrelating between objectives lends unity to the learning enterprise.

4. *Viability*

Since all learning is, in the final analysis, individual learning, the individual with his needs and interests should share in the establishment of his own objectives.

Objectives become drab and dead when divorced from the learner himself. They must be live options for him. He must see that they are desirable and attainable.

Also, when objectives deal with behavior, one should state them in behavioral terms. This allows evaluation to be more objective and accurate than otherwise.

---

21. Vieth, *Objectives*, p. 34.

E. The Functions of Objectives

1. *Objectives Determine Directions*

Without clear objectives, curriculum becomes a meaningless experience. Objectives determine and make explicit the goals to be achieved; they are the ends to be reached. Objectives are the targets toward which one aims in seeking behavior modification. Because the learner is central in curriculum concerns, objectives must relate to his needs, his interests, his potential, and his limitations. The curriculum must allow for purposeful experience for each learner.

2. *Objectives Determine Content*

Because objectives determine the ends to be sought, they determine the content that engages the learner in his search for new goals and experiences. The specific objectives will find expression in the learning activities. These, in turn, become the building blocks upon which the learner stands to engage in increasingly higher attainments until the comprehensive objectives are achieved.

The content to be studied and the resources to be employed are brought in when and as appropriate to the stated objectives.

3. *Objectives Determine Methodology*

If objectives determine content, they should determine methods also, because methods must be geared to content and to the ends sought. Methods are the activities by which information is conveyed, insights evoked, emotions expressed, choices fostered, and skills developed. The methods used must be those that most adequately facilitate learning.

4. *Objectives Determine Structure*

Curriculum begins at the local church level. The specific needs of real people must be studied. As these needs are cataloged and compared, there emerges a synthesis of the predominant and urgent needs. These needs are classified for each age level and become working objectives of the curriculum staff planning educational materials for the denomination. At the same time, the local church should organize its leadership to determine how and through what agencies pupil needs can best be met. Organization thus becomes an asset in the achievement of objectives.

5. *Objectives Determine Evaluative Criteria*

Finally, objectives provide the criteria by which the curriculum is evaluated. When we have set attainable goals in curriculum, we must ask, Have we reached them? Without this constant, constructive evaluation in the light of objectives, the curriculum becomes hodgepodge and stagnant. It can be powered to serve only when it is geared to individual needs and when its goals are being achieved.

When we use objectives as criteria for determining the effectiveness of content and methods, we must remember the total concerns of Christian education. Do the objectives express the shared aims of the home and church? Do they include the concerns of pupil and teacher? Does the curriculum assist in making God real to man? Does it provide an atmosphere that helps the learner reach toward God in loving obedience and toward man in loving mission? Does it meet the needs and interests of individuals and at the same time strengthen the ties of Christian community? Are all specific objectives subordinated to the comprehensive objective(s)? Is there unity, coherence, direction, selectivity, motivation, structure, and value in the entire battery of objectives? When these questions can be answered affirmatively, the curriculum design begins to take shape.

IV. Planning Curriculum

A. Levels of Planning

The following levels of concern for Christian education curriculum planning are listed in priority order:

> Personal
> Class or group
> Agency or program
> Local church
> District or area
> Denominational
> Interdenominational

In general practice, however, the reverse order is used in curriculum planning. The needs to be met are personal and local, but the task of preparing materials and guiding teachers exceeds the ability of most local church leaders, so interdenominational concerns take precedence.

Often several denominations will combine task forces to outline broad curriculum plans in accordance with surveyed needs of individuals and groups. One recent example of this combination of task forces may be seen in the gathering of representatives from 16 different denominations who participated in the Cooperative Curriculum Project:

Over the four-year period the Project's total membership of over 125 persons put in seven work sessions of one week each, to which were added months of work by subcommittees, special task groups, Administrative Committee, and the Project Staff.

This project has resulted in a Curriculum Plan usable by denominations nationally as a basis for designing curriculum and as a basis for developing materials to support curriculum. It is anticipated that denominations would use this resource both as single denominations and as denominations working cooperatively.[22]

Another even more closely knit interdenominational cooperative approach is the work of the Aldersgate Graded Curriculum Committee. In this arrangement much of the planning, writing, and printing of curriculum materials is done cooperatively by the participating denominations.[23]

In these cooperative ventures each denomination determines to what extent it will use the results of this combined labor. They also make whatever modifications or special adaptations are necessary. Each denomination decides whether to print and distribute its own materials or whether this can be done more effectively in cooperation with others.

Usually representatives from local churches, age-group specialists, psychologists, and theologians are represented on the denomination's curriculum advisory board. Spears's reminder for public-school curriculum planning is appropriate for Christian education as well: "Just as Clemenceau once said that 'war is too serious a business to be left to the generals,' so it can be said that curriculum planning is too serious a business to be left to the experts."[24]

Any materials or programs of Christian education prepared at the denominational level must be adapted to meet special needs that can be known only at the local level. These adaptations should include appropriate additions to and deletions from the resources provided. Central planners work diligently to envision typical needs in local churches. But they can plan only for typical situations—and for a few possible exceptions. The local leader must plan adaptations to be as helpful as possible to his group. Ultimately the teacher

---

22. *Cooperative Curriculum Project: A Design for Teaching-Learning* (St. Louis: The Bethany Press, 1967), p. xvii.

23. Churches of Christ in Christian Union, Church of the Nazarene, Evangelical Church of North America, Evangelical Friends Alliance, Evangelical Methodists, Free Methodists, The Missionary Church, The Wesleyan Church.

24. Harold Spears, *Curriculum Planning Through In-Service Programs* (Englewood Cliffs: Prentice-Hall, 1957), p. 50.

and the pupils become the final editors of all curriculum plans and resources.

B. Necessity of Planning

Curriculum is consciously planned. Such planning involves decisions regarding the organization, personnel, and tasks. It includes the coordination of all these facets and the outlining of a sequence of activities. Planning should lead to the progressive use of content in such a manner that the objectives will be achieved.

C. Coordination of Planning

There is a need for coordinating all the educational agencies and activities of the church. Those who plan the curriculum for the local church must include the teachers and learners, parents, department heads, pastor, and the official board of Christian education. It is only as these persons discuss the needs, the resources, the activities, and the materials that they can plan Christian education curriculum effectively. However, it is reassuring to know that there are many common human needs at each age level. Therefore centrally planned activities and materials may meet many of the needs that we find in our pupils in the local church.

D. Cooperation in Planning

It is a serious step when the curriculum of the denomination is disregarded in favor of other materials that are thought to be more attractive or easier to work with. The local church is thus cut off from its most helpful channels for doctrinal teaching and for denominational unity.

Adaptation of any activities and materials, to meet the needs of the individual, is expected and recommended. However, the serious decisions that go into curriculum design, materials, and procedures constitute an awesome task that should not be shouldered by any one person. Such decisions should be made only by the local board of Christian education after consultation with teachers, pastor, and denominational planners.

V. CONTENT IN CURRICULUM

A. Emphases in Content

If it is *Christian* education that is attempted, there must be a central place given to the Bible as the Revelation of God to man. However, to say that the Bible must have central place does not by itself give adequate guidance for curriculum development. Other related questions must also be answered.

Shall we select only a limited number of scripture passages and emphasize these to the exclusion of the rest of the Bible? Shall we study the Bible sequentially, book by book? Shall we approach it from a theological position, dealing with the major doctrines? Shall we come to the Bible from the social perspective, asking, What does it say to the needs of man in society? Shall we be individualistic and ask, What does the Bible say to my problems and needs? Shall we ask what each book was trying to say to the people for whom it was written?

Obviously, there are advantages and limitations in each of these approaches. The Bible is a large book, and human life is complex. From time to time the Bible needs to be viewed from each of these perspectives, according to the developmental and understanding levels of the learners. Human needs and interests are so varied that we must give some time for each of these perspectives to be explored.

1. *Bible-centered Content*

"We believe in the plenary inspiration of the Holy Scriptures . . . given by divine inspiration, inerrantly revealing the will of God concerning us in all things necessary to our salvation."[25] When evangelical Christians thus commit themselves to such a high view of the Scriptures, curriculum plans should make the Bible central and pervasive. Generous use of the Bible in curriculum materials enables the learner to know the Bible well enough to find strength, guidance, comfort, or warning as he has need. The Psalmist gave voice to the testimony of many persons when he declared, "Thy word is a lamp unto my feet, and a light unto my path" (Ps. 119:105). The Bible is the good news of God's redemptive plan. This diary of God's creation-engagement with man is indispensable to the curriculum of Christian education.

2. *Theologically Interpreted Content*

Christ and His gospel are essential elements that give all other emphases meaning, coherence, and perspective:

> In selecting curriculum materials insist upon a vertical dimension that allows God to be seen in the following terms: (a) the divine Initiative that reveals God as love seeking his own and

---

25. *Manual, Church of the Nazarene* (Kansas City: Nazarene Publishing House, 1976), par. 4.

reconciling the world unto himself; (b) the divine Encounter that builds relationships with mankind in order that a redemptive fellowship may be established; (c) the divine Revealer who confronts man with himself as expressed through Jesus Christ, the holy Bible, and the Christian fellowship; (d) the divine Redeemer who knows man's moral predicament of sinfulness and rebellion, but who still through love forgives and restores man in a relationship of faith and grace; (e) the divine Sustainer, the source of power which sensitizes, unifies, and strengthens the divine aspirations and commitments of all devotees; and (f) the divine Sovereign, who is the supreme Lord and Master over all mankind and the universe.[26]

The content of the curriculum must cover every area which helps to illuminate the revelation of God to His people. The curriculum will therefore include primary emphasis upon the Bible as the revealed Word of God. It will also use creedal statements, history, theology, and philosophy as necessary to explain and reinforce the Word of God. Curriculum content will include music, art, architecture, and choral reading to enhance the spirit and understanding of worship. It will use biography, social problems, and personal needs to enrich and make relevant the awareness of God's action in personal and corporate experience.

B. Presentation of Content

In selecting materials for curriculum, churches are becoming more discriminating. Once the emphasis for many was largely upon attractive format and easy teaching helps. Now workers are asking more pertinent questions of the literature they review. Appropriate concerns include: Are the materials graded to suit the interest and learning levels of those who will use them? Are they materials in which God's message comes through strong and clear? Is there a strong allegiance to the denominational articles of faith? Are they educationally sound in the teaching-learning methods recommended? Do the materials emphasize the vertical, spiritual dimension? Do they emphasize a loving, obedient relationship to God? Do they speak to the current needs of man in his world?

The form below is suggested as a useful device for evaluating curriculum materials. Because curriculum includes the content of the materials and also functions carried out by local teachers, both aspects need to be examined.

---

26. Schreyer, *Christian Education*, pp. 152-53.

Evaluating Curriculum Materials

As you examine curriculum materials, look for these 10 elements. Rate the materials on a scale of 1 to 10 on each question. A score of 1 will indicate your lowest possible rating on that item —it is very unsatisfactory. A score of 10 will mean that you judge the material to be entirely satisfactory at the point in question.

1. Does the material draw the learner to the Bible and to Jesus Christ as the Source of truth? *Bible/Jesus*
2. Do the materials consistently relate Bible truths to the life concerns of the students? *Bible → Life*
3. Does the material recognize and help teachers reach the need level of the learners? *Need Level Student*
4. Is the vocabulary on the learner's level of understanding? *Vocabulary*
5. Are the aims stated or interpreted so that they point teachers and students beyond knowledge to changed attitudes and behavior? *change attitudes*
6. Do session developments reflect the stated aims? *Follows through aims*
7. Do the materials clearly present and explain learning activities in which pupils will be involved? *Clear on learning activities*
8. Are there visual and audio aids to support learning activities? *Audio/visuals*
9. Are there questions or other devices to encourage teachers and pupils to evaluate progress? *good Questions*
10. Do teacher's materials include encouragement for a deepening life of devotion and motivation for continued Christian service? *life of devotion + motivation to service*

Evaluating Use of Materials

As you examine the teacher's use of curriculum materials, look for these 10 elements. Rate the teacher on a scale of 1 to 10 on each question. A score of 1 indicates the lowest possible rating on that item—very unsatisfactory at the point in question. A score of 10 will mean that you judge the teacher's function to be entirely satisfactory at that point.

1. Does the church furnish the teacher with all of the regularly recommended curriculum materials?
2. Does the teacher spend at least two hours each week studying the materials and preparing for the session?
3. Does the teacher understand that his leader's guide is a compilation of recommended helps? Does he add items that occur to him? And omit suggestions that do not fit his class?
4. Does the teacher regularly plan learning activities that involve student participation during the class hour?
5. Does the teacher use the visual aids provided—and plan some of his own?
6. Does the teacher know his students well enough to relate Bible truths to their life needs?

7. Does the teacher at least once a year read a book, attend a training class, or attend regular worker's meetings that are planned to help him improve his teaching?
8. Does the teacher spend some time each week evaluating his teaching procedures and class responses?
9. Does the teacher's life and manner make the Christian life appealing?
10. Does the teacher show concern for reaching new persons and for winning them to Christ?

1. *Focus of Content*

Materials now used by most denominations begin with the major concerns of life and relate the Bible to these themes. This procedure is an attempt to give Bible teaching its greatest impact by helping the learner see clearly how the Bible speaks to his needs.

2. *Appeal of Content*

In their serious consideration of curriculum, more churches are focusing on the learner in his total experience within the church fellowship. An integrated thrust of all educational agencies of the church is being fostered. More and better teaching materials are being provided. New, attractive formats encourage greater interest on the part of the learner. The individual is also receiving more attention in the planning of curriculum content. Serious evaluation, research, and field testing are being carried on by the denominations.

3. *Organization of Content*

Organization of curriculum content is receiving considerable revamping at present. To achieve unity and sequence, content is planned in units involving from 2 to 13 or more sessions dealing with a similar theme. These themes are arranged sequentially until a cycle of one year at the nursery level to three or more years at older levels has been completed.

Also coordination of topics from one age level to another is being attempted realistically. This plan makes it possible for the entire family to study similar themes at the same time, but for each to study it at his own level of understanding and application.

4. *Evaluation of Content*

Changing times and changing needs will continue to require changing curricula. We must be sure that God's message is put in understandable terms and that our Christian teaching is relevant to man's needs. Only thus can we help men to move ever closer to "the measure of the stature of the fulness of Christ" (Eph. 4:13). To accomplish this, the curriculum must be researched and evaluated continually.

In the words of D. Campbell Wyckoff:

> If the curriculum materials available to the local church for use in its Christian education program reflect an educational plan that focuses upon a sound objective, uses the full scope of Christian education, involves basic learning experiences, and is organized to involve the learner's use of all the resources of the faith within the fellowship of the church as it lives its life and fulfills its mission, then the choice and use of the right materials is of the utmost importance.[27]

VI. RESOURCES IN CURRICULUM

A. Scope of Resources

What resources are there for learning in the church? How may these be used effectively by the individual and by groups? For the most alert teachers, the whole world is claimed as resource material, but for the average Christian teacher little of it is used for effective teaching. For practical purposes the printed materials become the central focus for learning. These are prepared for the learner. The lesson includes a scripture passage and an exposition of its major thrust. Teacher's materials include a lesson outline for development, illustrations from life, applications to contemporary situations, activities for pupil involvement, and conclusion for reinforcement.

In addition to these periodical materials, most editorial centers recommend Bible commentaries, Bible dictionaries, lesson commentaries, and a variety of Bible versions and translations. Books on Bible lands, peoples, and customs broaden the understanding of teachers and pupils. Currently teaching pictures, film slips, tapes, and other audiovisual materials are available to more effectively involve pupils in the learning experience.

B. Choice of Resources

When we look for resource materials, we must ask, What is our objective? What resources will help us most? Is the cost manageable? Never before in history has there been such a wealth of resources for Christian education. Videotapes, cassette recordings, single-concept films, film slips, overhead projection, multi-media impact, micro-

---

27. D. Campbell Wyckoff, in Taylor, *Religious Education,* p. 108.

teaching techniques, and individualized instruction are only representative of the almost limitless helps that are available.

But resources must never become ends in themselves. They are only tools that may improve our learning, growing, and serving as Christian co-laborers of God. In a very real sense, the church is its own best curriculum. Local leaders may import materials of tremendous scope, yet find them ineffective. Those who use materials can either make or break the Christian teaching ministry.

C. The Essential Resource

We have mentioned resources available in the marketplace and in the talents and relationships of men. But there is another resource which cannot be purchased; it can, however, be encouraged and cultivated. This resource is the priceless presence of the Holy Spirit. Wyckoff graphically describes it in his discussion of the Word of God:

> Christian education deals with the vocabulary of the gospel and the Word of God. The Word of God is his way of revealing himself to us. It has been a spoken word; it is the word made flesh in Jesus Christ; it is the written word, the Bible, witnessed to by the Holy Spirit. God's own language is quite clearly a combination of the spoken and unspoken, the verbal and the nonverbal, a language of words and a language of relationships; he acts, he talks, he shows, he sends, he waits; he enters, he heals, he teaches, he preaches, he prays; he suffers, he dies, he rises, he ascends, he lives and reigns; he returns; and through it all he creates, he loves, and he redeems.[28]

VII. METHODOLOGY IN CURRICULUM

Specific consideration of methodology will follow in the next chapter. But because one cannot completely divorce method from curriculum, a brief treatment of that relationship is appropriate here. Without pupil involvement there is little learning. Ultimately one learns individually, but most learning processes are interpersonal and occur in an interpersonal setting.

The objectives reached are often due largely to the method chosen. Curriculum must have rich varieties in methodology. The learner must become involved in the action—questioning, analyzing, appraising, synthesizing, evaluating, responding, applying—in order to learn. The more closely the learning experience resembles a meaningful life situation, the more effective the teaching method is. Even

---

28. Wyckoff, *Theory and Design,* p. 119.

when factual data is taught, one finds greater retention when there is a demonstrated relationship between the information and its immediate usefulness to the learner. Always those methods should be used which facilitate learning while resulting in the fewest negative by-products.

VIII. SUMMARY

Curriculum is defined here as the church's planned experiences for the education of the learner. It must be concerned with the inculcation of knowledge, the incorporation of attitudes, the development of decision-making skills, and the involvement of Christian relationships.

Objectives are the keystone of curriculum. There must be one ultimate objective which gives centrality and support to all of our Christian concerns. In addition there must be many specific goals. They must be clear and practical if they are to be worthy and understandable. Our objectives determine the content desired, the methods and resources used, the organization and structure devised, and the evaluation criteria required.

Planning curriculum requires the coordination and cooperation of all agencies and persons involved in it. The integration of denominational and local emphases is necessary for coherent unity.

Content, whether considered as the central core of curriculum or as data for experience enrichment, must find an integral place in our planning. The place of the Bible, the experience of the past, the role of the church, the current development and future problems of individuals—all must find their way into the curriculum if it is to meet the needs of tomorrow's church.

The resources for curriculum are as varied as the boundaries of man's environment. They include all printed materials that would be appropriate—audio, video, and tactile. Resources also include both contrived and direct, meaningful experiences.

Curriculum must be concerned with methodology, because it is through methods that objectives are implemented, involvement is evoked, learning is facilitated, and relationships are fostered. But in all of the concepts, concerns, objectives, planning, content, resources, and methods, one more important element is needed. We must allow for the redemptive work of the Holy Spirit. He is the irreplaceable Key to the entire teaching-learning enterprise that we call Christian education curriculum.

BIBLIOGRAPHY

Colson, Howard P., and Rigdon, Raymond M. *Understanding Your Church's Curriculum.* Nashville: Broadman Press, 1969.

This small book fulfills its promise in attempting to make the curriculum plan of the church understandable to the average reader.

The Church's Educational Ministry: A Curriculum Plan. St. Louis: The Bethany Press, 1966.

The Cooperative Curriculum Project, reported in this volume, was a venture undertaken by 16 denominations to explore jointly curriculum development and to formulate a curriculum design upon which they could then build their individual denominational structures. The results of this study are both scholarly and extensive. It provides a good overview of the concerns and directions that many Protestant denominations have considered in framing curriculum revisions during the past two decades.

Joy, Donald M. *Meaningful Learning in the Church.* Winona Lake, Ind.: Light and Life Press, 1969.

Dr. Joy is eclectic and concise in his treatment of learning theories and their effect upon learning activities in the church. His is a refreshingly evangelistic treatment of the subject. Although he oversimplifies the learning theories, he depicts a good design for building a curriculum of Christian education.

Schreyer, George M. *Christian Education in Theological Focus.* Philadelphia: The Christian Education Press, 1962.

Dr. Schreyer stresses the need for theological content as the core of Christian education.

Vieth, Paul H. *Objectives in Religious Education.* New York: Red Label Reprints, 1930.

Dr. Vieth helped to pioneer the field of objectives in Christian education. His influence upon Protestant curriculum for Christian education cannot be measured. This book should be in every Christian educator's library both for its historical and its practical value.

Wyckoff, D. Campbell. *Theory and Design of Christian Education Curriculum.* Philadelphia: The Westminster Press, 1961.

Dr. Wyckoff has summarized the concerns of builders of Christian education curriculum. His book invites a second and third reading for thorough understanding. It is germane to workers planning and implementing a Christian education program at either the local or general church level.

CHAPTER 8

Methods and Media in Christian Education

I. INTRODUCTION

There is more than a grain of truth in the statement, "It's not so much what you do but how you do it that counts." This fact is trenchantly stated by McLuhan: "The medium is the message."[1]

Methods are means of communication. They are the vehicles by which teachers encounter learners, learners encounter other learners, and learners encounter problems and resources. Such encounter results in learning—and bringing it about is a basic concern of Christian education.

II. METHODS FROM FOUNDATION AREAS

Methods have a way of linking together the foundation and the goal, the teacher and the learner, the organization and the administration. Because methods are essential, they are purposefully chosen and carefully developed in accordance with foundation bases.

---

1. Marshall McLuhan, *Understanding Media: The Extensions of Man,* 2nd ed. (New York: The New American Library, Inc., 1964), p. 23.

A. Biblical

1. *Methods in the Old Testament*

The central purpose of the Bible is the unfolding of God's plan of salvation, but it also contains some delightful incidental truths. The Bible is a treasure trove of Jewish religious and educational history. Here we find examples of methods used for religious nurture. One can hardly read Exodus or Leviticus without sensing the careful attention given to each detail of procedure. It is a reservoir of case studies in interpersonal communications. The beautiful examples of educational methodology still attract serious educators today. The classic use of available audiovisual media by Old Testament patriarchs and prophets has been both pattern and challenge to those who wish to learn how to be effective in the teaching-learning encounter.

Bible teachers used descriptive language, models and objects, demonstrations, questions and answers, vivid and well-organized lectures, group dynamics, problem-solving, inquiry-discovery, individualized instruction, projects, assignments, storytelling, and discussion.

2. *Jesus' Methods*

We would do well to emulate Jesus' teaching practices. Let's look at one example of the many where He chose the best method for His specific purpose. Note the following hypothetical lesson plan from John 13:1-17.

The learners: 12 mature men of varying interests and backgrounds

The place: an upper room before the Passover meal

The objective: to enable the disciples to feel that importance lies in serving rather than in being served, and to act upon that insight

Lesson title: "Concern for Others"

Primary method: demonstration by footwashing

Our means of evaluation: immediate response of the learners, and the recorded memory of the writer of the book

In the setting of the Last Supper, stresses were great and emotions were at keen edge. Jesus had little time and only one opportunity to make an indelible impression. He could have chosen other methods to help change the disciples' attitudes regarding "place" and "rank." How about a convincing lecture? This would not necessarily have been a wrong procedure. Would a good discussion have worked as well? How about a moving story comparable in pertinence and poignancy to "The Good Samaritan"? What about role playing? Any one of the suggested alternatives may have worked well. Why, then, did Jesus choose to demonstrate and explain His demonstration? What clinching power did this method have that all the others would have lacked?

The clue seems to have been the moral dullness of the disciples. They needed to become aware that their attitude regarding position was so wrong that Jesus would take time from the important Passover preparations to deal with it. They needed to be stabbed wide awake. He embarrassed them by His selfless ministry in a lowly task that none of them had been willing to do.

B. Philosophical

Marcus Priester succinctly states the importance of an appropriate philosophical basis for the choice of methods in Christian education:

> The educator faces the ever-persisting problem of selectivity of ideas and descriptions that are deemed by him to be true and worthy of his commitment. Therefore, any valid theory and practice of Christian education must take into account philosophy as well as other disciplines that deal significantly with the human scene.[2]

One example of how much we are influenced by our philosophy and cultural heritage is our concept of education itself. What picture comes to mind when you hear the word *education?* Now, define *education* in your own words. Note the difference between the picture and the stated definition. Was not the picture related to a classroom or to a book? If so, this image connotes content more than activity. However, one meaning from the Latin origin of the word relates more to activity—*educare*, to lead out.

Historically, a central concern of education has been the transmission of information. Consequently, the organized lecture, recognized as an effective method affected little by place or facilities, was widely used. No other method was as highly recognized. Teachers seemed to feel that little education took place without lecturing. It became a part of their philosophy of education. But will critical examination support this position?

---

2. Marcus J. Priester, "Philosophical Foundations for Christian Education," in *An Introduction to Christian Education,* Marvin J. Taylor, ed. (Nashville: Abingdon Press, 1966), pp. 61-62.

On the other hand, a true philosophical spirit will push us to investigate Marshall McLuhan's thesis that "the medium is the message." There is an important connection between the method we use and the message we proclaim. But to equate the one with the other is fuzzy thinking. Critical consideration must be given to the philosophical base and to the practical and theological implications of this thesis. A wise evaluation of methods depends on clear thinking—and clear thinking is the business of a philosophy of Christian education.

C. Theological

The theological understandings and commitments of the Christian teacher affect his choice and use of methods. Because Christian education is biblical and theological in content, both teacher and pupil take it seriously. James Smart spoke to this issue when he wrote of theologically liberal Christian educators:

> What they do not realize is that their failure to hold young people and adults in their educational program is a direct consequence of their unwillingness to take the subject matter of Christian education with sufficient seriousness.[3]

We recognize that the attitudes and emotions of the teacher influence his ability to persuade. Also the attitudes of learners affect their openness to change. The supreme importance of our subject gives the Christian learning encounter this special dimension. As James Smart puts it: "Wherever education is taken seriously, the educator finds himself inevitably asking ultimate questions about the nature and destiny of man and about the meaning of the world in which he lives."[4]

Our understanding of the doctrine of God, of man, of sin, of inspiration, of revelation have a direct bearing upon the way we teach. Grimes points out that the genuinely Christian teacher "can both talk about God and witness to his own relation to God."[5]

D. Historical

The serious educator will be amply repaid for his diligent examination of the methods used by earlier educators, and the results that

---

3. James D. Smart, *The Teaching Ministry of the Church* (Philadelphia: The Westminster Press, 1954), p. 115.
4. *Ibid.,* p. 203.
5. Howard Grimes, "Theological Foundations for Christian Education" in Taylor, *Introduction to Christian Education,* p. 33.

attended their efforts. In order to be fair in this kind of exploration, we must always judge a method in the context which prompted its use. The situation itself has a bearing upon the choice of method. By the same token, the situation must be used to evaluate the effectiveness of that choice.

Today we are inclined to emphasize the acquisition of knowledge as a major, if not the prime goal of education. This approach is a part of our Greek and Latin heritage. For both the Greeks and the Romans, knowledge had its primary orientation in the scientific and intellectual realm. However, for the Hebrew of Bible times, knowledge took on much more of a moral, relational, and ethical coloration. In Christian education we must ask ourselves seriously, What is the right emphasis and the right balance between these two?

Perhaps it is too simplistic, yet the hypothesis is given for consideration: Is one of the major reasons for the ineffectiveness of Christian education today our adoption of the wrong branch of tradition to espouse as our model? Has this adoption resulted in the wrong methods? Is it any wonder that we are called one of the best informed but least Christian generations since the time of Christ?

E. Psychological

There is much closer relationship between educational methods and psychology than between methods and the other foundation areas. Psychological bases include considerations of human growth and development, how we learn, how persons are motivated, human defense and coping mechanisms, and personality theory.

1. *Human Development*

Young children enjoy repetition, activity, play, stories, and individual attention. Because of their limitations of experience and ability, they are not ready for such methods as discussion, complex projects, if-then reasoning, lecture, or assignment.

Older children and early adolescents are beginning to develop their rational and social skills. This means that they are attracted to methods that exercise these skills. Discussion, inquiry-discovery, projects, and role-playing provide the needed mental stimulation and social interaction appropriate to their developmental stage—a stage of exploration and testing.

Older adolescents and young adults are even more interested in varied types of discussion, projects, research, lecture, and symposia. They are beginning to establish their life patterns and need to make their own decisions. They have attained physical maturity but are still struggling with the demands of psychological, social, and spiritual maturation. Maturing young persons must compare alternatives, prove hypotheses, and make conclusions in order to establish personal autonomy and identity.

Middle and older adults tend to enjoy lectures, panels, symposia, and varied forms of discussion. They do not respond as quickly as they formerly did to methods involving physical activity, manual dexterity, or role experimentation. At this period, routine has tended to become a way of life.

Generally speaking, different age levels require different methods of teaching. We must be careful, however, not to assume that this is always true. There are some common laws of learning that apply at all age levels. People generally respond well to methods that involve and reward their participation. They also pay attention to visual presentations, and to exploration of Christian concepts related to their current interests. Wise teachers always try to choose methods that bring eternal truth to bear directly on some deep human need of their pupils.

2. How Persons Learn

Understanding how people learn different types of material helps the teacher to choose methods appropriate to the learning task. If one learns concepts best through testing, relating, and realigning, then we should use methods that not only present concepts clearly but which also allow for testing, relating, and realigning. If attitude formation is our goal, then role playing, discussion, and other methods involving emotional response become important. Understanding how persons are motivated and how motivation improves the educative process will also enhance the appropriate selection of methods.

How do motivation and learning theory relate to our theological tenets? Supposing one learns some things best by response-reward. Does that give the teacher the authority to use rewards to bring about behavior change whether the learner wants to have his behavior modified in that direction or not? How does the free moral agency of man accord with the stimulus-response learning theory? Are we justified in using methods just because "they work"?

These questions trouble many of today's humanistic theorists for whom life's highest value is the freedom to direct one's own life and make one's own choices. There is danger that persons may be psychologically manipulated to their hurt. But this danger is all but eliminated when a teacher acts in Christian love to guide a pupil into paths of righteousness. Furthermore, a Christian philosophy of life does not recognize our right to absolute sovereignty over our decisions as life's highest value. Rather in the Christian view of the world we find life's supreme good and our own greatest self-fulfillment as we surrender our supremacy claims to the will of God. The teacher who guides us to make this surrender of self is not cramping our style—he is setting us free.

How do the defense mechanisms of the teacher and the pupil affect the use of methods? Can we choose methods that will increase psychological safety within the group and reduce individual reliance upon defense mechanisms? Can we recognize the way the defense mechanisms of our pupils operate, and respond with methods that will not unmask the learner but will allow him to lower his barriers to change?

As we study the interrelationships of maturation intellectually, emotionally, physically, and socially, can we bring about corresponding spiritual maturity by the use of appropriate methods of teaching? It is only as we mature in these areas in mutually complementary ways that the personality will develop appropriately. Paul's vision is that the work of Christian education goes on until "we all at last attain . . . to mature manhood, measured by nothing less than the full stature of Christ" (Eph. 4:13, NEB). Some study of personality theory and a genuine love for persons will enable the teacher to avoid dangers of using methods that tend to destroy or nullify wholesome personality development.

F. Sociological

Education is primarily involved with changing the relationships of persons. For our choice of methods to be appropriate, we must be familiar with the individual as a member of a group—what he is, what he knows, how he learns, how he feels, how he responds, how he interacts, and what are his ties outside of the church. Because most people learn in relationships, the choice of method must consider these social relationships and interactions. Boelke says, "Learning is not 'something done to persons.' It is the action of a responsible self experiencing his relationships."[6] Sherrill reminds us that

> the self is formed in its relationships with others. If it becomes de-formed, it becomes so in its relationships. If it is re-formed or

---

6. Robert R. Boehlke, *Theories of Learning in Christian Education* (Philadelphia: The Westminster Press, 1962), p. 26.

trans-formed, that too will be in its relationships. . . . A community is a body of relationships which affect the becoming of its individual members.[7]

Methods can be chosen that pit persons against each other, that deprive persons of their freedom of choice, and that manipulate them toward a preconceived end. But there are other methods that lead participants to build each other to their highest potential as individuals and as a group.

A thorough awareness of the dynamics of group processes, of influence shifts, of group maintenance and support, of how to build a psychologically safe learning environment enables the teacher to choose those methods that enhance the probability of learning.

III. METHODS IN CLASSROOM EXPERIENCES

The first part of this chapter would be of little value without its application to the teaching-learning situation. We turn now to apply the principles already considered to classroom procedures.

A. Lesson Plans

Spontaneous experiences in life are often enjoyable. However, some of the richest experiences are those that have been planned—carefully budgeted for in terms of time, attention, and cost.

A lesson plan is usually prepared by the teacher or leader. It may, however, be prepared by a teaching team, by the class, or by the leader and group together. It is less important who does the planning than *how well* the methods fit the needs and interests of the learning group.

The lesson plan must fit the content to be learned, and it must allow for real change in the lives of the learners. It must also provide for evaluation and for linking with previous learning as well as preparation for future learning. Some of the essential elements of a lesson plan are included in Figure 1 (opposite page).

Often we think of a lesson plan as only an outline of content to be presented. A good plan includes such an outline but there is much more. The lesson plan is concerned with methods—how we expect to get the job done.

Note under III (Objectives or goals) that we must be clear in our

---

7. Lewis Joseph Sherrill, *The Gift of Power* (New York: The Macmillan Co., 1955), pp. 45-46.

LESSON PLAN SHEET[8]

I. *Subject* _____ Date _____

II. *Unit topic* _____
   A. Emphasis of last lesson _____
   B. Emphasis of present lesson _____
   C. Emphasis of next lesson _____

III. *Objectives or goals* (Be clear and specific.) _____
   A. Concepts or facts to be learned _____
   B. Attitudes to be changed _____
   C. Behavioral skills to be gained _____

IV. *Resources available* _____
   A. Assignments due _____
   B. Equipment and facilities to be used _____
   C. Materials prepared (films, records, pictures, charts, models, graphs, exams, etc.) _____
   D. Personnel involved (guest speaker, students, instructor, etc.)
   _____

V. *Lesson procedure* (Note outline in detail and exact time duration anticipated.)

Emphasis	*Methods/Materials*	*Time (minutes)*
Bridging from previous lesson		
_____	_____	___
Introduction _____	_____	___
Emphases _____	_____	___
Conclusion _____	_____	___
Responses anticipated		
_____	_____	___
Application and follow-through		
_____	_____	___
Next assignment		
_____	_____	___

VI. Evaluation _____ _____ ___

FIGURE 1

8. Chester O. Galloway, *Team Teaching with Adults* (Kansas City: Beacon Hill Press of Kansas City, 1972), p. 76.

aims; we must know what we expect to happen. In IV we list all of the materials and other resources that we plan to use. In the middle column of V we indicate the methods that we intend to use during the session. We plan exactly what method we will use to build a bridge from the previous lesson. We plan how we will introduce the new materials, and how we will make the main emphasis of the session. We then indicate what methods will be used in the conclusion, how we expect to elicit desired responses, stimulate follow-through, make the next assignment, and evaluate the results of the session.

In printed lesson materials all of these elements are usually included, but the teacher must make them his own before he can effectively guide the learning of his class. He must know his methods well enough to understand how to use the procedures recommended, or to substitute methods that he believes will work better for his group.

Unit or session planning by teachers in group meetings will often stimulate better teaching methods than will occur to the teacher working alone.

IV. METHODS OF TEACHING

The teacher has options in his choice of methods because there are so many ways that persons can learn. A recent Christian education text is titled *40 Ways to Teach in Groups*.[9] Just as a musician is neither satisfied nor effective with one song or one composer's style, so a Christian teacher cannot afford to be content with one style of teaching. Effective teaching at every age level demands that the teacher use a variety of methods.

Because there is such a variety of educational procedures, some system of arranging them is needed to help the teacher understand them and know when to use one instead of another. Several ways of classifying methods have been used; perhaps the best arrangement is to group them by their dominant form and by the dominant learning principles involved.

A. Telling

The oldest and still most widely used form of teaching is for the

9. Martha M. Leypoldt, *40 Ways to Teach in Groups* (Valley Forge, Pa.: Judson Press, 1967).

teacher who knows something useful to tell it to pupils who need to know it. Several methods involve these elements of human knowledge and human language.

1. *Lecture*

The time-honored lecture method originated in the early history of education before writing had been invented, and before printing made books available to students. When only the teacher's mind had a record of the truth to be taught, the only method of instruction available was to tell the pupil what he needed to know.

Today we have other ways of storing data and other methods of communicating it to students, but this ancient method still has merit. The lecture can compress maximum content into a minimum time. When we must say a lot in a hurry, we use the lecture. The lecture also has the motivating power of the teacher's personality. All of the elements of personal persuasion are open to the lecturer—if he knows them and uses them. Also the lecturer today has many ways to supplement and strengthen his presentation.

Among the alternatives to the straightforward lecture are visual aids such as (1) supporting the points of the presentation with slides or flat pictures; (2) using a flip chart, chalkboard, or overhead transparency to list the outline progression; (3) preparing tape-recorded supportive and illustrative comments to give audio reinforcement.

Added interest can be created by using more than one person to present spoken data. A dialogue lecture by two people, or a panel, or a forum adds attention value. Sometimes an interview is appropriate to become better acquainted with persons, ideas, or issues. It is easy for the visiting expert to be interviewed by the leader. However, more interest may be stimulated by a group interview, in a kind of "Meet the Press" format.

2. *Storytelling*

The lecture, with its variations, is used in Christian education today most often with adults and young people. Teachers of children seldom attempt to give large blocks of information by lecturing young learners. In Western culture children are simply too active and too stimulated to pay attention to ideas given in this form.

The story is the telling alternative for the teacher of children. She has a truth to be presented by being told, but her form of telling is unique. In the lecture, truth is presented in logical order, step by step. In the story, the idea is seen in its impact on the lives of persons. Because stories relate directly to human activities, they are inherently more interesting than lectures. The teacher of children seldom leads a session in which she does not tell one or more stories to communicate the truth and to help her reach the session goal.

Because the story is so effective and so widely used, the teacher of children strives to become a master storyteller. But the method is also a worthy tool for the teacher of teens and adults. A well-told story is often a superb launching pad for a discussion of Christian truth. An appropriate illustration is sometimes the best way to relate Bible teaching to human living. Therefore, every Christian teacher should seek to become a skilled teller of stories.

B. Involving the Learner

Because pupils learn best when they are involved, there are no better methods of teaching than those that give the learner an active role in his own education.

1. *Question and Answer*

Questions in teaching were probably used first to determine whether the pupil remembered and understood what the teacher had said. Today this testing device also lets the teacher know if a student understands what he has read in a textbook, or viewed on a screen, or observed on a field trip.

But the best use of questions goes beyond testing. A teacher's query can open the pupil's mind to explore the nature of God. A student's question can reveal to the teacher the pupil's point of interest and concern—therefore the point of his greatest readiness to learn. These questions bring the learner into the act—whether he is asking or answering. Such active involvement is almost always better learning procedure than is passive listening.

Good questioning is an effective method for Christian teaching with elementary children, teens, and adults.

2. *Discussion*

A question often triggers class discussion. This is frequently the teacher's purpose in asking it. Trigger questions usually take the form of "What do you think about ———?" or "How do you react to ———?" Such questions normally elicit discussion because they tap students' minds at points where they have opinions and personal preferences.

A discussion usually begins with interaction between the teacher and a pupil, but it should quickly spread to interaction between pupils themselves. In Leypoldt's diagram of the discussion procedure

(Figure 2)[10] count the number of pupil-to-pupil (P-P) interactions in contrast to only two teacher-to-pupil (T-P) interchanges.

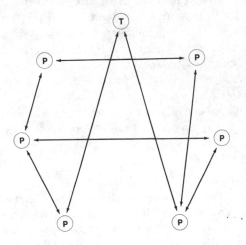

FIGURE 2

The educational strengths of the discussion are learner involvement and group interaction; its weakness is the danger of gaining no new information or insights. To avoid this breakdown the teacher usually:

> Introduces the topic
> Reminds the group of the purpose for the discussion
> Keeps the discussion on track
> Asks, What does the Bible say?
> Gives a summary of progress
> Suggests further study or courses of action.

For children, discussion techniques are less formal but the method is just as important as for teens and adults. In teachers' manuals the procedure is likely to be indicated by such phrases as "Discuss with the children . . ." or "Let the children talk about . . ." In treatments of techniques for preschool and elementary children the method may be listed simply as "conversation." The goal is to encourage children to express themselves so that the teacher can know what they are thinking and how they feel about the Christian issues being explored.

---

10. Modified from Leypoldt, *40 Ways to Teach*, p. 68.

3. Brainstorming

This is a special method of group interaction. It is designed to uncover every facet of information in the group that is relevant to the topic under discussion. The subject to be explored is presented by the leader, then every member is encouraged to express his thoughts. All ideas are recorded in full view of the group on a chalkboard or flip chart. Criticism and evaluation of suggestions are not permitted because negative evaluation tends to discourage free expression of ideas.

In a Sunday school class or youth group, brainstorming is useful to open up a new topic or a new unit of study. The list of ideas generated then becomes the basis for exploring how well the views presented reflect Bible teachings.

4. Buzz Groups

This is another special form of group interaction currently popular with teens and young adults. Small-group structure is the unique feature of this method of discussion. A class is divided into groups of no more than three or four students each. All groups may discuss the same question, or each group may be assigned a different question related to a common issue. After a few minutes of discussion each group reports its findings to the whole class.

The small-group structure allows time for every member to make his contribution. It also encourages participation from persons too timid to speak up in a discussion involving the larger group.

In *couple buzzing* the small group includes only two persons who explore together the question under consideration, and then report.

5. Inductive Bible Study

Here is a group method especially significant for evangelical Christian education. It is important to keep the group small (under 15) so that every member has opportunity to become involved and contribute. Instead of a discussion topic, the group explores a designated passage of scripture. Instead of the teacher telling what he *knows*, each member is encouraged to tell what he *finds* in it. The chosen paragraph or short chapter may be read aloud, then each one reads it silently and attentively several times. After 5 or 10 minutes of exploration, each member is encouraged to share with the group one or more insights that have especially impressed him.

6. In-depth Bible Study

Another special form of small-group interaction is that of in-depth study of the Bible. Each pupil paraphrases the verse or paragraph chosen for study. He expresses the thought in his own words, and as far as possible avoids using any of the key terms in the Bible text. The paraphrases are shared with the group, and each writer is questioned about his reasons for the interpretations he has chosen. At the close of the sharing period, each member of the group thinks about the personal relevance of the passage by considering the question, *If I took this passage seriously, what would I have to do?*

Inductive study and in-depth Bible studies are methods used especially with teens and adults.

7. *Presentations with Group Response*

Several other methods often used with teens and adults combine a group response with a presentation by a lecturer or by a small team of leaders. The values of these methods lie in the added interest created by a team presentation, and in the participation of class members.

a. The *symposium* is simply a formal group presentation method. Instead of one speaker presenting all phases of a topic, several speakers present the various aspects. The symposium *dialog* adds a resource person who responds to the presentations. In a *symposium forum* the entire group enters into a discussion of the topics presented by the symposium team.

b. The *panel* resembles the symposium in so far as it is a group presentation. However, instead of the set speeches of the symposium, a panel informally discusses the assigned topic. In a *panel forum,* the presentation by the panel is followed immediately by an open forum discussion of the issues. All class members are encouraged to ask questions or to offer responses. A *reaction panel* responds to a lecture, film, or other form of presentation. The panel is simply a small group designated to react rather than to initiate a topic of Christian concern. A *group response team* resembles a reaction panel except that team members interrupt a speaker at appropriate times during the lecture in order to clear up issues immediately.

c. A *forum* is a discussion by the entire group—but it is a discussion in response to a specific presentation. In a *lecture forum* the class responds to the ideas discussed by the speaker. A *debate forum* is group response to a discussion in which opposite views are presented by two or more speakers. The *interview forum* lets the class members ask their own questions after a designated leader has interviewed a class visitor. An increasing number of pastors are using the *sermon forum* (usually at a coffee session after the service) in order to secure sermon feedback from church members.

C. Visual Learning

Educational research shows that learning is improved when two or more senses are involved in exposure to the material to be learned. Thus far we have discussed methods that rely largely on hearing. But hearing seems to be less valuable in acquiring information than is seeing. Hearing with seeing is superior to hearing alone. Hearing, seeing, then repeating in your own words the essence of what has been learned seems to be still more effective.

1. Flat Pictures

Pictures are widely used in the Christian education of children from the nursery age up through the sixth grade and on into junior high school. Bible pictures help the child visualize stories and settings for events in Christian history. Pictures of modern settings help pupils apply Bible teachings to their own life situations.

For class use, pictures need to be large enough for all pupils to see details clearly. A widely used size for these teaching pictures is about 12" x 17". Pictures are often used in connection with stories, either to visualize an episode in the narrative, or to review the events after the story has been heard.

Picture study of a life situation scene can be used to introduce a discussion of Christlike attitudes in interpersonal relations between children.

Nu-Vu[11] and flannelgraph enlarge the teaching values of flat pictures. Pupil interest is heightened when separate figures in the total picture are added one by one as the story progresses.

Flat pictures have long been standard educational equipment for the Christian education of children. But in recent years they have been used increasingly in classes for teens and adults. Sometimes a picture such as the Crucifixion scene is displayed to help set the mood for a class session. Other pictures are examined and analyzed as a method to involve the group in Christian perception and reaction.

Leypoldt describes a teaching method for adults called *gallery conversations.*

> An art gallery atmosphere is created by displaying one or more paintings, or sculptures about a particular theme, to which a group responds by discussing the meaning which various members find in these.

---

11. *Nu-Vu* is a trade name for build-up pictures in the Aldersgate curriculum widely used in churches affiliated with the Christian Holiness Association.

The goal [is] to understand what the artists or sculptors are trying to say through the medium of art.[12]

2. *Teaching Packets*

Within the past decade publishers of Christian education curriculum materials have provided packets of visual resources for nearly every age level served by their courses. These resources include a variety of film slips, cassettes, booklets, and learning games. The strength of the packets lies in the visual teaching tools that they provide. Planners study methods of public education and printed advertising that can be adapted to visualizing Christian education concepts. For young children, teaching pictures are included for most sessions. Bible maps and charts support studies for adults. Mod posters of Bible verses and cartoons depicting Christian responses are designed to capture the interest of teens and motivate them to Christlike conduct.

3. *Projected Visuals*

As projected media have flooded the entertainment world and have been developed for public education, they are being used increasingly in Christian education. Films, filmstrips, slide sets, and videotapes are available to aid in many areas of the church's teaching ministry.

A major assignment for pastors, Christian education directors, and supervisors is to acquaint lay teachers with the values and techniques of these modern teaching tools. Leypoldt, for example, lists the method of a *film talk back*. This includes the showing of a film, filmstrip, or slide set followed by a time of free, open discussion by the group.[13]

Technology has revolutionized both the possibility and much of the nature of communication for the church. With the advent of transistors and solid-state equipment, the price on much of the electronic hardware is now well within the reach of budgets of most congregations. Projectors for filmstrips, film slips, slides, motion pictures, opaque and overhead images are found frequently in churches of modest size. Hardly a church is without some means of projecting images for educational purposes. The church that feels it cannot afford to purchase one or more of these machines can often borrow or rent such equipment from a nearby business, public school, or private family.

---

12. Leypoldt, *40 Ways to Teach*, p. 66.
13. *Ibid.*, p. 64.

In addition, the development of sound reproduction and amplification has tremendously enriched the possible educational resources during the past decade. Disc records for Christian education have multiplied; and the relative costs of manufacture and distribution have diminished greatly. The cassette age is upon us. A cassette recorder-player is within the price range of every church. The cassette allows for prerecording of locally prepared presentations. Also a vast array of Christian teaching cassette tapes can be purchased inexpensively.

The cassette recorder adds a further educational dimension; the student is enabled to record lectures, discussions, and other audio presentations. He can then rerun these recordings in privacy when he has more time to reflect on them and is able to pay closer attention to the content.

D. Music as a Method

Whenever Christian education seeks to change the learner's feelings and attitudes, music is an effective method. In preschool Christian education our objectives are usually more emotional than cognitive. The teacher knows that she can help a small child feel good about God's love even when she cannot expect him to understand it. Simple songs of gladness, accompanied by rhythmic movements, is standard nursery and kindergarten procedure.

For elementary children, songs with a chosen teaching theme are vehicles for communicating Christian concepts. When we explore the doctrine of creation, our children sing:

> *This is my Father's world.*
> *The birds their carols raise;*
> *The morning light, the lily white*
> *Declare their Maker's praise.*[14]

In experiences of worship we sing:

> *Praise Him, praise Him,*
> *All ye little children;*
> *God is love, God is love.*[15]

---

14. "This Is My Father's World," by Maltbie D. Babcock.
15. "Praise Him, All Ye Little Children," Anonymous.

When we would teach God's care, we sing together:

> *Jesus loves me! this I know,*
> *For the Bible tells me so;*
> *Little ones to Him belong;*
> *They are weak but He is strong.*[16]

Making these affirmations together in God's house with adults whom children love becomes profound Christian persuasion. The words themselves communicate the concepts of our faith. The tunes help to imbed the beliefs so deeply in our consciousness that they remain with us as long as memory lasts.

In evangelical youth services, with uplifted hand and index finger extended, young people joyfully affirm:

> *He is Lord; He is Lord;*
> *He is risen from the dead, and He is Lord.*
> *Every knee shall bow, every tongue confess,*
> *That Jesus Christ is Lord.*[17]

This is method—a procedure that Christian youth leaders use to help teens affirm their belief and declare their commitment.

And what of the use of music in the education of adults? Christian concepts are declared, Christian loyalties strengthened, and steadfast Christian behavior is reinforced when mature saints sing:

> *Fear not; I am with thee. Oh, be not dismayed,*
> *For I am thy God, I will still give thee aid.*
> *I'll strengthen thee, help thee, and cause thee to stand,*
> *Upheld by My gracious, omnipotent hand.*[18]

In a *music forum* teens or adults listen "to instrumental music and then respond to it by discussing the meanings of the moods and atmospheres that it creates. Or a group listens to choral music and follows this experience by discussing the meanings of the words and their significance to each individual."[19]

Similar learning occurs when children and teachers discuss the meaning of the words of a new song—or reflect on the Christian concepts when they sing a well-known hymn.

---

16. "Jesus Loves Me," by Anna B. Warner.
17. "He Is Lord" (Source unknown).
18. "How Firm a Foundation."
19. Leypoldt, *40 Ways to Teach,* p. 83.

E. Methods That Produce Change

Music perhaps more than many methods is effective in changing the learner's feeling tone. All of the methods that involve pupils most directly seem highly conducive to changes of attitudes and feelings. These include buzz groups, discussion, debate, listening groups, group writing, drama, role playing, sociodrama, simulation games, case studies, and response teams. The law of learning seems to be that when we get involved, we like it.

In Figure 3 (opposite page), Leypoldt outlines steps that we must help learners to take if our teaching is to bring about significant changes in them. These steps involve principles of learning that we must look for and seek to apply in any of the methods that we choose.

F. Individualized Learning

No discussion of methods is complete without exploring individualized learning. Ultimately all learning is individual; only individuals learn. But often persons learn together in parallel or in interacting experiences. We are here concerned with the possibilities for Christian learning outside of group interaction. Often individual learning is faster than learning in group experiences, but of course, one loses the values of class interaction and encouragement.

The development of individualized learning possibilities has increased greatly during the past generation. Prior to that time, reading of books, tutoring, and personal experience were the major avenues open to us. Current possibilities include:

Programmed-learning sequences developed by machine or print
Directed research
Workbooks
Instructional films
Filmstrips with audio or printed guides
Slides or flat pictures with audio or printed guides
Map study
Personal interview with consultants
Listening responses to music
Lecture
Sound film or filmstrip

STEPS THAT WILL PRODUCE CHANGE[20]

When there is a feeling of inadequacy:

Of Factual Information	Of Understanding	Of Feelings	Of Ways of Behaving
1. Become aware of need for new information	1. Become aware of need for new information	1. Become anxious	1. Become aware of need for new way of behaving
2. Seek adequate resources	2. Seek adequate resources	2. Reduce or remove barriers to change	2. Become aware of new ways of behaving
3. Perceive new ideas	3. Perceive new ideas	3. Seek new ways of feeling	3. Select a new way of behaving
4. Imitate the idea of another	4. Comprehend the meaning of the new idea	4. Select appropriate new feelings	4. Test the new behavior
5. Repeat the idea until it is memorized	5. Apply the new knowledge	5. Incorporate the new feeling	5. Get evidence of effectiveness of the new behavior
6. Practice what has been learned	6. Analyze situations involving the idea	6. Test it out	6. Use evidences to change self-perception
7. Incorporate the new idea	7. Synthesize into new patterns		7. Incorporate new behavior into lifestyle
8. Test it out	8. Evaluate the new idea in relation to purposes		8. See other uses for the new behavior

FIGURE 3

---

20. Martha M. Leypoldt, *Learning Is Change* (Valley Forge, Pa.: Judson Press, 1971), pp. 61-62.

Workshop
Book report
Case study
Inquiry-discovery

A much neglected method for individual Christian learning is providing research assignments for personal Bible study at home. The more we can stimulate pupils to do personal Bible reading and Bible study, the more likely they are to grow and develop as Christians. To be effective these assignments need to be specific; they should be related to the theme of the class studies; and there should be opportunity for the student to report his research discoveries to the group.

Church schools can foster individualized learning by providing in the classroom interest centers, bulletin boards, displays, and dioramas. A current trend is to develop in the church's educational area an instructional media center or learning resource center that includes a library of books, cassettes, films, slides, pictures, and maps, as well as equipment to use them.

G. Learning by Observation and Practice

We learn most effectively when we can observe directly what needs to be done and then practice doing it. Therefore, as often as possible, teachers choose methods that permit pupils to have direct experiences of Christian learning.

1. *Demonstrations in the Classroom*

When juniors need to learn to locate passages in the Bible, teachers show them how the Bible is arranged in books, chapters, and verses. The juniors then practice locating verse references and finding familiar stories. When junior highs need to understand the use of a Bible concordance, they observe how the teacher finds a passage; the students then practice finding assigned passages by using the concordance.

2. *Field Trips*

Effective Christian learning occurs when we can take our pupils where the action is. When nursery children need to see and feel the wonder of God's creation, we take them for a walk in the church yard or in a nearby park.

To help kindergarten and primary children understand elements of adult worship services, we visit the sanctuary to see, touch, and talk about the pulpit, the choir loft, the organ, the altar, and the Communion table.

3. *Work Groups*

When suburban senior high young people need to understand human squalor and Christian service ministry, we try to expose them to both. It was effective Christian education when a work team spent several Saturdays cleaning accumulated debris from ghetto streets and alleys of their city. They saw at first hand the power of good example when ghetto residents began cleaning debris from their adjacent yards.

It was effective Christian education when a teen team crossed the border to a nearby mission field to conduct vacation Bible schools; and when a young adult team from Idaho spent a week in Arizona helping build a home mission chapel.

H. Encouraging Creativity

God is the Creator, but the Bible teaches us that man has been made in His image. One of the goals of Christian education should be to stimulate this God-given capacity in the pupils we serve. But there is a further sound reason for using creative methods whenever they can serve our purposes. Creative expression is one of the most effective ways to open the human mind to new truth and to impress concepts deeply in the memory.

1. *Role playing*

Leypoldt describes role playing as follows:

> A problem situation is briefly acted out, with emphasis placed on individuals identifying with the characters. This is followed by a discussion of the problem presented. The following steps are necessary: Determine the exact circumstances of the problem situation; cast the players who in turn plan the method of presentation; act out the situation; stop the action at a climactic moment; analyze and discuss the role-play; and evaluate the results.
>
> The goal [is] to solve a problem and to have opportunity to enter into the feelings of others.[21]

Role playing by children often takes the form of dramatizing the Bible stories being studied. As children act out the parts in the story,

---

21. Leypoldt, *40 Ways to Teach*, p. 97.

they enter into the feelings of these Bible characters and express those feelings in ways that are natural to the child.

2. Drawing

Group drawing is a method used with pupils from primary through adult years. The teacher presents an idea related to the topic under discussion. Pupils individually, or in groups of two or three, express their concepts or reactions through drawings. Later the drawings are shared with the group and their meanings are interpreted.

A related method used with teens and adults is to create a sculptural reaction by forming figures from pieces of chenille wire. Sometimes other materials are used for sculpting.

3. Creative Writing

Creative writing, like creative art, can be used with pupils from third grade through adulthood.

The teacher and group decide on some common ideas related to a theme under discussion. These ideas are then expressed through a responsive reading, a poem, or prose. The leader prepares the group by suggesting ideas, reading some poems, and showing examples of what might be written. The compositions may be prepared by individuals or by small groups. Each person or small group is encouraged to share his contribution with the class.

V. The Holy Spirit in Human Methods

Methods are perhaps our most important human contribution to Christian education. The content comes from God, revealed to us in the Scriptures. The objective is a human life completely in tune with God, as modeled for us in Jesus of Nazareth. But methods are based squarely on the natural laws of learning. Our assignment as Christian teachers is to learn what methods work best, and then to use them as effectively as possible.

A. God-given

While methods are firmly based in the laws of psychology, does that make them any less the laws of God? Not at all. The Bible tells us, "Whatever is good and perfect comes to us from God" (Jas. 1:17, TLB). The laws of learning are the laws that God has established for interaction between the human mind and its environment. Men have only gradually discovered these laws and given them the names *psychology, learning, change, education.*

The important difference between the spiritual truths of our content and the psychological laws that shape our methods is in the way we learn about them. The spiritual and moral laws are given in the Bible by direct revelation. We are told in clear language, "Thou shalt love the Lord thy God with all thy heart . . . Thou shalt love thy neighbor as thyself" (Matt. 22:37-38). But we must study God's natural laws of learning, just as we must study His laws of chemistry and biology, to discover what they are and how they work.

B. Morally Neutral

These laws, like the law of gravity are neither morally good nor bad. They have good or evil consequences depending on how well the teacher understands them and applies them. Someone has quipped, "The world might be a safer place if Ph.D.'s, like M.D.'s, could be sued for malpractice."

The results of our teaching, however, are also greatly influenced by the teacher's motivation. If we have a perfect love for God and a genuine Christian concern for the welfare of our students, the Holy Spirit helps to compensate for our limited knowledge. As Christian teachers we may without guilt miss the mark through unintended ignorance, but God does not permit us to be unconcerned or unloving. In the eyes of God, human failure at this point is sin. The Holy Spirit works through the teacher's purified intention to accomplish His ministry to the pupil. James reminds us, "We who teach shall be judged with greater strictness" (3:1, RSV).

C. Spirit-guided Teachers

We believe that God's Holy Spirit normally works through human channels, and further that He works best through lives that are cleansed from all evil intention—persons who are most like himself. But does the Holy Spirit use the natural talents of the dedicated Christian teacher to achieve results that are better than the teacher by himself could accomplish? We believe that He does.

We cannot say precisely how the Spirit of God works through persons who have yielded themselves wholly to Him; but men of God testify that they are often conscious that the Spirit is working in this way. Wiley, in his discussion of the inspiration of Scripture, identifies three elements of God's work: (1) superintendence of the whole plan; (2) elevation of the human mind beyond its normal capabilities; and

(3) direct suggestion of thoughts to the minds of the writers.[22] We believe that the basic content of divine revelation has already been given in the Scripture. We may not expect the Holy Spirit to reveal truth that contradicts or supercedes what is written in the Bible. But has the Holy Spirit ceased His function of inspiring and teaching those who receive Him and walk in full fellowship with Him?

Is it unreasonable to expect the Holy Spirit to continue to illuminate human spirits that are fully open to Him? No. Jesus promised that this kind of illumination would be one of the ministries of the coming Comforter. "When the Spirit of truth comes, he will guide you into all the truth; for he will not speak on his own authority, but whatever he hears he will speak, and he will declare to you the things that are to come. He will glorify me, for he will take what is mine and declare it to you. All that the Father has is mine; therefore I said that he will take what is mine and declare it to you" (John 16:13-15, RSV).

When we are engaged in God's work, it is our right in Christ to expect the Holy Spirit to elevate our minds above their natural limits. We believe in the leadership of the Holy Spirit. When we are seeking the best method to influence a pupil toward God, we can claim our Lord's promise that the Holy Spirit "will take what is mine and declare it to you." The Holy Spirit does at times lead us directly; He suggests very specific thoughts and approaches that result in changed lives for those whom we teach.

D. Divine-Human Cooperation

How do Christian teachers qualify for this partnership with the divine Supervisor? By accepting His partnership; by submitting all of our "faculties to Him as a living and holy sacrifice" (Rom. 12:1, Weymouth); by consciously asking for His help; by depending upon Him; by expecting Him to show us what to do; by doing our work every day in the consciousness of His divine partnership.

He is the Supervisor and we are the teachers. When He has taught us, He expects us to learn. He is pleased when, after learning how to influence pupils for Christ, we are wise enough to use that method again. When one procedure has become a part of us, He can guide us into another part of that vast field of "all truth" which is

---

22. H. Orton Wiley, *Christian Theology*, 3 vols. (Kansas City: Beacon Hill Press, 1940), 1:170.

His area of operation. This is our Lord's promise; and this is the special ministry of the Holy Spirit to all who teach the things of God.

E. God Is God

Christian teaching is a growing partnership with the Supervising Spirit. But even under His guidance, we do not do all that is done. God is not limited to accomplishing His will through us. Sometimes we are aware that He himself has taken over direction of the class for the moment—or for the day! We believe that the Bible teaches both God's ministry through men and God's sovereignty over them. The Old Testament teaches that the work of God is done "not by [human] might, nor by [your] power, but by my spirit, saith the Lord of hosts" (Zech. 4:6). Our Lord himself reminds us, "The wind blows wherever it pleases. You may hear its sound, but you cannot tell where it comes from or where it is going. So it is with everyone born of the Spirit" (John 3:8, NIV).

The Bible teaches that God does His work through human lives that are wholly consecrated to Him, and through human methods that are dedicated to accomplishing His goals. It is supremely important to God that we consecrate our lives to Him, and that we consciously dedicate our methods to achieving His purposes. This is the divine-human partnership of Christian teaching. But we are the junior partners; He is the majority stockholder in the enterprise. He often shows us how to perform our ministries better than we have done before; and He helps us in those ministries. But sometimes He takes over, and we can only exclaim, "This work was wrought of our God" (Neh. 6:16).

Such a partnership has been God's purpose since the dawn of human life when He said, "Let us make man in our image, after our likeness. . . . So God created man in his own image, in the image of God created he him" (Gen. 1:26-27). In this partnership we are so deeply involved that at times we seem almost to lose our self-identity. Paul writes, "In him we live, and move, and have our being" (Acts 17:28). But in this partnership we find also the most complete sense of self-fulfillment known to a human being.

BIBLIOGRAPHY

Beal, George M.; Bohlen, Foe M.; and Raudabaugh, J. Neil. *Leadership and Dynamic Group Action.* Ames, Ia.: Iowa State University Press, 1962.

Part I describes the principles of a democratic theory of group inter-action. Part II explores a wide range of groups used for teaching and learning. A short chapter is devoted to each of 17 techniques useful to Christian teachers.

Edge, Findley B. *Helping the Teacher.* Nashville: Broadman Press, 1959.
Introductory information concerning teacher training and preparing a lesson. Differentiates between responses sought and develops over-views of eight different teaching methods: question and answer, dis-cussion, lecture, story or illustration, role playing, project, nonprojected and projected visual aids.

Leypoldt, Martha M. *40 Ways to Teach in Groups.* Valley Forge: Judson Press, 1967.
The author has provided outline forms for the 40 methods selected (involving definition, diagrammed relationships, goals, leader and group member responsibilities). The first two chapters relate to the teaching-learning encounter and criteria by which to choose and evaluate appropriate methods.

Leypoldt, Martha M. *Learning Is Change: Adult Education in the Church.* Valley Forge: Judson Press, 1971.
Martha Leypoldt has broken the standard mold of books on methods. She involves the reader immediately with information, reflection, exercises, sharing, and evaluation. She attempts to answer the familiar questions of Who? What? Where? When? and How? as they relate to the teacher-learner interaction for change. Her last chapter, "Has Change Taken Place?" provides several suggestions of evaluation devices.

Richards, Lawrence O. *Creative Bible Teaching.* Chicago: Moody Press, 1970.
Richards deals specifically with Bible teaching. He combines a conserva-tive, evangelical view of the Scriptures with an informed understanding of teaching-learning principles. There are guidelines for relevant teach-ing procedures at different age-levels.

Rives, Elsie, and Sharp, Margaret. *Guiding Children.* Nashville: Conven-tion Press, 1969.
A book of methods currently recommended for the Christian education of children. The authors explore the meanings of teaching and learning. They then describe learning through art activities, drama, creative writing, discussion, games, music, and research.

Sanders, Norris M. *Classroom Questions: What Kinds.* New York: Harper and Row, 1966.
Sanders's book should enable the teacher to develop the art of an old, dependable practice. But his development of the use of questions takes far deeper perspectives than asking for recognition or recall. He shows how to use them for translation, interpretation, application, analysis, synthesis, evaluation, and learning.

CHAPTER 9

Christian Education
of Preschool Children

The concern of this chapter is children who have not begun their public school experience as first graders. This dividing line has been established because starting to school launches the child into many new and complex experiences.

> Here he steps beyond the family circle into the larger world
> of the school and community. . . . Whereas in the home the child
> is loved and accepted because he is a member of the family group,
> he now finds that he must win acceptance among others of his
> own age.[1]

The preschool period is important in a child's life because during these years he is expected to master some of the most basic developmental tasks. One of these is learning to walk. Not only does walking involve complex combinations of muscular control and coordination, but it also changes a child's world. Prior to walking, his world is limited to a crib, a rug, or a room. If he goes beyond this environment, he is accompanied by an older person who can assist and protect him. But walking gives the child more independence. He can now explore beyond what he sees from one spot. In walking, the child has taken a giant step toward becoming an individual in his own right.

---

1. G. G. Jenkins, H. Shacter, W. W. Bauer, *These Are Your Children* (New York: Scott, Foresman and Co., 1953), p. 109.

Inevitably, however, he is also subjected to greater pressure to conform to the wishes of other individuals in his environment. Until he becomes aware of the hazards which he encounters, he is a source of worry to his parents and teachers as he insists upon finding out what is around the corner or down the street. Parents constantly warn him to stay here, not to go there. He finds limits put upon his newfound freedom.

A second basic developmental task that the child must accomplish is acquiring language skills. This involves learning how to understand what is said to him and how to communicate with other human beings in words. The ability to understand language precedes the ability to speak it, therefore verbal control of children by adults is possible before dialogue occurs.

Language acquisition opens a whole new horizon of possibilities to the child. Now he can command others to obey him, express his own inner feelings, and eventually verbalize abstract concepts. His ability to learn reaches fantastic new proportions because he has opened the door of communication.

No development in later life will be as important as this one. Stone writes:

> While the child's new powers of bipedal locomotion may be the most striking manifestation of toddlerhood, probably more important psychologically is his beginning to speak in his mother tongue. . . . We might insist that it is only by . . . understanding speech and by speaking, that the child gains access to full status as a human being.[2]

Preschool years hold special challenges for Christian educators because they introduce the child to his first non-family contacts. When he is brought to the church nursery for the first time, he is confronted with strange faces, an unfamiliar environment, and other children.

The emotional quality of these early experiences leaves its imprint upon his attitudes. If these initial encounters generate fear and insecurity, he may generalize them in later life to include the whole constellation of church-related persons and experiences. As an adolescent and an adult, he may not fully understand his reluctance to participate in the life of the church. And others may never surmise the cause of this negative reaction. On the other hand, his

---

2. B. T. Gardner and R. A. Gardner, "Teaching Sign Language to a Chimpanzee," *Science*, 165, pp. 664-72, cited in H. F. Harlow, McGaugh, and R. F. Thompson, *Psychology* (San Francisco: Albion Publishing Co., 1971), pp. 390-93.

early experiences can be a solid emotional foundation that will in later years encourage the child to devote himself to Christ and His work.

Adults who work with preschool children need to be alert to the child's sensitivity. These early learners are especially attuned to the feelings expressed by adults. This sensitivity is rooted in the child's dependency and the adult's seeming omnipotence. Children intuitively know that they must respond to adults in order to have their needs met.

No other task that faces Christian educators in the preschool years is of greater significance than creating a pleasant, accepting environment in which the child can use his developing skills of loco-motion and communication.

I. Objectives

In chapter 7 we saw that objectives for Christian education may be general or specific. Preschool objectives should always be consistent with the general objectives of Christian education. But also, these age-level goals must become more specific than the general objectives in order to meet the immediate needs of the pupils. The closer we move to the real learning encounter, the more specific our goals become. A preschool objective is more specific than the general objective; a kindergarten goal is more specific than a preschool one; the objective for a given class session, or pupil, is most specific of all.

Preschool objectives are important because they determine the curriculum, the methods, and the experiences provided for these young learners. What does the church seek to do for children before they are ready to enter the first grade?

A. Teach Some Beginning Foundation Truths

Christian educators are concerned that pupils learn the truths revealed in the Scriptures. Preschoolers, however, are limited in the number and kinds of facts that can be learned. Simple statements about God, Jesus, the Bible, the church—and simple Bible verses that support these truths—are within the learning capacity of children three to five years of age. During kindergarten years children soak up such facts and parrot them back easily to their teachers.

1. *God*

Truths taught during these years need to be related to familiar things or persons in the child's experience. When God is called

Father, children understand this image in terms of their family situation. If the home is normal, they absorb the concept of God as a kind and loving person. However, if the child lacks a stable father figure in his home, he will find it difficult to identify with the symbol of "God, our Father."[3] For such children other associations will be needed to form the concept of God as one who loves and cares for us.

2. *Jesus*

Preschoolers easily identify with Jesus as their Friend. The writer was listening to his Jewish professor discuss the problem of teaching religion to children. He remarked that Christians have a much easier task than Jews. Christians can teach children about Jesus, and they can identify with Him; Jews must struggle with the abstract concept of God.

3. *The Bible*

The Bible can be presented to preschoolers by using the analogy of a letter from their father. Most children are acquainted with letters and they can grasp this figure quite easily. When teaching the Bible to young children, we must be aware that:

(a) They do not grasp abstract truths.

(b) They cannot remember many facts for very long.

(c) They are not able to memorize many verses of Scripture— and the verses they learn must be short.

Children can, however, develop an attitude of reverence and respect for the Bible. In brief worship experiences they discover that the teacher treats the Bible differently from other books. As children watch her hold the Bible, move it carefully, and tell stories from it, they begin to feel what adults feel when we call the Bible sacred. On this foundation they will build the devotion that we know when we call the Bible the Word of God.

4. *The Church*

What does the church mean to small children? For them, it is a building, a place to which they go one or more times each week. If they find a clean, warm room and a loving, understanding adult awaiting them, they will begin to feel an affection for the church. From this early response their understanding and appreciation can grow until they sing with us:

---

3. J. D. Butler, *Religious Education* (New York: Harper and Row, Publishers, 1962), pp. 146-47.

> *I love Thy Church, O God!*
> *Her walls before Thee stand,*
> *Dear as the apple of Thine eye,*
> *And graven on Thy hand.*[4]

B. Encourage a Spiritually Receptive Attitude

Preschool children have limited capacity to grasp abstract truths. We, therefore, always try to associate the truths we teach with the child's life experiences. And we always try to make the child's experiences in the church enjoyable.

Children of this age should be told the principal events of Jesus' life—His birth, boyhood, deeds of kindness, and His mission. These stories need to be told in ways that help the child respond with the feeling, "I love Jesus." Children should hear that God created the world; that He gives us good food, warm clothing, and cool water because He loves us. They need to hear these truths again and again in a variety of contexts. As they hear them often, and bow their heads to thank God for His love, preschoolers are building a broad, receptive attitude toward Christian truth.

C. Experience Worship at a Preschool Level

Worship is a vital part of Christian nurture at every developmental level. For preschoolers, response to God is most often spontaneous and unplanned. They do not react very well to planned group worship. The most beneficial experiences are those that grow out of the wonders of an encounter with nature, or from singing a song, or receiving love from another person.

Christian teachers seek to help the preschool child make these worshipful moments meaningful. Adults who work with children must be sensitive to the critical moment when a child's eyes light up with tender response. Teachers must seize the opportunity to guide the children in thanking God for what He has given them. From these moments of wonder children develop a deep sense of awe. From their expressions of thanks they will sense God near them.

While planned worship is not very meaningful to preschool children, they should begin to experience group devotional exercises, especially during the kindergarten years. The child may be invited to join the group at the worship center. In this situation, he will begin to develop the cooperation and self-discipline necessary for

---

4. Timothy Dwight, "I Love Thy Kingdom, Lord."

group experiences. Such worship times need to be brief, interesting, and related to activities in the child's experience.

Usually one corner of the room is set aside as the worship center. On a low table there will be a Bible and perhaps a vase of flowers or an appropriate picture. Around this center the teacher and kindergartners gather on a rug to sing, pray, and hear stories and verses from God's Word.

D. Expose the Child to Mature Christian Adults

Adults serve as models of behavior for all children, but the younger the child, the greater the impact of the adults in his life. We influence the child's behavior more by our actions than by our words. Parents, of course, exert the greatest influence because they spend so much time in the company of their children. If the parents are godly persons who live their Christian values both in the home and out of the home, children will usually pattern their behavior along similar lines.

Contacts with other adults in the church will reinforce Christian home patterns. Children benefit greatly from observing these nonparental models outside the family. Every preschool child needs several adults in the church who know him well enough to call him by name, and who take time to talk to him when they meet at church. Such exposure provides additional Christian input and expands the child's perception of godly living. Thus, preschoolers come to understand that the term *Christian* applies to persons other than their parents.

Christian teachers and other adults in the church provide the young child with objective interactions. Parents tend to develop emotional biases and thus to overemphasize the child's strengths and understress his faults, or vice versa. Consequently, it is sometimes difficult for them to provide a good balance. Sunday school teachers are often able to perform this service. In the group, teachers can also observe children of the same age interacting with each other. They can thus assist children with problems that do not arise in the family or to which parents may not be sensitive.

In the Sunday school, preschool children will also begin to learn how to respond to public school teachers and to other significant adults outside of the church. They can learn to receive praise and also to accept guidance without resentment.

Christian teachers are in an ideal situation to supply encouragement and success to preschoolers whose parents have not done this for them. When parents are thoughtless or harsh, they often stress their children's failures more than their successes. They reinforce the child's poor self-concept by constantly pointing out his shortcomings. Sometimes these shortcomings are real faults in the child; at other times faultfinding may arise from the parent's failure to understand children. In both instances, the result is the same—a poor self-concept and low self-esteem.

Christian teachers who are sensitive to the needs of children with low self-concepts can praise them and insure them success in the tasks given to them.[5] From these experiences, children can learn to think of themselves in better terms. They develop more self-acceptance and self-confidence. Christian teachers may not be able to counteract the family influence totally, but they can help. In this area, as in every area of Christian nurture, improvement, though slight, is better than none at all.

E. Introduce the Child to Christian Group Experiences

Life is lived in social interaction, and persons learn to relate to groups through social experiences. Preschool children are introduced to group experiences in the life of the church. From such experiences they learn the values of adequate social interaction. In this specialized environment children are guided to fundamental Christian responses. Here in simple interpersonal relationships, preschoolers begin to learn the complex ways of getting along with other children. Christian adults help children develop a sensitivity to the rights and needs of others. These same adults gently guide the child into learning what Christ expects of us in these situations.

Christian teachers provide life models of justice and mercy, two important characteristics of God. When preschoolers quarrel over toys or act selfishly, teachers can insist on just treatment for the other children. At the same time wise leaders show mercy and love to the offenders. As these Christian social skills are practiced in the classroom, they are more likely to transfer to the broader arenas of life.

When the foregoing objectives guide our work, they help us toward our ultimate goal in Christian education. Parents bear the primary responsibility for the moral and spiritual development of

---

5. See James Dobson, *Hide or Seek* (Old Tappan, N.J.: Fleming H. Revell Co., 1974).

their children. The church, however, assists them in their task by providing a larger, more objective social context.

As we strive for these objectives, we lay a strong foundation for a child to accept Jesus Christ as his personal Saviour. He will have some basic knowledge, a receptive attitude, and an early motivation to make this important choice. As each child grows, he will arrive at the developmental level where it is appropriate for him to take this step.

Some children may never accept Christ. But, if Christian teachers have performed their task with love and skill; if parents have lived as consistent models of Christian character, we shall have done what God requires of us. Christian education has been successful when the Word has been shared and the seed sown. When this has been done, we confidently await the harvest, some 30, some 60, and "some an hundredfold" (Matt. 13:8).

II. The Child as an Individual

Preschool children are not miniature adults; they are unique individuals. Each one has his own rate of development and his own potential. Each grows at his own pace and matures in his own time. He is ready for learning new skills according to his own built-in timetable.

Adults who successfully work with children are keenly aware of these individual differences. They see the world through children's eyes and learn to think as children think. They are sensitive to the rapid changes taking place in each child. For these reasons they know preschoolers cannot be successfully grouped with older children. Rather they prefer children to be in smaller groups with approximately equivalent developmental levels. Jenkins writes: "Children are alike—and different. Alert teachers and parents will always keep the individual child foremost in their minds, seeing him against the background of the normal developmental picture."[6]

Adults who work with preschoolers are also aware of the differing average expectations for children who are two, three, four, and five years of age. We do not expect children to fit rigidly into all these norms, but we use the norms as guidelines to plan appropriate group activities.

---

6. Jenkins, *These Are Your Children,* p. 24.

A. Developmental Expectations

1. *Physical-Motor Skills*

Detailed information for this aspect of child development can be found in sources cited in the bibliography. Only a resumé of important changes is included here.

At birth the child has the necessary survival reflexes—sucking, breathing, bowel and bladder elimination, and crying. These responses are called reflexive because they do not need to be learned. Each is important to the continuing life of the baby.

Thus far psychologists have not been able to differentiate prenatal learning from reflexive responses. Experiments, however, have shown that conditioned learning is possible before birth. We know that the mother's emotional states during pregnancy affect the child. Mothers who exhibit continual anxiety are more likely to have babies who cry more than the average. These babies also have more than average feeding problems.

Immediately after birth, learning begins to shape the baby's responses. As the infant grows and his central nervous system matures, he acquires more specific responses and eliminates unnecessary movements. Soon he will develop the ability to use his thumb and forefinger in opposition to each other. This enables him to pick up objects.

Eye-hand coordination enables the child to reach for objects and to put them into cups or bowls. As he reaches, he is learning spatial relationships. He learns that *far* means *out of reach*. He acquires the sense of *beside, behind,* and *in front of.* By the end of the preschool years, he will be able to use pencils, crayons, and to paint with considerably more skill.

Toward the end of the first year, the child begins to stand alone and to walk with adult assistance. Most children learn to walk by the end of the 14th month. With the acquisition of this skill, the child is no longer confined to small areas for exploration. Walking, running, and climbing skills usher the child into a new world.

Near the end of the second year the child begins to acquire language. At first he communicates his needs by crying. Strangers cannot differentiate among the crying patterns, but his mother or father usually can. Crying, however, is not the precursor of language; explosive sounds are. At first these sounds are "coos," "gurgles," and "grunts." Why the child repeats them is not known. Perhaps he enjoys hearing them. Often his mother will say them back to him and thus encourage him to use them again.

Studies of language acquisition in many cultures show that children go through the same stages of symbol learning, regardless of their native tongue. For the first four months all children make the same basic sounds irrespective of their native language. At this point the cultural influence becomes discernible and moulds the type of verbal symbols used.

Language acquisition is a significant event in the life of the child. When he has learned to understand simple sentences, he responds better and more often to verbal control from adults. As he learns to say one-word sentences such as *eat, want,* and *give,* he gains greater control over other persons in his environment. He can thus begin to express his own inner feelings.

One of the great advantages of language is the accompanying increase in learning ability. Words enable the child to talk about his feelings, to repeat verses of Scripture, and to have vicarious experiences. After he goes to school, he will learn to solve problems by using number symbols. Later he will be able to solve equations and formulas.

During this early development the child learns to use his sphincter muscles involved in bowel and bladder control. Psychoanalysts regard toilet training as a critical process in the child's life. If he learns that his parents regard cleanliness with a high degree of emotion, he discovers that his bowel and bladder accidents upset them and thus become powerful weapons. If he feels that he is being denied adequate attention, he knows that an "accident" will get it for him. Some children regress to pre-toilet training when a new baby arrives in the family and challenges them for parental attention. When the child can achieve toilet training in stride without arousing too much parental emotion, he will be better adjusted and have fewer personality problems later in life.

As one looks at a newborn baby, he is amazed by the child's helplessness. By his sixth birthday, however, he is adept at moving about, feeds and dresses himself, has a large working vocabulary, and handles large crayons with skill. How marvelous is God's miracle of preschool development!

2. *Emotional Responses*

A newborn child shows no clearly defined emotional responses during the first two weeks of life. At this time, however, he will begin to display a generalized emotional response of excitement.[7]

---

7. *Ibid.,* p. 289.

A short time later, the child will exhibit distress. His mother will learn the difference between a cry of pain and a cry of attention seeking. When he is about 2 months old, he will display delight. From these two differentiations of excitement—distress and delight —all other emotions evolve. Delight develops into elation and affection. Distress becomes disgust, jealousy, fear, and anger. When the child is 18 months old, he will evidence all of these. As he grows and matures, he experiences even finer discriminations of emotion.

A young child feels his emotion intensely. It floods his whole behavior until the emotion of the moment completely blocks out rationality. Fortunately, the storm is quickly over and the child becomes amenable to adult direction again.

For this reason verbal guidance and argumentation are ineffective with a nursery child during his emotional outburst. Distracting his attention and seeking to provide a substitute interest are much more effective. The kindergartner is by comparison more susceptible to verbal control, but his emotions also lie close to the surface and can be aroused with little provocation.

3. *Social Relationships*

The baby comes into the world completely self-centered. He cannot distinguish between himself and his clothing, between his body and his environment. Everything he experiences seems designed for his comfort and ease.

Gradually he becomes aware of other persons around him. His mother seems to him to be the almighty provider. When he needs food, she has just what will satisfy him. When his diapers are wet, she can put dry ones on him. Gradually a father enters the child's awareness. Then come siblings, relatives, neighbor children, and adults. All of these pass through his life space with varying degrees of regularity and for different lengths of time.

By the time the child learns to walk, he is keenly aware of "mine" but not "yours." Consequently, whenever he sees a toy that he wants, he sees it as "mine." When he plays in groups, he struggles to take the toy from another. His behavior leads to frequent tussles for possession. Although these quarrels are bothersome to parents and teachers, they are essential to the child's development. As he learns what "mine" means, he begins to learn who he is. He begins his identity as a person.

During these years, until he is nearly four, he will play in "parallel." He sits beside another child in the sandbox but will carry on his own activities. He will learn to play associatively with others only as he nears kindergarten age. This change enables him to carry on an activity cooperatively. He begins to know what "yours" means. At this age he is introduced to cooperation, sharing, and concern for others.[8]

Adults who work with preschoolers often see them engaged in role playing. Much of the time when the kindergarten child is in group activity, he will be imitating adults. He plays house, bus driver, doctor, church. Such play activities teach the child what life is and how it feels to be one of these mighty adults. Wise Christian educators will provide play equipment in the nursery and kindergarten which encourages the children to act out these roles. Boxes make good busses or boats. Tables, chairs, doll dishes, and miniature cook stoves help children play house. Through these activities, Christian behavior is taught. Playing these roles is the way the child learns acceptable adult behavior.

By the end of the preschool period the child will be able to participate in group functions, share some responsibility for the group's welfare, and contribute to the success of the group. All such behaviors are marks of sound social development.

4. Intellectual Growth

At birth a baby's brain is about three-fourths its adult size. He has all of the brain cells he will ever have. But as his brain matures, his intellectual powers increase accordingly.

During the first year the infant's cerebellum and cerebrum increase about 300 times in weight.[9] The cerebellum is significant in motor coordination. As it matures, the child learns to walk. The cerebrum is the part of the brain involved in cognition, thinking, imagining, and perceiving. As it grows, the child is able to remember better and to think more clearly and creatively.

The last part of the brain to mature is the cerebral cortex. This is called the bark or covering—the part one sees as he looks at a whole human brain. It is convoluted or wrinkled and so has a larger surface than the inside of the cranial cavity. Just as one wrinkles paper into a ball to fit it into a smaller space, so the cerebral cortex is wrinkled to fit inside the skull.

The cerebral cortex is involved in abstract, conceptual thinking.

---

8. E. Hurlock, *Developmental Psychology*, 3rd ed. (New York: McGraw-Hill Book Co., 1968), p. 220.
9. *Ibid.*, p. 138.

It functions on a concrete conceptual level during childhood and will begin to mature fully during puberty and adolescence. As it does, the person is able to better understand and handle abstract ideas such as truth and patriotism.

Because the cerebral cortex is not yet developed, we do not introduce abstract theological concepts to preschool children. We talk more about concrete, tangible ideas that fall within their experiences.

A child's intellectual development enables him to grasp differences before he understands similarities. He knows that dogs bark and cats meow before he knows that they both have two eyes or four feet. All of his percepts are based on concrete, tangible characteristics. It is little wonder that he interprets adult abstractions erroneously. He cannot imagine a person wanting "a thousand tongues." How would he manage them?

Preschool teachers often check to see if the child is understanding what he hears by asking him to draw a picture of it. As the child tells what the picture is about, the teacher knows if he got the message accurately.

A preschool child resembles an inquisitive adult in that he likes to touch what he sees. In fact, he has not "seen" something unless he has touched it. For a child, tactile stimulation is a necessary part of seeing. Teaching pictures, therefore, need to be durable and touchable. Finger paints satisfy the child's need to feel wet, messy stuff.

The preschool child possesses an insatiable desire to learn. On this trait teachers of children build their curriculums and plan their teaching-learning experiences. The child is curious about his world. As a toddler he physically explored it. Now he explores it intellectually by constantly asking, "How?" "Why?" and "What for?" His concept of death will be vague. He will have little comprehension of time or distance. He will not understand property rights very clearly.

By the end of the preschool period, the child can repeat short Bible verses. How much of them he really comprehends is uncertain and will depend upon his individual level of maturation and intellectual ability. We are sure that the child understands Christian truths better when teachers help him. He grasps still more when parents support our Christian concepts by teaching in the home.

5. *Moral Development*

In addition to spoken language, the capacity for moral functioning sets man apart from the animals. Behavior involves morality when one's deeds are judged by biblical or by social rules of conduct.

Adult human behavior, therefore, involves the ability to weigh alternative courses of action and to make a decision about which option to pursue. Moral behavior means to be sensitive to the effects one's decision has on other persons, and to accept responsibility for the behavior.

Man's conscience is his monitor. This feeling tone is in the form of either self-esteem or a sense of guilt. Conscience is the feeling of oughtness, i.e., "I ought to do the right." It is integral to human nature and is universal. However, conscience as man's basic feeling of moral obligation requires in addition the discernment and guidance of the understanding in order to determine what is right or wrong. The Bible speaks of spiritually mature persons whose "perceptions are trained by long use to discriminate between good and evil" (Heb. 5:14, NEB).

Conscience thus involves "the incorporation of a set of standards valued by adult society."[10]

A young child does not have the intellectual skills nor the self-concept necessary for this level of functioning. Moral development is dependent upon his brain maturation and upon the socializing process which begins at birth. He develops his conscience as he matures. Sanford gives these definitions of conscience: "copying or modeling; adhering to a group of which an individual feels a part; acceptance of a cause; empathy and vicarious living; sympathy, love; closeness; and loyalty."[11]

Psychoanalytic theories stress the necessity of a young child identifying with his same-sex parent to achieve sex-role clarification. Later he will develop cross-identification with the opposite-sex parent. The personality of the adult with whom the child identifies—parent, surrogate parent, or other close adult—will in a large measure shape his conscience.

Studies which have investigated the role of identification in conscience development agree that

> the process of identification appears to be more complex for girls than for boys. Girls who are strongly identified with their mothers do not seem to be superior in adjustment to girls who are less strongly identified, although this relationship does hold for boys.[12]

Another significant factor in conscience development is the

10. Boyd R. McCandless, *Children and Adolescents* (New York: Holt, Rinehart and Winston, 1961), p. 421.

11. Cited in McCandless, *ibid.*, p. 338.

12. *Ibid.*, p. 349.

child-rearing practice of the parents. Peck[13] found that parents who did not set up a consistent pattern of rewards and punishments for misdemeanors, developed a child who was either morally insensitive or merely conforming. Parents who were extremely authoritarian developed either a conforming conscience or a conscientious-irrational conscience. A conforming conscience follows moral codes when parental or social pressure is inescapable; but whenever external authority is missing, the individual will not conform to his professed code. The conscientious but irrational conscience is legalistic. In later childhood, adolescence, and adulthood, the individual obeys his internal code but is legalistic in his interpersonal expectations.

Children of parents who are democratic in their child-rearing patterns usually develop rational-altruistic consciences. These children grow up to have an internalized moral code which they use with reason and sensitivity. This type conscience is the most mature kind. It reflects the kind of moral discernment that Jesus looked for in men.

Bible knowledge is also essential to moral development. The young child can be taught the content of the Bible and its moral precepts. One of our goals of Christian education is to lay the foundation and begin the development of Christian character in young children. Even though the child may merely parrot words and verses, he will store some ideas in his mind. As his understanding develops, these biblical passages take on new meaning and become building blocks for Christian character.

B. Implications for Christian Teaching

Individuals who work with children in the church are sensitive to the primary impact that parents and family exert upon the child. Consequently, teachers visit in the pupils' homes to become acquainted with the emotional climate, the cultural environment, and the spiritual needs. With this information they become more effective teachers. Also they can enlist the support of other persons in the church to win the family to Christ and to sustain the family's Christian foundations. The more the home and the church cooperate and reinforce each other, the greater impact they have upon the child.

Wise Christian educators seek to recognize the individual differ-

13. Robert F. Peck, *et al., The Psychology of Character Development* (New York: John Wiley and Sons, Inc., 1960), pp. 103-25.

ences of their preschool pupils. They provide a variety of teaching activities and enrichment opportunities. These enable pupils to have more effective learning experiences than if their experiences are narrowly conceived and strictly structured.

Planning for every phase of Christian educational activity must take these individual differences into account. Children who grow up in cultural deprivation require a different type of instruction than do the middle class, suburban children. The children of parents who have recently started to church have less Christian heritage to build upon than children who have been in the church all their lives.

Individual differences are important, but

> we must remember that if everyone were completely unique in every respect it would be most difficult for people to work together in groups or for teachers to teach groups of children and youth. Human beings of a given culture are more alike than they are different.[14]

We therefore group children in terms of common learning and developmental levels. Total uniqueness would cripple Christian education until it could function only on the tutorial basis. Individual differences cannot be ignored, but similarities enable formal education to function.

C. Needs

From the foregoing observations, several important needs of preschool children become apparent. Successful Christian education will seek to meet these needs.

1. *Variety of Activities*

Children in this age bracket have a short attention span and a great need for physical activity. From ages three to five there is a significant difference between the sexes. In most tasks girls have a longer attention span than boys. For simple tasks, the boys' span ranges from slightly over 5 minutes to 8½. For girls who are working on simple tasks, the span ranges from almost 2 minutes for three-year-olds, to 8½ for four years, to 10½ for five-year-olds.

Complex tasks elicit longer spans. Three-year-old girls have a span of a little over 14 minutes; four-year-olds, 15½ minutes, and five-year-olds, 12½. Boys at three years have a span of 8½ minutes, 10½ at four, and a little over 10 minutes at five.[15]

---

14. Morris L. Bigge and Maurice P. Hunt, *Psychological Foundations of Education* (New York: Harper and Row, Publishers, 1962), p. 110.
15. Jenkins, *These Are Your Children*, p. 291.

In the classroom, the teacher will be aware of these differences and will plan a variety of activities that do not tax the children's attention span beyond its normal limits. In addition she will be sensitive to her pupils' restlessness, a sure sign of lost attention. Wise teachers are careful not to demand attention when children have exhausted their normal limits.

2. Play

An uninformed person looking in on a Sunday school class of preschool children might respond with dismay that the children were not learning, just playing. But for small children, *play is learning.* As they imitate adults, they are learning about the world, their role as future men and women, and their social expectations. Children also enjoy reliving the Bible stories through play and drama. Usually these play activities use the creativity of children to its fullest extent. Christian teachers therefore seek to create environments in which the child's play contributes to his learning about the Bible, the church, God, and Jesus.

Teachers of preschoolers need to be aware of the natural play patterns of these children. At the beginning of this period they do not have a very good sense of sharing. For nursery children, each one must have his own toy. Even duplicate toys will be fought over. Teachers will spend many hours settling such disputes and helping children develop a sense of sharing with others. By the end of the preschool age, however, children will have improved greatly in this respect. Kindergarten children can sometimes play together using the same equipment.

3. Mobility

Preschool children have special need for physical activity. They cannot sit immobile for very long, certainly not beyond the limits of their attention span. If adults exert enough pressure, they may force children to sit still, but such demands create frustration. These frustrations generate hostility and aggressiveness that explode into quarrelsomeness, pushing, and teasing. Such behavior problems destroy the learning climate and force the teacher to become a direct disciplinarian.

If long continued, these emotions can generalize from a dislike for the teacher to a distaste for Sunday school and resentment toward the church. Later in life when the parental pressure can be safely disregarded, these frustrated children become church dropouts.

The best teaching for nursery children is almost entirely free and informal activity. Procedure for the kindergarten includes periods of sitting and listening interspersed with times of active singing and free movement. The need for activity will be met as children move from small group to large group and are permitted times when they can pursue their own interests.

4. Individuality

Children need to be treated as respected persons, not as inferior adults. Because preschool children resent being talked down to, perceptive teachers will avoid baby talk. Such language is poor vocabulary training and it is an insult to the personhood of the child.

Children also need to learn to make decisions in order to become self-directing individuals. These skills grow from an early childhood in which children are allowed to make as many decisions and choices as their intellectual development will allow. Christian educators can assist parents in this area of childrearing by encouraging them to give their children choices and then respecting the choices that they make. In the classroom children can be allowed to choose crafts or other individual activities. Also they may often choose songs they would like to sing, and roles in the stories they are dramatizing.

5. Models

Children need adequate adult Christian models. They need to see Christian love in the behavior of the persons closest to them, especially in their parents and Sunday school teachers. Research has shown that children also develop their negative aggressive behavior by watching aggressive adult models.[16] The principle of imitation applies to most areas of life. Christianity is caught more than taught. As small children see kind parents and loving Sunday school teachers, they model their lives after these significant adults. If parents are not in the church, the teacher may be the only adult Christian model in the life of the child. When parents are Christians, Sunday school teachers can further enrich the lives and spiritual perceptions of children and thus supplement and extend the godly parental influence.

---

16. A. Bandura, D. Ross, and S. A. Ross, "Transmission of Aggression Through Imitation of Aggressive Models," *Journal of Abnormal and Social Psychology*, no. 3, 1961; reprinted in *Readings about the Social Animal*, E. Avonson, ed. (San Francisco: W. H. Freeman and Co., 1973), pp. 210-25.

6. *Environmental Challenges*

Developmental psychologists stress the importance of children living in an environment that provides maximum opportunities for them to use their developing skills. As preschool children acquire language skill, they should have the opportunity for conversation. The same principle applies for reading and writing. The environment should be arranged so that children can use their newly developed abilities. There must be sensitive limitations but enough freedom to meet properly the challenge of their environment.

Obviously these tasks must be suited to the child's age, ability, and experience. Words spoken to children must be within their comprehension. But this level exceeds the child's own speaking vocabulary because children often understand twice as many words as they use.

Emotional experiences must also be on the level of the child's own feelings. Children cannot make fine discriminations in complex moral and ethical situations because they have not reached that level of intellectual maturity. For this reason stories, illustrations, and moral problems must be clearly outlined in simple, right or wrong terms. Otherwise children miss the point and become frustrated.

III. CHRISTIAN EDUCATIONAL EXPERIENCES

The Christian educational experiences of children need to be planned from the perspective of wholeness. Sunday programs, weekday experiences, and home educational activities need to be seen together. When leaders understand the overall objectives and interrelatedness of every activity that the church provides, they will correlate activities so as to reinforce each other. In this way children best acquire the lasting learnings essential to lifelong devotion to Christ and the church.

A. Characteristics of Learning Experiences

The scope of this chapter precludes discussion of specific methods to be used with preschool children. But some essential elements of the teaching-learning experience may be explored. The exact methods chosen will be successful to the degree that these criteria are observed.

1. *Satisfaction of Developmental Needs*

a. Preschoolers need educational experiences that allow them freedom for physical movement. Their recently acquired physical mobility and their reservoir of energy provide teachers with access to an almost exhaustless capacity to learn.

b. Young children are curious about the world. They learn most efficiently when their interests are recognized and when they have a variety of activities.

c. Older preschoolers learn efficiently when they experience a balance between large- and small-group settings, also between structured group activities and individual learning.

d. Play is an essential activity for this group because play is the child's method of learning. As children imitate adult roles, they are learning about the world in which they live. As they play with other children, they learn how to reconcile their personal desires with the interests of other persons.

2. *The Experience of Worship*

As we have seen earlier, deep worship experiences for young children more often emerge spontaneously out of their experiences than out of formally planned activities. We do, however, plan some worship experiences.

When music is used in planned worship activities for children, it will be chosen carefully. Simple tunes without complex harmonies are most effective. The range of notes should be limited to the narrow range of children's voices—normally from E, the first line on the staff, to D, the fourth line. If accompaniment is used, it will highlight the melody. The words will reflect the children's concrete experiences rather than abstract thought patterns.

3. *Improvement in Social Relationships*

Nursery-age children are egocentric. They are mainly interested in meeting their own needs and carrying out their own activities. Group projects and cooperative activities are normally not suitable for them.

Kindergartners, on the other hand, are learning to play cooperatively. While struggles over "mine" and "yours" will be frequent, they can often be resolved by talking about them. These children can learn to take turns and to help each other. True friendships will develop and preferred playmates will be recognized. Teachers will use every opportunity to help kindergartners respect the rights and welfare of others.

4. *Opportunity for Expression*

Nursery-age children have not developed good control over the small muscles in their arms and hands. Consequently pencil and paper activities will not be judged by their ability to stay precisely within the lines of figures. Nursery children usually express themselves better by body movements and by manipulating blocks.

Kindergartners have some improved finger control but in general they are still capable only of large mass movements with the hands.

If finger painting or coloring is used in the classroom, kindergartners often do better with large spaces without meticulous boundaries. They are permitted to fill up the spaces as they choose. Even though the adult may see the completed projects as meaningless, the children sense them as being their own.

Some Christian educators use rhythm bands as vehicles for expression, permitting children to beat on various instruments more or less in rhythmic sequence. Such activity helps children develop a sense of accomplishment and improves eye-ear coordination.

5. *Projects for Service*

Preschoolers are not skillful enough to produce fine-quality, useful objects for the church or home. Yet they should be encouraged to do simple, creative things that express love for their parents, for the church, and for God. Such projects use and develop the natural creative ability of children. Adults will find that children's work lacks the preciseness of more mature individuals. Teachers should, nevertheless, be careful to praise the children's efforts and to encourage them to express themselves.

B. Learning Environment

1. *Groupings*

Christian education has commonly used two methods of dividing children into classes—chronological age and public school grade. For young children who have not begun school, chronological age provides the only practical option. Even so, it is not always ideal because children change rapidly during the first six years of life. Also, individual differences are great and development is uneven. However, the techniques of personality assessment are too sophisticated and expensive in time and training for the average church to be able to use them. Thus chronological age is the most practical approach despite its limitations.

Preschoolers include all children who are not attending public school. As some denominations define the terms, the *Cradle Roll* is for children up to four years of age whose parents do not attend church regularly. The Cradle Roll ministry is largely a monthly or quarterly visit to the home.

The *Nursery* includes all children under four whose parents attend Sunday school. The Crib Class is for children not yet walking, who spend most of their time in cribs provided. Toddlers are free to walk about the nursery. For these children, the church provides supervisory care in a room with some play equipment and a religious motif. Little formal education is attempted.

The Nursery Class is for two- and three-year-olds. In larger churches nursery children are separated into classes for twos and for threes. Curriculum materials are usually published for both age-groups. Music, storytelling, worship, and play are the major sources of learning experiences.

Kindergarten includes children four and five years of age. Their curriculum provides for more formal instruction than for twos and threes, but less than for older children. Larger churches usually have separate classes for fours and fives; smaller churches normally combine them.

2. *Physical Environment*

The physical environment in which Christian education is conducted is highly important. Preschoolers need more space per pupil than do other age-groups. The floor needs to be clean and warm. Carpet is highly desirable because it provides a comfortable play surface. However, the carpet needs to be adequately cleaned each week to avoid collecting and harboring disease germs.

The room should be well lighted with plenty of windows to open and to see through. Walls should be clean, well painted in pastel hues. Furniture should be sturdy, mobile, in good repair, and brightly painted.

All furnishings in the room should be appropriately sized. Picture rails should be low, on the eye-level of children. Pictures should appeal to children's interests and should be changed often.[17]

A bathroom with child-sized fixtures should be included or readily accessible to the classroom. Adequate sanitary measures should be rigidly followed.

If cribs are used in the nursery, they should be constructed so as to prevent children from falling out. Painted surfaces should be lead

---

17. This aspect of preschool Christian education is too complex and detailed to be discussed fully in this chapter. Sources for specific information will be found in the bibliography. Also see Appendix I.

free. Clean linens must be used every week; they should be changed after each child has used the crib. Churches should avoid crib designs that resemble pens along and up the wall. Such arrangements save space but are less desirable than movable cribs.

The nursery room should have steps to climb, wooden or plastic blocks to build with, various sized boxes to pile up, sit on, climb in and out of. In children's imagination, these become trains, buses, ships, or fire engines.

Toy household furniture, kitchen fixtures, and dolls should be available with which children can imitate adult behavior and try out adult roles.

3. *Emotional environment*

While physical environment is important in preschool experience, the emotional climate is even more vital. If the teacher is anxious, tense, or irritable when she is working with children, she will generate the same feelings in them. They are too young to understand her feelings and cannot empathize with her. Thus they subconsciously interpret her reactions as directed against them.

Also, if the leader does not understand the emotional needs of children and is harsh and authoritarian, she will create an unfavorable emotional climate. Little desirable learning will occur. The net result will be adverse to our goals for Christian education.

Adult leaders who express confidence in preschooler's abilities to learn and to cooperate inspire more learning and elicit more cooperation than those who tell children they are stupid and naughty.[18]

Preschoolers are perceptive about adults' feelings toward them. John was four and attended the church-sponsored weekday nursery and kindergarten. When his mother came to pick him up one afternoon, a teacher overheard him say, "Mother, Mrs. Brown likes me, but Mrs. Wilson loves me."

C. Important Characteristics for Preschool Workers

1. *Personality Traits*

Not everyone is suited emotionally or intellectually to work with preschoolers. Perhaps the most important qualification is how one feels about children. Persons who do not like or understand young children, especially in groups, will not be successful children's

---

18. Robert Rosenthal and Lenore Jacobson, *Pygmalion in the Classroom* (New York: Holt, Rinehart, and Winston, Inc., 1968).

leaders. Also adults who find other persons' children inferior to their own are not suited for this important task.

Effective work with preschool children demands adults who sincerely love them. Teachers must see the world through the eyes of children and see children as individuals who have their own distinctive and worthy mental processes.

Adults who can let children be spontaneous, creative, and joyous contribute most to their development. At the same time, leaders who set limits based on the children's developmental level and who kindly but firmly guide them within those limits lay a sound basis for personality development.

2. *Intellectual Traits*

Adults who work with preschoolers should have intellectual curiosity, be knowledgeable in Bible information, and well informed about the world. They need to be able to answer children's questions correctly. Children who are started right during preschool years are less likely to leave the church during adolescence.

Preschool teachers need to be creative and have the initiative to implement their ideas. Children respond to a variety of learning experiences.

Adults who work with children should be able to perceive the implications of a child's behavior. Often children who are cross and unruly are not reacting against the teacher. They may be struggling with anxiety and insecurity in their world outside of the church.[19] Unless adults sense these inner motivations, they may increase the children's anxiety by being punitive in response to their misconduct.

3. *Communicative Traits*

Adults who teach must be able to communicate with preschoolers. They need to enunciate clearly and speak precisely on the level of the children's understanding. Emotionally, adults need to be able to portray feeling and excitement. Otherwise their storytelling will not evoke the interest of the children.

4. *Spiritual Traits*

Because children are perceptive, they quickly pierce any facade of hypocrisy and inconsistency in adults. Every admonition written about adults as models applies in this context. Preschoolers need

---

19. See F. F. Wise, "The Goldfish Incident," *Church School Builder*, vol. 27, no. 7 (March, 1973), p. 22.

leaders whose lives are Spirit-filled and completely dedicated to God. If religion is caught, not taught, the process begins in the preschool years.

VI. CONCLUSION

The Christian education of preschool children is one of the critical educational tasks of the church. Some educational theorists hold that one's personality is formed during the first five years of life. This position may be extreme, but in any case, these are important years. Hymes writes:

> Good early living is no sure guarantee of strength and stability as life moves along. Later trauma can be so overpowering that, no matter how supportive early childhood was, life confronts man with more than he can stand. But good early experiences strengthen the human, they do not weaken him. In reverse, unsatisfactory early experiences weaken the human, they do not prepare him.[20]

Every later development is built on this initial thrust. Is it any wonder that we say these years deserve the best the church can provide?

BIBLIOGRAPHY

Barrett, E. *Storytelling: It's Easy.* Grand Rapids, Mich.: Zondervan Publishing House, 1960.

> The author shares her secrets and techniques as a master storyteller. Since storytelling is so important at this age level, teachers of children should fully develop their skills in this area.

Coopersmith, S. *The Antecedents of Self-esteem.* San Francisco: W. H. Freeman and Co., 1967.

> This book is an intensive study of what affects the development of the self-concept and self-esteem, such as child-rearing practices and religious orientation.

Gesell, A., and Ilg, F. A. *Child Development.* New York: Harper and Bros., 1949.

> A very precise description of how children develop from birth until age 10. It is quite detailed, but a solid book in the field on how the child develops intellectually, physically, socially, and emotionally.

---

20. James E. Hymes, Jr., *Teaching the Child Under Six* (Columbus, Ohio: Charles E. Merrill Publishing Co., 1968), p. 16.

Gilliland, A. H. *Understanding Pre-schoolers*. Nashville: Convention Press, 1969.

Relevant information that has been derived through study and research by specialists in various fields of early childhood. It is useful to all who have association with preschoolers at home, church, nursery school, or kindergarten.

Rowen, Dolores. *Ways to Help Them Learn: Early Childhood, Birth to 5 Years*. Glendale, Calif.: Regal Books, 1972.

In each of the five chapters on methods, the author includes a significant section on "Bible Teaching/Learning Opportunities."

Sutton-Smith, B. *Child Psychology*. New York: Appleton-Century-Crofts, 1973.

A solid but easily understood book that discusses human development from conception to adolescence. It includes the results of recent research.

Young, Leontine. *Life Among the Giants*. New York: McGraw-Hill Book Co., 1971.

Teachers who want to communicate with children need to understand their thought processes. The author draws from her wide experience working with children to explain what it is like to be a child facing a confusing and complicated grown-up world.

CHAPTER 10

Christian Education
of Children

This chapter deals with the Christian education of children commonly associated with the Primary, Middler, and Junior Departments of the Sunday school. Chronologically, they are from 6 to 11 years of age. Their public school classification begins at the first grade and concludes with the sixth. If they attend a 6-3-3 school system, they comprise the elementary grades.

While these children are discussed separately from the preschoolers, they do not demand a new set of learning laws. All individuals learn in the same way. Many of the principles discussed in the previous chapter are applicable to this adjacent age-group. However, developments in the child's neuromuscular maturation provide new options of teaching-learning for the teacher. Learning experiences for elementary children can be more specifically focused by the teacher and can be more structured than in preschool years.

This chapter will highlight these new options in learning. Only those principles that are most relevant to the Christian education of elementary children will be covered. The reader is directed to chapters 5 and 8 for discussion of the broader educational principles and general methods.

I. Objectives

The ultimate objective for elementary children is the same as for the whole of Christian education. However, we need to identify some cific goals to be achieved during elementary years. The child's expanding mental capacities and movement toward abstract thinking makes possible the ongoing process of developing Christian character and churchmanship. To the basic receptivity that Christian education seeks to foster in preschool years, we can now add growing concepts and a measure of self-responsibility.

The specific objectives for elementary years may be identified as follows.

A. To Enlarge Christian Attitudes and Knowledge

In their earlier teaching preschoolers are encouraged to feel that the Bible and the church are helpful factors in one's life; that Jesus and God are kind and benevolent Persons. Older children need to be led to identify themselves with these factors and these Persons.

B. To Broaden Perspectives of Christian Truth

Elementary children have an expanding social environment because of their attendance at public school. Here they meet other people who have value systems different from their own. As they identify with peer groups, they are subjected to intensifying pressures to conform to group mores. Our teaching must help children know how to confront these non-Christian value systems.

C. To Introduce the Missionary Enterprise

Juniors are able to comprehend both historical and geographical percepts. They can understand the meaning of "1,000 years ago." They can also grasp both geographical and cultural concepts of India, China, and Africa. Because of these developments, children at this age can benefit from missionary education. They can empathize with children from other lands and can respond to their needs. Habits of sharing with less fortunate children around them can be developed—and these habits may continue through life.

D. To Give Opportunities to Accept Christ as Saviour

A few children will be able to have a meaningful relationship with Christ at the preschool level; many more will be able to experience this relationship during the elementary years. Adults must be sensitive enough to detect when the child is ready to respond to the Holy Spirit. On the other hand, we must not emotionally manipulate children to imitate a conversion experience or to simply parrot a confession of faith. Children at this age are very susceptible to adult desires;

they may go through the motions of coming to the altar simply because they want to please the adults. Wise leaders will provide adequate opportunities for conversion but will not create undue emotional or group stresses that bring the children to this step prematurely. To act prematurely without understanding the significance of the event sometimes creates hindrances to a real conversion experience later in life. It is probably true, however, that we fail more often by delaying too long than by encouraging children too early.

E. To Involve in the Life of the Church

At what age should a child be admitted to church membership? This question is not easily resolved. Some groups, such as Jews, Roman Catholics, and Lutherans, set 12 years as the minimum. Other denominations do not have an age limit but require a confession of faith in Christ as Savior. Most evangelical conservative churches follow this pattern. In any case when the child joins the church, he should want to take this step, and the experience should be as meaningful as possible.

Elementary children can learn a great deal about their church's beliefs and standards. They can participate in children's choirs, special programs, and service projects. These experiences make later adult participation easy and natural.

F. To Provide Opportunities to Serve God and Others

Wise leaders use many types of group projects to let children experience Christian service. Vacation Bible school projects can be chosen that will beautify the church, such as making doormats and wastepaper baskets for classrooms. Children can experience the satisfaction of beautifying God's house and in this way enjoy serving God.

They can plan and execute projects at Thanksgiving and Christmastime: food, toys, candy, and clothing may be shared with the poor, the aged, and the shut-ins. Elementary children respond well to these challenges, provided the leaders involve them at every stage of the planning and the execution. Such activities help children to learn the joy of sharing.

G. To Increase Knowledge of the Bible

These are years in which children like to assimilate and to memorize. They are therefore golden years for acquiring factual knowledge of the Bible.

Teachers can stimulate middlers and juniors to acquire the basic facts that will enable them to use the Bible as their resource Book. When they leave the Junior Department, children should know the names of the books of the Bible, their sequence in the Old and New Testaments, the major personalities of each Testament, and the major events of Christ's life. They should know how to locate scriptural references and how to use a concordance. These children should be encouraged to memorize passages recommended by the church and some of their own choosing. Some can be challenged to memorize extensive amounts—"crammed like you would cram an ox with corn" is the way the Jews would say it.

This is also a good age to teach children scripture verses they can use in witnessing to others. Such knowledge will lay the foundation for a lifetime of finding spiritual support in the Scriptures.

II. The Individual

A. Importance of School Years

Learning in the church is basically of two types: informal and formal. Informal learnings are those that the pupils pick up from interactions within the group and from adults who are responsible for the program. Attitudes, values, and self-concepts are either acquired or strongly influenced by these contacts. Both adults and children are often quite unaware that such shaping of the personality is taking place. Often the informal learning is more life-changing than the formal lessons. For example, positive or negative attitudes toward the church or the pastor can be learned in one exposure of such feelings by adults. Few of us can recall detailed information learned in Sunday school, but most of us who went regularly can recall a specific person who influenced us.

Formal learning is planned by adults and is consciously pursued in a suitable environment. It involves definite objectives and chosen methods to achieve them. Formal learning that is effective is based upon congruence between the content taught and the developmental level of the pupils. Its effectiveness is directly proportional to this match between the educational efforts and the developmental needs.

Elementary children are characterized by consistent development. During early and late childhood they will continue the self-development begun earlier. At the same time, early individual differences are accentuated. Physical development and resulting skills sharpen individual differences in contrast to others of their own age.

The same processes are at work in the earlier and later elementary years. However, successful Christian education for primaries will not automatically be successful for juniors. Ten-year-olds are different from six-year-olds. Different types of formal learning experiences are essential for these groups.

Age six is significant for most children. For many of them it is the gateway to a much broader world. Most American children of six years enter public school. Even though half of them have been in kindergarten, first grade is something of a landmark. They now begin the long, arduous task of becoming literate members of human society. Barbara Biber writes: "The preschool child becomes a member of the human race, while the school child becomes a member of his society."[1] Erikson says of this process: "Literate people, with more specialized careers, must prepare the child by teaching him things which first of all make him literate, the widest possible basic education for the greatest number of possible careers."[2]

In a sense the six-year-old is a member of two societies—the adult-teacher society and the peer group.

> On the one hand, teachers and parents are indoctrinating him in the ways of society at large with its adult-made rules. Among his friends, on the other hand, he lives in a special childhood culture marked by its own traditional games, rhymes, riddles, taunts, and so forth, transmitted virtually intact from one childhood generation to the next, sometimes over a period of centuries, with no help from adults and sometimes in spite of them.[3]

The elementary school years are critical for the children and for the church. In these years children learn much about the world, about society and social institutions, and about themselves. From the conflicts and stresses of this developmental period the finished foundations of character and personality emerge. On these foundations the child builds the rest of his life.

B. Critical Developmental Areas

Children in the elementary years are emerging into social beings. They are experiencing the awakening of critical personality factors, such as conscience and self-concept. They must refine their skills in

---

1. Cited in L. Joseph Stone and Joseph Church, *Childhood and Adolescence* (New York: Random House, 1957), p. 203.
2. Erik H. Erikson, *Childhood and Society*, 2nd ed. (New York: W. W. Norton and Co., 1963), p. 259.
3. Stone and Church, *Childhood and Adolescence*, pp. 203-4.

order to cope with basic motives and resolve essential conflicts. In these tasks, adults often expect children to act as if they understood the abstract concepts of honesty and property rights. In reality, the child's intellectual development has sometimes not proceeded to the point where he can deal with these concepts in acceptable behavioral terms.

> The school child, as we have suggested, has reached a point in his development where he can be aware of his essential human aloneness in a vast, powerful and . . . unpredictable world. He has to deal with this awareness in two ways. First as an individual he must master and control reality. Second, he must find emotional strength in the company of his peers. His childhood culture meets both these needs exactly on the level of his capacities.[4]

1. *Industry Versus Inferiority Conflict*

One of the basic tasks of children is to resolve the developmental conflict between industry and inferiority. Children at this age become extremely concerned with how things work, both mechanically and socially. They develop a strong need to formulate rules, to organize groups, and to know what are the limits of social behavior.

If adults support the child in these efforts by assisting him to develop communicative, social, and physical skills, the child becomes industrious and active—a contributory member of society.

> He develops a sense of industry—i.e., he adjusts himself to the inorganic laws of the tool world. He can become an eager and absorbed unit of a productive situation. To bring a productive situation to completion is an aim which gradually supersedes the whims and wishes of play. . . . Thus the fundamentals of technology are developed, as the child becomes ready to handle the utensils, the tools, and the weapons used by the big people.[5]

On the other hand, if adults constantly thwart children's efforts to join their gangs, to learn how to make and do things, and to achieve orderliness, children develop a sense of inferiority and blind conformity.

> The child's danger, at this stage, lies in a sense of inadequacy and inferiority. If he despairs of his tools and skills or of his status among his tool partners, he may be discouraged from identification with them. . . . The child despairs of his equipment in the tool world and in anatomy and considers himself doomed to mediocrity or inadequacy.[6]

---

4. *Ibid.,* p. 213.
5. Erikson, *Childhood and Society,* pp. 259-60.
6. *Ibid.,* p. 260.

Tools, as Erikson uses the term, refer to a wide range of physi objects, to mental and physical skills, as well as to concepts. Children of this age need to manipulate things—crayons, paintbrushes, balls, pencils, wood, paddles. Their creative efforts when recognized and praised by adults can help them achieve a sense of adequacy. Their participation in both play and task-oriented group activities enlarges their understanding of the rules of social endeavors and increases their sense of accomplishment. As new facts are learned, they become mental tools to solve the riddles of life. As children expand their vocabularies and develop their ability to use words effectively, they are less likely to have a sense of inadequacy and incompetence.

Christian education can enhance children's sense of industry and competence through its handwork activities, workbook assignments, Bible memorization, field trips, and class cooperative projects. Adult leaders are educating children when they recognize and reward significant activities as well as significant achievements. Teachers can provide tactful guidance for groups to work effectively together, while allowing the children to assume as much responsibility as they can for the planning and execution of these projects.

In class activities, adult leaders should be sensitive to the social structure of the group with which they are working. Children tend to form close friendships, often excluding others from their clique. The stars are the popular leaders of the group; the isolates and rejectees are the children excluded from participation. Quite often they are the quiet, compliant, conforming children.

Teachers must be alert to identify the rejectees and isolates and then help the group learn to accept them into its membership. Every child needs experiences with social success. These shy children can be given places of responsibility and leadership in areas where they have competence. Sometimes they have developed unusual hobbies, acquired special skills, or travelled widely. When they have the opportunity to share their unique experiences with the group, they will be more readily welcomed and respected as peers.

2. *Intellectual Development*

Jean Piaget's studies[7] of the intellectual development of children

---

7. See bibliography for some of Piaget's works. Usually it is better to read authors who restate or interpret the theories because his own writings are difficult to understand. See "The States of the Intellectual Development of the Child," *Readings in Child Development and Personality,* Paul H. Mussen, John J. Conger, and Jerome Kagan, eds., 2nd ed. (New York: Harper and Row, Publishers, 1970), pp. 291-98.

has attracted widespread attention. He has probably influenced current educational trends in England and America more than any other person. By carefully planned experiments with children, Piaget classified their intellectual development into four major stages: sensorimotor, preoperational, concrete operations, and formal operations.

Elementary school children are in the stage of concrete operations. This means that the children can classify objects according to their size, color, or weight and can arrange them into sequential order on the basis of their appearance. They have not yet reached the stage of formal operations where they can handle symbolic thinking. Piaget's greatest contribution to religious education has been to reaffirm the fact that primaries and juniors usually cannot deal effectively with abstract truths or solve problems by applying highly conceptual principles. These children think best when dealing with concrete facts—they are at the developmental stage of concrete operations.

Christian education ministries for children must be planned to work within the limits set by the child's intellectual development. For this reason the curriculum and teaching methods stress factual learning and memorization of biblical material essential to Christian living. In the words of Donald M. Joy,

> It is likely that in the church we will continue to find many "formula" quality bodies of information that should be committed to memory for permanent use. High on the list will be a variety of Bible passages which are useful in sustaining the courage and the commitment of one's own faith. There are other passages one should know if he wants to share his faith with other persons. . . .
>
> Names of Bible books, catechism, the Ten Commandments, the Lord's prayer need to be memorized even before the words are meaningful. . . . Nevertheless, in the classroom with its limited time, we must devote our energies more often to helping our young and ourselves find the deep meaning of our faith. And that meaning is rarely guaranteed by memorization.[8]

3. Motives

According to Kagan,[9] people behave as they do because of four basic motives; these grow out of their attempts to resolve uncer-

---

8. Donald M. Joy, *Meaningful Learning in the Church* (Winona Lake, Ind.: Light and Life Press, 1969), p. 68.

9. Much of the material in this section is based on Jerome Kagan, *Understanding Children* (New York: Harcourt, Brace, Jovanovich, Inc., 1971).

tainty, mastery, hostility, and sexuality.[10] Adults who understand the role of these motives and who acquire the necessary skills to use them may accomplish behavioral changes and expedite learning in children. Of the four motives that Kagan discusses, the resolution of uncertainty and the achievement of mastery have the greatest implications for Christian education of children. Sexuality has not been, at least to this time, an area to which churches have given much educational attention. Christian educators, however, cannot ignore its secondary influence upon their programs, especially in the junior age-groups.

a. Uncertainty. People experience uncertainty for three basic reasons: (1) they meet the unfamiliar idea, or the strange event; (2) they are confronted with inconsistency between their own ideas and those of another, or their behavior deviates from their own self-ideal; (3) they cannot predict the future with any great degree of confidence. In these situations learning is very likely to take place.

Most children respond readily to the force of this motive. Adult leaders who work with them will constantly look for situations in which they can expose children to ideas that are new. They will also help children to explore facts by simulating moral situations in which there is no simple answer. When teachers see primaries or juniors behaving in a self-centered manner toward other children, they will help them to rethink their inconsistencies of Christian behavior. Or, if children call attention to adults who profess to be Christian but do not act consistently, teachers will use the occasion to confront children with the importance of a loving appreciation for others, and the need for Christian growth even in adults.

Also, children may equate membership in their particular denomination with being a Christian. Teachers can help clear up the error by carefully guiding the children's thinking. Together they may explore what the essential differences are between Christians and non-Christians. Children will then be able to handle the problem of differences among various Christian groups.[11]

b. Mastery. Another motive with which Christian educators are deeply concerned is that of mastery. This urge includes secondary motives such as "the desire to perfect a skill, finish a task, or solve a challenging problem."[12]

---

10. *Ibid.*, p. 33.
11. For a fuller discussion of the implications and principles involved, see Donald M. Joy, *Meaningful Learning*, pp. 69-80.
12. Kagan, *Understanding Children*, p. 47.

The mastery motive is triggered, first, by the desire to achieve certain goals: "the desire to match behavior to a standard, the desire to predict the environment, and the wish to define the self."[13] In order for children to match their behavior to a standard, they must know clearly what the standard is and how their behavior is different from it. The teacher's role is to explain to children what is God's standard of behavior. They must learn how His standards are different from the world's. Children get this picture, in part, by talking about it and in part by seeing it in adult lives. Specific teacher guidance will help children understand the basic principles involved in Christian living. Then as they see God's love in the lives of parents and teachers, they will want to live in accordance with those principles.

Too often Christian teaching has been content to impose solutions to problems without providing principles to guide children in the complex issues they face outside the church. Often in adolescence they have abandoned the attempt to live as Christians because of this deep uncertainty and confusion. A more effective Christian education tries to equip children with strategies for solving their moral and ethical problems. In this kind of goal seeking, principles predominate and rules are minimal in number.

Kagan says the second basis for the mastery motive is the desire to predict future events. Both children and adults engage in this predicting process. Children like to envision their success in games; they enjoy thinking about what they would do in imaginative situations. Perhaps this is the basis for so much fantasy and hero worship in childhood. Also the ability to project themselves into an imagined role is the cognitive basis for mastering a new skill and for establishing a new response to a worthy challenge.

Christian teachers use games, riddles, and simulations of social situations in order to help children predict their reactions in similar circumstances. These aids provide a variety of experiences from which students can draw understanding about real life. To be assured of best carry-over, teachers must help the children to clearly articulate some principles to use as they meet practical situations in their own lives.

The third basis for the mastery motive is the desire for self-understanding. Everyone wishes to know his competencies, his uniqueness, and his similarities to others. Too often children know

---

13. *Ibid.*

their differences and similarities only by comparing themselves with others, rather than by having an adequate self-concept for evaluation. Children usually need adult guidance in this area. Kagan writes:

> Perhaps psychological maturity should be defined as that time in life when a person has established such a well-articulated understanding of himself that he can decide on the quality or morality of an action without showing it to anyone or comparing it with the action of others.[14]

This search for self-definition may help explain the tendency of juniors to "test the limits." Children actively seek from adults a clear picture of the rules. They tattle on other children whom they observe breaking them. Boys playing softball will argue strenuously about the rules of the game, though they may frequently change them to suit a particular situation. As children learn the limits, they develop a working knowledge of the rigidity and flexibility of rules. They are thus better able to adjust to life around them, and to move toward fuller self-definition.

Adults who work with children will be sensitive to their unique characteristics and be careful to reward them for their achievements. Teachers can create work groups within which the children can use their skills to the fullest extent. They will assign to these groups tasks that challenge their abilities. Always adults should praise the successes of the children more often than they criticize their failures.

In these ways the child's desire to achieve can be used to increase learning. Kagan affirms, "The more unique the profile of competencies, the better delineated the self-concept."[15] The better the self-concept is delineated, the better adjusted is the individual. And the better the adjustment of the individual, the greater productivity and happiness he will enjoy.

c. Sexuality. Sexuality and the role of sex identification have not been as directly the concerns of Christian education as have uncertainty and mastery. But with the increasing openness of American society in regard to sex and with the greater emphasis upon sex education in the public schools, the churches are giving more attention to sex-role definition. They feel that the church has a responsibility to generate a sense of the Christian stewardship of sex among children. The junior age seems an appropriate time for this learning

---

14. *Ibid.*, p. 51.
15. *Ibid.*

before children develop the emotionality about sex that comes during adolescence.

One of the prominent characteristics of junior children is their affinity for same-sex gangs. Girls prefer girls as playmates; boys prefer boys. In any free-choice situtation, both seem to disdain involvement with the opposite sex. Each sex tries to ignore the other. However, careful observation will show that in reality junior boys and girls are keenly aware of the opposite sex. But these heterosexual interests are disguised. Each sex is unsure of its identity and its roles. Each, therefore, forms strong same-sex group identity to support them while they learn the rules of life regarding boy and girl roles.

In organizing for Christian education, we must decide whether junior-aged children should be separated into groups by sex or put into mixed classes. There does not seem to be a compelling case for either plan. Psychologically and developmentally juniors seem to fit better in sex-segregated groups. However, public schools do not appear to encounter any difficulty in mixed groups; also many local churches combine boys' and girls' classes successfully. Each local church will need to weigh the factors of available leadership, space, and the number of children, then decide which plan to follow.

4. *Self-concept*

In recent years psychology has shown an active interest in the self-concept and its critical role in human learning and behavior. It is defined simply as the picture one has of himself. Perkins writes:

> The *self-concept* is the highest integrative level of the self-struc-
> ture and is defined as those most highly differentiated perceptions,
> beliefs, feelings, attitudes, and values which the individual views
> as part or characteristic of himself. Behavior tends to be consistent
> with the self-concept and reflects the individual's effort to main-
> tain and enhance the self-concept. The student's self-concept
> appears to be the most important single factor influencing learn-
> ing performance—more important than intelligence, aptitude, or
> difficulty of the material to be learned.[16]

Controlled studies in public education have shown conclusively that the self-concept plays a critical role in the learning process.[17]

---

16. Hugh V. Perkins, *Human Development and Learning* (Belmont, Calif.: Wadsworth Publishing Co., Inc., 1969), pp. 220-21.

17. Helen H. Davidson and Gerhard Lang, "Children's Perceptions of Their Teachers' Feelings Toward Them, Related to Self-perception, School Achievement, and Behavior," *Journal of Experimental Education*, 29 (1960), pp. 107-18.

Also changes in the self-concept occur when teachers purposely work for them.[18]

As we deal with elementary pupils in Christian education, we must take the self-concept into account because one's self-concept tends to shape his personal development. Everyone organizes the various percepts of himself in terms of his self-concept so that his personality is consistent with itself.[19] If we know the basic values that a child holds, we can predict his behavior in many situations. We will also be able to understand the mystifying behavior of some children. What appears on the surface to be highly inconsistent behavior would be clearly explained on the basis of underlying consistency.

Children develop their self-concept out of the input that they receive about themselves from their social relationships. Parents are the earliest and most powerful shaping factors. Parental approval and disapproval, love and acceptance, or indifference and rejection are highly significant. These parental attitudes provide the basis for children to feel that they are loved, adequate, and lovable—or unloved, inadequate, and hard to love. Also from the age of six on through adolescence, the physical growth and appearance of the child's body assumes an increasingly critical importance in his self-concept.[20]

Children do not leave their self-concepts at home when they come to church. Teachers can be sure that children will respond to them and to their ministries in behavior patterns that are consistent with their present self-concept. It is important, therefore, that we discover how each child sees himself.

A child's self-concept can be partially known by observation. He reveals how he sees himself in his conversation, his emotional responses, and his behavior. Adults who want to work with children effectively will carefully observe them in as many different environments as possible—in Sunday school classes; in informal, recreational settings; and in the home. By listening to the child's comments about his work and himself, we gain insight into his self-concepts.

---

18. Robert Rosenthal and Lenore Jacobson, *Pygmalion in the Classroom: Teacher Expectation and Pupils' Intellectual Development* (New York: Holt, Rinehart, and Winston, Inc., 1968).

19. Prescott Lecky, *Self-consistency* (New York: Island Press, 1945).

20. Paul H. Mussen and Mary C. Jones, "Self-conceptions, Motivations, and Interpersonal Attitudes of Late-and-Early-maturing Boys," *Child Development*, 28 (June, 1957), pp. 243-56.

As we really know individual children, we can assist them in their growth and learning.

Perhaps the most important aspect of the self-concept for Christian educators is its implications for conversion. "One interpretation of conversion sees it as the development of new self-concepts."[21] When children experience genuine conversion, they find themselves in a new relationship to God. As they come to Christ, they become aware of their sinfulness before God and see themselves as they can become—one of His children. They also find themselves in a new relationship to other people. They move from an ego-centered selfishness to a Christ-centered life which includes concern for others.

5. Conscience Development and Moral Behavior

Conscience is a "mark of humanity."[22] Christian education is therefore faced with the task of trying to understand both the origin and the development of conscience. If this task can be accomplished, our program of Christian teaching can be planned to guide more effectively the development of the child's conscience.

It is essential, at this point, to understand the difference between conscience in the absolute sense (an innate capacity) and conscience in the relative sense (a learned content). Conscience as an inborn sense of oughtness—an unvarying awareness of moral obligation to do the right—is absolute and "beyond the power of education or development." In the relative sense, however, conscience involves a process that is "subject to education and moral development."[23] Conscience as a sense of oughtness to do right is an essential part of man's constitution, as a creature made in the image of God, and is absolute. On the other hand, conscience as the activity of a human being dealing with perplexity in moral decisions is relative.

From the relative viewpoint conscience may be described as pure (1 Tim. 3:9), evil (Heb. 10:22), defiled (Titus 1:15), weak (1 Cor. 8:7), or seared (1 Tim. 4:2). It is therefore obvious that in the relative sense conscience may be distorted by ignorance and vice. Thus one may form false judgments. Conscience very much needs Christian education and guidance in order to be healthy rather than morbid, good rather than defiled. We must also remember that in issues of

21. David O. Moberg, "Some Social Aspects of the Self-concepts," from *Proceedings of the Eighteenth Annual Convention*, Christian Association for Psychological Studies, William L. Heemstra, ed. (Grand Rapids, Mich., 1971), p. 112.

22. Joy, *Meaningful Learning*, p. 111.

23. H. Orton Wiley, *Christian Theology*, 3 vols. (Kansas City: Nazarene Publishing House, 1943), 3:33-35.

right and wrong, "it is the will of God not the conscience of man that is the final judge. Only in so far as the conscience is illuminated by Christ is it reliable."[24]

Since moral behavior is learned, what are the principles involved in the learning? On the basis of their research, psychologists maintain that the content of conscience develops in much the same manner as all other behavior is learned.

Piaget[25] describes two major stages in conscience development—the objective and subjective. In the objective stage children attend to and judge the moral quality of an act in terms of its objective damage to physical property with little regard to the intent of the act. In the subjective stage they are more concerned with the intention of the act than with the damage.

Piaget feels that younger children are in the objective stage; older children in the subjective. The child is capable of moving from the objective to the subjective stage at 7 years of age. Research by Bandura and McDonald shows that children of 5 to 11 years are capable of making both types of judgments. The significant factor was what an adult model did. Knowing the behavior of the important adults in their lives was the most potent factor in shaping the patterns of children's generalized social behavior.[26]

Out of the wealth of research that has been conducted in this area, several basic principles have emerged.

a. Development and maturation. Conscience, moral behavior, and character are subject to the same principles of growth and development as all other aspects of human personality. Moral behavior is learned. As children mature, they are capable of higher levels of abstract thinking. They become increasingly able to learn appropriate moral principles and behavior.

When children disregard or disobey their moral principles, they experience guilt and shame. Younger and older children, however, have different reasons for their feelings. Younger children are mainly afraid of adult disapproval. Older children also desire adult approval but they become increasingly sensitive to peer group expectations.

---

24. William Hordern, "Conscience," *A Dictionary of Christian Theology,* Alan Richardson, ed. (Philadelphia: Westminster Press, 1969), p. 675. (See also 1 Cor. 4:4.)

25. Jean Piaget, *The Moral Judgment of the Child* (Glencoe, Ill.: Free Press, 1948). Cited by Hiriam E. Fitzgerald and John P. McKinney, eds., in *Developmental Psychology* (Homewood, Ill.: The Dorsey Press, 1970), p. 415.

26. Albert Bandura and Frederick J. McDonald, "Influence of Social Reinforcement and Behavior Models in Shaping Children's Moral Judgments," *Developmental Psychology,* Hiriam E. Fitzgerald and John P. McKinney, eds., p. 424.

As they are able to understand the approval and disapproval of God, they may experience a sense of guilt for real sin. At this stage they can also learn the release from guilt that comes with forgiveness.

b. Intelligence. Some research has shown that the correlation between intelligence and honesty is about .50. This low correlation indicates that intelligence alone is not a safe basis for predicting honesty.

A child of 9 years with a high intellectual capacity is able to make moral discriminations that are normal for a 14-year-old of average intelligence. Such brighter children can see the implications of a situation more sharply than can the average child. They may also be more sensitive to the better rewards that come to those who make proper choices. High intelligence permits better moral discrimination, but more than discrimination is involved in moral choices.

c. Sex. There seems to be little difference between boys and girls in their ability to make moral decisions.

d. Parental influence. Parents are the most influential persons in the conscience development of children. If parents are warm, accepting, and loving, children will be more likely to develop high identification with them. Families of this type, especially those in which the father displays warm acceptance toward his son, rear children who seem able to resist temptation more effectively. These children also carry out assigned tasks without adult supervision better and are more likely to confess to failure and guilt.

Introjection is also important in conscience development. It is the psychological process of accepting the attitudes and values of authority figures. Children adopt their parents' values and expectations in order to avoid parental displeasure. They conform to the attitudes and rules of parents in order to avoid punishment or to win their favor. Early in life children learn what parents approve and disapprove. Out of this knowledge emerge their moral judgments and their moral behavior.

e. Peer group. During middler and junior years, the peer group takes on an increasingly important role. The society of children engenders deep emotional attachments. Because of the deep loyalties they evoke, same-sexed informal gangs and cliques exert a strong influence on children's behavior. The peer group to which children feel they belong is a much more significant factor in their moral behavior than are other groups or other considerations. Hartshorne and May[27] report that in tests measuring deception, children's scores showed a higher correlation when compared with those of friends in their homeroom at school than with friends in other rooms. These correlations were .66 and .23 respectively.

Moral behavior seems highly specific rather than generalized. Children in one group setting may exhibit a high level of honesty, helpfulness, and courtesy. In another setting they may not exhibit these traits nearly as well.

f. Bible and moral knowledge. Considerable research has been done in trying to discover the correlation between Bible knowledge and moral behavior.[28]

In secular education we have traditionally assumed that true knowledge would result in right behavior. In Christian education we have likewise assumed that the more biblical knowledge children possess, the higher will be the level of their moral behavior. Empirical studies on these issues have yielded disappointing results. Children in a controlled situation who scored high on tests of Bible knowledge also showed a higher level of moral behavior than others. However, their moral behavior was not much different from those with lower scores. Bible knowledge points the way to moral character—but more than knowledge is necessary to assure ethical ideals and right conduct.

g. Church and Sunday school attendance. Families that attend church and Sunday school regularly are more likely to have children who show high levels of moral behavior. But the high rate of Sunday school dropouts in teen years is evidence that attendance alone is not enough. We know that the influence of the home and family is primary in forming moral character. The church therefore offers ministries that assist the parents in the moral and spiritual development of children. We also know that the influence of the peer group is powerful; the church therefore seeks to provide significant peer groups through Sunday school classes and weekday activities.

III. METHODS

From the foregoing discussion, a few principles concerning methods to be used with elementary children become apparent.

---

27. Hugh Hartshorne and M. A. May, *Studies in Deceit* (New York: The Macmillan Co., 1928), cited by Cecil V. Millard, *Child Growth and Development in the Elementary School Years*, rev. ed. (Boston: D. C. Heath and Co., 1958), p. 343.

28. Several such studies are cited by Millard, *Child Growth*, pp. 339-42.

A. Suitability

The methods that are chosen should be selected on the basis of their suitability to the age and developmental level of the children. Objectives will be achieved to the degree that the methods are suited to the learners.

Teachers may find that their own personality and habits are also critical elements. Adults who work with children find that they cannot adopt uncritically someone else's method. We are, however, responsible to explore new methods, to try them out, and to develop skill in using those to which children usually respond most readily.

B. Variety

Many young adults are disenchanted with Christian education because as children their experiences lacked variety. There is no one best method that should be used every Sunday to present a lesson or during the week to conduct a Caravan session. Variety and change will add zest and interest to any program.

Elementary children can help adult leaders plan many of their own Christian education experiences. As children are involved, they will give the leader feedback on previous programs. They will also reveal the level of their own spiritual development, thus enabling adults to know how to relate to the children's vital interests.

C. Discovery and Experience

Teachers can enhance the learning of children when they see their roles as stimulators of the search for truth, rather than as fountainheads of wisdom. Children, especially juniors, dislike being talked down to. As Kagan[29] points out, elementary children should be trained in skills to discover answers, and be helped to find answers rather than always being given facts to remember.

During primary years children can be challenged to use their newly acquired skills in reading and writing. Later, they should do more than look up verses in the Bible and jot down obvious and routine answers. Middlers and juniors should be challenged to think about tough questions and to discuss the complex social and moral problems they meet in everyday life.

D. Creative Arts

One of the most productive methods of helping children to learn is

---

29. Kagan, *Understanding Children*, p. 51.

through the creative arts. As they prepare their own skits about contemporary life or dramatize Bible stories, they acquire vast amounts of knowledge as well as insights into practical Christianity. Why not let children write and produce a film of their own? Some super-8mm cameras are simple to operate and are readily available. In these creative activities children learn a great deal more than by merely reading and reciting in class.

IV. ADULT LEADERS

Adults who work with children play a critical role in their character development. Leaders should therefore be carefully selected.

Many of the traits necessary to successful teaching can be learned. Persons are not born as expert teachers; they perfect their gifts. Church leaders who find adequate adult leadership in short supply must develop and train those who are willing to engage in this rewarding work with children.

The primary requisite is a consistent Christian life and character. Social learning theory supports our intuitive hunch that adult models are the one most important factor in developing moral character. Above every other consideration, therefore, Christian education demands consistent, clear-cut Christian lives.

Adults who lead children must also understand them. They should be acquainted with the developmental sequences of childhood and thus be able to see the world through the eyes of children.

Because children are sensitive to adults, successful teachers must love children. They can tell when a teacher really cares for them or merely tolerates them. Equally important is good personal adjustment. Nervous, high-strung people create tensions in children. Nervous children added to nervous teachers results in poor learning environments.

Adult leaders also need to be energetic and imaginative. They should be creative in planning their programs, possess the initiative to carry out those plans, and have the sheer physical energy required to work with children.

Elementary children need adult leaders who have a sense of destiny and eternity. They need leaders who see each learning experience as crucial in building Christian character. When teachers see the inherent possibilities in children and eagerly seek to aid in their development, they overcome many handicaps in achieving their goals.

V. CONCLUSION

Children begin their school years with the necessary skills to be members of the children's society. At the end of the junior age, many will be physiologically and emotionally adolescents. Others will be on the edge of this critical period. Their Christian education experiences as children will enhance or weaken their desire to trust themselves to Christ. Our prayer is that all of the children whom we touch will find Christ and stay with the church. Not all will, but ours is the joyful privilege of praying and working to that end.

BIBLIOGRAPHY

Bolton, B. J., and Smith, C. T. *Bible Learning Activities.* Grades 1 to 6. Glendale, Calif.: Regal Books, 1973.

> This small book is filled with suggestions of ways teachers can help children learn the Bible by doing interesting learning activities. Most of the materials can be teacher-made.

Carpenter, R. D. *Why Can't I Learn?* Glendale, Calif.: Regal Books, 1972.

> Carpenter presents a total view of the cause, diagnosis, and treatment of learning disabilities among children. Parents and all educational specialists will find a variety of courses of action available to help the child with learning problems.

Cully, J. V. *Children in the Church.* Philadelphia: The Westminster Press, 1960.

> This book approaches Christian education of children from the viewpoint of the best in psychological, biblical, and theological thinking. The whole child is involved in learning about the Christian faith.

Joy, Donald M. *Meaningful Learning in the Church.* Winona Lake, Ind.: Light and Life Press, 1969.

> Joy's book is based on the premise that lay-volunteer teachers are the most potent educative force in the church. He presents concepts of teaching and learning that laymen can master and use in their teaching activities. The author explains complex concepts clearly and gives them practical applications.

Muller, Phillipe. *The Tasks of Childhood.* New York: McGraw-Hill Book Co., 1969.

> For teachers who do not want to read through a highly technical book about the development of children, this book is a straightforward description of developmental psychology.

Peck, Robert F., *et al. The Psychology of Character Development.* New York: John Wiley and Sons, Inc., 1960.

This book discusses the results of research on how character develops. It cites five stages of conscience development and shows the connection between parental child-rearing practices and character development. Implications for religious education are pointed out.

Sapp, P. W. *Creative Teaching in the Church School.* Nashville: Broadman Press, 1967.

The author draws on her own experience to explain things teachers can do to encourage children to become involved in the Sunday school lesson. Dramatization, creative art, language arts, music, and pupil involvement are explored.

CHAPTER 11

Christian Education
of Youth

This chapter concerns itself with the period of human development begun at puberty and extending to adulthood. It is a traumatic period for most persons because it is characterized by transition. These are the in-between years.

> The young adolescent's status in our modern society is vague and confused. At one time he is treated as a child, and when he acts like a child, he is reproved and told to "act his age." When he attempts to act like an adult, he is often accused of being "too big for his britches." This ambiguous status presents a dilemma for the teen-ager.[1]

A further evidence of ambiguity is the uncertainty that we adults experience in referring to youth. At times we call them "teens" or "teenagers"; sometimes, "youth"; frequently, "young men" and "young women." Adolescents themselves often refer to their peer group as "kids."

In our organizations for Christian education, this group includes junior highs, 12 to 14 years of age, and senior highs, 15 to 17. Junior highs usually represent grades 7 to 9 in public school; senior highs, grades 10 through 12. Young people 18 to 23 years of age are also sometimes included in the youth division. This is because psychologists recognize age 23 as the close of a period known as later adoles-

---

1. Elizabeth B. Hurlock, *Developmental Psychology*, 3rd ed. (New York: McGraw-Hill Book Co., 1968), p. 392.

cence. Today the trend is to class the 18 to 23 age-group as young adults.[2]

Youth are more easily categorized by school grades than by their psychological and developmental stages. They begin their transitional journey on a highly individualized schedule and progress through adolescence at different rates. Our organizational divisions are useful when working with groups, but we must always remember that a particular individual may or may not fit our general descriptions.

I. THE CHALLENGE

Of the various groups to which the church ministers, none poses more critical challenges nor faces more destiny-dictating choices than teens. Each age level has its unique array of alternatives and choices, but youth faces more critical issues in a shorter time span than does any other group. It is frightening to remember that these issues must be resolved by youth themselves; and many of them are unprepared to face the awesome tasks.

Another evidence of the teen challenge to the church is that these are the years of spiritual and moral decision. Three out of four drop out of church during adolescence. In recent years arrests for first offenses in this age span have risen sharply. In contrast, youth who stay with the church are evidence that these years are the most fruitful times for conversion. After age 21, the number of persons who are converted and join the church sharply declines. About one-half of persons in specialized Christian service felt their call during these teen years.[3]

Another facet of the teen dilemma is reflected in the questions they ask of themselves and of the world. This searching is reflected in some of their songs. The mood of youth is seeking, probing, searching. They are wrestling with five basic questions for which the church can help them find answers.

A. Who Am I?

This question reflects what Erickson describes as the identity crisis

---

2. A. F. Harper, *The Nazarene Sunday School in the 70's* (Kansas City: Beacon Hill Press of Kansas City, 1969), p. 159.

3. J. O. Percy, "Where Are the Recruits?" *Missions Annual, 1959* (Ridgefield Park, N.J.: International Foreign Missions Association, 1959), p. 33; Roy G. Irving and Roy B. Zuck, eds., *Youth and the Church* (Chicago: Moody Press, 1960), p. 18.

of youth in Western culture.[4] It is seen predominantly in complex, interdependent cultures in America. In these cultures the period of transition from childhood to adulthood is an arid, no-man's-land. Teens are neither children nor adults. There is no clear-cut ritual that unmistakably says to them, Now you are an adult with all of its rights and privileges. Primitive cultures do not leave youth in such a prolonged uncertainty. Puberty rites for girls usher them into marriageable status and household responsibilities. For boys, the initiation rites require a feat of courage or skill which, when completed, permits them to sit with the elders in council.

In contrast, our suburban society has few built-in identification-developing processes. How does a teenager who lives in a high-rise apartment find a contributing function in the family or society? It is hard to see emptying the wastepaper once a day as a really significant adult contribution!

The search for identity is reflected in the various styles of clothing worn by many youth. Long and shabby hair, together with casual, often bizarre clothing, reflects a rejection of adult values, but it may also reflect youth's search for themselves. Frequent changes in the teen's mode of dress unconsciously says to himself and to the world, "How do you like me now?"

B. What Is True?

Because of their developing intellectual powers teens attempt to examine the values and philosophies to which they have been previously exposed. They are internalizing their own systems of truth. Some see total rejection and activistic rebellion against their childhood training as the only way to achieve intellectual certainty.

The scientific climate of our modern world stimulates this testing of truth. From elementary school onward youth are constantly challenged to use the scientific method, to believe only those things that can be proved experimentally. This materialistic emphasis presents youth with a dilemma. They are intrigued by the objectivity of science but are also appalled by its ruthlessness and destructive power.

We need to help them learn that scientific facts are cold and impersonal; in themselves they do not lead to God. We must help them discover what we have learned—that the most important

---

4. E. N. Erikson, *Childhood and Society,* 2nd ed. (New York: W. W. Norton and Co., Inc., 1963), pp. 261 ff.

values of life and the foundations of Christian faith cannot be scientifically proved. As Tennyson said, "For nothing worth proving can be proven, nor yet disproven."[5]

C. What Will I Become?

What vocation can I follow that will give my life meaning? As technology has increased its development of electronic gadgets, the vocational options open to youth have increased significantly. At the same time, other occupations have diminished. Automation has created new jobs but at the same time has eliminated many of long standing. Youth face difficult choices as they try to match their abilities and interests with a job market that is changing constantly and whose future demands are difficult to foresee.

D. Whom Will I Marry?

A fourth question concerns the life partner. Shall I marry? If so, whom? The normal expectation is for young women to marry. Of those who do not date and marry, many become severely preoccupied with their self-concept and their sense of adequacy. Such young women become vulnerable to temptations to immorality, to illegitimate pregnancies, and to ill-advised marriages. In any case, they must face lifelong societal censoring—"Why aren't you married?" And they find themselves ostracized from many social groups.

Young men who remain single do not face quite as much social disapproval. However, modern society raises more questions about young men who live together than about young women in similar circumstances.

E. What Is to Be My Philosophy of Life?

During these critical years teens are confronted with choosing the value system upon which their total life structure will be built. As they advance through school experiences, they are exposed to the diverse values of their peer groups. As young persons mature intellectually, they compare the value systems of their peers with that of their family. But as adolescents they must do more than compare— they must decide which set of values is best for them. In the process of deciding, they question, rebel, or conform. Out of this painful process—painful both to youth and to the significant adults around

---

5. Alfred Lord Tennyson, "The Ancient Sage."

them—adolescents will shape their life philosophy. Some will accept Christ and the Christian view of life; others will turn away from Him.

Sensitive Christian educators are aware of these questions and of the consequences for human destiny that rest on how they are resolved. Careful planning for ministry to youth must be guided by this awareness.

II. TEEN CHARACTERISTICS

Leaders who minister to youth will plan their educational experiences in the context of youth's developmental characteristics. The aspects most relevant to the church's task are discussed here.

A. The Influence of Heredity and Environment

A teen brings to this stage of his development an accumulation of hereditary and environmental factors. Psychologists have long discussed the relative importance of these two. Obviously, both aspects of growth and development are influential. Heredity largely determines one's general physical characteristics, his intellectual potential, and his temperament. Environment provides the experiences and interactions through which persons develop their social, spiritual, and personality patterns.

We must not think of adolescence as a mere parenthetical interlude of development interjected between childhood and adult years. It is a continuation of personal inherited traits begun at conception and shaped by childhood environment. Adolescence, however, adds novel intellectual and physical dimensions to these earlier patterns.

One task for Christian leaders is to help youth escape the delusion of fatalism. Teens often think of their past experiences as wholly controlling their present behavior. Consequently they regard themselves as relieved of any personal responsibility for their behavior. They can justify to themselves, and hopefully to others, their unchristian and antisocial behavior because of what happened to them as children.

Actually, adolescence presents persons with a great opportunity to move from the dominance of their environmental past. As new intellectual powers are acquired, they open a young person's life to the transforming power of Christ which enables one to become his best self. Adolescence brings understandings that point the teen in the direction of becoming a Christ-centered, autonomous, fulfilled adult.

Jenkins writes:

> Our interest in the very real strains and adjustments involved have made us highlight the adolescent years, setting them apart from the rest of the growth process. As a result, the difficulties which children may have at this time have often been over dramatized and over-emphasized. . . . Rather than fearing them, we should consider carefully the role which we as adults can play in guiding young persons who are going through them, so they will be able to step with some confidence into their places in the adult world.[6]

B. Gonadal Maturation

Adolescence begins at puberty, which marks the beginning of the maturation of the sex glands. It is the most significant physiological change that happens to children after birth. Maturation of these glands starts the transitional process from childhood to adulthood. During this stage the individual begins the physiologically generated process of moving from an asexual individual to a sexual person.

Puberty is signaled by the beginning of the menstrual period in girls and by nocturnal emission in boys. About 50 percent of girls mature by age 13; 50 percent of boys by 14 or 15 years. The other 50 percent of both sexes mature during the next few years.

This process signals physical and psychological changes that profoundly affect the teen's behavior, self-concept, and social relationships. He does not understand himself. If Christian educators do not adequately understand him, they will not be able to provide effective leadership for him at this most critical period of his life.

1. *Increased Height and Weight*

Puberty is the result of the close relationship between the pituitary gland, located at the base of the brain, and the sex glands. The pituitary, triggered by the hypothalamus, stimulates the gonads to increased activity which results in the appearance of the primary and secondary sexual characteristics.

Because the pituitary gland also produces the growth hormone, it releases this hormone during puberty in greater amounts than previously. Consequently, pubescents often experience a growth spurt, a dramatic increase in height and weight. Their arms and legs

---

6. G. G. Jenkins, J. Shacter, and W. W. Bauer, *These Are Your Children,* exp. ed. (Chicago: Scott, Foresman and Co., 1953), p. 200.

grow faster than their skills of controlling them. As a result, adolescence is a period of clumsiness. Teens stumble over objects in plain view, drop dishes, or knock over glasses at the table—much to their own embarrassment and the consternation of their parents.

2. *Primary and Secondary Sex Characteristics*

Puberty initiates the development of characteristics closely related to sexual maturity. Primary characteristics involve the growth of sexual organs in each sex. For the female this growth is internal and invisible; for the male external and visible. Maturity of the reproductive apparatus makes procreation possible. From two to four years is required for persons to complete gonadal maturation and thus to be able to conceive life.

Secondary characteristics are those which identify a person as an adult male or female. The hair on the male's face coarsens and grows. His voice deepens as the vocal chords thicken. He is often embarrassed by the "cracking" of his voice (the sudden shift between the higher tones of the child and the lower adult tones). Boys' chests become more like adults'. Their heavy muscles increase in size and strength, and body proportions begin to assume those of an adult.

Girls evidence puberty by the first menstrual period, the menarche. As puberty progresses, their bodies become more feminine. Their breasts enlarge. The hips broaden and the whole body assumes more feminine contours.

3. *Common Adolescent Problems*

Both sexes begin to experience problems as a result of their moving from the asexuality of childhood to the sexuality of adolescence. Some of these problems are rooted in a hormonal imbalance. One of these problems is the increased activity of the oil glands, especially on the face. Adolescents are plagued with acne.

Another problem is mood swing. Teens shift from elation to sadness rapidly. For no apparent reason they sometimes burst into tears, then in a short time may be elated.

Adolescents are also confronted with the problem of accepting the body as it is. On the one hand, they must learn to accept their sex. They must adjust to being a male or female, with all of the demands that our culture associates with it. Also they must accept their size, appearance, and proportions. Because adolescent bodies develop so rapidly, this adjustment often assumes a high priority for teens. If they make the adjustment and learn to live with themselves, they will solve the identity crisis much easier than if they do not.

In the midst of rapid physical growth teens often become very sensitive about their bodies. Some take pride in self-display—boys going shirtless, girls wearing tight sweaters and short skirts. Most of them develop intense feelings over real or imagined inferiorities of appearance. They are very sensitive to criticism about their appearance or skills; derogatory remarks wound them deeply.

During these years, parents and youth leaders should be unusually sensitive to this developmental crisis. Most evaluative remarks about an adolescent's behavior, dress code, or physical appearance should be supportive. Adverse comments, direct or implied, should be carefully worded and couched in kindness rather than in harsh rebuke.

C. Brain Maturation

Along with sexual changes, adolescents are profoundly influenced by a less obvious growth and development in the cerebral cortex. This gray mass of billions of cells lies just beneath the skull. It is involved in the higher types of cognitive activity related to conceptual thinking. Until it is mature, the person cannot assimilate highly abstract ideas, such as truth or beauty. Prior to puberty this part of the human brain is immature, but in early teen years it begins to ripen and will be quite mature by middle adolescence.

Jean Piaget[7] called this level in cognitive development the stage of "formal operations." It is the level at which a person can deal with hypotheses.

Ausubel points out:

> Beginning with the adolescent period children become increasingly less dependent upon the availability of concrete-empirical experience in meaningfully relating complex abstract propositions to cognitive structure. Eventually, after sufficient gradual change in this direction, a qualitatively new capacity emerges: the intellectually mature individual becomes capable of understanding and manipulating relationships between abstractions *directly*, that is, without any reference whatever to concrete, empirical reality. . . . Since his logical operations are performed

---

7. Jean Piaget, "The Stages of the Intellectual Development of the Child," Paul H. Mussen, et al., *Readings in Child Development and Personality*, 2nd ed. (New York: Harper and Row, Publishers, 1965), pp. 291-98.

on verbal propositions, he can go beyond the operations that follow immediately from empirical reality . . . and deal with all possible or hypothetical relations between ideas.[8]

This development of the mind provides the basis for understanding several adolescent characteristics: their high idealism, their rebellion, their questioning of traditional values, and their openness to conversion. Prior to this time they accept adult expectations and generally conform to parental and societal values. With their newly developed powers of abstract conceptual thinking, they test, question, and internalize their own value system.

All of these physical developments have a direct influence on the emotional, social, and psychological behavior of adolescents. Youth leaders and others who have frequent contacts with young people will be effective to the degree that they understand these factors. A failure to understand will often cause us to miss the implications of a teenager's actions.

The ease with which this can happen is readily seen in the following statement:

> In order to cope with . . . conflicts, the adolescent must create a device which keeps him from being hurt and from hurting himself. . . . The easiest thing for him to do is to build a wall. This can be done by maintaining a high level of cynicism or sarcasm all the time, or by pretending not to care or to take anything seriously. Anything that puts the adolescent at a distance from people also protects him from losing control, or from dependence on others. . . . He can create another wall by becoming preoccupied in being "hopelessly messed up." This draws the attention of others (which he needs to keep from becoming lonely) and protects him from having to come out of himself or forget about himself.
>
> By having a wall, the adolescent is exercising a tight control over himself. He cannot easily forget himself or get involved in someone or something else. . . . The safe distance between himself and others is too safe. His isolation leads to loneliness, when he finds himself much farther away than he need be.[9]

In summary, youth is a period of highly significant physiological changes. These changes are accompanied by emotional instability ranging from withdrawal to vocal hostility, and from depression to

---

8. D. P. Ausubel and P. Ausubel, "Cognitive Development in Adolescence," *Readings in Adolescent Psychology*, ed. by M. Powell and A. H. Frerichs (Minneapolis: Burgess Publishing Co., 1971), pp. 62-63.

9. Tina DeVaron, "Growing Up," *Twelve to Sixteen: Early Adolescence*, J. Kagan and R. Coles, eds. (New York: W. W. Norton and Co., Inc., 1972), p. 345.

elation. Adolescents rebel against rules but are dismayed by their absence. Childishness is repudiated but often displayed.

III. Implications for Church Leaders

All of these changes have a bearing on our tasks in Christian education. Teens do not bring their souls to church and leave their bodies and minds at home. They are whole persons who respond in the totality of their being.

A. New Social and Emotional Experiences

Adolescents turn increasingly to peers to discuss their problems. By the time they become seniors in high school, they talk over their concerns with parents much less frequently than before. Also, because teens lack personal skills to handle developmental conflicts, the peer group assumes a more significant role in their lives. Among peers they find an understanding of their own confusions and a support in their searching which they feel most adults do not give. The peer group reinforces their self-concept and accepts them. In the group they feel able to make a worthwhile contribution, and they learn how to function as participating members. Also among peers they feel freer to experiment with various roles and identities to find the one that satisfies them most.

Thus, as adolescents search for economic, social, and emotional independence, they find security in the peer group. Even though they wish less parental authority, they feel insecure without some structure. This structure they feel and accept in the rigid control of the teen group. Peers thus serve the basic function of providing emotional and social support.

B. Critical Resultant Problems

Pastors and youth leaders who wish to successfully minister to youth will be sensitive to their problems. They will seek to plan programs that assist in resolving their concerns. Some may require only a minimum of information in a group discussion—helping youth to understand themselves better. Others will need personal counseling. Some problems require programs of Christian peer-group activities.

1. *Emotional Shifts*

For no apparent reason adolescents move rapidly from periods of depression to delight, from doubt to idealism. Such emotional reverses are both a boon and a bane. In youth meetings the group can move rapidly from peaks of hilarity and humor to periods of soul-searching solemnity and worship. Skillful youth leaders plan group activities that provide for such changes and use this teen characteristic to advantage.

On the other hand, the individual teen may be moody without apparent cause. The observant youth leader will not pass off such emotional changes as unimportant. Rather he will recognize them and try to assist the teen to understand himself better. Too frequent extremes in either direction are ominous, as are sustained periods of depression or elation. In such cases professional counselling may be necessary.

2. *Sexual Feelings*

Curiosity and the desire for novel experiences link up with the sex drive in youth to make this a critical problem area. Society, the church, and the Bible surround sexual behavior with strong regulations. In late teens when young men experience their most intense drive, they are not permitted sexual expression. Thus, Christian young men are faced with the challenge of finding ways to redirect their energy into approved avenues.

While girls do not usually experience sexual feelings in such direct ways as boys, they do experience warm feelings of tenderness, love, and sympathy. If girls do not date, or rarely do so in high school and college years, they develop inferiority feelings and negative self-esteem. Because of the American dating and courting patterns, these feelings vitally affect a teen's sense of adequacy, acceptance, and security.

In both boys and girls sexual drives can become powerful weapons of rebellion. In what other way can rebellious adolescents hurt their parents and the church more than by immoral behavior? Obviously such conduct hurts the offender most, but the adolescent in confused rebellion cannot see that far ahead.

We live in a society obsessed with sex. Public portrayal of sexually deviant behavior and the availability of pornography indicates the lowering of moral controls in society. In an overpermissive society Christian leaders must seek ways to help youth accept and internalize the biblical code of moral purity. At the same time we must help teens to understand sex as one of our most precious God-given drives.

3. *Developmental Concerns*

One basic fact of human development is the wide range of individual patterns and timetables. We know the average age for a certain characteristic to appear, but no one can forecast precisely when Johnny or Susie will demonstrate that trait. In adolescence, deviation from the average timetable often concerns the individual, especially in his social relationships.

Early developing girls usually date much earlier than do later developing girls. Late developing girls, however, are regarded by the boys as being prettier, and are more often selected for leadership roles based on popularity elections such as homecoming queens and cheerleaders.

Among boys, early developing fellows also date earlier than late developing boys. But, in addition, the early developing fellows may exhibit leadership qualities, group popularity, and stardom in athletic contests. Some late developing fellows are retiring, shy, and socially immature.

Early developing girls and late developing boys are more likely to have emotional problems, to be overly concerned with acceptance by others, and to suffer from serious questions about their self-image. A few of the girls may try to use sexual promiscuity to prove they are whole, capable, and attractive persons. Boys may try to compensate by being Don Juans. Such adolescents need sensitive support during these critical years until adulthood lessens the divergence and impact of the developmental pattern.[10]

Related to these differences is the fact that girls are, on the average, about two years more advanced in their social and emotional interests than are boys. Twelve-year-old girls may have more in common with 14-year-old boys than with 12-year-old boys. Programs that are too rigidly structured by age groupings may therefore prove incompatible with the needs and interests of the teens.

Another factor affecting ministries in Christian education is the earlier age of maturation that has occurred in the past half century.

> The sequence of the biological events remains the same. But there has been one considerable change; the events occur now at an earlier age than formerly. Forty years ago the average British girl had her first menstrual period (menarche) at about her fifteenth birthday; nowadays it is shortly before her thirteenth.[11]

To the degree that these figures apply to all of Western culture,

---

10. Hurlock, *Developmental Psychology*, pp. 367-71.//
11. J. M. Tanner, "Sequence, Tempo, and Individual Variation in Growth and Development of Boys and Girls Aged Twelve to Sixteen," *Twelve to Sixteen, Early Adolescence*, J. Kagan and R. Coles, eds..

and assuming that they suggest similar changes in males, they are of vital importance to Christian education. First, the curriculum of Christian education has traditionally been geared for the later development of youth. Consequently we need to be sure that the social and emotional level of our ministries is in step with the development of modern adolescents.

Second, today's youth have stronger heterosexual interests at an earlier age than many adults realize. As a result, pastors and youth leaders need to approach the area of sex with a candor that is understood and appreciated by today's adolescent. The church cannot afford to neglect its responsibility to counteract the immoral permissive input of today's society. This is best done by stressing biblical principles of morality and chastity. Specific biological information given by the church may be superfluous for most youth. But the stewardship of sex and its blessing when channelled according to God's plan is a major contribution that Christian education can make to youth.

4. *Ambivalence Toward Authority*

On the one hand, youth proclaim that they want to be free. They resist the authority of parents, society, institutions, and traditions. On the other hand, they are unhappy and feel unloved if no one sets down definite guidelines for them. Some rules, democratically established, provide teens with a sense of security and a feeling of being loved. Total freedom in a period of identity uncertainty and value internalization may result in too much uncertainty.

Wise youth leaders will provide some guidelines in consultation with the teens themselves. Violation of these expectations will be consistently and impartially handled. What better way to teach youth the bipolar concepts of justice and mercy than by insisting that they assume personal responsibility for their deeds?

5. *Intellectual Changes*

Adolescence brings with it a whole new range of intellectual processes that were not previously possible. Most children think concretely. Adolescents can think propositionally. Principles of law and morality are now more readily understood and handled.

This means that youth are capable of moving from legalistic interpretation of Christian rules toward an understanding of the principles behind them. They are capable of applying basic principles to different social situations and moral dilemmas which previously they could not do.

Pastors and youth leaders see in this enlargement of propositional thinking an opportunity to promote the internalization of the principles of Christian living. Such guidance is most effective when it uses the teen's questioning mood. Leaders who dogmatically lay it on the line—to be accepted or rejected—will probably find it rejected most of the time. Those who skillfully help youth explore the behavior alternatives and their consequences in the light of Christian revelation will help teens acquire a dependable value system.

IV. The Aims of Youth Work

Developing a set of overall objectives for youth work is a complex task. Such objectives are a sincere attempt to express the Christian faith and life in terms of their meaning for youth. Several examples are given for consideration. Each is worded differently, but a careful exploration of any one of the three will point the way to significant youth ministries.

The objective of Christian education for senior high young people is stated below (1); then three corollary educational principles (2, 3, 4) are given.

(1) The objective of Christian education is to help persons to be aware of God's self-disclosure and seeking love in Jesus Christ and to respond in faith and love—to the end that they may know who they are and what their human situation means, grow as sons of God rooted in the Christian Community, live in the Spirit of God in every relationship, fulfill their common discipleship in the world, and abide in the Christian hope.

(2) Christian education takes place in a setting that has natural, human, historical, and divine dimensions.

(3) Christian education engages the person in certain learning tasks.

(4) The individual bears a responsibility for engaging himself in these learning tasks.[12]

One evangelical denomination states its goals for youth work thus:

---

12. Adapted from Marvin J. Taylor, ed., *Religious Education* (New York: Abingdon Press, 1960), p. 125, citing "The Objective of Christian Education for Senior High Young People" (National Council of Churches, 1958).

The purpose of NYI shall be to build up its members in Christian faith and in holy character and to instruct them in the Word of God and in the doctrines of the church. It shall also be the purpose of NYI to bring others to Christ and to provide ways for equipping youth for the total mission of the church.[13]

The writer suggests that the goals of youth ministries are to:

1. Lead into a definite experience of salvation and entire sanctification.
2. Provide opportunities for the development of heterosexual skills in a Christian context.
3. Examine the basic tenets of the Christian faith in a constructive manner.
4. Assist in vocational choices consistent with Christian commitment.
5. Counsel youth who have problems.
6. Interpret the ethical implications of the gospel.
7. Develop skills of churchmanship.
8. Create Christian peer groups.

The development of suitable aims for youth ministry is especially difficult in the rapid change of our society. As worthy as the above statements are, the question is still valid, What kind of adaptations will be necessary in our society in 1990, or in 2000? Those generations of teens are now small children, or they are yet unborn. What patterns of education will be effective in promoting Christian maturity in a space-age, computer-based society?

The current situation is rapidly changing, and the future promises little abatement in technological, social, and economic shifts. The Christian education of youth in the past has been interested in helping teens become effective Christians in their world. The goal has not changed, but today's demands increase the necessity for Christian teaching skills to a greater degree than ever before.

In his assessment of the impact of technological and social changes on the educational strategy of the future, Jerome S. Bruner arrives at four general policies.

It would seem . . . that principal emphasis in education should be placed upon skills—skills in handling, in seeing and imagining; and in symbolic operations.

---

13. Constitution and Bylaws, Nazarene Youth International (Kansas City: General NYI Office, 1976-80 edition).

A curriculum should involve the mastery of skills that in turn lead to the mastery of still more powerful ones, the establishment of self-reward sequences.

If there is any way of adjusting to change, it must include . . . a metalanguage and "metaskills" for dealing with continuity in change.

Finally . . . we shall have to bring far greater resources to bear in designing our educational system.[14]

While Bruner was pointing his remarks to public education, he suggests a direction for Christian teaching. The best youth ministries will achieve these aims: (1) the review, acquisition, and use of new information, (2) the development of the skills essential to effective Christian living, and (3) guidelines for Christian stability in a world of change.

V. The Life Skills

In any kind of world, if youth are to be effective Christians, they need to have a solid spiritual base from which to operate. This base includes a certainty concerning their relationship with Christ. Teens must be led into a vital experience of conversion and a meaningful experience of entire sanctification. Some will come into these crisis experiences during their childhood years; more will come to know Christ as teenagers. The whole ministry of the church is built around these life-changing experiences. For those who do not yet know Christ, we try to bring them to Him. For those who have found Him, we seek to expand and enrich their life in Christ.

Two key factors in successful youth ministry are being increasingly recognized today. First, the youth fellowship must become a significant peer group. Its ministry must center around involving and nurturing teens in Christian experiences. A youth group becomes a peer group when it employs the processes of frequent gatherings for well-defined purposes and uses the techniques of unique identity, such as having a name or wearing a label. It becomes the young person's own peer group when he exhibits loyalty to the group and desires to participate.

Second, the significant adults of the church must be models for the teens to observe. Young people need live, authentic, and consistent incarnations of biblical experiences of grace. These models

---

14. Jerome S. Bruner, *Toward a Theory of Instruction* (New York: W. W. Norton and Co., Inc., 1966), pp. 34-37.

include pastor, youth leader, parents, adult friends—the more the better. Our doctrine may be sound, but if youth see inconsistencies or rigid, unloving attitudes in us adults who profess these experiences, they become disillusioned and distrustful of the whole system. Youth who have screamed about the adult population as phonies may have overcompensated. Their cries, however, certainly remind us that teens are searching for models who act consistently with their words.

After we have provided a supportive teen fellowship and worthy adult model, what skills do youth need to become effective Christians in a changing world? What skills are basic for today? And for the future?

A. Meaningful Bible Study

Youth succeed in the Christian life to the degree that they understand the principles of the Bible and apply those always-relevant truths to their lives. When they lack this skill, they see Bible study as useless and dull. When they acquire these skills, Bible exploration becomes an exciting discovery.

One of the hurdles to be cleared is that the language of the Bible ranges from clear, forthright statements, such as the Ten Commandments, to highly symbolic, poetic passages, like the 23rd psalm.

The specific directions and commandments of the Bible are easy enough to understand, but transfer of training into life must be taught. The youth group can look intently at a commandment, such as, "Thou shalt not steal." They can discuss the reasons why stealing is detrimental to group life, then ask, What happens to us when personal property is not respected? They can explore the emotional effects of losing a cherished possession.

A drama written by the group or a movie produced with 8mm film would make the effects of honesty and dishonesty more vivid and real to them. Obviously such an intensive study cannot be completed in a 40-minute Sunday school lesson. However, if teens choose the topic, plan the method of approach, and become actively involved in carrying out such a project, they will concentrate their activities for several weeks on this one item. A final public presentation and a group evaluation are essential elements of such a learning experience.

The poetic passages of the Bible are more difficult because the imagery and symbolism are drawn from an ancient society. Sometimes parallels in today's urban life are more difficult to see. However, the search for meaning in the poetic passages can also be exciting and rewarding. Teens can be asked to write their own versions of such passages. Together teens and teacher can discuss their efforts, distill the eternal principles from the passage, and relate those truths to their own life situations.

When Bible study is approached creatively in this manner, it comes alive. Teens discover the values of cooperation, research, evaluation, and the applications of knowledge that are so essential to a Christian's witness in the modern world. The Bible becomes a guide to life and a useful tool; it is seen as more than an authoritative set of rules. When teens find the Bible applicable to modern life, they have discovered a source of stability even in the relativistic morals of our times.

B. Internalization of Controls

Teens face the critical task of moving from dependence upon outside forces toward inner controls of behavior. This movement is slow, but it is essential if young people are to become autonomous Christian adults—persons who dare to follow a distinctive life-style in a hostile world.

This skill becomes increasingly important as society becomes permissive to a greater degree than ever before in its history. When the forces of public immorality become more brazen, Christians must be more vocal and more aggressive in proclaiming Christ. Today's social trends reveal that passive Christian witness is rapidly becoming less meaningful. Tomorrow's Christian youth will be compelled to identify himself openly as Christ's follower.

The internalization of controls is necessary if teens are to base their ethical decisions on something other than common practice and popularity. Christian life can be lived effectively only on the level of total obedience to God's will. Our Christian education must be sensitive to the need for this commitment and seek to help young people develop it.

1. *A Personal Value System*

Internalizing Christian controls is directly dependent upon the teen's development of a personal value system. In this he is aided by his growing ability to do abstract thinking. Youth cannot become internally controlled until they have made their own decision about what is most important in life. A teen's value system may be incomplete but some foundations are necessary. He must have committed himself to Christ, to basic Bible teachings, and to the principles of

Christian morality. However, along with this commitment, the process of questioning the reasons for rules and codes of conduct must go on. When teens ask the reasons for adult restrictions and do not accept mere assertions as sufficient answers, they are working at internalizing their values.

2. An Adequate Self-concept

To the degree that the young person sees himself as an adequate, accepted person, he will achieve internal control. A recent study indicates that the more a person believes he can control his own behavior and destiny, the more he is likely to be a nonsmoker, able to quit smoking, influence others to change their minds, resist hidden manipulation, and become engaged in activities he believes will change society.[15]

3. Group Interaction

Open, honest group interaction under the guidance of an adult leader who has maturity and confidence in the Christian life is an important factor in developing inner controls. As youth interact with each other and as the leader provides balance, stimulates discussion, and raises critical issues, teens mature in their thinking. Under these conditions, they have a better opportunity to develop a life philosophy and value system that will be consistent with the Christian gospel.

Pastors and youth leaders will depend heavily upon group discussions to stimulate this growth. Many group methods can be helpfully used—debates, panels, and committee reports. All result in teens asking questions, expressing opinions, and evaluating various points of view.

Especially important in establishing inner controls are the personal qualifications of the youth leader. He must himself be a model of the consistent, mature Christian. The adult who is rigid, defensive, or critical will have little success. Rather the youth leader must win the confidence of teens by being approachable, and he must know how to communicate verbally and emotionally with young people. He must stand for what he believes but allow the developmental processes of maturing youth to proceed under loving guidance.

---

15. Julian B. Rotter, "External Control and Internal Control," *Psychology Today*, vol. 5, no. 1 (June, 1971), pp. 37 ff.

C. Improvement in Reality Testing

Reality testing means to think through a situation carefully before passing judgment. It subjects a situation to testing and searching before action is taken. An example would be how one might react if he saw his youth leader emerging from a bar. The snap judgment would be to express disbelief, to lose confidence in him, and to spread mischievous rumors about him. The person who had developed the skill of reality testing, however, would first ask what reasons other than patronizing the bar might have prompted this person to be there. Was he searching for an alcoholic friend whose wife had asked him to look for her husband? Did he have some business with the proprietor? The reality tester would withhold judgment until he had been able to talk with the person involved and discover the facts.

Another example would be a young person who was pressured to do something neither quite right nor clearly wrong. If he refused, he would be subjected to a great deal of unfavorable peer ridicule; if he went along with the group, he would suffer adult criticism. The young person trained to test reality would refrain from doing anything until he had thought through the situation in the light of biblical principles. Only when he was convinced of what Christ wanted him to do would he act.

Psychologists regard the ability to test reality especially important in efficient functioning of the human personality and in achieving mental health. To the degree that an individual is able to test the reality of a situation he will be freed from impulsive behavior and acceptance of propaganda.

Again, group discussion techniques plus information-gathering procedures are useful in developing this skill. Use of church libraries and resource persons can provide pertinent information on the problems youth face.

Also, creative activities such as short skits enable teens to explore the alternative outcomes and make teaching more effective. Role playing enables youth to see the multifaceted aspects of another person's behavior. They are then better equipped to subject their own decisions to reality testing.

D. Increase in Self-understanding

A basic life skill necessary for successful Christian living is to keep in close touch with one's real self. Persons who are alienated from themselves are not able to assume responsibility for their actions.[16] They tend to be impulsive. A wider than normal discrepancy exists between their ideas and their actions. On the other hand, a greater awareness of their own feelings and motives increases the likelihood that teens will behave in ways that are authentic. Their public image will be less camouflaged from their real selves.

One goal of Christian education is to help teens develop an authentic Christian witness. The young people themselves have high ideals in this regard, and many of their spiritual defeats arise from the inability to fulfill their lofty ideals. As we help them to verbalize their feelings and to keep in closer touch with their real selves, they will become more genuine and better adjusted Christian persons.

Sometimes the process of developing real self-understanding involves honestly disclosing oneself to another.

> It may seem paradoxical, but one comes best to know one's real self, and to be able to introspect honestly, as a consequence of unselected, spontaneous disclosure of the self to another person. The individual who has a trusted friend or relative to whom he can express his thoughts, feelings, and opinions honestly is in a better position to learn his real self than the one who has never undergone this experience, because as he reveals himself to another, he is also revealing himself *to himself.*[17]

The psychological values of honest self-disclosure are not new to Christian practice. One of the benefits of prayer, especially for conversion and entire sanctification, is honest confession. Teens need quiet moments of self-searching and prayer when they talk honestly to God about themselves. It may be at the end of a class session, at the close of a social evening, or around the fire at camp. Whenever self-disclosure occurs, it will be most effective when it is the natural outcome of the group's activity.

The pastor or youth leader can often fulfill the role of the significant, helping other person. Youth typically turn to persons outside of the home for guidance and support. Therefore, youth leaders who cultivate warm confidence and an accepting relationship with their group will be in a better position to encourage the self-disclosure process.

Some youth groups find it helpful to plan times of openly and

---

16. Karen Horney, *Neurosis and Human Growth* (New York: Norton, 1950) cited in Sidney M. Jourard, *Personal Adjustment,* 2nd ed. (New York: The Macmillan Co., 1963), pp. 158 ff.

17. Jourard, *Personal Adjustment,* p. 160.

honestly sharing their feelings. Christian groups would avoid the negative, critical "confrontation encounter." Rather they would express sincere appreciation for what Christ has done for them, and for what other members of the group mean to them. Perhaps such self-disclosure times may lead to humble confessions of negligence or wrong feelings toward others. The Bible urges us: "Confess your faults one to another, and pray one for another, that ye may be healed" (Jas. 5:16).

VI. SUMMARY

The Christian education of youth is especially critical in today's increasingly secular society. Adults who love teens and who are adept at using youth's unique developmental experiences are needed as Sunday school teachers and youth group leaders. Ideally, such leaders combine zeal, skill, and commitment. Today's youth will become tomorrow's adults no matter who guides them. But Christian leaders offer the best possible climate for them to become devoted, witnessing Christian adults!

BIBLIOGRAPHY

Erb, E. D., and Hooker, D. *The Psychology of the Emerging Self.* Philadelphia: F. A. Davis Co., n.d.

> Psychology with its principles of mental health are interpreted and applied to the development of a fuller functioning, happier self.

Gesell, A.; Ilg, F. L.; and Ames, L. B. *Youth: The Years from Ten to Sixteen.* New York: Harper and Bros., 1956.

> This book is a companion volume to the one by Gesell *et al.* on childhood. It is a definitive analysis of human growth and development. Rather than reading it in its entirety, one should use it as a reference book for special aspects of youth development.

Irving, Roy G., and Zuck, Roy B. *Youth and the Church.* Chicago: Moody Press, 1968.

> A survey of the church's ministry to youth from the perspective of evangelical leaders working with youth in evangelical churches.

Powell, M., and Frerichs, A. H., eds. *Readings in Adolescent Psychology.* Minneapolis: Burgess Publishing Co., 1971.

> A collection of essays which reports research on adolescents in today's society. The self-image, value formation, and attitudes toward today's culture are explored.

Richards, L. O. *Youth Ministry.* Grand Rapids, Mich.: Zondervan Publishing House, 1972.

A practical guide to working with youth in the local church. It is aimed for the youth minister, sponsor, or leader; tries to help Christians understand the effects of the culture of the 1970s and how to work with youth who are a part of that culture.

Stone, L. J., and Church, J. *Childhood and Adolescence.* 2nd ed. New York: Random House, 1968.

The authors are well known in their field. They have tried to compile all the facts they feel are important for understanding adolescents in today's school situation.

Strommen, M. P. *Research on Religious Development.* New York: Hawthorn Books, 1971.

A comprehensive study of the developmental factors involved in the religious experience and maturation of individuals. The book is the report of a cooperative effort within the Religious Education Association.

CHAPTER 12

Christian Education
of Adults

Until recently little research has been conducted on adulthood. Several reasons account for this lack of interest. For one thing, children were more exciting to observe because they change rapidly. Observing them was so intriguing that psychologists expended enormous efforts to expand our knowledge of child development. Another reason was the importance of childhood adjustments for improved adult personality. Psychologists felt that persons would avoid many adjustment problems in later life if corrective techniques of child training could be instituted early enough. Lastly, adults seemed so homogeneous and slow paced developmentally that they did not attract much attention.

Recently, however, several factors have aroused researchers' interest. One of the most important is the rapid increase in the number of older persons. In 1976, every day in the United States 5,000 more persons reached 65 years of age. The total population above 65 was nearly 23 million![1] Between the years 1850 and 1940, the average life expectancy of an American citizen increased 9.2 years. During the next 14 years, the life expectancy had jumped a dramatic 20.4 years.[2]

---

1. United States Census Bureau, 1977.
2. Elizabeth B. Hurlock, *Developmental Psychology,* 3rd ed. (New York: McGraw-Hill Book Co., 1968), p. 778.

At present a vast amount of information is being accumulated as researchers focus on elderly persons and the aging process. Greater interest is also being shown in young adulthood, with its strains and stresses. In the church, special plans are being developed for the young adult, and special ministries for the aging.

I. CLASSIFYING ADULTS

There are few valid chronological classifications in adulthood, although Christian educators usually think in terms of three major divisions: young adults, middle adults, and senior adults.

Early adulthood begins at the end of adolescence when the average person is socially mature and vocationally equipped to assume the responsibilities of marriage, family, and independent existence. An adult, therefore, is an individual who has completed his growth and is ready for his place in society with other adults.

Usually an individual reaches this age legally and experientially at about the same time. In the United States and in other countries the legal age for voting is 18.

Young adulthood closes at about age 40. At this age, if the individual married in his early twenties, he has adolescent children who are themselves about to become young adults. This experience brings adjustments that are new to the 40-year-old person. Thus he becomes a middle-aged adult.

Middle age extends from about age 40 to 65. During these years, important family, vocational, and physiological changes occur which are critical factors in social and emotional adjustment. How successfully the adult handles these crises will vitally affect his adjustment to the later years of life.

Older adulthood is the last period of life. We date it rather arbitrarily at 65, and it extends until death. Age 65 has been chosen because in most jobs retirement is mandatory at that birthday. Of greater importance is the aging process that brings on degeneration of the brain and body. Not all persons experience a sharp decline of physical powers precisely at this age. However, noticeable declines are universally observable.

In this chapter we will follow the generally accepted classifications. These age limits, however, are not to be regarded as rigidly applying to all individuals. Persons age psychologically, emotionally, socially, and physiologically at their own rate and to their own degree. Chronological age is the least significant factor even though it is the easiest to handle.

II. YOUNG ADULTS

A. Characteristics

One of the first issues of young adulthood is determining when an individual is no longer an adolescent and should be considered an adult. The distinction is subtle and involves more than the number of birthdays he has celebrated. In recent years the criteria for defining adulthood have changed. This has happened because the average age of marriage has dropped, one may serve in the military at 18, and he begins voting at the same age.

Wright suggests that the criteria of adulthood include age, maturity, occupation, interests, and social role.[3] He divides young adulthood into two categories, college age and young adult. The college age includes youth who have finished high school and are either going to college or are working at a job. Most are single. Young adults include those who have married, are establishing a family, and are getting started in a vocation. Each group has its unique needs and interests that must be considered in structuring an effective Christian education program.

Hurlock[4] describes young adulthood as the "reproductive age," the "settling-down age," the "problem age," and the "period of emotional tension." These are the reproductive years because in this period most adults begin their families and conclude child-bearing before the era is over. Young adulthood is the time of settling down because family responsibilities, vocational endeavors, and financial involvements occupy so much of one's time and energy. One must channel his energy into fewer activities than in teen years if he expects to achieve success.

For the young adult this is a problem age because now, for the first time without parental guidance, he must face his problems, solve his conflicts, and experience the results of his own decisions. If he has had previous experience in decision making, he is better equipped to handle life's problems than if he has not had that training. In either case the consequences of his decisions are his own.

---

3. H. Norman Wright, *Ways to Help Them Learn: Adults* (Glendale, Calif.: International Center of Learning, 1971), pp. 4-5.
4. Hurlock, *Developmental Psychology*, pp. 530-34.

Young adults often live under great emotional strain. Hurlock writes:

> In early adulthood, the individual is faced with more adjustment problems than he has ever had to face before, even more than during the early years of adolescence, and he is less well equipped to deal with these adjustment problems than he will be later.[5]

Among the causes of his worry are money, personal appearance, health, and vocational success. The anxiety generated by these concerns pervades all of his social relationships. And the young adult has a right to be concerned because his achievement in each of these areas will affect his adjustment in middle life and on into old age.

Erikson[6] characterizes young adulthood as the stage of intimacy vs. isolation. He sees these years as the time for committing oneself to another individual in emotional intimacy, learning to live with a marriage partner, starting a family, rearing children, managing a home, getting started in an occupation, taking on civic responsibility, and finding a congenial social group.

Christian ministries to these young adults should be structured around their developmental tasks. We must help them to undertake these tasks in the light of the gospel. Our overall goal will be to help young adults meet their challenges in a Christian manner, so that they become true disciples of Christ in the 20th century.

B. Assets

Young adults have many assets to offset their tensions and adjustment problems. Prior to this era they are developing physically and intellectually; later, in middle adulthood, they begin to decline in physical powers and reach a plateau in intellectual development. But in young adult years they are in the age of prime physical and intellectual abilities.

1. *Physical*

During the decade of 22 to 32 years, men achieve their peak development. They have the necessary physical skill to meet emergencies. Many professional athletes reach their prime in the twenties. The young adult learns new skills easily because of efficient reaction times and ease of learning.

This physical skill is important in vocational and social adjust-

5. *Ibid.*, p. 532.
6. Erik H. Erikson, *Childhood and Society*, 2nd ed. (New York: W. W. Norton and Co., 1963), pp. 263-66.

ments. Because the young adult can learn new job skills, he has greater vocational mobility. Consequently he has more opportunities to seek a different job should he become discontented. He can move around until he finds a job that pleases him. This job satisfaction is important in family relationships because incompatible work can mar family harmony.

2. *Intellectual*

Studies indicate that adults reach the peak of their intellectual capacities in the mid-twenties.

> The important mental abilities needed for learning and for adjustment to new situations, such abilities, for example, as forming comparisons, reasoning by analogy, recall of previously learned information, and creative imagination reach their peak during the twenties and then begin a slow and gradual decline.[7]

Thus young adults reach the peak of intellectual development at a time that is most important for adjustment to novel situations. While the ability to memorize may decline somewhat, it is not enough to seriously impede learning. These are fruitful years to challenge the young adult with new areas of Christian service, and to help him acquire new skills in Christian ministry.

3. *Achievement*

Late in the young adult years persons reach the peak of their achievement—between 30 and 39. It is then they produce their best work. However, success may require so great an investment of time and energy that young adults neglect their commitments to Christ. Pastors and lay leaders need to keep the challenge of Christian ministry before these young people. At the same time there must be enough innovation and flexibility that young adults can be active in ministry while advancing in their chosen vocations.

C. Problems

Young adults encounter their own unique stresses. Family adjustments that involve the marriage partner and children exact their toll of anxiety. Enlarging families require more living space, more furniture, more health care, and more food. With added expenses comes the pressure to work more to earn more.

1. *Financial*

Financial stability may be achieved by the wife and husband

---

7. Hurlock, *Developmental Psychology,* p. 537.

both working, by the husband working longer hours, or by the husband moving up the economic ladder through promotion. Each solution brings its own toll of added stress. When both parents work, the children see less of them, and parents are tired when they come home. Irritability increases between them and the children; the harmony of family relationships may become strained.

Should the husband moonlight, he has less time and energy to invest in the family. He cannot help manage the home or take the children on outings. His wife feels neglected and the emotional intimacy between them lags. Also the children see less of their father —often when they need him most.

Promotion in one's vocation means moving to a higher socioeconomic level. Even though the paycheck is larger, the increased family expenses may more than counterbalance the financial gain. Often the family must move to another city. More and better clothes may be needed. The obligation of entertaining the boss and his friends may rise sharply in order to meet company expectations.

2. Social-ethical

At this point the young adult's commitment to religious and ethical standards may be tested. If the boss likes to drink at the party, should the Christian serve liquor in his own house when he himself is opposed to social drinking? Can he maintain his upward movement in the organization if he stands for what he believes? Or, is it more important to stay in the boss's favor by compromising? These situations test the strength of the young adult's ethical standards.

3. Marital

Tension in young adulthood often centers around marriage. For married young adults, stress may come from the intimacy of sex life and interpersonal relationships, as well as from the advent of children. Many marriages do not survive these critical years. L. J. Bischof says, "There appears to be some evidence that the vulnerable years for divorce are in the first few years of marriage and in the early 40's (approximately 41-45)."[8]

Divorce is on the increase at an alarming rate. Exactly what is causing the change is unclear. Some writers feel that couples are simply affirming by their civil divorce an emotional divorce of long

---

8. L. J. Bischof, *Adult Psychology* (New York: Harper and Row, Publishers, 1969), p. 72.

standing. They believe that couples today are less willing to keep a facade than were the older generation.

Probably the reasons for divorce have changed little, even though the rate has. Infidelity and lack of communication are major occasions. But often they are symptoms of basic underlying problems, more than real causes. Self-centeredness and emotional immaturity often lie at the root of marital conflicts that lead to the "other woman" syndrome and to inability to communicate.

Many writers believe that divorce rates are highly influenced by socioeconomic conditions. Divorce is more apt to occur during times of prosperity. Our present high degree of urbanization and rationalization are also involved; the higher these two factors, the greater the incidence of divorce.[9]

For some unmarried young adults, stress is directly related to their single status. Society expects young women to marry; and certainly most single girls hope to have a husband and family. Because there are more women than men in our society, there are simply not enough men to go around; some girls are faced with disappointment. It is true, of course, that many single women have voluntarily turned down opportunities to marry for various reasons: parents who need care, professional pursuits, disillusionment with their friends' marriages, or a personal preference. They remain single by choice. Men who do not marry have also chosen to remain single. Whatever the reasons, single young adults are not necessarily unhappy, nor should Christian educators assume them to be. Bischof says:

> In the writer's counseling experience, it is sheer idiocy to assume that it is necessary to be married to be happy. . . . To rule that being unmarried naturally begets unhappiness and misery is to place oneself in the ridiculous position of stating that nuns and priests, for example, know no happiness. This is patently not true.[10]

Nevertheless, the single young adult has special needs because of his singleness. The unmarried who are still hoping to marry need opportunity to meet eligible companions within the church. Those who remain single by choice need opportunities for social contacts with other Christian adults. In recent years many churches have sponsored special organizations and programs to meet this need for companionship. They find ready response from the singles.

9. *Ibid.*, p. 73.
10. *Ibid.*, p. 72.

These single young adults present problems to the typical Sunday school organization of the small church when there are too few to have their own class. Their interests and concerns are markedly different from those of married persons. Their age and vocations do not help them fit into the older teen class or into the adult Bible class. Many churches seek to use them in leadership roles until there is a large enough group to form a separate class.

4. *Sex*

Sex is an especially acute problem for single adults. The peak age of the sexual drive in males is from about 18 to 22 years. Young women, too, are emotionally open to seduction. Unmarried young persons must find ways to control and express sexual urges in socially accepted ways. Christian young people must do so within the context of Christ's teachings.

A contributing factor to sexual problems in our times is the permissiveness of modern culture. The TV, movies, and popular literature are highly saturated with sexually stimulating material. Constant bombardment of the public with sexually deviant acts, proclamations of approval for homosexuality, and plots that highlight extramarital affairs, subtly change sexual values of all age-groups.

Some insight into the magnitude of the resulting contemporary problem is seen in research statistics. Moore reports:

> Illegitimacy, premarital coitus, and infidelity score high among persons eighteen to thirty. For example, up to fifty percent of young women and an even higher percentage of young men experience premarital sexual intercourse.[11]

These statistics, of course, represent a cross section of the population. Young persons with Christian backgrounds would certainly rate better, but church young people are not immune. Christian educators are concerned to preserve Christian homes. And because illicit sexual experiences prior to and after marriage impose severe strains on the marriage, teachers and pastors must stand prepared to assist individuals in these problems.

5. *Home Management*

Society provides the least training to young persons for their most important life task—home and family management. Many

---

11. Allen J. Moore, in *Introduction to Christian Education*, Marvin J. Taylor, ed. (Nashville: Abingdon Press, 1966), pp. 195-96.

young adults enter the family level of life ill prepared to manage money. As a result they often find themselves in serious financial problems. Easy credit is an everpresent temptation. In recent years bankruptcy proceedings have risen sharply in spite of the affluence of our society.

Neither are young parents well prepared to rear children. Usually they adopt the techniques of their parents. Today they often strenuously avoid authoritarianism, and so may give little profitable guidance to their children's behavior. Consequently children become emotional tyrants and socially insensitive adolescents who disrupt society and clog the juvenile court system.

One of the church's urgent current needs is a strong ministry in family guidance and counselling. The Christian home can use every good principle employed in the best non-Christian homes. But the Christian home needs added elements that the family's commitment to Christ entails—family prayer, Christian love, and church involvement. Excellent training courses in family life are available to the local church. Special Christian Family Life programs are denominationally prepared and recommended. One evangelical denomination provides that its local board of Christian education shall "elect a local director of Christian family life."[12] He seeks to strengthen the church's ministry to its families, to help the home and church work more closely together, to encourage parents to make their homes more truly Christian, and to challenge church families to win non-Christian families to Christ.

6. *Rootlessness*

Young adults are especially vulnerable to rootlessness, and our modern society is mobile. The train, bus, airplane, and automobile have made it so. Many companies expect their young executives to move frequently to a different city. Because of vocational, health, or family situations, on an average one out of five families moves every year.

The result of this mobility is rootlessness. When a family moves to a new city, they often find it difficult to get involved in the church in their new location. It is easy for them to become lost in the complex, impersonal suburban ghetto. Without the constant fellowship and nurture of the church, they lose their fervent love for Christ and cease effective involvement in His work. To help meet this need,

---

12. *Manual, Church of the Nazarene,* 1976, Par. 157.16.

some denominations have programs for "moving Christians." Pastors are urged to notify a denominational agency when a family moves. The agency immediately alerts the pastor nearest the new home, letting him know of the arrival of the family in his area. This opens the way for an early contact and for immediate involvement of the family in the life of the church in the new community.

D. Programs

We turn now to a consideration of the elements that need to be included in the church's program. Effective Christian education for young adults can come only from realistic goal setting and careful planning to meet their needs.

> The church is the custodian of religious and moral instruction. The young adult has a right to look to the church to serve him in his hour of need. . . . It has the tremendous obligation and opportunity to devise plans for undergirding the young adult in his struggle to live a moral life in this unmoral world.[13]

1. *Bible Teaching*

Because modern society bases its moral and ethical codes on statistical surveys, pragmatic utility, and relativistic principles, Christian education for young adults must be increasingly centered in the Bible. Bible study in the Sunday school class, in the home, and in other settings provides a counterbalance to the worldly value system.

Young adult Bible teaching focuses on the principles found in the Bible and on its relevance to today's society, more than on the formal acquisition of facts. The authority of God's Word must be constantly recognized. If the teacher lacks total commitment to this authority, he will communicate uncertainty to his class. Paul writes: "If the trumpet give an uncertain sound, who shall prepare himself to the battle?" (1 Cor. 14:8). If we wish to communicate confidence in an authoritative revelation, we must feel that confidence and testify to it.

2. *Fellowship*

Young adults need strong social ties within a homogeneous group. In order for these ties to grow stronger, the church must develop an adequate program of social activities both within the Sunday school structure and beyond it. Retreats for the family, socials

---

13. J. A. Charters, *Young Adults and the Church* (New York: Abingdon-Cokesbury Press, 1936), p. 25.

for fellowship, mutual problem discussions, and community service involvements are all viable ministries that develop the social cohesiveness so essential to young adults.

3. *Christian Family Skill Training*

The church has not fulfilled its responsibility to these young adults until it has provided programs that assist them in easing their family stresses. Christian Service Training classes and discussion groups are good. Some congregations arrange banquets or seminars in which qualified resource persons are brought in. The resource persons lecture, discuss, and counsel with young adults about child-rearing, interpersonal conflicts, sexual drive management, and financial responsibility.

All such attempts are most fruitful when the atmosphere is pervaded by a sense of trust and mutual respect. Unless these conditions exist, communication occurs on a superficial level only; the real problems go undiscovered and unresolved.

The church's significant input will be the Christian perspective on these interpersonal relationships. The findings of sociology and psychology are valuable, but they must be tested against the "Thus saith the Lord."

4. *Counseling*

Whenever the church's pastors and Christian education leaders are qualified, young adults have a counseling resource available when problems arise with which they cannot cope alone. The threat of divorce, parent-child conflicts, and financial stresses can often be eased by talking them out with a qualified counselor. For this reason pastors and Christian education specialists can enlarge their ministry by being prepared to be significant helpers to persons under stress.

III. MIDDLE-AGED ADULTS

A. Characteristics

In many ways middle age is an attractive period of life. By this time the financial struggles of starting a vocation, furnishing a home, and beginning a family are about over. For many adults it is a period of adequate income and job security. The children are becoming or have already become self-sufficient and are less dependent upon their parents for emotional and financial support. The years of living have provided these adults with more skills to handle life's problems and frustrations. They have begun to accept more realistic goals for their lives and are, therefore, under less success-stress. Real need, rather than impulsiveness and status achievement, directs their spending and buying habits.

At 40 years of age normal persons should have had sufficient experience through education and human contacts to have developed sound judgment in social relationships. Their financial and social positions should be established, and they should at least begin to have a clear vision of the future and the goals which they wish to attain. If these accomplishments are complemented by good health, life can indeed begin at 40.

For the church this age-group is indispensable. They provide the major share of the financial resources and serve in leadership roles as teachers, board members, and in other ministries. They are more likely to be emotionally stable and objective in their appraisal of situations, yet forward-looking enough to cooperate with growth endeavors, and flexible enough that minor change does not upset them.

B. Problems

As is true in other periods of development, middle age has its own specific problems along with its peculiar blessings. Some of these problems also occur at other periods of life, but the probability of their occurrence at this time is significantly greater.

1. Developmental Tension

Erikson describes the psychological conflicts of middle years as generativity versus stagnation.

> Generativity, then, is primarily the concern in establishing and guiding the next generation. . . . Where such enrichment fails altogether, regression . . . takes place, often with a pervading sense of stagnation and personal impoverishment.[14]

Middle adults must decide whether they will focus their life energies, economic resources, and social privileges only upon themselves or whether they will invest them in their family, society, and future generations.

2. Physical Health

The incidence of cardiovascular diseases rises sharply. Cancer is a greater risk. Diseases that require surgery are more frequent at this period of life. Where surgery necessitates removal of body parts

---

14. Erikson, *Childhood and Society,* p. 267.

vitally connected with sexual adequacy or attractiveness, the middle adult may experience strong feelings of inadequacy and incompleteness. In such instances, the person requires extra support and reassurance from the marriage partner until new self-acceptance has been achieved.

Loss of hair by men, and the loss of teeth by both sexes, may be accompanied by traumatic shocks to self-image. All such changes remind middle-aged adults of the loss of youth, the passing of years, and the irreversibility of aging.

In a society that places great emphasis on the advantages of youth, any reminders of its loss create adjustment problems to persons who resent the certainty of becoming old.

One especially important physiological change in middle life is the climacteric. In women it is called menopause or change of life. It marks the slowdown of the reproductive system and eventually terminates the child-bearing capacities. As a result, women's hormonal balance becomes disturbed, and they suffer flashes—periodically feeling flushed and overheated. In addition they may be subjected to periods of depression and anxiety. Fortunately today, medical treatment with hormones reduces the physiological and psychological effects of menopause.

Women enter change of life in their early to mid-forties. Hurlock says, "The average age . . . is around forty-five years, though this varies widely among women, depending on hereditary endowment, general health conditions, and variations in climate."[15] Five to 10 years are needed for this change to be completed.

Men undergo a similar though far less severe change in their late forties and early fifties. For them the change of life is less dramatic and little is known about it. Most of its symptoms are psychological—a realization of diminishing physical strength, a fear of loss of physical attractiveness along with doubts concerning their sexual adequacy. Many men adjust easily with a growing complacency about life. Some, however, are tempted to prove their masculine adequacy by extramarital affairs with younger women. Others lose themselves in compulsive vocational pursuits.

The basis for much of the decline in sexual powers is the social and psychological pressure abetting the physical deterioration. The social and psychological factors are more significant than is the physical.

---

15. Hurlock, *Developmental Psychology*, p. 688.

3. *Emotional Stress*

As a result of physiological changes, the middle years often bring periods of depression and doubt. When such changes are accompanied by drastic family alterations, they produce even greater shock. As children become independent, marry, and move away, parents experience the empty-nest syndrome. The house is quiet; mother's family maintenance chores are greatly diminished; both parents feel useless and neglected. If the mother is not employed away from home, she may feel this more than the husband.

Some couples find this a time of renewed self-discovery. They develop new dependency upon each other and find renewed enjoyment in each other's company which was impossible when the children were at home. Other couples cope with the emotional readjustment by getting more deeply involved in the church and in Christian social service activities. In some families the wife secures employment, or both increase their visits to friends and families.

4. *Goals*

After middle-aged individuals have achieved many of the vocational and financial successes they have set for themselves, they feel a sense of futility. Where does life go from here? Unless they find some new and challenging purposes, these men and women start to live in diminishing circles of activities and interests. Life begins to turn in upon itself, losing much of its zest and meaningfulness.

Christian couples can find new fulfillment by investing their lives in the welfare of others. Today's complex society offers ample opportunities for creative self-expression and worthwhile social service activities.

5. *Contingent Stress*

Another significant problem of middle-aged adults is dealing with contingent stress. This is the anxiety that persons must endure because of the decisions or actions of other individuals whose choices they are powerless to alter. Contingent stress is usually sustained over long periods of time and drains psychic, physical, and spiritual energy. When children are small, they are less mobile, more dependent upon parents for life necessities, and more compliant to parental authority. As they grow into adolescence, they develop their own life-styles. Some of them challenge the value system of the parents and the church. As youth learn to drive, they associate more with their peers who may or may not be known to the parents. Some teenagers, of course, never depart drastically from the expectations of their parents. But others do an about-face. They reject the values and life-style of the home. Many identify with the youth culture. A few turn to drugs, illicit sex, and violence.

The following examples are typical of thousands of parents whose hopes and dreams for their children have been shattered by teenagers who have disdained their Christian heritage. A fine Christian layman reported that his son was expelled from college because he was involved in the use of drugs. Later, the boy had to marry a girl because she became pregnant by him. A Christian minister, whose life radiates the spirit of Christ, said, "I hope you can help my daughter in your class. We raised her in the Christian way, but she has turned to an oriental mystical religion."

Parents of such adolescents must cope with the inner personal stresses engendered by their children's bad decisions and activities. Some will return to Christ later in life; others will not.

Contingent stress also comes from another source. As parents advance in age and eventually come to the point where they can no longer take care of themselves, middle adults face difficult decisions. How can they care for parents? If they take them into their own home, they require a heavy investment of time and energy. The family's freedom is severely limited. Who will stay with Mother and Dad? If the elderly parents are bedridden, they must be fed, bathed daily, helped to the bathroom, and given their medicine.

On the other hand, if the elderly are sent to a nursing home, the children face different problems. The cost may run $1,000 per month or more. Frequently, residents of the home are boisterous and insensitive to others' rights. Often the elderly cannot adjust to the institutional routine when they have been accustomed to the privacy of their own homes.

Thus, middle-aged adults face severe stress. If they commit their parents, they feel guilty for making the parents' lives more difficult. If they keep them in the home, they feel guilty for imposing a heavy burden of work on others in the family.

Middle adults also face the psychological stress of becoming grandparents. While this experience offers many satisfactions, it also induces contingent stress. The birth of the first grandchild reminds middle-aged adults of the reality of advancing age, a fact persistently blocked from consciousness throughout youth and early adulthood. Suddenly the grandparents must pause and review the direction of their lives. Look how far we have come! How much longer do we have?

Today many middle adults also face contingent stress from the prospect of possible job changes. Some experts predict that because of our fast-moving technological society, the average adult will need to be vocationally retrained four times during his working years. Persons in their forties and fifties are not only threatened by the specter of unemployment should their job be phased out; they are also faced with increasing difficulty in changing jobs if they become dissatisfied. Company hiring policies, insurance regulations, slowed personal reactions, and the difficulty of acquiring new skills all contribute to the sense of being trapped—locked into a job without a chance to move.

C. Ministries

The Christian education ministries for middle-aged adults should attempt to meet the foregoing needs. Too often, however, middle adults are taken for granted because they are seen as the strength of the church. Leaders may not be sensitive to their problems, either because we are not aware of them or because we expect mature adults to have the necessary skills to cope with them.

Pastors and ministers of Christian education who are young and oriented toward youth programs may also find it difficult to identify with the needs of the middle-aged. Consequently, the church's ministries will not be designed to meet their needs.

1. *Social Needs*

Christian ministries should provide for the social needs of the middle-aged. All groups have common interests and problems that are alleviated by mutual sharing; this age is no exception. The Sunday school class and small prayer or Bible study cell provides a convenient vehicle for middle adults to get together on Sunday and during the week.

Small groupings, sometimes called "Links of Love," "Circles of Concern," or some such name, offer opportunities for these adults to meet informally or to visit on the telephone. Sometimes the conversations are simply to share an item of good news. At other times friends will interact to mutually distressing concerns. Such occasions provide an outlet for frustrations; they also develop understandings that enable adults to face their own problems with greater self-confidence and spiritual strength.

2. *Elective Courses*

Middle adults respond well to the program of meeting together to study a common topic of mutual interest. Elective courses at the Sunday school hour will often draw a diverse group. But adult interest in the same topic surmounts whatever disadvantage is presented by differences in age or occupation.

4. *Adult Bible Class*

Too often the adult Bible class is overlooked or downgraded as an unimportant avenue of Christian education. But if this is our view, we are wrong. Here adults, grouped more or less by chronological age or some other organizational pattern, meet to study God's Word under the stimulation of a teacher. Where else and by what other means can adults caught in the dilemma of decision, find the foundations upon which to stand? We need exposure to the eternal truths of the Bible when other foundations appear to be subtly and slowly eroding in an ungodly world.

The average adult Bible class, however, has not begun to take hold of its psychological and spiritual potential. Teachers need to realize that adults can learn throughout life; there is no real obstacle to their taking part in genuine educational activities. An alert teacher can help provide adults with a continuous experience in Christian learning.

The adult Bible class has many critics and many weaknesses. But we have yet to see an equally helpful instrument for spiritual nurture. At its worst the class brings adults to the church once a week to talk together and to think for a little while about some significant passage of scripture. At its best, the Bible class seeks to help adults to:

1. Know and love the Bible
2. Help the unsaved find God
3. Encourage Christians to grow in grace
4. Build class members into the life of the church
5. Reach new people for Christ
6. Challenge all class members to Christian service
7. Encourage all to become effective Christian witnesses.[16]

Miller writes:

These Bible classes have an inherent value, for they have been the means whereby the content of the Bible has been made

---

16. A. F. Harper, *The Nazarene Sunday School in the 70's* (Kansas City: Beacon Hill Press of Kansas City, 1969), pp. 183-87.

relevant to life. Their continuing popularity indicates that a need is being met and that this is more than simply an absorbing of content.[17]

5. *Christian Service*

Many middle adults can be recruited for active roles in the life of the church. Christian service training courses help them prepare for Sunday school teaching, for witnessing, and for other important ministries in the church.

IV. SENIOR ADULTS

A. Aging

What is the aging process? The results are observable and easy to distinguish, but the causes are less easily understood.

> The most widely used current definition of aging stems from the biological sciences. Any biological processes which are time related, irreversible, and deleterious in nature are considered to be manifestations of aging.[18]

Dovenmuehle, however, goes on to explain that this concept of aging is very difficult to apply, even in the laboratory. Disease, illness, and aging are so similar in some biological respects that it is difficult to clearly differentiate between them.

Many definitions of aging are descriptive rather than analytic. One describes aging as:

> ... a process of changes involving all aspects of the organism. ... The term "aging" is meant to denote determinant patterns of late life changes, changes eventually shown by all persons though varying in rate and degree. ... Aging ... is defined as a progression of adult changes characteristic of the species and which should occur in all individuals if they live long enough.[19]

B. Terms Used

There are several terms frequently used in connection with aged adults that should be defined.

---

17. R. C. Miller, *Education for Christian Living* (Englewood Cliffs, N.J.: Prentice-Hall, Inc., 1956), p. 313.
18. R. H. Dovenmuehle, *Normal Aging*, E. Palmore, ed. (Durham, N.C.: Duke University Press, 1970), p. 40.
19. J. E. Birren, *et al., Human Aging: A Biological and Behavioral Study* (Bethesda, Md.: U.S. Department of Health, Education and Welfare, 1963), pp. 150-61. Cited in Hurlock, *Developmental Psychology*, p. 778.

1. *Senescence* refers to the gradual decline of physical and intellectual abilities which occur toward the end of life, but which occur so slowly that the individual can make compensatory adjustments. Senescence occurs earlier in some individuals than in others. It is illustrated by the older person who knows that his night vision is becoming inadequate and consequently he refuses to drive at night.

2. *Senility* is the more or less complete failure of the physical structure; it includes the mental disorganization that results from an inadequate supply of oxygen reaching the brain. Senility is exemplified by mental confusion, absent-mindedness, and the eccentric behavior of aged persons.

3. *Gerontology* refers to the science of aging whether it be physical or nonphysical. The major concern of gerontology in the area of human personality has been to study aged adults and to gather data concerning them. Such information is important to help counteract the stereotyped images that prevail and to provide the aged with as much emotional security as possible in a culture that places a high premium upon youthfulness. Prevailing stereotypes have strongly influenced society's treatment of aged persons in respect to housing, employment, and family life.

4. *Geriatrics* is the term that designates psychiatric interest in the physiological and illness problems of the aged. It includes all attempts to improve the quality of life for older persons by improving their health. "The goal of geriatrics is, therefore, to *add life to the years* of the elderly, not just years to their lives."[20]

C. Psychological Aging

In order to adequately understand older adults, one must recognize the relationship between chronological, physiological, and psychological aging. The three phases of growing old are not necessarily contiguous and concomitant. Chronological aging marches on relentlessly and irrespective of other factors. Physiological aging, however, is greatly affected by heredity, health, occupation, and socioeconomic factors.

Psychological aging is dependent upon adjustment, self-concept, and motivation. If the individual maintains an active interest in the world, keeps involved in social relationships, feels needed, and lives independently, he will keep young in spirit; retirement will be a

---

20. Hurlock, *Developmental Psychology*, p. 783.

fruitful period in his life. On the other hand, if he withdraws from reality and social relationships, pities and becomes preoccupied with himself, he will age psychologically long before his years or physical condition would warrant.

D. Stereotypes

Aged people are often stereotyped as cranky, unhappy, mentally ill, rigid, unteachable, and incapacitated. Due to physical problems and social rejection, many of the aged fit these descriptions. However, other elderly persons do not fit the stereotypes at all. They are active, sociable, happy, learning, well-adjusted persons who function very well in society.

One of the tragic consequences of these stereotypes is to alienate young people from a valuable resource of skills and knowledge available in aged persons. When young people are encouraged to really communicate with older persons, they find the experience to be an immensely rewarding one. Also, the older people enjoy being made the focus of interest.

Perhaps one of the most helpful but untapped dimensions of Christian education is to initiate and encourage this communication between generations. For example, a children's class or a youth group may invite an older person to become its prayer partner.

To be effective, communication between generations must be on the emotional and empathetic level. Sometimes when youth visit the nursing home, they flit from person to person. A greater ministry is rendered by the one who sees these older persons as individuals who like to reminisce, to share ideas, and to know younger persons' points of view.

E. Characteristics

Older adults are best characterized as an accumulation and extension of their younger selves. Those who were cooperative usually continue to be congenial and compliant. Adults who were intractable and rigid become even more so with advancing years. Individuals who kept abreast of current developments and persisted in expanding their mental horizons, normally continue to be alert in old age. Persons who were withdrawn, self-centered, and narrowly focused on their own concerns become even more preoccupied with themselves. In such persons emotional responsiveness and social orientation narrow faster than their physical deterioration would normally dictate.

Often aged adults are less interested in pleasing other people than they were in earlier years. Their lowered social inhibition may make them blunt in speech and insensitive to the opinions of others.

Younger persons, especially their own children, are often mystified by personality changes that occur as their parents age. One of the milder changes is forgetfulness. In extreme cases, aged adults develop senile psychosis, overt aggression, and hostility. Their deteriorating physical condition causes such a reversal of personality traits that Christians may seem to act in unchristian ways. One family was concerned because their saintly father in his old age began to swear. They felt he had forsaken God. The truer explanation was biologically based. The blood vessels to the brain become hardened and constricted. The resulting diminished oxygen supply causes behavioral changes. As the condition worsens, persons lose touch with reality, become mechanical in their responses, and are unable to engage in intelligent conversation.

Aged parents also sometimes seem to suddenly reject their children and express dislike toward them. They do not really mean it. Understanding will help to insulate the emotional hurt. Children need to understand that because of these physical changes, their aged parents are mentally incapacitated and are not, therefore, morally responsible.

Erikson has called this the age of ego integrity versus despair. During this period adults look over their lives and evaluate their choices. If they feel they have made the proper key decisions and are satisfied with them, they feel a sense of integrity. If they feel they missed some golden opportunities and their lives are not personally fulfilling, they often turn in on themselves.

> Only in him who in some way has taken care of things and people and has adapted himself to triumphs and disappointments adherent to being, the originator of others or the generator of products and ideas—only in him may gradually ripen the fruit of these severe stages. I know no better word for it than ego integrity. . . . The lack or loss of this accrued ego integration is signified by fear of death. . . . Despair expresses the feeling that the time is now short, too short for the attempt to start and to try out alternative roads to integrity.[21]

---

21. Erikson, *Childhood and Society*, pp. 268-69.

F. Problems

1. *Physical*

One of the paramount problems with older adults is physical health. Their vigor, stamina, and reaction time are greatly diminished. Vision and hearing are sharply reduced. Loss of finger dexterity makes the handling of small items difficult. Hypertension, cancer, stroke, heart attack, arthritis, and rheumatism are all found more frequently in the aged.

2. *Financial*

For many adults, old age is a time of severe financial stress. Health problems necessitate constant medication, expensive hospitalization, and frequent visits to the doctor. Thus expenses soar when income diminishes. Some find their social security benefits too meager to provide them with even the barest necessities. Unless these persons own their home, they live in poverty. Without financial assistance they cannot survive.

3. *Emotional*

While some aged adults have the capacity to adjust to change and to be genuinely interested in others, many have not. They do not fit into the families of their married children. They cannot live alone, and they cannot adjust to the regimentation of a nursing home. When they develop feelings of being unwanted and unneeded, even their children find it difficult to talk with them. Consequently the older adults' world begins to close in upon them as they disengage themselves from it.

4. *Acceptance of Death*

A great deal of research is being done on death, how it is faced by the aged person, and its impact on the family. The inevitability of death makes it man's "last enemy" (1 Cor. 15:26). But diminishing physical vigor, poor health, and the death of friends prepare adults to accept death more easily.

Resignation is evidenced by such statements as "I have had a good life," "I can hardly wait to see Jesus," and "All my friends are over there." Each statement is an attempt to cope with the irreversibility of death. The better one has adjusted to life, the easier he finds it to accept death as a part of life. A vital Christian faith is the most powerful factor in contemplating death; faith makes us confident that the life beyond is an extension of all that has been best in our lives while here.

5. *Social*

Older adults often face critical social problems. Their positions of leadership in the church and business are given to younger persons, and they feel left out of things. They find their former circle of friends diminishing, friends and associates become infirm, move to retirement homes, or die.

If the spouse dies, they are faced with severe crises. The adjustment to life without their companion is extremely difficult, especially if they have been heavily dependent upon them. If both received social security, the income is sharply reduced. Should they marry again? Some older adults do and have a happy relationship for several years. Others who marry find they cannot adjust to the new partner's demands; they separate or divorce.

As the world moves on, many older adults feel more and more alienated from it. They reminisce about the good old days, and become unsettled by the rapid changes they see. More and more they withdraw from social contacts, from younger people, and from their own children. For them, their own age-group provides the essential companionship.

G. Ministries

The church that feels Christ's compassion for all persons will not neglect older adults. While the aged may not be able to contribute financially as much as young and middle adults, they deserve their share of attention. Many of them have sacrificed, labored, and witnessed in bygone days to enable the organization to survive and to become the strong, affluent church of the present. Christian gratitude will not forget the investment of these older adults. An effective program of Christian education will minister to their special needs.

1. *Senior Adult Clubs*

Many churches organize older adults into clubs and help them plan activities that meet their needs. Activities include Bible study and prayer groups, trips to museums, and social times. Weekly or monthly gatherings in the local church are supplemented by annual district get-togethers. NIROGA is a national gathering of adults over 55. Nearly 2,000 from evangelical churches gather in the fall at three locations for a week of Christian fellowship and study.

2. *Service Opportunities*

Older persons need to feel wanted and needed. Christian education programs ought to make use of their rich resources of experience and skills. Some older women provide nursery care one afternoon a week at the church; young mothers leave their small children while they go shopping. Couples have been organized into "helping others" cells. They visit other older adults, pray with them, and provide needed attention and help. Retired men often assist in maintenance of the church, construction projects, ushering, and finance committee work.

3. *Sunday School Classes*

The wishes of older adults should be observed in the structuring of their classes in the Sunday school. In some instances the men and women will want to meet together; in others, they prefer a class for the men and one for the women. If they meet separately, the teacher will usually be the same sex as the class. This preference is sometimes due to the effect of aging on hearing. Older men have difficulty hearing higher pitched voices; older women have trouble hearing sounds in the lower ranges.

Study materials and Bibles should have large print. Chalkboard writing needs to be large and bold. Older persons enjoy teachers who are relaxed and who do not move about too much while teaching. Classrooms for these older people need to have plenty of light.

Pressure for learning new facts and for memorizing are not appropriate at this age. Instead, ample opportunity should be given for the class to discuss the lesson. Exploration of concepts and testing of ideas may generate heated discussion because these elder citizens have strong ideas about the correctness of their opinions. Thus teachers of older persons will need tolerance and tact to handle emotionally charged opinions and to guide discussions into productive thinking.

4. *Visitation*

Nursing homes, retirement villages, and housing complexes for older adults provide opportunities for visitation and service. Nor should we forget the inactive older adults living in their own homes or in the homes of their children. Christian educators should serve these aged adults by promoting frequent and consistent visitation to them.

H. Conclusion

As the present youth generation grows older and the current birth rate continues to decline, middle-aged and older adults will be a growing segment of the population. Creative Christian education must conceive of ministries for every age level of adults and thus prepare them for a rich and rewarding old age. Well-conceived programs, administered in the spirit of Christ, will enable adults to rise to their unique opportunities and to cope with the stresses peculiar to them.

BIBLIOGRAPHY

Galloway, C. O. *Team Teaching with Adults.* Kansas City: Beacon Hill Press of Kansas City, 1970.

The effectiveness of team teaching is contrasted with the usual one-teacher model. The author stresses the importance of team planning and evaluation; he also points out dangers that may be encountered and ways to avoid them.

Minor, H. D., ed. *Techniques and Resources for Guiding Adult Groups.* Nashville: Abingdon Press, 1972.

A compilation of 46 articles dealing with leadership of adults in the church. The topics are arranged under the headings "Group Life," "Guiding a Study Group," "Ways of Learning," and "Resources for Learning."

Robb, Thomas Bradley, *The Bonus Years.* Valley Forge, Pa.: The Judson Press, 1968.

The subtitle is "Foundations for Ministry with Older Persons." The author devotes three chapters to the emerging data on aging. In them he explores the characteristics and needs of older persons. The climax comes in his discussion of the role of the church and the suggestions for organizing local church ministries for the elderly.

Wright, N. H. *Ways to Help Them Learn.* Glendale, Calif.: Regal Books, 1971.

Part One explores the characteristics of adults, with special attention to their unique needs in earlier, middle, and older years. Part Three discusses methods—emphasizing good lecturing, discussion, and inductive Bible study.

PART III

Structures
for
Christian Education

Preamble

We come now to the last main division of our venture in *Exploring Christian Education*. In the first section on foundations we asked, Why are we concerned? What are the basic truths of the Christian faith and what are the universal needs of human life that send us on our mission? In foundations we assume the role of evaluators and long-range theorists, planners for Christian education.

In Part II on curriculum, we raised the question, How do we achieve our goals? There we explored the role of the teacher and the educational supervisor. We asked, What are the ways that we can best help human learners with their deep needs to expose themselves to God's truth and to God's people who have found the answers to those needs?

Now in Part III we step into the role of the administrator—the pastor, Sunday school superintendent, and minister of Christian education. We ask, How can persons be best organized to carry out our Lord's commission to "Go . . . teach"?

We shall look first at the tested principles of human organization and administration. We need to know how any successful human enterprise is structured in order to function smoothly and to achieve its goals. But because ours is an educational ministry, we especially need to understand the principles employed in general education. What are the best ways to organize and administer learning enterprises?

Finally, because we are exploring Christian education, we must always ask, How do the accepted guidelines for successful secular organization and administration stand up when tested by Jesus' guidelines for Christian relationships? What would our Christian education organization look like if Jesus were our Administrator? Reflecting on His earthly ministry, we are sure that there would be leader-follower roles. We would also find respect for the inherent worth of every person, regardless of his role in the organization. We would find every phase of the structure geared to achieving the fulfillment of the Great Commission. And we would find the spirit of perfect love permeating every relationship.

In this exploration of structures we shall look chiefly at organization and administration within the local church—because that is where Christian education finds its focus today. *Organization* is the way that persons are grouped to best achieve Christian learning. *Administration* refers to the activities of leaders dedicated to achieving those same goals.

Three final chapters take us beyond local church ministries. In chapter 17 we explore the opportunities and God's call to full-time ministry in Christian education. These opportunities are open both to ordained ministers and to laymen. Normally this ministry does not include an every-Sunday preaching schedule—but there is a rewarding full-time Christian calling.

In chapter 18 we examine organizations devoted to the ministry of Christian education beyond the local church, and sometimes outside of denominational affiliation. We shall examine their purpose, try to understand their contributions, and learn what services they may offer us to enrich our own ministries in the church.

In a final chapter the author examines the contributions of higher education to our cause. We look at the role of the Christian liberal arts college, the Bible school, the graduate seminary, and Christian ministries on secular campuses.

For every organization committed to Christian education, we give thanks. For all of us placed in positions of leadership we pray, "Since we have special gifts which differ according to the grace bestowed upon us, if it is . . . administration, let our hearts be in our ministry" (Rom. 12:8, Weymouth).

CHAPTER 13

Organization for Christian Education

God chooses human instruments to accomplish His work on earth. In His sovereignty, He is not limited to this plan, but most often "He has no hands but our hands." An exploration of Christian education includes a consideration of the organizations that men use to accomplish the task of discipling. But teaching is done in and through the church. Therefore organization for Christian education must be viewed in the light of the nature and purpose of the church.

I. THE NATURE OF THE CHURCH

A. The Foundation

Jesus declared that He would build His Church upon people like Simon Peter who had received a personal revelation of Jesus Christ and who were willing to confess it openly (Matt. 16:13-19). Such persons hold the keys to the kingdom of heaven; they will be given as large a supply of divine resources as they are willing to assume responsibility for. Not even hell can prevail against their assault. So the church begins with "revelation responders" and continues to exist on divine power.

B. The People of God

It is the desire of God to have a distinctive people (see Deut. 26:18-19). They are to be a "chosen generation, a royal priesthood, a holy nation, a peculiar people . . . the people of God" (1 Pet. 2:9-10).

All organizations in the church should allow Christians to be this kind of people—people who are holy and "set apart for a purpose." Their task is to show forth the praise of God who has called them from darkness into light. Because light is the traditional symbol for knowledge and truth, this phrasing suggests the ministry of Christian education.

C. The Body of Christ

The Church is the Body of Christ (Eph. 1:22-23). As such, it is an extension of the Incarnation. The incarnation of God in Christ is His most effective means of revealing himself to men. The Church extends this communication as the Holy Spirit whom Christ sent dwells in each man. Here is the "deepest and most effective form of communication of the Gospel today."[1]

One expression of the Incarnation may be seen in the results of Pentecost when each person heard about Jesus in his own tongue (Acts 2:8). This is not an unattainable ideal for the Church today. The goal of missions is to show every man the truth of the gospel in his own language and culture.

Another achievable expression of the Incarnation in the life of the Church should be the self-emptying quality of Jesus Christ (Phil. 2:7). Here is a demanding ministry, but many Christian educators and organizations set such examples in their faithful service to less fortunate persons.

To be the Body of Christ in the world is to be the visible expression of God and to do His will. This demands the maintenance of a vital relationship with God because it is He who gives power and effectiveness to persons in our organizations.

D. The Fellowship of the Spirit

Koinonia, translated "communion" or "fellowship," is the Greek term used to describe the work of the Holy Spirit in uniting men to work together; today it is probably one of the most popular phrases used to describe the work of the church. It identifies many of the close-knit groups actively endeavoring to do God's will and work.

Koinonia is used in several contexts in the New Testament. It describes a contribution to the poor (Rom. 15:26). In Heb. 13:16 and Philem. 6, the term describes sharing or communicating the faith.

---

1. Carroll P. Wise, *The Meaning of Pastoral Care* (New York: Harper and Row Publishers, 1966), p. 11.

Paul uses the word to explain his partnership in the gospel (Phil. 1:5) and his desire to share in the sufferings of Christ (Phil. 3:10). From such a study of the term Donald Butler concludes that "the Church is not a place to which we retreat for rest . . . but . . . to get burdens, compulsions, imperatives, urgencies, and responsibilities."[2]

E. The Worshiping-Learning Community

The word "teach" is important because the church is a learning community. The preaching *(kerygma)* and teaching *(didache)* are not in conflict; rather, as Franklin Segler observes, teaching is "making explicit all that is implicit in the kerygma."[3]

F. The Commissioned Community

A careful study of the Great Commission (Matt. 28:16-20) reveals the purposes of the church to be: (1) worship, (2) evangelism, (3) education, and (4) fellowship. When we consider the commands of Jesus to give a cup of cold water and to feed the hungry, we can add (5) service. The church is commissioned to fulfill these commandments.

II. CONCEPTS OF ORGANIZATION

A. A Divine-Human Structure

There are some who prefer the church to remain merely an ideal, spiritual force; they suggest that it needs no material structure. But human organization need not be in conflict with the demands of the Kingdom. The church must be a "functioning institution set in the midst of non-idealistic conditions."[4]

B. Definition

Human organization is an arrangement of persons to achieve chosen objectives. Figure 1 (p. 316) represents unorganized pieces of wire. Figure 2 shows the same wires pulled taut and organized into a piece of screen or grill. Organization arranges and makes the pieces more meaningful. People, like materials, are at cross-purposes unless they organize themselves into some cooperative pattern. These planned arrangements become effective methods to achieve objectives.

---

2. J. Donald Butler, *Religious Education* (New York: Harper and Row, 1962), p. 17.
3. Franklin M. Segler, *A Theology of Church and Ministry* (Nashville: Broadman Press, 1960), p. 28.
4. *Ibid.,* p. 4.

FIGURE 1

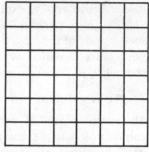

FIGURE 2

C. Hierarchical Arrangement for Responsibility

Armies have groupings from privates to generals. Universities have rankings among professors. Within the church some recognition of responsibility is desirable. Vertical and horizontal relationships in an organization chart spell out inner structure and the assignments of responsibility.

In diagramming these structures, the pyramid with vertical and horizontal lines has usually represented organizations with one central authority (Figure 3 below). In this diagram "A" would represent the pastor, where he is designated as head of the church. "B" to "D" represent department or supervisory personnel. "E" would represent the congregation. Each level shows lines of both vertical and horizontal relationships and responsibilities.

Some church organizations have a structure that makes a difference between policy-making groups and other functioning workers. Figure 4 represents this type. "F" would represent the policy-making group and "H" would be the other workers. "H" could be organized comparable to Figure 3. In Figure 4, "G" represents the pastor or the chief administrator of the organization.

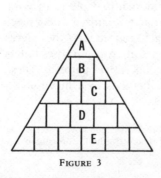

FIGURE 3

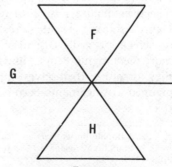

FIGURE 4

D. Simplicity and Democracy

One of the criticisms of modern organizations is that they tend to become too complex. Therefore, simple and direct lines of responsibility should be designed.

Because organizations tend to become outdated and inflexible, growth and progress depend on built-in provisions for change. A system that allows for remodeling and overhaul lessens the possibility of stagnation or revolution.

We believe that democracy is the best form of government for the human spirit. Being party to a decision makes us more ready to be governed by it. Also helping to reach church decisions is one of the ways that we nurture Christian growth. The more people involved in the decision-making process, the more there are who accept responsibility in the church. This makes communication extremely important in all forms of democratic church government. People in the church need to be informed.

III. Church Organization

Denominations have varying organizational structures. Patterns differ in accordance with the degree of congregational freedom. Denominations with a congregational form of government may show considerable variation even from church to church. Those with an episcopal type of government will not normally have so great a variety.

A. Church of the Nazarene

Figure 5 depicts the representative form of government found in the Church of the Nazarene.[5]

The entire congregation carries responsibility for its affairs, but the local membership elects a church board to represent them between meetings of the church. It is composed of ex officio members (pastor, chairman of the board of Christian life, Nazarene World Missionary Society president, and Nazarene Youth International president); also from 6 to 22 persons are elected to the board as trustees, stewards, and (if desired) members of the board of Christian life. In

---

5. As this book goes to press, the Church of the Nazarene has launched a major restructuring of its entire organization for Christian education. See Appendix V for a representative structure of an organization for church education based on age-level ministries.

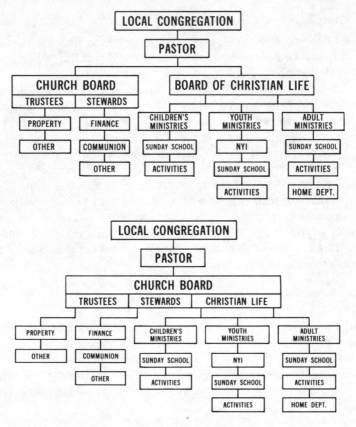

FIGURE 5

smaller churches the church board as a whole may serve as the board of Christian life. Also churches may elect a board of Christian life separate from the church board; in this case there is no education committee within the church board.

The education committee coordinates the educational efforts of the Sunday school, the missionary society, and the young people's society. Each organization chooses most of its own officers, but the education committee, in cooperation with the pastor, nominates or chooses leaders for other special educational organizations that meet on weekdays or in summer ministries.[6]

---

6. *Manual, Church of the Nazarene* (Kansas City: Nazarene Publishing House, 1976), Pars. 134, 154-171.

B. The Wesleyan Church

Figure 6 shows the organizational structure of the Wesleyan church.

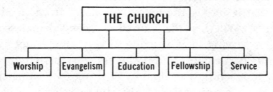

FIGURE 6

The Annual Conference of the local congregation elects a church board to care for business between conference sessions. This board is composed of ex officio members—pastor (chairman), associate pastor, secretary, treasurer, Sunday school superintendent, and board of trustees. Ten additional members-at-large may be elected.

The Discipline indicates that a board of Christian education composed of the pastor, employed assistants, and the heads of educational organizations plus others elected by the church board is to be organized with the pastor as chairman.[7] Other committees within the church may be organized as follows: Missions and Evangelism, Finance and Stewardship, Witness and Membership, Music, Ushering, Communion, and Judicial. A member of the church board serves as chairman of each committee.

The board of Christian education is responsible for the direction and coordination of the activities of the Sunday school, Wesleyan Men, Wesleyan Women's Missionary Society, Wesleyan Youth, Christian Youth Crusader, and Young Missionary Worker's Band. The president or chief officer of each group would be a member of this board.

Three age-level divisions—children, youth, and adult—are possible in the local Wesleyan church when the board of Christian education so directs.

The church board elects the Sunday school officers with the exception of the Sunday school superintendent. It also elects directors of other Bible schools, secretaries of education and literature, as well as adult youth counselors. Nominations for many of these offices come through the board of Christian education.

---

7. *The Discipline of the Wesleyan Church* (Marion, Ind.: Wesleyan Publishing House, 1972), Par. 361.

IV. Organization for Church Education

A. Concept

Some educational theorists think of the entire church as a school; everything that it does is, therefore, considered from an educational point of view. Whether the church is evangelizing, worshiping, socializing, or serving, it is teaching. Everything it does has some effect upon its participants and observers. Each activity becomes an opportunity to teach how to do it or how not to do it. Each activity is therefore a process of Christian education—either positive or negative.

However loudly one may protest such a concept, he is still confronted with the fact that teaching is happening under these conditions. There is a sense in which the entire ministry of the church is educational. But we are not helped by thus oversimplifying our analysis of the work of the church.

There is another and better interpretation of the church education concept. This view gathers all of the planned educational activities into one of the major functions of the church. It confines Christian education to those activities that deal with deliberate teaching or training. This is a narrower view but probably more helpful—and certainly the most widely accepted organizational pattern.

It is probably true that some organizations for Christian education sprang up outside of the church because the church neglected its reponsibility of teaching.[8] It is certainly true that the Sunday school was started outside of the church and later was adopted by it. We may argue just as cogently, however, that most of today's organizations for Christian education represent the church's search for the best means to perform her nurturing task.

Today's church school concept recognizes the church as a communicating agency. We have a life to be lived, a work to be done, and a message to be shared.

B. One Central Planning Group

In most churches there is an official board consisting of key elected or appointed leaders. This is a smaller group than the entire congregation; it is designated to make decisions between meetings of the

---

8. Oliver DeWolf Cummings, *Christian Education in the Local Church* (Philadelphia: Judson Press, 1942), pp. 22-25.

full body. For best structure, all functions of the church should ultimately be responsible to this official board. Financial, program, and personnel policies should be settled here. The entire work of the church can thus be coordinated, balanced, and adequately planned.

C. Room for Small Groups

Small groups are needed for special functions. That is why the whole church board names a committee for Christian education. Smaller units are also needed to encourage close Christian fellowship so essential to Christian nurture. The individual may feel lost as the organization grows larger. Sunday school classes for adults probably should be divided when enrollment reaches 25-30. With younger ages, the groups are much smaller, ranging from 4 or 5 in the preschool to 10 or 15 in the teen classes. Normally the younger the pupil, the smaller the class.

D. The Fullest Participation Possible

Along with intimate group fellowship there should be participation by each member. All should be involved, but with consideration for personal differences. Some people desire to be limited in activity; the organization should therefore allow for different levels of service. All persons, however, should be encouraged to accept responsibility and to serve in keeping with their ability and personality. Carefully prepared job descriptions assist organizational planning at this point.

E. The Need in Christian Education

Organization in Christian education offers the following values:
- Serves as a means of enlisting and using persons
- Makes collective thinking and action possible
- Gathers resources in a way not otherwise possible
- Assigns responsibility
- Assures stability and continuity.[9]

V. The Board of Christian Education

Christian education in the local church usually centers in a board of Christian education, an educational committee, or a church schools board. In the more integrated organizations, the Sunday school is

---

9. Frank M. McKibben, *Christian Education Through the Church* (New York: Abingdon-Cokesbury Press, 1947), p. 45.

only one—but often the largest—arm of the board's responsibility. These boards are composed of persons elected by the congregation or appointed by the appropriate bodies. Some members such as the Sunday school superintendent serve by virtue of their offices. The board of Christian education makes policy, coordinates activities, and guarantees leadership to accomplish the educational objectives of the church. Much of its work may be initiated by the pastor, educational director, or chairman.

The board should include representation from all important educational organizations in the church, also leadership from every age-group. And of course some should be elected from the congregation who are most familiar with educational theory and philosophy. It should be large enough to be representative, but small enough to assure efficient functioning.

This board of Christian education should be distinguished from the Sunday school cabinet. The board supervises the total program of Christian education in the local church. The cabinet, on the other hand, is responsible for the organization and operation of the Sunday school. The cabinet normally includes the superintendent, secretary, treasurer, and departmental supervisors. Sometimes in smaller churches the cabinet is enlarged to include all teachers and officers of the Sunday school. When this is done, the larger group is often known as a workers' conference. The proper function of the cabinet or this workers' conference is limited to the operation of the Sunday school.

The board of Christian education makes key decisions concerning the proper functioning of the church schools. It sets basic philosophy and long-range plans, develops standards or adopts those suggested by its denominational agencies. It establishes permanent record systems and regular visitation programs. The board plans for training of workers and for the most effective ministries of the Home Department, Cradle Roll, and other outreach departments. It approves the purchase of audiovisual equipment and determines the curriculum materials to be used throughout the church schools.

This board provides for the financing of the educational program and encourages the practice of good stewardship on the part of the members. It would encourage the establishment and use of a church library. The board is responsible for policies of grading and promotion, also for the use of school facilities and equipment including buses. It should establish efficiency measures and evaluation procedures.

The board would recommend home, church, and community cooperation and explore the best ways for these three to work together. It should cooperate in procedures of follow-up for new converts and the educational programs necessary to bring them into the full fellowship of church membership. In the overall concept, the board of Christian education is responsible for a comprehensive and balanced program of Christian teaching and discipling.

VI. The Sunday Church School

A. Origin

The Sunday school, as we know it, had its beginning predominantly in England and in the United States. In England under Robert Raikes it became a substitute for the public education of poor children. Raikes hired teachers in order to get the boys and girls off the streets on Sundays, and to teach them how to read and write. Thus the Sunday school began outside of the church. But under John Wesley and others, it early became a major arm of the church for Christian education. It had great success in the United States in the latter part of the 18th century. During the 19th century it became a uniting force among many denominations through the cooperative study of uniform Bible lessons. After reaching its zenith in the second and third decades of the 20th century, its influence began to wane. However, in spite of its limitations, the Sunday school is still one of the church's most effective organizations for Christian teaching.

B. Evaluation

The Sunday school has been criticized for poor teaching methods— and the criticism is often justified. The better response to this fault, however, is improvement rather than abandonment.

There will certainly be some changes for the Sunday school in the days ahead. Information retrieval systems and knowledge explosion instruments are affecting methods and language. Emphasis is being placed upon doing the faith, engagement, and involvement. But hearing Christ's call and responding to it are still supremely important objectives.

Sharing the faith in many new specialized ministries connected with homemaking, health education, and social action may be ways to meet some of the needs of the times by a return to the concept of Robert Raikes. Nevertheless, teaching the life-giving truths of the Bible continues to be of utmost importance. It is God's Word telling of the past, meeting present needs, and pointing the way to the future. Perhaps today, as never before, the sharing of the faith demands the study of the Bible and allowing the Holy Spirit to speak to us through it.

C. Personnel

An important consideration in the success of any organization is the enlistment of appropriate personnel. The success of a Sunday school depends upon the selection of a competent superintendent and enough assistant superintendents to care for various phases of its activities. In addition, the school needs a general secretary for records and reports; a librarian for keeping and distributing literature, books, and other materials; a treasurer; departmental supervisors; department secretaries, treasurers; song leaders; pianists; ushers; greeters; parking attendants; teachers; assistants; and class officers. Organization leaders have no more crucial task than finding and recruiting colleagues for these ministries of Christian education.

D. Grouping and Grading

Grading by age and school grades is probably the most democratic and interest-centered method of grouping. Even in the smallest Sunday schools classes are provided for preschool children, elementary pupils, teens, and adults. In larger schools each of these age-groups is further subdivided. A complete classification includes groups or classes for:

Cradle Roll:	birth until enrolled in the nursery
Nursery:	crib babies
	toddlers
	2-year-olds
	3-year-olds
Kindergarten:	4-year-olds
	5-year-olds
Primary:	1st grade (6 years)
	2nd grade (7 years)
Middler:	3rd grade (8 years)
	4th grade (9 years)
Junior:	5th grade (10 years)
	6th grade (11 years)
Junior High:	7th grade (12 years)
	8th grade (13 years)
	9th grade (14 years)
Senior High:	10th grade (15 years)
	11th grade (16 years)
	12th grade (17 years)

Young Adult:	18-34 years of age[10]
	college youth
	working or professional youth
	young married—childless
	young married—with children
Middle Adult:	35-65
Senior Adult:	65 and older
Home Department:	shut-ins, Sunday workers

1. Grouping Children

There are several sound reasons why the age limits below the adult level should be carefully observed in class divisions. The division between kindergartners and primaries is often the point at which the child starts to school. Nursery and kindergarten children are taught as preschool children, while primary teachers must always keep in mind the child's school experiences. Also up to adolescence the mental ability of the child increases each year much as his body grows larger year by year. Mental differences of three years are about the maximum that can be effectively grouped together for effective teaching and learning—groupings of only two years are even better. Another very practical reason for observing the recommended groupings is that publishers prepare lesson materials for these specific age-groups.

2. Grouping Teens

Grouping of teens into junior high and senior high classes is based more on social reactions than on continued development of intelligence. Younger junior highs will be inwardly shy and overawed by senior highs. On the other hand, sophisticated youths of 17 are likely to resent the presence of "12-year-old kids" in their group activities. There are such marked differences in maturity and interest that wherever possible junior highs should have their own class or department and senior highs should have a separate organization.

3. Sex Grouping

Grouping children and teens according to sex has been highly controversial. Some separation of the sexes occurs in many churches at the junior or junior high ages. Proponents of separate classes argue that while boys and girls are at the competitive age, it is wise

---

10. There is a variation of several years in the points at which theorists and organizations divide their adult levels. Many, as above, classify 18-year-olds as adults; others maintain an older youth division from 18 through 23. The young adult division thus begins at 24 years. Some would extend the young adult period until 40.

to separate them. Others contend that because girls mature more rapidly than boys, some separation is desirable during the junior and junior high period. Most theorists today would recommend mixed classes, though some urge separate classes for junior boys and girls.

4. *Grouping Adults*

Probably there is less agreement in classifying adults than any other age-group. We recognize many experiences other than age that influence adult groupings: youth movements, marital status, and vocation. But it may still be that classifying adults roughly on the basis of age differences is the best way to meet their common needs and interests. Certainly hard and fast age classifications are not necessary and not always the most helpful.

The current emphasis upon individualism and "doing one's own thing" has had its influence upon grouping adults. Elective course offerings tend to encourage a changing organizational structure, and these changes help to meet the needs of the restless. Unless carefully chosen, however, elective courses and shifting classes do not provide a balanced diet of Christian teaching for adults.

Southern Baptists have had acknowledged success in Sunday school work. Contrary to most recommendations, they have organized adult classes both on sex divisions and on relatively narrow age spans. They contend that while some married couples might not attend unless they can be together in the same class, it is difficult to gain a response from both partners if they are in a class together. One may talk while the other is silent or both may be silent to prevent disagreement publicly. In some areas, it is reported that Southern Baptists are moving away from sex-divided adult classes because couples want to be together.

E. Department Organization

1. *Importance*

Persons best informed in the ministries of Christian education regard departmental organization essential to growth and effective nurture in the Sunday school.

a. Greater growth. The need for departmentalization develops as schools grow, but department organization is primarily a cause of growth rather than a result. The best way to have continuous growth is to develop an adequate organization that involves a maximum number of people within the framework of a departmentalized school.

b. Better teaching. The values of departmentalization, however, are greater than simply providing growth. A departmentalized school can provide better Christian nurture. When all pupils in a department are approximately the same age so that classes can study the same lesson, the whole hour is planned for effective teaching. Presession activities and the content of department worship are built around the day's lesson, so that pupils get a full hour of planned and integrated learning experience.

c. Better supervision. Without departmentalization it is difficult to give teachers adequate educational guidance. An experienced teacher may be willing to supervise a group of her fellow teachers in an age-group department, but few workers feel adequate to give guidance to teachers working with widely varying age-groups. In a graded department the supervisor and other workers become a team of Christian nurture specialists.

d. More workers. Departmentalizing the Sunday school creates jobs that inexperienced persons can and will undertake, even when they do not feel qualified to teach a class. Each new department requires additional helpers—pianist, secretary, and assistant teachers. Training in these positions opens the door to more responsible ministries. Many a person who never dreamed he could teach has agreed to serve as a department secretary or a helper in a class taught by someone else. That experience and training has encouraged him to become an active teacher with a class of his own.

2. *The Supervisor*

The supervisor is the key person in the departmentalized Sunday school. As the school grows and its organization is expanded, it becomes increasingly difficult for the superintendent and pastor to keep in personal touch with each teacher. The teacher is the one who in the final analysis is doing the work of Christian nurture. The teacher, however, cannot do the job alone. He needs help to keep up morale, provide guidance, and supply materials. Since it is impossible for the superintendent and pastor to provide this personal contact, the supervisor becomes the essential person in the organization. That is why departmentalized schools with efficient supervisors are growing—and developing a highly effective ministry of Christian education.

3. *Organizational Guidelines*

Organizing a Sunday school by departments depends on several key factors. In addition to securing supervisors, attention must be given to the size of the school, the space available, and the number of pupils attending—or planned for in each department. The chart on the opposite page gives guidelines for setting up department organizations in schools of varying sizes. In every case the chart suggests how many pupils and how many classes should be planned for in the departments recommended.

E. Organization for Outreach and Attendance

In evangelical circles the Sunday school has been used as an outreach arm. Often the Sunday school enrollment greatly exceeds the church membership as reflected in the following statistics from the *Yearbook of American and Canadian Churches for 1976* (overseas churches not included).

	Church Membership	Sunday School Enrollment
Churches of Christ in Christian Union	8,771	16,182
Church of the Nazarene	404,732	992,668
Free Methodist Church	65,167	116,976
The Missionary Church	20,078	44,161
The Wesleyan Church	84,499	212,463

1. *Contests*

Sunday school contests have often been used to stimulate attendance. In depression years, even small contest prizes stimulated great numbers. In times of affluence, the prizes take on larger proportions such as trips to a mission field or to Palestine. When prizes are related to personal improvement or to educationally stimulating ends, it is easier to see them as spiritually worthy tools.

2. *Rallies*

Rally days continue to be a means to stimulate attendance. Such rallies are beneficial when people respond to the challenge and seek to reach outsiders. Goal setting is helpful, but goals should always be based on previous attendance rather than on reaching the highest percentage of class enrollment present. When awards are based on enrollment figures, classes are tempted to keep enrollments low in order to make contest percentages easier to reach.

On rally days, one must plan for enough additional workers and materials to show that the school is interested in more than counting

Departmentalizing a Sunday School

DEPARTMENTS

Approximate Attendance: 25 — Department Rooms: 1

Department	Children	Youth	Adult
Ages	2-11	12-23	24 and up
Pupils	10	5	10
Classes	2	1	1

Approximate Attendance: 50 — Department Rooms: 2

Department	Children	Youth	Adult
Ages	2-11	12-23	24 and up
Pupils	19	10	20
Classes	4	1	1

Approximate Attendance: 75 — Department Rooms: 3

Department	Preschool	Children	Youth	Adult
Ages	0-5	6-11	12-23	24 and up
Pupils	12	21	13	29
Classes	3 groups	3	1	2

Approximate Attendance: 100 — Department Rooms: 4

Department	Preschool	Children	Junior High	Senior High/Career Youth	Single Young Adult—Adult / Married or Singles
Ages	0-5	6-11	12-14	15-23	24 and up
Pupils	16	28	9	8	40
Classes	4 groups	4	1	1	2

Approximate Attendance: 150 — Department Rooms: 6

Department	Nursery	Kindergarten	Primary	Middler	Junior	Junior High	Senior High/Career Youth	Single Young Adult—Adult / Married or Singles
Ages	0-3	4-5	6-7	8-9	10-11	12-14	15-23	24 and up
Pupils	12	12	14	14	14	13	12	60
Classes	3 groups	2 groups	2	2	2	1-2	1-2	3

Approximate Attendance: 200 — Department Rooms: 7

Department	Nursery	Kindergarten	Primary	Middler	Junior	Junior High	Senior High	Career Youth	Single Young Adult—Adult / Married or Singles
Ages	0-3	4-5	6-7	8-9	10-11	12-14	15-17	18-23	24 and up
Pupils	16	16	18	18	20	18	17	9	70
Classes	3 groups	3 groups	3	3	3	2	2	1	3

Approximate Attendance: 300 — Department Rooms: 9

Department	Nursery	Nursery	Kindergarten	Primary	Middler	Junior	Junior High	Senior High	Career Youth	Single Young Adult—Adult / Married or Singles
Ages	0-1	2-3	4 / 5	6-7	8-9	10-11	12-14	15-17	18-23	24 and up
Pupils	9	8	12 / 12	27	27	27	27	25	14	105
Classes	2	2	3	4	4	4	3-5	2-4	1	4

Approximate Attendance: 400 — Department Rooms: 13

Department	Nursery	Nursery	Kindergarten	Primary	Middler	Junior	Junior High	Senior High	Career Youth	Young Adult	Older Adult
Ages	0-1	2-3	4-5	6 / 7	8 / 9	10 / 11	12-14	15-17	18-23	24-40	41 and up
Pupils	10	10	16	18 / 18	18 / 18	18 / 18	36	32	20	70	70
Classes	2	2	3	3 / 3	3 / 3	3 / 3	3-6	3-6	1	3	3

500 and over

Schools 500 and over organize a department for each age or grade from nursery through junior.

people. Also follow-up of visitors is necessary to realize full outreach benefits from rallies.

3. *Advertising*

Advertising through direct mail, dodgers, parades, newspapers, radio, and television is usually helpful.

4. *Visitation*

By all counts the most effective method of outreach is personal visitation. Most visitors come to our Sunday schools as the result of a personal invitation from a relative, friend, or other person in a close primary relationship such as an employer, employee, teacher, or pupil.

5. *Guidelines for Growth*

What principles account for Sunday school growth? Some years ago the Southern Baptists identified the following guidelines:

> New units grow faster; classes reach maximum growth in a few months; small units must be provided; visitation is necessary; teachers and officers in a one to ten proportion to enrollment; grouping by age is the most democratic way of adding new units; the building determines the growth to about seventy-five per cent of capacity.[11]

In a more recent study of the 10 largest Sunday schools in the United States, Elmer Towns discovered that these schools use master teachers to build large classes, write their own literature, have weekly teachers' and officers' meetings, employ staff members to head most departments, set goals, promote contests, and advertise. They also establish branch units in new locations and use buses to transport pupils to a central building.[12]

A study of 300 larger Sunday schools in the Church of the Nazarene concludes that:

a. Attendance figures are related to the starting and closing time.

b. Pastoral leadership over a long period of time aids growth.

c. Being near a public school is the most significant location factor.

d. More frequent teachers' and officers' meetings aid.

---

11. J. N. Barnette, *The Pull of the People* (Nashville: Broadman Press, 1953), pp. 38-62.

12. Elmer Towns, *The Ten Largest Sunday Schools and What Makes Them Grow* (Grand Rapids, Mich.: Baker Book House, 1969).

    e. A five- or six-point record system is helpful.

    f. Growing schools survey their community at least once a year.

    g. Promoting pupils twice a year helps.

    h. A continuous leadership training program is necessary for growth.

    i. Publicity through a weekly newssheet is important.

    j. Fellowship and social contact outside the classroom stimulates attendance.

    k. Supplementary materials stimulate attendance of young people and adults.

    l. Employment of paid professional assistant ministers is necessary.

    m. Separate classrooms are not always necessary. Face-to-face contact in a crowded and noisy cafe seems not to deter interesting conversation and could be used as a means for learning and teaching when necessary.

    n. Fluctuation in gains or losses is normal.

It is almost impossible to maintain growth every year over a long period of time. Growth often exceeds the ability to provide adequate space and to train added personnel to do an effective job of teaching. Those who employ the master teacher concept with large classes probably depend heavily upon the lecture method and audiovisual aids.

It is easy to depend entirely upon human methods and to forget that real growth comes only by the power of the Holy Spirit. We honor God when we tarry in prayer and seek His blessing upon our efforts. When He works, man must stand in awe. God is not restricted to any one plan or method to do His work. One can find souls in the Kingdom to justify the use of almost any method. Some methods, however, are better than others. The secret is to seek God's blessing upon the best methods that we can discover.

F. Workers' Conferences

A regular workers' conference is one organization for enlarging and improving the work of the school. The most successful schools hold them weekly. Many are held in connection with a midweek family night, with supper for all. The choir and youth meetings are often held while the workers' conference is in session.

These conferences are planned for the purpose of inspiring workers, praying together, studying next Sunday's lesson, preparing and sharing materials. Here workers tackle and solve problems as quickly as possible.

In a departmentalized school it is highly important to provide major time in the workers' conference for department supervisors to meet with their staffs for department planning. Under these circumstances a general meeting of the entire staff may take up to 30 minutes, reserving 45 minutes to an hour for the department meetings.

Some schools find the weekly meeting impossible, so they schedule monthly or quarterly meetings. Whatever the schedule, it is important that meetings be held regularly.

G. Evaluating the Organization

Every phase of the Sunday church school should come under the scrutiny of some evaluation instrument. Statistics over a period of time will reveal gains and losses. Studies made from adequate records may show weaknesses and strengths. Local records compared with previous achievements or with standards set by denominational or interdenominational agencies will be valuable.

Few achievement tests have been used to evaluate learning in religious education—and none have been widely standardized. Because Sunday school attendance is voluntary, we have been reluctant to impose testing and evaluation procedures. Where achievement tests have been used, close home and church cooperation has usually been necessary. The difficulty of measuring Christian growth, however, should not stop us from trying to devise adequate forms of testing. The success of such programs can always be evaluated by informed leaders. Also the use of self-evaluation forms by teachers and officers can be encouraged.[13]

In recent years church growth studies have evaluated the effect of the type of community, its economy, and the location of the church. Such studies also evaluate the influence of room sizes and kinds of literature used. In institutional evaluation it is often wise to bring in an outside expert who has been trained in these techniques. Supervision and follow-up can be carried on by trained local leaders. The importance of such skills in educational leadership is one of the reasons why many churches have employed ministers of education in addition to the pastor.

The future of the Sunday church school has been doubted by

---

13. See Appendix II.

some. It is certainly permissible to question details of the precise organizational form it should take, but its objectives cannot be faulted. Much of the population of the world is still unreached and needs to be taught the way of Jesus Christ. The future of the church depends upon how effective we are in proclaiming the Good News and in teaching Christ's commandments. We had best use the Sunday school that we have at hand until some better alternative is provided.

VII. YOUTH SOCIETIES

Youth societies in the present era are so many and so varied that it is difficult to remember that they had a beginning. Perhaps in an earlier period it was not quite so difficult to make them a part of the church. But in spite of their current proliferation and independence, one must realize that there may never be enough. We have a never-ending task to reach and train youth for service in the Kingdom.

A. Historical Survey

Throughout the history of man, friendship groups have probably existed among youth. Schools of the prophets were used by Elijah and Elisha to gain and train young men. But youth societies as we know them today have existed for only about 100 years.

During the 19th century some early youth organizations were formed; they centered in singing schools and in temperance, missionary, and devotional activities. The Young Men's Christian Association was established in England in 1844. The YWCA followed in 1855. Both became popular in the United States. But the first distinctly religious society for young people in the church probably traces its origin to Theodore L. Cuyler in Brooklyn, N.Y. He modified the YMCA motto and pushed the concept of "Young People for Young People."[14]

The best known interdenominational group was the Christian Endeavor Society, organized by Francis E. Clark in Portland, Me., in 1881. The Brotherhood of St. Andrew in the Episcopal church followed in 1883. The Methodists organized the Epworth League in 1889. The Baptist Young People's Union was started in 1891 and the Walther League of the Lutheran church in 1893.

Many of the younger denominations organized at the turn of the

14. J. M. Price, *et al., A Survey of Religious Education* (New York: The Ronald Press Co., 1959), p. 252.

century probably included youth groups in their original structures. The Church of the Nazarene, starting under P. F. Bresee in 1895 in Los Angeles, Calif., had two groups, the Brotherhood of St. Stephen for the boys, and Company E for the girls. These groups met on a weeknight as much for evangelistic purposes as for study, fellowship, and devotion. The young people were identified by a pin of silver in the form of a Maltese cross upon which was written 1 Tim. 4:12 ("Let no man despise thy youth").

These crosses were used as conversation openers to witness for Christ in the city. They were called "Shiners" because they reflected the light.

Most of these denominational youth programs have developed into worldwide organizations with district, state, national, and sometimes international officers and programs.

B. Purposes

Probably the main purpose for youth groups was to give young people a place in the church. They met for inspiration, study, training in service, fellowship, evangelism, and improvement of devotional life.

As organizations in the church multiplied and the programs became more sophisticated, they tended to duplicate the work of the Sunday school or vice versa. Moreover, as young people grew into adulthood, it was difficult for their societies to restrict membership to youth. Also, as the societies ran out of inspirational topics, the programs took on more of a training emphasis. To solve these problems, in 1934 the Southern Baptists changed their BYPU into a Baptist Training Union. Other denominations found similar problems. Some drifted into mere Sunday evening fellowship hours, while others deliberately followed the Baptists in their Sunday evening training programs.

C. Training Versus Inspiration

Questions centering in purpose and programming arose rapidly. Do we provide programs of the novelty type merely to entertain? Do we confine young people's societies to the teenagers? Do we try to attract all age-groups within the same organization? Where does one place a "learning by doing" program within the organization of the church?

Answers to these questions are still shaping organizational structures. Groups that emphasized training have faced duplication of educational activities; within 25 years they have found their youth attracted to outside organizations that provided inspiration, excitement, and novelty programming. Also, a strong emphasis on training has often resulted in attendance of church members only; outside young people were not attracted. On the other hand, when the youth service has been highly inspirational, it has sometimes duplicated the singing and excitement of the Sunday evening evangelistic service.

The distinctiveness of youth societies is usually not found in methodology because buzz sessions, panel discussions, skits, reports, brainstorming, and symposiums are used in good Sunday school classes. Zuck finds the difference in objectives. He says the Sunday school class seeks to communicate God's Word through study and exposition, while the youth society seeks to train.[15]

Youth societies that have concentrated on outreach programs in personal and mass evangelism have attracted wide interest. Training in evangelism is accomplished by *doing* evangelistic work. Perhaps this model holds the key to the future in combining training, expression, fellowship, and a place in the evangelistic outreach ministry of the church.

D. Organization

Most training and youth societies follow the age groupings of the Sunday school. However, the youth groups elect their own officers and tend to carry a larger share of responsibility for their own programs. The teacher becomes a sponsor who guides indirectly from behind the scene. In the most effective training groups, each person carries some definite responsibility to participate each time the group meets.

Much of the planning and work is done through committees formed for these purposes. Committee planning sessions may be held once a month or once a quarter to prepare assignments and to provide opportunity for evaluation of effectiveness.

To secure an integrated age-group ministry in the local church, adult leaders are often chosen or assigned to care for all of the agencies and activities of the age-group.[16] The Sunday school teacher may also serve as a sponsor of the youth society. To relieve one person from overwork, several couples may be assigned to share these responsibilities.

---

15. Roy B. Zuck in *An Introduction to Evangelical Christian Education*, J. Edward Hakes, ed. (Chicago: Moody Press, 1964), p. 322.

16. See Appendix V.

Also a youth council is often used to coordinate all phases of the program. Each youth group is represented on the council, along with adult sponsors and the pastor or youth director.

E. Program and Curriculum

The objectives of the society determine its program. If the purpose is inspiration and fellowship, a variety of program kits or booklets offer skits and contest ideas. To those desiring more formal and purposeful training, quarterly journals are available from denominational and independent publishers. Training textbooks consisting of 6 to 12 session plans are also available from most publishers. Some materials provide unrelated lessons from Sunday to Sunday, but most periodicals and training texts offer units or series of related studies that continue for several weeks, sometimes up to three months.

VIII. MISSIONARY EDUCATION SOCIETIES

A. Historical Development

In 1792, William Carey was sent to India by the "Missionary Society for the Propagation of the Gospel Among the Heathen." This society was born in the home of a widow, Mrs. Belby Wallis in Kettering, England. The monthly meetings for prayer aroused interest to the point of revival and gave an emphasis to financial support for missions. After Carey's work was publicized, the interest in such missionary groups grew. The objectives were "prayer and giving, with a view to supporting mission work."[17]

During the first part of the 19th century interest and participation in missions grew rapidly. By 1817 there were 110 women's societies, and by 1860 they had been organized on an interdenominational level. Denominational groups followed: Southern Baptist and Congregational (1868), Methodist Episcopal (1869), Northern Presbyterians (1870), and American Baptist (1871).[18]

Sewing circles and missionary interests are still carried on faithfully by women of most denominations. In some churches the organizational structure has been expanded to include men, youth, and children. The World Missionary Society of the Church of the Naza-

---

17. W. Forbes Yarborough, *et al.*, *A Survey of Religious Education* (New York: The Ronald Press Co., 1959), p. 72.
18. *Ibid.*, p. 273.

rene is an example. At the time of the union of three groups in 1908, women from the Eastern group brought along emphasis on a specialized concern for missions. The Women's Foreign Missionary Society remained their exclusive concern for approximately 40 years. But gradually the feeling grew that missionary interest, study, and giving is the responsibility of the total church. Therefore, since 1952 the society has expanded to include the whole church family in its program.

B. Purposes

The objectives of missionary societies center in three areas:

1. *Missionary Education*

The missionary thrust is certainly found in God's love expressed in the Bible. We see it in the Book of Jonah, in the Great Commission, in the Gospels, in Acts, and in the Epistles. The outreach for all men is clearly revealed.

Missionary study groups are concerned about the history of missions and about the development of mission fields by their own denominations and by others. Members usually meet once a month to study books and other program materials describing what is happening in the missionary enterprise.

2. *Missionary Service*

As a result of such interest and study, missionaries have received their divine calls to serve. Others who stay at home are stimulated to pray and to carry forward practical projects for missions. These include box work, bandages for hospital use, and books for schools. The projects may vary from denomination to denomination and from one field to another, but they all have one thing in common: missionary projects enable those who stay at home to become vital partners of missionaries on the field.

3. *Support for Missions*

Prayer and service are parts of a good program of missions, but there is another area that most societies have in common—they are actively financing the cause. Scripture calls for the tithe as God's plan to finance His work. In addition, offerings are encouraged above the tithe to support more projects. Often the entire missions budget of a local church is raised by the missionary society.

C. Organization and Program

The names and numbers of missionary organizations and officers vary from church to church. Small churches may have only one organization. In larger congregations missionary societies may include adult, youth, and children's chapters.

Officers normally include a president or chairman, vice-presidents or other assistants as necessary, a secretary, and a treasurer. Some organizations provide for chairmen of committees, or secretaries designated for each phase of the program. The number of persons involved is determined by the size of the organization and the availability of personnel.

Regular monthly meetings seems to be the most widely used pattern. Other meetings are called for special projects. Some groups meet in the mornings or afternoons. Men's missionary fellowship groups may meet at a mealtime. In organizations that include the entire family, graded groups usually meet separately on prayer meeting night or prior to the Sunday evening service. A combined age-group meeting once a month at the midweek hour is the practice of still other groups.

The program and activities of each society are determined largely by the objectives and purposes. Study quarterlies or books are common missionary education media. Reading books covering various phases of missionary work are made available to members. Often standards are set by denominational agencies to guide the quality of the program. Also various recognition devices are used to encourage participation. The missionary society work has often been highly effective even though it normally operates without direct pastoral leadership and sometimes without a regular worship service.

BIBLIOGRAPHY

Byrne, H. W. *Christian Education for the Local Church*. Grand Rapids, Mich.: Zondervan Publishing House, 1963.

Chapter 1 explores the nature of the church as it relates to the educational ministry; also principles of organization are examined and various patterns are described for organizing Christian education.

Gangel, Kenneth O. *Leadership for Church Education*. Chicago: Moody Press, 1970.

Five chapters in Part I deal with the nature of the church, a biblical approach to education, a balanced program of Christian education, organizing and evaluating the educational work of the church.

Harper, A. F. *The Nazarene Sunday School in the 70's.* Kansas City: Nazarene Publishing House, 1972.

A current interpretation of the Sunday school ministries of one evangelical denomination with organization and programming common to most evangelical schools. A chapter is given to the program for each age level, nursery through adult.

Rice, Kenneth S. *Sunday School, the Growing Edge.* Kansas City: Beacon Hill Press of Kansas City, 1964.

This book supports the thesis that in today's world the Sunday school is the growing edge of the church. It is organized to reach new people, to share God's Word with them, to win them to Christ, and to provide them with places for service in the Kingdom ministries.

Richards, Lawrence O. *Youth Ministry.* Grand Rapids, Mich.: Zondervan Publishing House, 1972.

The author writes: "This book on youth ministry is a renewal book. In it I seek to draw from Scripture and to explore principles on which youth ministry can be confidently based." The book examines contemporary youth culture, youth as a time of life, the processes of youth ministry, and programming for youth work.

Wiseman, Neil B. *The Sunday School Supervisor.* Kansas City: Beacon Hill Press of Kansas City, rev. ed., 1977.

This book applies current principles of organization to the departmentalized Sunday school. Chapter 4 deals specifically with "Organizing the Department."

CHAPTER 14

Christian Education Organizations

In this chapter we shall look at organizations that use weekdays or special seasons of the year for Christian education. When these organizations are related to the local church, they are responsible to a board of Christian education.

I. Vacation Bible School

The vacation Bible school is usually a local church program that uses summer months when public schools are closed. It occurs in an informal setting where one can wear everyday clothes for work and play. During these summer months one finds fewer competing demands; also interest can be sustained more easily than in the Sunday school because of the consecutive daily sessions.

A. Historical Development

Vacation Bible schools, like the Sunday school, began because someone noticed neglected children and became concerned. The work actually started in Boston (1866) and in Montreal, Quebec (1877), when concerned Christians saw Bible reading, memory work, hymns and songs, military drills, calisthenics, manual work, and patriotic exercises as ways to occupy the time of idle children for a purpose.[1]

---

1. Mavis Anderson Weidman, in *An Introduction to Evangelical Christian Education,* J. Edward Hakes, ed. (Chicago: Moody Press, 1964), p. 332.

However, Mrs. D. T. Miles of Hopedale, Ill., is considered to be one of the first to have organized a vacation Bible school (1894). Mr. Walter A. Hawes, of the Epiphany Baptist Church in New York City, conducted a school four hours daily each summer from 1898 to 1904. Robert G. Boville, a Baptist city missionary, promoted Mr. Hawes's idea into a movement that spread to an international organization beginning in 1901.[2]

The denominations gradually took over this ministry. After 75 years the number of schools indicates that they are considered one of the most worthwhile educational activities of the church.

B. Purposes

The objective has been more than merely providing something for idle children to do. VBS seeks significant goals of Christian education.

1. *To Supplement Other Educational Activities*

When Protestants count up the time children spend in the Sunday school, they generally find it pitifully small. Even when we add other Sunday educational activities, it is still not enough. The vacation Bible school supplements these few hours with a concentrated period of about three hours daily for one or two weeks.

This consecutive block of time provides a basis for more concentrated units of study than can be provided through Sunday programs. In a well-planned curriculum these units are designed not to duplicate the Sunday ministries. Rather they supplement Sunday school teaching. When this happens, the student's Christian education is enlarged and enriched.

2. *To Reach the Unchurched*

Many churches have found the vacation Bible school to be an excellent outreach for enlisting unchurched children and their parents. Boys and girls not ordinarily attending Sunday school can be persuaded to join in the vacation activities. A public program at the end of the school to display the work and activities of the children has been a time to invite and involve the parents.

Schools in which churches cooperate across denominational lines give opportunities for community-wide enlistment. All participating churches benefit from the added emphasis on Bible study; also more persons are enrolled in other church activities.

---

2. W. Forbes Yarborough, *et al.*, *A Survey of Religious Education* (New York: The Ronald Press, 1959), pp. 292-94.

3. *To Evangelize*

It is not enough to enlist persons in Bible study; the church's task is to bring them to a confrontation with Jesus Christ. Proclamation of the Good News and decision-making have been characteristics of revivals; but evangelical Christian education should also lead persons to the point of decision. The vacation school provides an excellent opportunity for winning pupils to Christ.

Revivals are excellent methods for adult evangelism. Also children attend and are often won to Christ, but many preachers find it difficult to meet the needs and interests of all ages. Therefore, some churches plan vacation Bible school as revival time for children. The curriculum materials are designed as a unit of study building toward a time of decision. The natural time for the invitation to accept Christ comes in one or more of the concluding sessions. The truth is presented so as to build toward a climactic moment in the session. The leader then gives the invitation to receive Christ through a definite crisis of decision and public profession.

4. *To Enlist and Train New Workers*

Many persons who have never taught in Sunday school or other Christian ministries have been persuaded to help in the vacation school. These new recruits have been given training. This instruction and experience has prepared them to make further contributions. Confidence has been achieved where fear prevailed. Interest in and love for pupils have been aroused. To maintain and preserve this spirit some have accepted positions of leadership with these pupils in year-round teaching ministries.

5. *To Gain New Members for the Church*

If evangelism is successful, it leads to involvement. The public profession of faith leads to a deepening interest in the life of the church. The VBS may be followed by a pastor's class for new converts. Such a unit should be climaxed by receiving new Christians into church membership.

C. Organization and Leadership

1. *Sponsoring Groups*

To make the vacation Bible school an integral part of the whole educational work of the church, the most inclusive educational board should be responsible for its supervision. The Christian education committee usually serves in this capacity. It is responsible to appoint or elect a director, choose the curriculum, approve the leaders, and provide financing and facilities for the program.

In community-wide schools, a committee made up of representatives from each cooperating church becomes the sponsoring organization. In some communities a church council or ministerial alliance serves this purpose.

2. Director

The key to an adequate school lies in the person chosen as the director. He must be one who can inspire and work well with others. For summer programs it is extremely important that such a person be selected as early as January. This allows time for the choice of curriculum materials and for the training of workers.

In smaller churches either the pastor or his wife usually serves as director; in larger churches it may be the minister of Christian education. This arrangement often provides more qualified leadership than could be had otherwise, but it may deny some qualified layman an opportunity for service. Whoever the director, the pastor should be responsible for a service of dedication of the workers and for giving spiritual guidance throughout the school. The pastor may also carry responsibility for the evangelistic services.

If necessary, the director can teach one of the classes in the school, but it is better if he is free to supervise others, to give support and encouragement, and thus to improve the quality of the entire school.

3. Workers

In addition to the director, the school will need supervisors for each age-group. After teachers are recruited, supervisors can assist the director in helping to train workers for their own departments. Availability of teachers sometimes determines when the school can be held. A good policy is to schedule the VBS at a time when the most workers are available.

A great many helpers are needed for VBS: recreation and handicraft leaders, musicians, secretaries, playground supervisors, and street crossing guides. These assistants are recruited from parents, teenagers, and other church members who may never before have been involved in the educational work of the congregation.

Public school teachers and college students home for the summer are likely sources for expert help. Night shift workers have been used in morning schools. No definite ratio between workers and pupils has been adequately determined, but a general rule might be at least 1 worker for each 10 pupils. For preschool groups the ratio should be 1 to 4 or 5.

4. *Organization*

The organizational pattern usually follows that of the Sunday school: nursery, three years; kindergarten, four and five years; primary, first and second grades; middler, third and fourth grades; junior, fifth and sixth grades; junior high, seventh, eighth, and ninth grades. Senior high students are usually used as helpers. Many night schools also provide adult classes for parents who bring their children.

D. Curriculum

1. *Materials*

The board of Christian education, as the most responsible educational group in the church, should select the curriculum. Materials are available from denominational and independent publishing firms. It is usually wise to use denominational materials or to follow denominational recommendations because general leaders have given careful attention to coordinating the VBS courses with other Christian teaching curricula used in the church. Most publishers have developed materials in a cycle covering several years. Whoever publishes them, the materials should be graded according to the age, interests, and needs of pupils. This provides an educationally sound program. They should also be evangelistic in emphasis and help students advance in the Christian life. All materials should be evaluated according to the biblical content as well as for theological and educational soundness.

Most publishers encourage the local church to adapt, revise, and supplement the printed materials to fit the local situation. Much of this adaptation is planned in training sessions when workers study the materials together.

2. *Activities*

Activities in VBS are usually the key to the excitement and challenge of the program. Learning opportunities are increased by the joyous, relaxed atmosphere of the vacation period.

The basic activities of worship, Bible study, and evangelism are enhanced by innovative methods. Choral reading and rhythmics add excitement. Creative writing and drawing, along with handicraft, help eager pupils to learn. Trips, exploration, and service projects aid the student in observing or putting into practice what has been taught. Recreational periods and light refreshments provide opportunities to develop friendships and enjoy fellowship.

Parades to advertise the Bible school have been increasing in recent years. Bicycles, wagons, floats, pets, and signs add to the excitement. When parades are used, good judgment is advised, so that the cause of Jesus Christ is apparent and served.

E. Financing

Finances are needed for curriculum materials, supplies, postage, promotional materials, transportation, refreshments, and any remuneration paid to special directors or teachers. However, volunteer service by the teachers and workers should be encouraged.

Expenses for the school vary from one community to another. A national VBS director quotes a 1976 average cost of $1.65 per pupil. Supplying craft packets, of course, raises the cost. With careful planning and budgeting, however, one should provide adequate materials and program for $1.50 to $2.50 per pupil.

Finances for the vacation school should become a part of the regular educational budget of the church. Funds should be provided by the appropriate church finance committee or board. Special offerings to finance the program may need to be taken prior to the meeting of the school. However, offerings taken during the school collected from the pupils should be applied to some special missions or service project. Giving to support the work of the church thus becomes a part of the Christian learning experience of the pupils.

F. Standards

Most denominational departments set up and publish standards for evaluating vacation schools. These criteria involve length of the school, finance, curriculum, training for workers, organization, balanced program, attendance, records, evaluation, and follow-up.

For many years the standard length for vacation schools was 10 sessions of two and one-half hours daily over a period of two weeks. However, increasing employment for women and a growing number of summer activities for children have brought pressure to shorten the VBS. Many churches are experimenting with adapted schedules. Some have endeavored to condense the program into five double sessions in one week. Others, finding more workers available at night, have included the whole family in the program with a night school from 6:30 to 9 p.m. In these schools young people and adults are also often engaged in Bible study and service projects. Many churches have found it necessary to reduce their programs to one week whether conducting morning or evening sessions. Others are using day camps and backyard Bible schools.

Evaluation and follow-up have become increasingly recognized as important for securing enduring values from the vacation school. An evaluation session following the school aids future planning. Careful follow-up includes recruiting VBS pupils for Sunday school attendance and preparation of VBS converts for church membership.

II. Weekday Christian Education

The Protestant Reformation increased the demand for democratic government and for public education. As a result, in many countries the state has gradually assumed responsibility for general education. Whenever government has replaced the church as the sponsor of schools there has been a gradual separation between religious instruction and public education.

A. Religion and Public Education

1. *Issues*

The United States serves as an example of this gradual separation. In the New England colonies, one of the main objectives of public schools was to teach reading so that students could read the Bible. The first textbooks were filled with biblical quotations and stories. The first colleges, Harvard and Yale, were established to prepare men for the ministry. But as the colonies united and the Constitution was established, the church and state were separated. Gradually the biblical elements were deleted from curriculum materials, and the public schools became almost entirely secular.

As the main thrust of this separation was felt, some communities experimented with programs of religious instruction. In public schools pupils were released to attend religious instruction in their own classrooms. In the state of Texas, credit was allowed for the study of the Bible as a part of the regular elective curriculum. Elsewhere pupils were released early from school or during designated periods to attend religious instruction in the church of their choice.

A number of Supreme Court decisions have brought about fundamental changes in these programs. In the 1947 decision, *Everson* v. *Board of Education,* the Court ruled that public funds could be used for busing pupils to private schools. In the now famous "Champaign Case" (Champaign, Ill.) *McCollum* v. *Board of Education,* the

Court's decision prohibits sectarian religious instruction on school time and property. However, in 1952 in the *Zorach* v. *Clauson* case, pupils were permitted to be released from school control to take sectarian religious instruction on school time but off of school property.

The landmark "Prayer Case" came in 1962 as *Engel* v. *Vitale*.[3] The decision prohibits school-sponsored prayer. But we must be careful not to interpret this ruling more broadly than its specific intent. The case involved a particular prayer being prescribed for the entire school. The Court has not ruled against all forms of prayer and Bible reading in a public school; the prohibition applies only when the activities are part of a state-sponsored practice of religion.

The *Abington* v. *Schemp* case[4] prohibits school-sponsored religious exercises. This, however, does not prohibit school-sponsored study of religion. *Study* may be possible while the *practice* is prohibited.

Much has been written concerning these decisions and their effect upon the teaching of religion. One nonprofit group has been formed to serve as a clearing house and consultant service.[5]

2. *Types and Experiments*

Weekday religious instruction in the United States has had more than a 50-year history. The most prominent type is probably the *released time program*. Through a written request from parents, pupils are excused from the public school to go a nearby church to receive religious instruction. Community schools have been conducted under the auspices of church federations or ministerial associations. Usually these schools are financed by the sponsoring association or by voluntary contributions from churches or individuals. In some instances employed teachers are certified in the same way as regular public school personnel. Other schools use volunteer teachers. Often these teachers are pastors or associate ministers from local churches.

The *shared time program* is still in an experimental stage. Some attempts have been made in Chicago, Ill., and in the state of Vermont. The Chicago experiment was conducted by a parochial high school located near a public high school. The parochial students

---

3. *Engel vs. Vitole,* 370 U.S. 421 (1962).

4. *Abington School District vs. Schemp* and *Murray vs. Curlett,* 374 U.S. 203 (1963).

5. Religious Instruction Association, Inc., P.O. Box 533, Fort Wayne, Ind. 46801. This association has prepared a practical handbook for teachers, published by Harper and Row: *Religion Goes to School.* They also have mimeographed reprints of articles regarding the relationships between religion and public education, relevant curricula, and materials adaptable for classroom use.

attended both schools. They received instruction in the natural sciences and technical subjects at the public school; their instruction in the humanities and religion was given at the parochial school.

In Vermont, a community solved the problem of separation of state and religion by erecting two public buildings. One was used for ordinary public school instruction; the other was used by the churches of the town as a place for religious instruction.

Court cases testing the constitutionality of these plans are yet to be heard.

3. *Materials and Programs*

The Religious Instruction Association of Fort Wayne, Ind., lists persons in more than 30 states who have experimented with various types of materials and programs. Courses most often include Biblical Literature, Biblical History, History of Religions, Comparative Religions, and Ethics. Units within these courses include study of selected Bible passages or books, and the history of religious movements. Speech courses have included studies of biblical personalities and biblical allusions in contemporary speeches. The influence of the Bible and religion upon music and art has also been of widespread interest.

B. Parochial Education

With the separation of church and state growing wider, some have turned to the parish-sponsored school. However, the expense involved in salaries and equipment has caused others to abandon the effort. Even the Roman Catholic church and the Missouri Synod Lutheran church, strong advocates of parochial education, have recently been forced to close some of their schools because they were unable to finance them.

There is increasing pressure to secure more public funds for private schools. Court cases are pending, and the outcome is difficult to predict. Some believe that individual tuition script will be the solution, thus allowing the student to choose his own school. If this should happen, it could be that in some highly religious communities public schools per se would be forced to close for lack of students.

Busing pupils to achieve racial integration in public schools has caused some communities to turn to private schools as a means of continuing segregation. No doubt a few parochial schools have been started or have increased enrollments as a result of these decisions.

Government money has been available to some religious organizations to support educational and social service activities. These include day-care centers, colleges, nursing homes, and homes for the aged. Buildings have been erected and equipment has been purchased through government loans or grants.

Nursery and child care schools have been the most popular in recent years because of the increased interest in childhood education and because working parents have had fewer available babysitters. Government money has been available, but government inspection and licensing have also been imposed in many locations. Minimum standards have been set, and additional paid personnel have been required. When local churches sponsor these day-care centers, the director of Christian education often serves as administrator. In some instances, the pastor himself has become the director. This arrangement may be a temporary expedient, but the pastor must be careful that these related agencies do not jeopardize his primary work as a preacher and minister of pastoral care.

Kindergartens and the primary grades are also quite popular in parochial education. Perhaps these schools for younger children are more frequent because they are less expensive in terms of equipment and facilities. As one enters the upper grades and secondary education, the subjects taught become more technical; therefore, more expensive equipment is needed, particularly in the libraries and science laboratories.

The current unrest and financial difficulties in both public and parochial education make it difficult to foresee guidelines for the future. Certainly education will continue, but what forms it will take are still to be determined.

III. Youth Clubs and Character-building Organizations

Mallet is credited with establishing one of the first clubs for young men in 1708 in Basel, Switzerland. Industrialized societies with the growth of cities have made these clubs possible and necessary. Those dealing with children and youth have been frequently identified as character-building organizations.

A. Essential Characteristics

Clubs for these ages hold certain essential elements in common.

1. *Code of Behavior*
Whether identified as rules or as values to be upheld, each group

has certain expectations that affect behavior and character formation.

2. *Recognition*

Achievement is recognized by some form of reward. It may be a badge, insignia of rank, or a ceremony honoring the accomplishment. By these rewards the member is made aware that he is expected to improve, to grow, and to develop.

3. *Loyalty*

Belonging to the group is important to the member. This importance is enhanced by rituals and pledges of allegiance. Initiation ceremonies also serve to reinforce the promises made. Close fellowship between members enriches and strengthens the loyalty.

4. *Identification*

Insignias, badges, or ribbons may be used to show common identification. Sometimes elaborate uniforms, including caps or scarfs, are used to increase the prestige of belonging to the group.

5. *Voluntary Association*

Compulsory attendance in any organization tends to produce negative reactions. On the other hand, when one joins of his own choice, his interest is heightened and his chances of being influenced favorably by the activities is increased. Discipline and codes of behavior are more easily enforced because of this voluntary association.

6. *Structured Experiences*

Planning the learning experiences in successive steps of increasing difficulty makes progress possible for club members. Achievement is also more obviously recognizable in this manner, and less is left to chance or to indirect methods.

7. *Self-development*

Most of the character-building groups, because of their voluntary nature, leave development and progress up to the individual. He is responsible for his own achievement. Competition may be encouraged in some activities, but each person is expected to be capable of reaching his goals under his own motivations.

8. *Goals*

These goals are achievable. Some are placed in a simple sequential arrangement that is completed in the early stages of membership. Other goals are expandable into lifetime challenges. Many have carry-over value that stimulates personal growth long after one has graduated from the organization.

9. *Adult Leadership*

Mature guidance and direction are necessary in all forms of education. Such characteristics are therefore among the qualifications for club leaders. Because this is true, training programs for leaders are a requirement in the best character-building groups. Also continuing education renews the leaders and enlarges their capacity to serve.

10. *Home Cooperation*

Character-building clubs recognize the importance of parents and guardians in the home. Active cooperation between home and club is encouraged. Some clubs dealing with younger groups insist upon parents as leaders. Others involve them on appropriate occasions and insist upon their attendance at award ceremonies.

11. *Whole-Person Emphasis*

It is difficult to divide the self into parts because character is affected by changes in every aspect of the personality. Thus development in body, soul, and spirit are included in club objectives. This triangle is often represented symbolically in the club ideals and is reflected realistically in its activities.

12. *Supreme-Being Emphasis*

While God may not always be explicitly recognized, a reverence for the spirit is clearly seen. Many groups indicate belief in God as a necessary part of their program. The importance of the spirit and achievement in these higher values is fostered through progressive steps of endeavor.

13. *Personal and Group Growth*

Character clubs recognize that each individual is different, therefore members have a choice of activities and projects. At the same time, they move up from one rank to another, each according to his own ability and achievement. At the same time, some common group action is made possible. The group is important but the individual does not lose his identity. All levels of the program may be achieved by any member willing to discipline himself to put forth the necessary effort.

14. *Openness*

Fraternal organizations tend toward exclusiveness, but the

character-building groups are structured to include as many persons as possible. Clubs are open to all who choose to join. No one is denied membership because of race, class, or religion.

15. *Learning by Doing*

Education is important in the character-building club. The mind is challenged, but knowledge for the sake of knowledge alone is not an objective. Learning is associated with training. Knowledge is coupled with practical experiments in ways calculated to change one's life. Often head, hands, and feet are combined in learning activities. The five senses are windows to planned experiences that stimulate growth for the whole person.

16. *Drama*

Glamour is a part of club ceremonies, and excitement is created by dramatic activities. No work or step of progress is unimportant. Everything is worthy of notice, therefore dramatic experiences are planned and appropriate ceremonies are conducted.

B. Church-sponsored Community Agencies

Churches often sponsor these organizations because they stress character building and place an emphasis on belief in God. Most often the church will use these clubs as supplements to its own Christian education activities.

The following list of agencies is not exhaustive but representative.

1. *Boy Scouts*

This is an organization that had its start in England. Robert Baden-Powell became concerned about the lack of training he observed in young men during the Boer War in Africa. Upon his return to England he founded the Scouts and in 1903 published a book, *Aids to Scouting.* His Brown Sea Island Camp was established in 1907, and the experiences there led to publishing *Scouting for Boys.* Organizing them into patrols, he early emphasized current features such as the scout oath, promise, laws, and a good turn daily. The motto "Be Prepared" still serves as a reminder of the necessity to make progress.

As a result of refusing a reward for doing a good turn to an American businessman, an unknown scout became the instrument that caused William D. Boyce to bring scouting to America. A charter came from the U.S. Congress on June 15, 1916.

Scouting has expanded and reached around the world. At an

international meeting of scouts, political differences are forgotten. Exchanges of trinkets and gifts are a prominent part of the display of friendship.

Scouting includes Cub Scouts, Boy Scouts, and Explorers. Each ministers to a different age-group. In Cub Scouts, the boys 8 to 10 are arranged in Packs and Dens with a Den Mother. Their activities center in the home.

Boy Scouts attract youngsters from 11 to 13 years of age. They are arranged in Patrols and Troops. Troops are bound together into area councils.

The older boys, 14 and up, can join the Explorers. Some of these groups are connected with sea or air motifs. A Ship or a Post are the basic units of organization.

Each scout group must have a sponsoring institution. The adult leader is called the scoutmaster.

Besides the various learning activities, the scout is encouraged to obey the scout law which states, "A scout is trustworthy, loyal, helpful, friendly, courteous, kind, obedient, cheerful, thrifty, brave, clean, reverent."

He takes this oath:

> *On my honor, I will do my best to do my duty to God and my Country, and to obey the Scout Law; to help other people at all times; to keep myself physically strong, mentally awake, and morally straight.*

The scout begins as a Tenderfoot. He can progress through several stages to the highest rank of Eagle Scout. In each stage there are required achievements and also optional enrichment projects. The *God and Country Award* is a highly desirable medal; to earn it, a boy must complete requirements including service to God and to his church. Here the church and the Scout Troop cooperate to help the boy complete the necessary requirements.

Another close association with the church is seen in the insistence of the scout movement on worship services. On any weekend trip, worship services must be provided or arrangements made for the scout to attend worship services of his choice.

2. Girl Scouts

Girl Scouts were first introduced as "The Girl Guides" by Mrs. Juliette Lowe in Savannah, Ga., March 12, 1912. In 1915 the name was changed to Girl Scouts. Their aim is to develop each girl into a well-rounded individual and an intelligent participating member of her own group and community.

The organization includes Brownies for girls 7-9 years of age, Girl Scouts 10-14, and Senior Girl Scouts 15 and older. These groups are sponsored by community organizations from which adult leaders are recruited.

Although not officially connected with Boy Scouts, many of the Girl Scout activities and progressive stages of development are similar but appropriately adapted to girls. Girl Scouts place equal emphasis on character building and services rendered.

3. *Camp Fire Girls*

This group was founded in 1910 by Dr. and Mrs. Luther Halsey Gulick. William Langdon was conducting a meeting for Boy Scouts in Vermont when girls came asking for a meeting. Learning of this desire, Dr. and Mrs. Gulick constructed a plan to use leisure time, to perpetuate the spiritual ideals of the home, and to stimulate the formation of habits for health and character.

Camp fire emphasis is upon learning by doing. The insignia of the crossed logs and flame symbolizes a fire on the hearth of the home; the campfire signifies the out-of-doors. The watchword is "Wohelo," a combination of the first letters of the three words work, health, and love.

The Law of the Camp Fire Girls reminds each girl to: "Worship God, Seek Beauty, Give Service, Pursue Knowledge, Be Trustworthy, Hold On to Health, Glorify Work, Be Happy."

Three divisions are maintained: Bluebirds, for girls 7-8; Camp Fire Girls, 9-13; and Horizon Club, for girls 14 years and older.

These units are sponsored by at least one to five persons or by some organizational group. A mother, friend, teacher, or sister over 18 years of age must be secured to serve as the adult leader, known as a *Guardian*.

4. *FFA, 4-H, FHA*

These organizations have developed primarily in rural and farming areas, but recently they have spread to suburban and urban locations. The federal government and some state agencies have encouraged organization and participation in these clubs through various grants and programs.

The Future Farmers of America (FFA) is an organization of, by, and for farm boys. It encourages the study of vocational agriculture in high school and is a part of its curriculum. High schools in the program usually hire a vocational agriculture teacher who serves as the sponsor. The purpose for FFA is to develop leadership, cooperation, citizenship, recreation, and patriotism as well as to improve agriculture. The motto is "Learning to do and doing to learn; earning to live and living to serve." Each student conducts a project in supervised farming; he applies on the farm what he has learned in the school. Regional, state, and national meetings provide opportunity for members to display talents and achievements.

The 4-H Club takes its name from its purpose to help its members develop in head, hand, heart, and health. It is a coeducational organization for young people who are engaged in farming, homemaking, and community activities. All 4-H clubs are a part of the national system of Cooperative Extension Work in Agriculture and Homemaking. The Smith-Lever Act of 1914 gave the Department of Agriculture authority to develop this work. Many county agents actively assist the clubs. The 4-H member pledges "my head to clearer thinking; my heart to greater loyalty; my hands to larger service; my health to better living for my club, community, and country." Each boy and girl chooses a piece of work or a project that will help him to become a better farmer or homemaker. Their motto is "to make the best, better." They are encouraged to better their own best records and to display their projects in county, state, and national fairs.

The Future Homemakers of America (FHA) are mostly girls who are interested in home economics and who are taking the subject in high school. Boys enrolled in home economics are also eligible for membership. The club's purpose is "to help individuals improve personal, family, and community living now and in the future." The motto is "Toward New Horizons." Local chapter advisors are usually homemaking teachers in the local schools.

5. *YMCA and YWCA*

These are separate organizations for men and women; however, some of the activities in each have been expanded to include the entire family.

The Young Men's Christian Association was born in England in 1844, but has now expanded into more than 68 countries. It began with a group of young men engaged in the drapery and other trades who met to improve their spiritual conditions. The work began as an organization to conduct religious services. George Williams, the founder, reaped a bountiful harvest. By the end of a year the program had expanded to include mental as well as spiritual needs; physical activities were gradually added. Today few of the original spiritual activities remain, although one could not say that the YMCA is completely void of a religious emphasis. The membership has been expanded to include members of other faiths as well as the Christian religion.

The YMCA has served in two world wars, cooperating with the United Service Organization to meet the needs of military personnel.

The Young Women's Christian Association came into existence in 1855. In the beginning it had spiritual concerns similar to those of the YMCA. Following the Civil War and during the great religious revival of the 1880s and the industrial revolution, the organization grew in importance. It was fostered by church women who sought to find suitable lodgings and to otherwise care for the young women flocking to the growing factory towns. It, too, expanded its program to include social, recreational, and educational activities.

6. Boys Clubs of America, Inc.

This is another club which, like the YMCA, has endeavored to reach city youth. It was founded in the 1860s in factory towns of New England, but its official charter was issued in 1906. Its purpose is to reach the most needy, but it is open to all boys regardless of their status or background.

Group activities are a part of the program; but attention is given to individual needs, and personal development is encouraged. The building of physically fit, self-reliant, tolerant, and all-around good citizens is the purpose of this group.

C. Church Weekday Groups

Quite often the church expands its ministry to include groups started outside of its jurisdiction. In other instances the church itself has launched these ministries. This has been done to supplement the work of its Sunday agencies and to provide a ministry to the whole personality of persons in its constituency.

The Salvation Army has its *Red Shield Clubs* to attract youth and to minister to those within its fellowship.

Organizations similar to Scouting have been developed by numerous church groups. The Christian Service Brigade began in 1937 in Glen Ellyn, Ill., and Pioneer Girls was started in 1939. These have been popular weekday programs among independent churches and a number of small evangelical denominations. The local church is directly involved in planning the Christ-centered activities.

A similar approach has been followed since 1940 with the Caravans in the Church of the Nazarene. Its policy has been to confine this activity to the younger groups while encouraging older youth to participate in a church-sponsored Scout troop. However, some Caravan activities and programs extend from primary ages through high school. Local, zone, and district powwows are held. A national director encourages the organization and promotes the program, but no national meetings have been held other than training and promotional sessions.

D. Camps

1. *History*

The Todds have declared that camping is "uniquely American."[6] The Pilgrims and also the pioneers who pushed westward sought out campsites on high ground. The Mexican War and the Civil War encouraged the ballad "Tenting Tonight on the Old Campground."

Frederick Willis Gunn is considered to be the father of the American camping movement. It began when he established a school for boys in which they could camp out in tents like soldiers. The first venture was a two-week summer program in 1861.

In the church the revivals of the latter part of the 19th century led to the establishment of camp meeting sites. The National Camp Meeting Association for the Promotion of Holiness was begun in Vineland, N.J., in 1867. Entire families would tent on the campgrounds in those days. The brush arbor camp meeting tabernacle and the sawdust floor and tent meeting in the last part of the 19th century gave impetus to the modern church camping movement.

2. *Societal Influences*

The American tradition is an outdoor tradition, but it took the city to create the great need for camping. Crowding people into the city's asphalt jungle enhanced the pleasure one receives from a week or two in the camping areas. In a technological society the gadgets cause persons to yearn for simpler pioneering experience and for the opportunity to work with one's hands. The reduction of hours in the work week has also created more time for the pursuit of leisure. This increased leisure coupled with a mobile society and affluence have placed camping within the range of many persons.

3. *Values*

A camp may provide the child his first opportunity to spend a

---

6. Floyd and Pauline Todd, *Camping for Christian Youth* (New York: Harper and Row Publishers, 1963), p. 3.

night away from home and parents. This is a maturing experience that can give opportunity to develop self-reliance.

Living out of doors also enables one to enjoy what God has created. It can deepen the sense of God's wonders and awaken respect for the way man is made.

Camps often become laboratories in living. One may learn how to survive on his own; but on the other hand he may also develop his feeling of interdependence with others. The camp thus provides a chance for democratic decisions to be made.

Living in a camp with Christian leaders deepens and enriches Christian experience and fellowship. Opportunity to observe oneself and others under a variety of circumstances fosters growth in Christian understanding and maturity.

Learning takes on a new dimension in the outdoor environment. Often barriers are broken that would not have been conquered in any other way. The sheer joy of a camping experience seems to create a desire to inquire. Thus the educational role is an important part of organized camping.

Attention to health is also often a part of camp life. Habits of clean and wholesome living are taught and encouraged.

4. *Types of Camps*

Informal camping may be experienced by an individual or a family in campsites or in the woods following one's own desires. But normally Christian education is concerned with organized camping.

Day camping is held during the daylight hours where no sleeping quarters are involved. Many city groups find that open space in parks and campsites without housing offer excellent opportunities for Christian outdoor experiences.

Organized camping takes on various forms depending on the purpose for the camp and on the age-group being served. Boys' and girls' camps, youth institutes, and weekend retreats are familiar programs. Conferences are also sometimes combined with a camping experience.

In evangelical circles the revival atmosphere is often combined with camping. Services are planned to give campers opportunity to accept Jesus Christ as Lord and Saviour. These may be in the open air, by a campfire, or in a tabernacle or brush arbor built for the purpose.

5. *Organization and Leadership*

There must be some sponsoring group for the Christian camp.

It may be a district board or a local church group of interested persons. This group plans the overall objectives and arranges financial backing for the camp.

The governing board usually chooses the director. He in turn is responsible for the day-to-day planning and operations. He chooses other personnel as needed.

Assistant directors may be appointed to care for various phases of the program: athletics, education, handicraft, recreation, and transportation. Cooks and kitchen helpers are designated to care for food services. Usually professional help will be needed in the health services. A camp nurse is important to care for first aid, insect bites, and minor illnesses. If the camp is not large enough to have a full-time camp doctor, a physician ought to be on call or nearby for major problems.

Counselors to care for campers and to assist them in their learning experiences should be chosen and carefully trained. The younger campers need more personal attention, and therefore more time is required from counselors.

Some camps require each camper to assume work responsibility. This becomes a learning and character-building experience. Some of the more unpleasant jobs such as cleaning the rest rooms and washing dishes are alternated. Cleaning the cabins and making one's own bed are usual chores for most campers.

Adequate leadership is the most important factor in the success of a camp. A good director, spiritual advisors, and other personnel can go far to make up for lack of facilities and equipment.

6. *Campsites*

To own a site is expensive, but it provides more opportunity to set advantageous dates for camps. Renting relieves one of responsibilities and saves making an investment, but he is at the mercy of another person's calendar to decide when the site is available.

In choosing a campsite, a number of factors may be considered. For some, locating close to a center of population and transportation would be most important. Farther from the beaten path may be the answer for others. Ample space is important for the development of living, dining, educational, and recreational areas. To most camps a stream or lake is vital. Trails and woods provide opportunity for hikes and for outdoor camping. In country areas, sewage and water treatment facilities have to be considered. Many groups now look for sites that can provide year-round activities.

7. Programs

The program should serve the purposes of the camp and also take advantage of the out-of-doors environment. What is available from the natural surroundings and campsite help to determine the program. Also weather conditions sometimes force postponement or changes in activities planned.

Ample time should be provided for rest and sleep. For children and teens, attention needs to be given to good eating and health habits.

Some camps demand a rigid schedule. Others follow a more relaxed and informal program. The purpose of the camp determines the schedule. Also the age of the campers affects the time allotted to any activity.

Suggestions for programs, activities, and schedules are available from denominational headquarters and from other sources.[7] Conferences for camp leaders are held periodically, and denominational resource persons can give aid in the solution of problems.

E. The Church and Recreation

Organized recreation is one phase of Christian education that is of fairly recent origin. The name itself suggests its Christian significance —to recreate rather than to wreck creation. To renew one's self in mind and body through physical or social activity means giving attention to the whole person. This emphasis is in line with sound psychology and with biblical principles.

The Scriptures support the role of play. Zechariah declares that in the restored Jerusalem "the city shall be full of boys and girls playing in the streets" (8:5). In biblical history, occasions of celebration brought joy and physical movement. When David returned from victory over the Philistines, "the women came out of all the cities of Israel, singing and dancing to meet King Saul, with tabrets, with joy, and with instruments of musick" (1 Sam. 18:6). Paul teaches the importance of the whole person when he writes: "Know ye not that ye are the temple of God, and that the Spirit of God dwelleth in you?" (1 Cor. 3:16). Jesus himself took part in social events even though some religious people criticized Him for it (Luke 7:34).

Today recreation is often used as a Christian outreach and wit-

7. Christian Camp and Conference Association, 14312 Runnymede, Van Nuys, Calif. 91405. National Recreation Association, 8 W. 8th St., New York, N.Y. 10011.

nessing program. Many young people are attracted for the first time to Christ through a social occasion or an athletic event under the auspices of the church.

In the early development of the First Church of the Nazarene in Los Angeles, P. F. Bresee, the pastor, had numerous types of activities including social and recreational events, but all of these had an evangelistic purpose. Trips to the beach on holidays became opportunities for rejoicing in singing and witnessing for Christ.

Every athletic or social activity in the church's program must serve some worthy purpose. Paul gives us the guideline, "Whether you eat or drink or whatever you do, do it all for the glory of God" (1 Cor. 10:31, NIV). It may be simply vigorous exercise in company with fellow Christians, or people getting acquainted with each other, sharing a responsibility, enjoying fellowship, or acquiring new skills. Such purposive activities can be sound Christian education: they produce changes that make us better persons.

Participation is the key to successful recreation. Too many of our modern activities involve only observation and spectator roles. Such vicarious experiences have some recreational value, but active involvement on the part of every participant is most desirable.

IV. RETREATS

A. Historical Background

The retreat has become a popular experience in modern Christian education. It is not, however, a recent discovery. In 1554, Ignatius Loyola began recommending "spiritual exercises"—later called retreats. These spiritual exercises purposed to provide the atmosphere where an individual could (1) reform his life, and (2) seek the will of God in solitude. "The Society of Jesus was the first active religious order in which the practice of the retreat became obligatory by rule."[8]

Originally, retreats were offered as occasions when one could decide, with "the help of the Holy Ghost," what he should do with his life. One came to consider the choice of a vocation for life— marriage, priesthood, monastery, business, etc.[9] Although the retreat was established initially for "pious ecclesiastics," it has evolved into a

---

8. *The Catholic Encyclopedia*, s.v. "Retreats," by Paul Debuchy, pp. 795-97.
9. Roy T. Howard, *Liturgical Retreat* (New York: Sheed and Ward, 1959), p. vii.

time of renewal conducted for employees, workingmen, teachers, and laymen as well as clergy.

In modern times, the retreat is most often geared to "helping a person put into practice the requirements of the state of life which he has already chosen."[10] It has become a time for renewal and rededication to one's values.

B. Definition

Two types of retreat are defined by James Michael Lee:

1. *The Closed Retreat*

This is "that period of prayer and spiritual reflection conducted in an environment devoid of any contact with the outside, temporal, everyday world." Such retreats are typically held in some isolated place where one may withdraw from his usual contacts. "Retreat houses" or lodges often serve as places of meeting.

2. *The Open Retreat*

This is "that period of prayer and spiritual reflection conducted in an environment in which there is contact with the outside world. Retreatants in such milieu watch television, read secular magazines —all in addition to the regular 'time' of prayer and spiritual reflection."[11]

In the truest historical sense a retreat is not meant to be a workshop, study conference, or promotional meeting. It is not primarily for planning, study, promotion, or getting out of doors; rather, retreat focuses on relationships—with God first and through Him with others.

A retreat is:

a. A planned *spiritual encounter*.

b. A time to experience, actualize, or embody truths of the faith.

c. An experience of *community* in which the intent is renewal.

d. A time and place of conversing and listening between oneself, God, and fellow retreatants.

e. A time to withdraw oneself from the routines of daily living, to devote oneself to God in exceptional communion, and to fellowship and share life and experience with others.

---

10. *Ibid.,* p. viii.

11. James Michael Lee, *The Shape of Religious Instruction* (Mishawaka, Ind.: Religious Education Press, Inc., 1971), p. 220.

 f. A time to engage in a special spiritual discipline for a specified period of time.

 g. An attempt to discover the true meanings of faith and to prepare for a renewed witness and service to the people of the world.

 h. A small-group experience. According to some, it should seldom involve more than 25 retreatants. Of course, a large group of 100 could be divided into groups of 25.

C. Elements of a Retreat

There seem to be at least six elements common to most retreats:

1. *Withdrawal*

The first type is physical. One literally withdraws from the usual routines and demands of living at home, on the job, or in school. There is also a separation of the whole person—body, soul, spirit—from the pressures and cares of normal living.

2. *Content*

Most retreats provide a variety of content sessions. Such times offer guidance as well as unity of purpose and thought for the retreat. There need not be a special speaker. The retreat leader may provide content in the form of Bible passages, portions of a book, printed handouts, pamphlets, films, filmstrips, audio-cassettes, and other input material.

3. *Interaction*

The total retreat group is usually divided into small groups for conversation and nonverbal exchange of meanings. The interaction often focuses on ideas and concepts from the content sessions. Dialogue may revolve around the attempt to clarify an issue, to solve a problem, or to share an insight. Interaction also denotes interrelationships; retreatants may share times of planned or spontaneous recreation and fun.

4. *Freedom*

A central concern of retreat is the provision of freedom. One should be free to spend some of his time as he desires. He should be free to create situations for his own renewal and recreation. The schedule should have built-in flexibility. Excessive time demands and agenda requirements are the great cripplers of true spiritual retreat.

5. *Silence*

Silence is probably the most overlooked element in modern retreats. It should be programmed in. Silence means listening to God and responding to His Spirit. Verbal communication is suspended for a time. Retreatants find places to be alone and to reflect on the meaning and values of existence. Often individuals and groups walk in silence and meditate. Too much talk obstructs hearing what God has to say to me. It may be my talk. It may be the talk of others. In times of silence, there is opportunity for me to breathe deeply from fresh winds, to find new direction and purpose, to reflect on the meanings of Scripture, to face my anxieties and problems, to wait on the Lord and be strengthened, to be still and know that God is God, to rest, relax, and find renewal. At first many are frightened by the "sound of silence," but it is a necessary retreat element.

6. *Worship*

Worship involves both formal and informal expressions of devotion to or dependence on God. Personal and corporate prayer are vital parts of the experience. There is also a place—especially toward the end of retreat—for formal and informal celebration. One may wish to celebrate his newfound purpose and life. He may desire to celebrate the resolutions he has made to God, to others, and to himself. Such celebration often takes the form of music or a Communion service.

Probably the greatest reason for the success of retreats in our day is the urgent necessity for renewal. Paul Debuchy suggests: "In the fever and agitation of modern life, the need of meditation and spiritual repose impresses itself on Christian souls who desire to reflect on their eternal destiny, and direct their life in this world towards God."[12]

V. SUMMARY

The church through the centuries has expanded its ministries to include the whole personality and the entire week. Often some of the ministries that the church has started, such as schools and hospitals, have been taken over by other agencies. When this happens, the church rejoices because good work that needs to be done is being

---

12. *The Catholic Encyclopedia*, p. 797.

done. Sometimes, however, these ministries have lost their religious purpose and Christian motive. As a result, the church has been forced to return to the field.

Paul's Christlike passion to be "made all things to all men, that I might by all means save some" (1 Cor. 9:22) serves as a model for the church. No doubt there are other ministries that the church will attempt. They will be organized into purposeful activities that are yet to be dreamed and fashioned. It is the work of the Spirit of God to challenge each generation to perceive the spiritual needs of people and to devise ministries to meet those needs.

BIBLIOGRAPHY

Fakkema, Mark. "The Christian Day School Movement," in *An Introduction to Evangelical Christian Education* (J. Edward Hakes, ed.). Chicago: Moody Press, 1964.

> A man involved in parochial school work discusses its historical background, the urgent need for it in today's social structure, the solutions to be found in Christian schools, and a report on the church affiliations of these schools.

Latham, Mary E. *Vacation Bible School—Why, What, How?* Kansas City: Beacon Hill Press of Kansas City, revised edition, 1972.

> A complete guide for VBS planning. How shall a VBS be set up? What should be included in the daily program? How shall teachers be secured? The author presents objectives and proven methods—all centered in the ministry of the church.

Russell, Eunice. "Weekday Youth Clubs," in *An Introduction to Evangelical Christian Education* (J. Edward Hakes, ed.). Chicago: Moody Press, 1964.

> An unusually good overview of the ministry of weekday youth groups. The author outlines their importance, unique values, programming, and administrative principles.

Todd, Pauline H. and Floyd. *Camping for Christian Youth.* New York: Harper and Row, 1963.

> A guide to methods and principles for evangelical camps.

Young, Bill. *The Caravan Ministry.* Kansas City: Beacon Hill Press of Kansas City, 1973.

> A guide to one evangelical denomination's weekday ministries with boys and girls.

CHAPTER 15

Principles of
Administration

I. Introduction

Of all human enterprises, the Church has always been the most dynamic. No other social organization has made such claims about its origins, purposes, authority, and source of truth. No other has made greater demands on the personal resources of its members. None has existed for so long with the same unity of command and mission. No other social organization has done as much to shape the thinking of persons and nations. None has been so uniquely characterized by a blending of the human and the divine.

"Its task is to persuade people to become Christians in order that they might make other people Christians, and so on to the end of the age."[1] The Church is the divine-human society by which God does His work in the world. With all of its problems—many of which are common to all human enterprises—the Church has made a difference in every social milieu in which it has existed. John Seamands calls it "a living fellowship where the Spirit of God is present and working, not just a club where members pay dues and attend meetings."[2]

Although the Church is an organization, it may be more correctly thought of as a highly complex organism. An advertisement on

---

1. Arthur F. Glasser, in A. R. Tippett, ed., *God, Man, and Church Growth* (Grand Rapids, Mich.: Wm. B. Eerdmans Publishing Co., 1973), p. 59.
2. John T. Seamands, in *God, Man, and Church Growth*, p. 95.

the radio proclaims that a certain precision watch is "the world's most perfect timepiece." The listener then hears an amplified ticking —the sound of a smooth-running mechanism designed to tell the time of day. But a stethoscope placed on the chest of a patient by his physician reveals another steady sound—the beating of the human heart—an organism but finely organized. The Church at its organized best is like the human heart—dynamic, life-sustaining, pulsating, reliable, and very well put together.

The Church has always depended upon human leadership to accomplish its mission. While operating under the lordship of Jesus Christ, it has functioned under the leadership of men. In the inner city as well as on the mission field, God works through key personalities. The church that is alive and pulsating seldom operates spontaneously—i.e., unadministered and unplanned. God always works through men with plans.

This chapter concerns the men and women through whom God works to organize and maintain His Church. It deals with leadership and management—the administrator and his tasks.

II. Administration: What It Is

For better coverage, the topics of organization and administration are treated separately in this volume. Organization, discussed in the previous chapters, is the structural dimension of an institution. It is to the whole Christian education enterprise what a skeleton is to the human body. Organization is the design; it shows how the parts fit together and relate to one another.

Administration, on the other hand, is the muscle of the organizational body. It is the functioning, managing, and achieving side of Christian education. Administration includes all of the processes by which the policies of the organization are carried out. In short, administration is the *action* dimension of organization. It is the means of making the organization work. In Christian education, especially, administration must always be highly personalized.

A. Definition of Terms

Beyond defining the key words, *organization* and *administration,* one must consider the meanings of other terms in order to grasp the central thrust of this chapter.

1. *Organizing*

The administrative function of organizing is the process of distributing, dividing, or grouping the work into individual tasks, and establishing the relationships between the individuals performing those tasks.

2. *Responsibility and Accountability*

Although these terms are often used as synonyms, there is a clear distinction between them. The term *responsibility* refers to the function or performance expected of a member of the organization. Ordinarily it is used to describe a set of functions for which a person is expected to answer. *Accountability* implies that there are persons in authority *to whom* a member of the organization answers for the work he is expected to do.

3. *Evaluation*

The process of evaluating is the question-asking task of administration. Evaluation attempts to find answers to at least four questions: (1) Where are we now in our Christian education program? (2) By what strategies and activities did we get here? (3) Where are we likely to end up if we continue in this direction? (4) What is necessary for improvement?

4. *Planning*

Planning is projecting the course of action. It is the process of deciding in advance what is to be done, and how. Planning is the strategy-setting side of administration. Such a strategy is not just any way to reach a goal; it is the *best* way. A good plan is one calculated to reach the goal with a minimal expenditure of resources.

5. *Purpose and Goals*

Before an enterprise can set out on a meaningful course of action, it must establish a set of objectives or aims. These become its purpose or mission. Without a statement of objectives, one has no basis for making plans. As Gulick has well said, "A clear statement of purpose universally understood is the outstanding guarantee of effective administration."[3] Before a church launches itself into a sea of homes and businesses, it must answer the question, Why are we here? Are we here to evangelize? To instruct? To disciple? To meet community needs? To attack social issues? To provide a holiness

---

3. L. Gulick, *Administrative Reflections of World War II* (Montgomery, Ala.: University of Alabama Press, 1948), p. 77.

witness? Just what *is* our mission? An objective, then, is a statement of the church's intention to act.

Once the purpose of Christian education is determined, goals can be established. Goals are plans expressed in terms of results to be achieved. They are the targets toward which one aims his efforts.

There may be a difference between an objective and a goal. An objective is often thought of as a long-range and general purpose. In contrast, "Goals are specific, measurable milestones which show a church's progress in moving toward its objectives."[4] However, it should be noted that the terms *goals, objectives,* and *aims* are often used synonymously, as elsewhere in this text.

III. THE LEADER-ADMINISTRATOR

Churches that are growing are usually characterized by three important qualities: (1) a clear sense of mission; (2) high morale within the congregation; and (3) an administrator-leader around whom enough people rally to achieve success in the various ministries.

Jesus spoke a great deal about leadership. He contrasted the religious leaders of His day with His own example of servanthood when He said, "Whoever among you wants to be great must become the servant of you all, and if he wants to be first among you he must be your slave—just as the Son of Man has not come to be served but to serve, and to give his life to set many others free" (Matt. 20: 26-28, Phillips). For a man to wear the mantle of leadership humbly, his character must equal his accomplishments. The Apostle Paul's instruction to Timothy regarding bishops and deacons sets a standard no less demanding than that set by Jesus (cf. 1 Tim. 3:1-13).

If the servant-leader is to follow the example of Jesus and lose himself in service to others—in contrast to the superior attitude of the scribes and Pharisees—he must see himself as simply one among those for whom Jesus died. "Leaders are not different from others in the church, but like them in all respects, and are to be deeply involved in the lives and experiences of individuals."[5]

A. Supervision as Stewardship

Paul believed that church leaders have the responsibility to help

---

4. Reggie McDonough, *Church Administration* (Nashville: Baptist Sunday School Board, Jan., 1967), p. 11.

5. Lawrence O. Richards, *A New Face for the Church* (Grand Rapids, Mich.: Zondervan Publishing House, 1970), p. 115.

church members become equipped for their own work of ministering. He writes, "And his gifts were that some should be . . . pastors and teachers, for the equipment of the saints for the work of ministry" (Eph. 4:11-12, RSV). For this reason God gives gifts to men and gives gifted men to the church. Whether one is a leader or follower, he is to heed the admonition to be a good steward. "The biblical concept of stewardship is that of a person responsible for his leadership under a higher authority. The elder shepherds, or lesser shepherds are to feed the flock of God responsibly . . . until the Chief Shepherd comes."[6] Until Jesus returns, the mantle of supervising will fall to chosen men. If they are faithful in their stewardship, they will wear that mantle with humility.

Supervision and management are synonymous terms. Both refer to overseeing designated responsibilities. Both are involved in the task of putting the strengths of people to work. Success in Christian education is related to the number of persons thus involved in the pursuit of its goals. Christian education, therefore, always requires active lay participation throughout the full range of the administrative processes. "Effective churches are built on involved, active, and responsible membership, not merely on a membership that is involved by participation in programs that are conducted by church leaders."[7] This participation increases a person's level of satisfaction and enthusiasm for the various projects of Christian education.

The superior-subordinate relationship often characteristic of secular organizations is neither commanded nor allowed by New Testament guidelines for church leaders. The servant-administrator performs his role of supervision under authority given him by Christ. That role is ratified by the members of the congregation who then look to him for sanctified leadership in equipping them for their own work of ministering.

B. Maintaining Lines of Communication

Effective church communication involves the transmission and reception of ideas, objectives, plans, and reactions by both leader and followers. The purpose is that goals shall be reached through understanding, agreement, and favorable response. Effective communication:

- Builds a climate of understanding in the church;
- Encourages interaction among members of the congregation;
- Creates an atmosphere of participation;
- Improves coordination of ministries;
- Articulates the goals and plans for Kingdom building.

C. Developing Morale

Josiah, king of Judah, during the seventh century B.C., not only appointed "the priests to their offices," but also "encouraged them in the service of the house of the Lord" (2 Chron. 35:2, RSV). God's leader apparently had learned that giving people a direct assignment and expecting them to work willingly was only part of his administrative role. He also had to give encouragement and praise when they deserved it—and sometimes when they did not.

A wise leader-administrator will strive to help his workers at three points. He will keep them—

1. *Informed*

Workers need to be informed. Communication regarding what is going on, even in areas that may not be their specific assignments, will keep everyone involved in the total effort. Information may be communicated either informally, or formally by announcements in staff meetings or through newsletters.

2. *Inspired*

Informed workers have a better chance of being inspired workers also. Motivation is the one gear without which Christian education ministries will not function with optimum power.

3. *Involved*

It may not be true that all involved people are happy people, but it is true that all happy people in the church have discovered the importance of their own involvement in its life. Happily involved workers usually have high morale. Businesses generally observe the following principles for maintaining the morale of their workers:

- Realization of the importance of the assignment;
- Confidence in leadership, from the immediate superior up;
- Participation in what is going on;
- Recognition as a person, not just a cog in the machinery;
- Appreciation and recognition for work accomplished;
- Opportunity for improvement;

• Good communication to and from leadership;
• A congenial group with which to work.

Fred Smith, formerly an executive with the Gruen Watch Company, said:

> I have never met a lazy man; I have only met unchallenged men. Challenge is the thing that releases energy into a man. Challenge creates energy and gives direction. It makes a man willing to pay the price of discipline. A football coach does not get many young men to cut out excess sweets and dates, to go to bed early and to sweat out practice, who have no dream of getting on the squad. . . . The game becomes the goal. . . . That is what is wrong with the Christian life as we often present it today. . . . We offer no challenge. . . . We just tell people to stop enjoying themselves, join the church and be miserable. We ask them to stay in rigorous training when we don't even have a game scheduled. We may have a huddle coming up, or a meeting of the team, but no real face-to-face, toe-to-toe encounter.[8]

D. Decision-making

In most human enterprises decision-making is a function of management. Subordinates may make limited decisions for the implementation of the work, but making policies is usually reserved for executives or boards of directors. This is also true in the church, but with one difference. Decision-making in Christian education must answer to biblical imperatives. Christ is the Head of the Church, which is His Body (Col. 1:18). All decisions in Christian education fall under His lordship.

While there is room for individual decisions in personal matters, the principle of joint decision-making should apply to matters that affect the whole church. Biblical precedents for this principle may be found in Acts 5:12 where the church met and acted "with one accord." Also we read in Acts 6:1-4 that the apostles "summoned the body of the disciples" together to settle a difficulty. In the midst of another crisis "the apostles, the Elders, and the whole Church agreed to choose representatives and send them to Antioch with Paul and Barnabas" (Acts 15:22, Phillips). New Testament leaders did not act on their own in making decisions that affected the entire fellowship of believers.

Kilinski and Wofford suggest that church leaders typically face three kinds of decisions: cyclical, confrontation, and innovation.[9]

---

8. Fred Smith, "Power into Your Life," *Decision* (June, 1963), p. 3.
9. Kilinski and Wofford, *Organization and Leadership*, p. 214.

Cyclical decisions are those routine matters that recur frequently, e.g., ordering church school materials each quarter. *Confrontation* decisions are forced upon an administrator by unexpected circumstances, e.g., expanding the parking facilities in order to take care of rapidly increasing attendance. *Innovative* decisions are those that do not confront the administrator—he seeks them out. Decisions to launch a new bus ministry or to begin a day-care nursery school are typical examples of innovative actions.

Unfortunately, cyclical and confrontation decisions often demand so much time and effort that the typical leader in Christian education has little time left for innovation. "We misplace the bulk of our time, effort, attention, and money on problems rather than opportunities . . . We spend at least 90% of our time making the routine decisions that account for not more than 10% of the results."[10]

If decision-making is important in Christian education, the phases of the process should be considered.

Griffiths suggests six steps:

1. Recognize, define, and limit the problem.
2. Analyze and evaluate it.
3. Establish criteria or standards by which the solution will be judged acceptable and adequate to the need.
4. Collect necessary data not provided.
5. Formulate and select the preferred solution.
6. Put the preferred solution into effect.[11]

The creative leader is one who has an appreciation for the biblical imperatives relating to decisions that affect the church. He is sufficiently organized to handle cyclical decisions in stride, and he gives optimum time and effort to confrontation and innovative decisions.

E. The Pastor-Administrator and His Paid Staff

1. *The Multiple-Staff Concept*

The concept of a shared ministry is not unique to the 20th century. In Exodus 18 an incident is recorded that has become accepted as the first biblical precedent for a team ministry. Jethro warned Moses that he was near exhaustion from his efforts to rule the people by himself. That counsel led to the first division of administrative responsibility in the Exodus events.

---

10. *Ibid.*, p. 214.
11. Daniel E. Griffiths, in Andrew W. Halpin, ed., *Administrative Theory in Education* (Chicago: Midwest Center for Learning, 1958).

Multiplied thousands of churches today function smoothly with only one employed minister. To some degree these men manage to multiply their ministries by equipping volunteer workers to share in their responsibilities and tasks. However, as churches grow beyond 250 active members, maintain Sunday schools requiring scores of workers, establish bus routes, organize multiple choirs, and develop elaborate ministries for all ages, the pastor-administrator discovers that he needs professional help.

In dynamic situations like these the multiple-staff ministry is often born. Associates are employed by the church to serve in roles requiring time and special skills not available to the church through volunteer workers. As staff members are added, the pastor-administrator becomes "senior minister," administering the work of all associates who share in his ministry. The larger a paid staff becomes, the more important is the selection of persons adequate for the roles expected of them. "Choosing the right man to share the same yoke with others is of utmost importance. In a sense, it is a vocational marriage."[12]

2. Communication Responsibility

Twofold communication is necessary for the development and maintenance of a multiple-staff ministry. The senior minister is the key to both.

First, he is responsible to establish and maintain lines of communication between himself and members of his staff. While it is true that an experienced staff member will help bridge any gap in communication, the responsibility still belongs to the senior minister. Several psychological factors enter into such successful cooperation between the pastor and his associate(s):

a. Leaders need to maintain a sense of task. No associate should have to ask of himself, "What am I doing here?"

b. Individual differences among staff members must be accepted. Each person brings certain strengths, as well as weaknesses, into a multiple-staff relationship. For a strong team effort, strengths must be built upon—and weaknesses built around!

c. There must be personal and emotional maturity in members of the staff. The prima donna mentality—extreme temperamentality —in any member has no place in good communication.

d. A sense of loyalty toward each other and toward the joint effort must supersede concern for individual assignments.

---

12. Kilinski and Wofford, *Organization and Leadership*, p. 173.

e. There must be frankness and humility in all verbal and written agreements, memoranda, and assignments.

The second essential phase of communication is for the senior minister to convey to his congregation the philosophy, goals, and benefits of the staff ministry. If the pastor understands his role as pastor-teacher and sees his relationship with his paid staff as that of a team ministry, he can better educate his congregation to understand that relationship also.

Most associates do not favor a rigidly compartmentalized ministry, in which the pastor does his work and the associates do theirs, with little or no communication regarding what is going on. Some division of responsibility is necessary. But also some sharing of all pastoral ministries usually strengthens a team effort. And certainly constant joint planning, encouragement, and mutual support are necessary for best relationships.

A reasonable work load and sufficient time to accomplish goals should characterize the multiple-staff ministry. Educational results take time—sometimes years. The motivation for beginning a multiple-staff ministry should be, "The labor demands a shared ministry," not "We'll double our Sunday school in a year with this new man." The former reflects honest task evaluation. The latter may indicate a goal that is too narrow and an expectation that is too high.

IV. Functions of Administration

Administration has been defined as "the guidance, leadership, and control of the efforts of a group of individuals toward some common goal."[13] This definition delineates the purpose but tells little about the functions of the administrator in achieving those results.

One way to analyze administration is to think of it in terms of what an administrator does. Newman suggests five processes that are basic:

1. Planning—determining what shall be done
2. Organizing—grouping activities into administrative units
3. Assembling resources—obtaining things needed to execute the plans in terms of men, money, and materials
4. Supervising or directing—issuing instructions
5. Controlling—seeing that the results conform to the plans[14]

---

13. William H. Newman, *Administrative Action* (Englewood Cliffs, N.J.: Prentice-Hall, Inc., 1951), p. 4.

14. *Ibid.,* p. 4.

As one looks at Christian education and attempts to relate Newman's outline for its administration, seven functions emerge: *planning, calendaring, organizing, delegating, coordinating, budgeting,* and *evaluating.*

A. Effective Planning

Planning is "the organized application of systematic reasoning to the solution of specific practical problems."[15] It is deciding in advance what is to be done—and in what order.

Seen in its broad context, effective planning is a microcosm of the full administrative process. The steps are often cyclical, beginning with ideas and dreams, filtering these through the institutional *purposes* and imperatives, *setting goals* which reflect these purposes, *choosing methods, establishing target dates, determining the persons responsible* for carrying out duties, *setting the plans in motion,* and *evaluating the results.* The Christian educator should then reexamine the original purposes, which could lead to revised goals, new methods, and so on through the cycle.

1. *Examining Purposes*

Planning often begins with a leader dreaming dreams, outlining objectives, and establishing purposes. Henrietta Mears was a magnificent blend of the dreamer and the doer in Christian education. Her primary objective in programming was for quality, not just quantity.

When Miss Mears accepted a staff position at Hollywood Presbyterian Church in the late 1920s, she discovered the church was ready to grow with its 450 enrolled in Sunday school, but the church had crowded facilities, pictureless curriculum materials, and inadequate training for teachers. Once her priorities were established, she set some ambitious goals.

> The first thing I did in Hollywood was to write out what I wanted for my Sunday School. I set down my objectives for the first five years. They included improvements in organization, teaching staff, curriculums, and spirit. I wanted a closely graded program, a teaching material that would present Christ and his claims in every lesson, a trained teaching staff, a new education building, choirs, clubs, a camp program, a missionary vision, youth trained for the hour.[16]

---

15. Peter Drucker, "Managing for Business Effectiveness," *Harvard Business Review* (May-June, 1963).

16. Ethel May Baldwin and David Benson, *Henrietta Mears and How She Did It* (Glendale, Calif.: Regal Books, 1966), p. 77.

As the quality of her Christian education improved, the number of persons increased also. In two and one-half years the enrollment grew to 4,200.[17] Her goal for a new educational building went unfulfilled for 22 years, but it was still a priority goal for her.

2. *Setting Goals*

Goals are desired results toward which money, leadership, and time are allocated. "Planning in terms of goals," says Newman, "contributes to the constant vigilance that is necessary to keep the enterprise pruned of unproductive or overgrown branches."[18] Goals, then,

- Articulate results desired;
- Narrow the effort range;
- Relate effort to purpose;
- Give logic to pursuit;
- Give reliable measurements of the effects and validity of decisions.

Goals are frequently thought of in terms of *time*. In their time dimension, they are often expressed as immediate goals (now to 3 months ahead); short-range goals (the coming year); intermediate-range goals (1 to 5 years); and long-range goals (5 to 10 years).

Goals may also be expressed in terms of *kind:* numerical, financial, staff (personnel), facilities, and program.

3. *Choosing Methods*

Methods are strategies of action. They tell how a Christian educator intends to reach his goals. Within a planning cycle, the administrator should obtain a maximum number of methods that could possibly be considered in the pursuit of the goals desired. Once a list is compiled, the best methods should be selected. For example, an outreach committee seeking ways to evangelize its community might brainstorm in one meeting, compiling several pages of ideas for evangelism. Then from this list would be culled the most effective methods to achieve the group's goals.

4. *Establishing Dates*

Target dates are sometimes considered to be goals, but they flow naturally from the methods chosen. They are the intermediate planning stages necessary if the overall goals are to be reached. Target dates are sequential; they reflect the partial completion of the

---

17. *Ibid.*, p. 77.
18. Newman, *Administrative Action*, p. 28.

project in stages or steps. As the project's methods are put into action, target dates may be adjusted as necessary, but the administrator should consistently aim toward the accomplishment of given goals by the dates set.

5. *Determining Persons Responsible*

A major potential for success in the administrative process comes at the point of choosing persons responsible for the tasks to be done. Whether these persons volunteer or are otherwise assigned is not important. What is important is that someone accepts the responsibility for completing each stage of a series of tasks.

6. *Setting the Plans in Motion*

Once persons accept responsibilities, action should begin. And once action begins, the administrator must generate sufficient leadership skills to insure that all assignments are followed through to completion. Follow-through can be checked by persons reporting back to the administrator in periodic group meetings, by keeping adequate records of all important functions performed, and by frequent review of all plans in the cycle.

7. *Evaluation and Planning*

One sure mark of a strong administrator is regular evaluation of the results of group and individual efforts.

> Most ailing organizations have developed a functional blindness to their own defects. They are not suffering because they can't solve their problems but because they won't see their problems. They can look straight at their faults and rationalize them as virtues or necessities.[19]

Every organization should have built-in provisions for self-criticism—an atmosphere in which uncomfortable questions can be asked without threatening relationships. The future cannot intelligently be charted without an honest evaluation of the past and present.

Planning may be the difference between administrative success and failure. "Planning promotes consistent, integrated, and purposeful action."[20] Through careful planning, mistakes may be avoided, crises anticipated, and goals are more likely to be achieved. A good plan leaves little to chance.

---

19. John W. Gardner, "How to Prevent Organizational Dry Rot," *Harper's* magazine (October, 1965).
20. Newman, *Administrative Action*, p. 56.

B. Establishing the Calendar

No Christian education program can function efficiently without a master calendar of events, plans, and activities. Administratively, preparation of the master calendar falls under the heading of *coordinating activities,* but its importance to general administration is so significant that it warrants double mention. A current master calendar serves the following purposes:

1. Visually shows the distribution of activities over one-month time blocks;
2. Relates activities to each other during the month;
3. Assists families in planning their own social calendars;
4. Stimulates communication among the auxiliary departments of the church;
5. Helps establish program priorities;
6. Encourages advance scheduling for immediate and short-range plans;
7. Assists persons who serve in coordinating roles;
8. Shows the entire program ministry of the church.

C. Organizing the Organization

While organization for Christian education is discussed elsewhere in this volume, the function of organizing is clearly an administrative role. Organizing ministries in Christian education consists of (1) dividing and grouping the work into individual jobs, and (2) defining the established relationships between individuals filling those jobs.[21]

Job descriptions are an important ingredient in the process of organizing. Both lay and professional workers in the church deserve to know their specific responsibilities, their limit of authority, their relationship to other workers, and their place in the total educational effort. Job descriptions serve the following purposes in Christian education:

1. Prevent many misunderstandings of assignments;
2. Improve efficiency in the team effort;
3. Assist both the congregation and the workers to understand more clearly their particular ministries;
4. Orient new workers more quickly to priority assignments;
5. Serve as administrative guidelines so that less direct supervision is required;

---

21. *Ibid.,* p. 123.

6. Clarify objectives and reduce buck-passing;
7. Provide some protection against an overload in assignments;
8. Establish formal lines of communication;
9. Delineate reporting relationships between leaders and workers;
10. Identify qualifications required for the job.

Establishing working committees is also an important organizing function. Forming committees should be considered in light of the following principles.

Committees will:

1. Involve a greater number of persons in decisions;
2. Tap a wide range of opinion and experience;
3. Provide opportunities for training and growth for inexperienced workers;
4. Give a broad objective base for evaluating church programs;
5. Improve coordination of programs represented by persons on a committee.

Committees will not:

1. Always operate efficiently;
2. Speed decision-making;
3. Centralize responsibility;
4. Maximize accountability;
5. Guarantee implementation of plans.

Typical tasks of the education committee in a local church might include: establishing objectives, surveying needs, determining the curriculum, enlisting workers, planning and coordinating the program, preparing a Christian education budget, and evaluating the results of programs within its range of responsibility.

D. Delegating

Distributing work among leaders and workers is called *delegating*. When Moses divided the work of judging the children of Israel, he delegated authority. Each person in a place of leadership was to have authority over his division of the people. Only the most difficult problems were to be brought directly to Moses' attention. The principle that was established then is still relevant.

> The authority for decision-making should be placed as far down in the organization as the scope of the decisions will allow. . . . The worker should be able to make final decisions about any

matter that concerns his own activities. If a decision or action will influence others, those individuals should be involved. A few matters of a truly critical nature should be referred to the board. It should be emphasized that more important decisions are made at the top of the church structure, not because of inherent superiority of individuals, but because of the assignment of responsibility.[22]

An administrator learns by experience that responsibilities cannot be totally delegated. He may want to let out quite a bit of string, but he must remember that the whole ball is not his to give away. The man who is ultimately responsible needs to be close enough to the program to know what is happening.

E. Coordinating

Coordination deals with "synchronizing and unifying the actions of a group of people."[23] While coordination may be regarded as a distinct activity, it is a part of all phases of administration. Coordination is achieved when organizations for local Christian education work together harmoniously to achieve the goals established by the church.

Coordinating the program of a Sunday school with 50 members obviously demands less attention and skill than coordinating one of 1,000 members. Also, coordinating a congregation's whole program of Christian education calls for more skill than coordinating the ministries of the Sunday school. There are, however, some common principles.

1. A simplified structure with committee responsibilities;
2. Agreement by workers on the overall purpose, priorities, and goals;
3. A calendar of activities kept current;
4. Well-designed methods of communication;
5. Supervision through a central authority figure;
6. A sense of proper timing;
7. Consideration of long-range as well as short-range plans.

F. Budgeting

Establishing and maintaining budgets is part of the administrative function known as *controlling*. Most Christian educators look upon budgeting as part of our stewardship of the money that God has given to the church through tithes and offerings. Therefore, in our

---

22. Kilinski and Wofford, *Organization and Leadership*, p. 168.
23. Newman, *Administrative Action*, p. 390.

budgeting and expenditure we are responsible to the leadership of the Holy Spirit. "If there is imbalance or waste in the financial area of church operation, this will strongly tend to effect an imbalance or loss in the use of time, talent, and other resources."[24]

Newman cites seven benefits of budgetary control:

1. Stimulates thinking in advance
2. Leads to specific planning
3. Promotes balanced activities
4. Encourages exchange of information
5. Discloses unbalance early
6. Provides inclusive standards
7. Uses available reports on performance.[25]

G. Evaluating

Evaluating is a form of self-criticism. It is the question-asking function of administration. Too often we are tempted to ask such questions of groups or individuals only when a program has been less than successful. "Where did we go wrong?" is a typical query. When a program goes right, few questions are asked. But if secular enterprises make so great an issue of evaluating all results of projects attempted, can Christian education do less?

Kilinski and Wofford suggest that evaluation has four main purposes: to (1) foster initiative, (2) encourage imagination, (3) develop a sense of responsibility, and (4) intensify efforts to meet organizational goals.[26]

Evaluation helps a worker appraise his performance, particularly if the procedure is allowed to be self-appraisal. A teacher sees his performance and understands his motivation for Christian service better than anyone else in the church. He knows his weaknesses and strengths. He has probably prayed more about his leadership needs than has anyone else. And he will be willing to evaluate his efforts honestly if an atmosphere of acceptance and support is provided in the church.[27]

---

24. Kilinski and Wofford, *Organization and Leadership,* p. 197.
25. Newman, *Administrative Action,* pp. 431-33.
26. Kilinski and Wofford, *Organization and Leadership,* p. 181.
27. See Appendix II for a self-evaluation instrument for teachers, and Appendix III for an evaluation instrument to guide Sunday school organization and administration.

V. Administering the Facilities

There is one further function of administration that is different from those already outlined. It is serving as a leader-administrator of the church buildings and equipment.[28] Two significant topics are included here—the place of buildings in the ministry of the church, and the stewardship of their use.

A. Buildings That Minister

It is interesting that the New Testament Church had no buildings at all. The early Christians had no sanctuaries, educational buildings, or parish houses. The first distinctly Christian buildings did not appear until around A.D. 200. Hence there are no biblical directives regarding church buildings. It seems natural, however, that the facilities used by a congregation should fall under the general principles of biblical stewardship.

The buildings belong to God, and the use of church facilities should be an extension of His ministry. A building should be an expression of a congregation's commitment to Christ and His work. In short, the buildings should be a part of ministry. They are not shrines to an architect, a builder, a pastor, or a prominent contributor. Property of the church should say to a community, "We care enough about you to erect buildings. We hope they will be of service to evangelize, nurture, and provide fellowship. We want them to be a place of service to you and your family as together we worship and serve God."

B. Using God's Buildings

Those responsible for the administration of such buildings should ask frank questions about their use. How many days or hours of the week do our church buildings go unused? If a person desired the services of the pastor, would he be able to find the church office? If he found the office, would anyone there be able to answer his questions? How accessible are our facilities to the community? Is our baptistry or gymnasium available to other churches that are less fortunate? How early before services does the caretaker open the buildings? How soon after services does he turn off the lights and suggest to those lingering in fellowship that it is time to leave? How

---

28. See Appendix I for a detailed list of guidelines for buildings and equipment recommended for effective Christian education.

concerned are we about the normal wear and tear that our buildings receive during the week? What age-groups receive priority consideration when a new addition to the church is planned?

Answers to these questions reveal what a church board thinks about the ministry of its buildings and grounds. The administrator-leader should carefully develop a philosophy of use of facilities. He should then, just as carefully, lead his board and congregation to understand the possibilities of what God can do with His buildings when dedicated men and women give Him a chance.

*   *   *

Administration involves planning, organizing, staffing, initiating, delegating, directing, supervising, coordinating, motivating, evaluating, leading, controlling, assembling resources, budgeting, calendaring—all of these. Administration is the church in action.

BIBLIOGRAPHY

Adams, Arthur Merrihew. *Pastoral Administration.* Philadelphia: Westminster Press, 1964.

> A practical guide for the minister who wishes to increase his effectiveness in each of the many administrative functions his role demands—planning, organizing, recruiting and training, and working with employees and lay workers.

Bower, Robert K. *Administering Christian Education.* Grand Rapids, Mich.: Eerdmans Publishing Co., 1964.

> The book is similar in content and philosophy to William H. Newman's classic, *Administrative Action* (Englewood Cliffs, N.J.: Prentice-Hall, Inc., 1951). Dr. Bower wrote with the seminarian and serious pastor in mind, and the result is a technical, generally theoretical approach to church management. However, it is an important work and widely read by church administrators.

Dudney, Bennett. *Planning for Church Growth.* Kansas City: Beacon Hill Press of Kansas City, 1970.

> Written from the author's background as pastor and Christian education director. Its strengths lie in its practical, systematic approach for evaluating the total church program including organization, administration, and finance.

Fickett, Harold L., Jr. *Hope for Your Church.* Glendale, Calif.: Regal Books, 1972.

The story of the growth of the First Baptist Church of Van Nuys, Calif., from 15 members in 1914 to over 9,000 in 1972. The main focus is on 10 principles of church growth that Dr. Fickett followed as pastor of this church.

Gangel, Kenneth O. *Leadership for Church Education*. Chicago: Moody Press, 1973.

A study of the general principles of management and their relationship to the educational program of the local church.

Getz, Gene A. *Sharpening the Focus of the Church*. Chicago: Moody Press, 1974.

The chapters on leadership in the New Testament Church and on the principles of biblical administration and organization are particularly applicable to the student of educational administration.

Parrott, Leslie. *Building Today's Church*. Kansas City: Beacon Hill Press of Kansas City, 1971.

Dr. Parrott has blended theory and practice in this book designed to help a pastor plan and program for the pastoral and educational ministries of the local church. His central emphasis is the "how to" of organizing the church board, public services, finances, and counseling.

Sweet, Herman J. *The Multiple Staff in the Local Church*. Philadelphia: Westminster Press, 1963.

For over a decade Dr. Sweet's book has been one of the books read most often by pastors and their associates involved in multiple-staff ministries. His primary emphasis is on the common problems that develop in staff relationships and how they can be solved.

CHAPTER 16

Leadership and
Enlistment
of Leaders

God has chosen to depend upon the cooperative efforts of His people
to accomplish the work of His Church. As people work together to
build the Kingdom, Christian leadership is a natural outcome. This
chapter explores the nature of leadership and the best ways to enlist
and develop leaders among Christ's followers.

I. LEADERSHIP

A. Bases of Leadership

1. *Native endowment*

Whenever men associate in groups, we see some of them as
leaders and others responding to leadership. Some persons seem
naturally to assume dominant roles wherever two persons are together. This natural tendency provides the psychological basis for
leader-follower roles in human society. The leadership role of a man,
however, may shift when groupings change. A recognized leader in
one group may be overshadowed by a stronger leader in another
setting. These natural tendencies to dominance and to reticence
underlie human leadership and its followers.

2. *Agreement on goals*

God's prophet suggests another basis for leadership in his question, "Can two walk together, except they be agreed?" (Amos 3:3). When persons agree on a common objective, it is natural for someone in the group to begin to suggest ways to reach their goal. If the suggestions seem wise, the group accepts them. In doing so, leadership develops naturally. The person who knows where he wants to go, and how to get there, almost inevitably attracts followers.

3. *Learned Leadership*

Not all men have the same talent and ability to lead; some prefer to be led. Others seem naturally to rise to the occasion and grasp opportunities to lead. But the church cannot depend upon these natural leaders for all of its work. As we understand the principles of leadership, we can develop the talent of influencing others. Because this is possible, we in the church want to learn all that we can about leadership and how we can best use this understanding to accomplish God's work among men.

B. Definitions of Leadership

Charles Titus says, "Leadership is the art of getting people to do what you want them to do and making them like it."[1] At first this definition seems demeaning and dictatorial, but it correctly depicts one key responsibility of a leader. The first duty of government is to govern. Ordway Tead defines leadership as "the art of influencing."[2]

Milhouse emphasizes the element of moral responsibility when he writes: "Leadership is skill in guiding a group to work together toward a desirable end."[3] But the Christian leader must go even further; he must be sure that the goal he seeks is a goal that God desires for His people.

Paul displayed a model for every Christian leader when he invited the Corinthians, "Be ye followers of me, even as I am of Christ" (1 Cor. 11:1).

C. Qualities of Leadership

Natural talents for leadership are always the gifts of God; and God

---

1. Charles Hickman Titus, *The Processes of Leadership* (Dubuque, Ia.: Wm. C. Brown Co., 1950), p. xiii.
2. Ordway Tead, *The Art of Leadership* (New York: McGraw-Hill Book Co., Inc., 1935), p. 20.
3. Paul W. Milhouse, *Enlisting and Developing Church Leaders* (Anderson, Ind.: The Warner Press, 1947), p. 9.

is always looking for men who will dedicate those gifts to the tasks of His kingdom. From among His followers, Christ chooses leaders for His work. To the disciples He said, "I have chosen you and ordained you, that ye should go and bring forth fruit, and that your fruit should remain" (John 15:16). We believe that the Spirit of God enlarges and strengthens our natural gifts as we exercise them in His service. God in His sovereignty gives gifts to men and calls those whom He will into His service. But there are also times when Christian men choose their leaders—and when men elect leaders, they look for qualities of leadership. By observing over a period of time leaders whom God has called and whom men have chosen, it is possible to identify the qualities that lend themselves to this ministry.

1. *Intellectual Capacity*

Leaders are not always the most intellectual, but they seem to possess a capacity to apply knowledge. The task of leadership demands a capacity to grasp, analyze, evaluate, and use facts.

2. *Physical and Nervous Energy*

Every task demands an output of energy, but the church leader often finds his physical and nervous resources taxed to their limits. Those who would lead men need an extra supply beyond what may be sufficient for their followers.

3. *Purpose and Direction*

In our definitions of leadership we have seen the necessity of goals. The leader must be able to see further than others. His objectives must be clear in his own mind, and he must be able to help the group see those objectives and desire to achieve them.

4. *Motive of Service*

Jesus says to His followers, "Whoever would be great among you must be your servant . . . even as the Son of man came not to be served but to serve" (John 20:26-28, RSV). Leadership in Christian life and work requires a desire to serve. Any other dominant motive dooms a man to eventual failure.

5. *Friendliness and Knowledge of People*

The leader should love his followers. This requires a knowledge of people and a willingness to share their interests. One who would be a Christian leader cannot escape involvement in the lives of persons.

6. *Technical Mastery*

Intelligence is an asset, but one who has a capacity to master details can overcome some handicaps in native ability. It is at the point of acquiring relevant knowledge that leadership can be enhanced by training. A concerned leader is willing to pay the price to acquire whatever skill is necessary to aid him. In Christian education, leadership training institutes and courses are readily available today.

7. *Initiative*

Ideas originate with the leader, and plans must be suggested by him. The first step belongs to the man at the head of the column. One who is unclear and uncertain ceases to lead. The church wants someone who knows where the group should go. Jesus displayed this characteristic when He called His disciples (Matt. 4:18-19); when He showed them what were the right attitudes (Matt. 5:38-42); and when He contradicted current low levels of morality (Matt. 5:20-24). Jesus also required initiative from His disciples when He commanded them, "Go ye therefore and teach all nations" (Matt. 28:19).

8. *Integrity*

Followers learn to depend upon the leader, and his word must be trusted. The person who betrays confidences is not fit for leadership. Integrity is imperative; and obvious sincerity is heartwarming.

9. *Adaptability*

An effective Christian educator has said, "One qualification for being a college president is to get enough rest so that you are able to meet a new emergency." A leader must always be prepared for the unexpected. His plans may not develop as projected. His followers may not respond as he had desired, so he adapts to the situation. When necessary, he is willing to settle for half a loaf. Circumstances beyond one's control may prevent completion of plans. When this occurs, a leader changes to meet these conditions and is able to blaze an alternate path.

10. *A Sense of Humor*

A leader who can laugh at himself has a quality that produces staying power. Also tensions are often relieved and a friendly atmosphere created when one is able to laugh with others. Wise leaders, therefore, look for occasions when they can let the laugh be at their expense; they also seek to cultivate a leavening sense of fun in the group.

11. *Faith and Prayer*

These essential qualities for Christian leadership are interrelated. Faith in God is the basis for much of our prayer, but also prayer stimulates faith. Dependence upon the spiritual resources that God gives often restores the sagging spirits of Christian education leaders. A pastor said to his denominational leader, "We are looking to you, Dr. ———, to guide us in this new area." With sinking spirit the elected leader said to himself, "And to whom shall *I* look?" In a moment the voice of the Holy Spirit whispered, "You can look to Me." God helps those who depend upon Him. The Christian leader believes in prayer and in trusting God. Prayer and faith change things; therefore, we pray and we believe.

12. *Christian Life and Character*

There is no substitute for the crises of conversion and entire sanctification when one considers the qualifications for leaders in Christian education. One cannot lead where he has not gone. Sanders considers the filling of the Spirit to be "the indispensable requirement" for spiritual leadership.[4] A denomination concerned for qualified leadership has ruled, "We direct our local churches in selecting their church officers to elect only such as are clearly in the experience of entire sanctification."[5]

Godly character and Christian virtues are thus assumed to be present in Christian leaders. But one must cultivate these virtues lest while leading others he himself be lost. No leader is exempt from the temptation to depend upon his own works and his own strength. Paul himself climaxes his claim to apostleship with this personal testimony: "I keep under my body, and bring it into subjection: lest that by any means, when I have preached to others, I myself should be a castaway" (1 Cor. 9:27). Personal devotion and reliance upon God and His Word are the means by which we maintain spiritual strength.

D. Methods of Leaders

1. *Giving Suggestions and Information*

Information given by pastors and superintendents helps teachers to accomplish their tasks. Some potential workers never assume tasks in the church because they do not know how. A wise leader, therefore, offers a suggestion here and a little key information there as the basis upon which the follower may act.

---

4. John Oswald Sanders, *Spiritual Leadership* (Chicago: Moody Press, 1967), pp. 70-84.

5. *Manual, Church of the Nazarene* (Kansas City: Nazarene Publishing House, 1976), par. 38.

How much information is given depends on the follower. For some, no more than a gentle hint is necessary. For others, only careful guidance will enable them to minister effectively. The skilled leader is always alert to discover where his experience and knowledge can be useful in motivating people to serve.

2. *Personal Attachment and Imitation*

Christian leaders seek to cultivate in their followers loyalty to Christ and to the church. At the same time the leader knows that very often children, teens, and even adults are motivated by the example of a leader. Today, therefore, experts in leadership talk about providing models to be imitated. Taking a new Christian along on a call and allowing him to observe the pastor has been a method of influencing laymen to witness.

Where admiration and love exist, there is a tendency for the follower to imitate and act like the leader-model he observes. This fact calls for worthiness on the part of Christian leaders—and such worth should be every leader's goal.

3. *Exhortation and Persuasion*

These methods have been used by religious leaders throughout the history of man. At times they have come under criticism, but they continue to be effective motivators. "Thus saith the Lord" is an exhortation used by both the prophet and the Christian teacher.

Every church leader needs to cultivate the art of persuasion. There are, of course, dangers. The persuader can become argumentative and the overzealous can manipulate another's mind. But the Christian leader avoids both. He presents the truth lovingly and depends upon the Holy Spirit to convict and convince.

4. *Publicity*

The best publicity is success. Jesus found fame because people talked about His miracles. Men came to Him out of curiosity because they had heard others tell of His work.

Today we live in a world of opportunities for publicity. Mass media abound in our culture and most persons have come to accept them as a way of life. Church advertising and Christian broadcasting have become sciences in themselves. Every alert Christian leader will acquaint himself with the special books that have been written to aid him at this point.

5. *Time and Sequence of Events*

Timing is important for those who lead men. Jesus understood this principle. He knew that the mob in Nazareth were not the ones to take His life (Luke 4:28-30). On the other hand, when the timing was right, "he stedfastly set his face to go to Jerusalem" (Luke 9:51).

Relying on the logic of events becomes a method of leaders. There are times when one does not need to act; unfolding events themselves will turn things in the way they should go. The leader discerns these movement and hence knows when to act and when quietly to wait.

6. *Visualizing Needs*

Men sometimes will not move until a crisis arises or at least until they see a need clearly. A wise leader occasionally precipitates the crisis. A Sunday school superintendent needed some new furniture in the Primary Department. The church board was unconvinced until the superintendent took them on a tour to see the need. A pastor anticipating church growth made a point of crowding out the sanctuary on a rally day in order to help the congregation see the need for expansion of the building.

E. Practices of Leaders

An exhaustive list of Christian leadership practices would be difficult to compile, but the following are often used.

1. *Concentration*

The music of the one-man band has never been as popular or as proficient as the music of the man who concentrates on one instrument. Leaders do not try to do everything at once. They decide what is most important, and concentrate their efforts there. Paul declared, "This one thing I do" (Phil. 3:13). Also a wise leader encourages his people to concentrate on the ministries where they function best. The work of the Body of Christ is accomplished by persons whose gifts are distributed by the Holy Spirit. To each man something is given, but all are bestowed "for the equipment of the saints, for the work of ministry, for building up the body of Christ" (Eph. 4:12, RSV). Since all gifts are for the common good, one does well to concentrate upon his gift and to perfect it.

2. *Helping Others Discover Truth*

A leader does not always give every detail or make complete plans. He avoids the appearance of a know-it-all and a dictator. This quality of leadership stimulates others to grow. Any truth that a learner discovers for himself is more exciting and self-fulfilling than if a teacher simply tells him. Therefore, if a learner can discover truth for himself, the leader does not tell him. The wise teaching-leader knows when to be still—and when to answer questions in a way that turns the inquiry back upon the inquirer. Jesus often used this strategy effectively. After telling the story of the Good Samaritan, He asked, "Which of these three, do you think, proved neighbor to the man who fell among the robbers?" (Luke 10:36, RSV). Today's wise Christian leader follows the strategy of his Lord.

3. *Action and Rest*

There is a human tendency to grow weary in well doing. Any great leader considers the fact that men need rest when weary; therefore alternate periods of work and rest are a part of his plans. Sometimes pastors are reluctant to stop a program while it is going well. But it is better to close at a high peak than to allow participation to dwindle to a handful. Some persons will continue out of sheer loyalty, but planned rest periods and change of pace provide refreshment and save others from guilt feelings.

4. *Outsider Doing the Disagreeable Task*

In man there is a natural resistance to change; therefore friction sometimes develops when we try to improve church ministries. Deep emotional reactions sometimes transfer to pastors and other elected leaders. Under these conditions, leaders are reluctant to make needed improvements. One way to avoid some harmful results from negative reactions is to allow an outsider to do the unpleasant task. An evangelist is sometimes able to speak directly to local problems and then carry the negative feelings away with him when he leaves.

Suggestions for changes in the Sunday school are often more readily accepted from the outside expert. Such a consultant prepares the way for the needed improvements. If there are hurt feelings, the minister of Christian education may not be held responsible for the injury. Also he is freed to apply salve to the wounds and to direct the healing process.

5. *Rotate Assignments*

In small organizations there is a tendency for persons to find fault with each other. In these smaller groups people become so well acquainted that each fault is magnified beyond proportion. This tends to dissatisfaction, discouragement, and lack of progress. Under these circumstances it may be wise to rotate assignments occasionally. Empathy for the other person develops as each one faces the responsibilities of a task where he has been critical of another's efforts.

In larger organizations the problem is not as great because one is not so often subjected to the close scrutiny of the group. However, in the smaller units of the larger organization this rotation principle may be used to increase strength and to stimulate growth.

6. *Listening and Speaking*

Someone has observed that man is made with two ears and one mouth. He should therefore spend twice as much time listening as speaking. A leader who uses this advice will find that the practice allows him to know what his followers are thinking. Also, when a minister of Christian education listens to a teacher, the teacher is more inclined to pay attention to the minister's counsel and requests.

7. *Accepting Loneliness*

No one should attempt to be a leader who is not willing to suffer loneliness. To lead, one must be ahead of his followers. Decisions made by him sometimes involve facts that he cannot share with others. This places him in a lonely spot. Jesus experienced this loneliness in the Garden of Gethsemane when He implored His disciples, "My soul is exceeding sorrowful, even unto death: tarry ye here, and watch with me" (Matt. 26:38). In Christian service strength comes when we remember the call of God which He has placed upon us. The work must be done, and God's man is willing to pay the price of loneliness when it is necessary to assure the completion of the task.

8. *Planning for the Future*

No one continues to lead who has not planned the second step before he takes the first. In church work it is important to have some long-range plans that may reach as far as 10 or 15 years into the future.

It takes time to become acquainted with people. For most pastors and Christian education leaders it takes several years to know a congregation. It takes equally long to become acquainted with the community. Only then is one best able to inspire people and bring about lasting improvement and progress.

9. *Division of Responsibility*

Paul uses two figures of speech that suggest a division of responsibility in the work of God. In the first he reminds us that the Church is like the human body. Persons have different needs such as walking, hearing, and seeing. To meet these needs God has given feet, ears, and eyes. So in the Church, God has given persons special abilities to meet the needs of His people for wise leadership, courageous faith, miraculous answers to prayer, and still other ministries (1 Cor. 12:4-18).

Paul's second illustration is the process of sowing and reaping. In 1 Corinthians 3:6 he writes, "I have planted, Apollos watered; but God gave the increase." The work of the Church is done by many men cooperating together with God. This is the method that God blesses and through which He gives growth.

10. *ITTOCKS*

This nonsense combination of letters carries good advice: *In the time of crisis, keep still.* Here is especially good counsel when one does not know what to do. Doing nothing and saying nothing may allow tension to ease, and give time for the group to find its way through to the most desirable solution. A calm and patient leader keeps a crisis from reaching greater proportions than necessary.

11. *Support Subordinates*

Confidence is encouraged between leaders and followers when a subordinate knows that his leader supports his work. In churches where there is more than one paid leader, this principle is especially important. But it is also important no matter how small the congregation. The superintendent is bolder and works more aggressively when he is confident that the pastor supports his efforts. The teacher works more effectively when she is assured of the superintendent's support. Giving commendations and other appropriate recognitions are strategies used by wise and effective leaders in Christian education.

12. *Essentiality of Unity*

It is important that a church be united on all of its major decisions. Paul admonished the Corinthians, "I appeal to you, brethren, by the name of our Lord Jesus Christ, that all of you agree and that there be no dissensions among you" (1 Cor. 1:10, RSV).

It is especially important that leaders present a united front. There is a time for discussion of differences of opinion. This should be done in planning sessions and in small groups. But the time should come when differences are resolved or forgotten in support of majority opinion and the unity of the whole body. The united assault upon sin is too important for us to allow personal and petty differences to divide.

There are strengths in unity. Moses taught that one shall "chase a thousand," but that two shall "put ten thousand to flight" (Deut. 32:30). Jesus teaches us the same principle of cooperation in Kingdom tasks: "I say unto you, That if two of you shall agree on earth as touching any thing that they shall ask, it shall be done for them of my Father which is in heaven. For where two or three are gathered together in my name, there am I in the midst of them" (Matt. 18:19-20).

II. ENLISTING AND DEVELOPING LEADERS

Christian education is the task of Christian leaders: pastors, associates, Sunday school superintendents, department supervisors, teachers, and class officers. The task is big enough to employ every worker now on the job—and we could minister to twice as many persons in any local church if we could enlist and train new leaders equal to our present force.

This need for adequate leaders in Christian education has existed since the beginning of the Church. In the day when Jesus trained the Twelve He exclaimed, "The harvest truly is plenteous, but the labourers are few: pray ye therefore the Lord of the harvest, that he will send forth labourers into his harvest" (Matt. 9:37-38). Marion Lawrence, secretary of the World's Sunday School Association, wrote in 1924, "Leadership is the only problem of the church."[6] Paul Vieth, one of the leaders in the Christian education movement, said in 1957 that the enlistment and training of workers was the church's number one problem.[7] In 1970, Kenneth Gangel declared, "The necessity of harvest laborers began in the days of Christ and continues on to the present."[8]

Three basic leadership problems are involved in recruiting laymen for the redemptive mission of Christ. The first is using people with inadequate training for their task. The second deals with the small nucleus of persons in the church who are overworked. The third brings into focus the great majority of church members who never become involved. Someone has determined that 10 percent of the people in the church do 90 percent of the work. Let us consider some of the ways we can overcome these problems.

6. Marion Lawrence, *My Message to Sunday School Workers* (New York: George H. Doran Co., 1924), p. 279.

7. Paul H. Vieth, *The Church School* (Philadelphia: Christian Education Press, 1957), p. 189.

8. Kenneth O. Gangel, *Leadership for Church Education* (Chicago: Moody Press, 1970), p. 325.

A. Discovering Leaders

1. *Concept of Ministry*

Along with Luther and the Reformation came the idea of the priesthood of all believers. It found its rightful place in biblical theology but is just now beginning to be recognized significantly in practical theology. Chafin says, "The discovery of the laity as the church's greatest resource for ministry is the greatest discovery of this day."[9]

A recent emphasis in this area has been called "body life." It is based on the various ministries discussed in 1 Cor. 12:4-31; Rom. 12:3-8; and Eph. 4:11-16. Every Christian person has an assignment. This assignment is related to the ministries of others, and all working together make up the Body—the Church. Ayres says, "If you are a baptized Christian, you are already a minister. Whether you are ordained or not is immaterial."[10]

The church has long emphasized the stewardship of possessions, but we have been delinquent in failing to keep before the people God's ownership of life and our stewardship of service.

It is important in our recruiting process that we be concerned with the potential of people more than with the filling of a position. Only thus can we help a person find God's will for his life. When all persons in the church find God's will for their lives, we shall have the leaders needed to carry out God's mission. Henrietta Mears, who led a great advance in Christian education at the Hollywood Presbyterian Church in California, capitalized on this principle. She said:

> My job as a trainer of leaders is to spot the potential of a person: What are his talents? What is his potential? It doesn't matter if he is doing anything now or not. I must see where he is capable of going. Then I encourage him along that line.[11]

2. *Talent and Interest Survey*

God operates according to law and order. Consequently, His will for our lives will normally correlate with our own interests and talents. To help a person invest his life in Christian service to his highest potential, it is essential that we know the experience he has had, the kind of work he would like to do, and the things for which

---

9. Kenneth Chafin, *Help! I'm a Layman* (Waco, Tex.: Word Books, 1966), p. 32.

10. Francis O. Ayres, *The Ministry of the Laity* (Philadelphia: The Westminster Press, 1962), p. 25.

11. Ethel May Baldwin and David V. Benson, *Henrietta Mears and How She Did It* (Glendale, Calif.: Regal Books, 1966), p. 162.

he desires training. On pages 400-401 is a reproduction of both sides of a typical form designed to secure this information.

After a message by the pastor or minister of Christian education on the biblical basis of the stewardship of life, these survey cards may be distributed. The cards should be completed in the service and placed on the altar suggesting the presenting of self as a living sacrifice to the Lord (Rom. 12:1-2). This can be a highly significant service.

Edwards calls the procedure an "inventory of the congregation" and says it should be taken at least annually. It may then be kept up to date during the year as new members join the church.[12]

3. Organization and Task Survey

A periodic review of the organization to determine areas for expansion will reveal leadership needs. Also a tally of new tasks that could be accomplished with qualified workers will highlight other needs. The positions open for leaders will determine the talents and abilities that can be used.

Personnel committee members should keep these surveys constantly before them as they seek the guidance of the Holy Spirit in recruiting workers and in matching need with talent.

4. Service Survey

One of the most productive areas for leadership talent is the Sunday school class. Youth and adult officers in Sunday school classes display their interest and abilities in working with people, in taking initiative, and in showing general leadership ability. Successful accomplishment of lesser tasks is one of the best prerequisites for larger leadership responsibilities.

A review of local leaders should be made at least annually to determine those who should be advanced to positions of greater responsibility. Such a policy will provide motivation for workers as well as give personnel committees evidence of proven abilities.

5. Publicity

The Bible tells us, "Ye have not because ye ask not" (Jas. 4:2). This could be said of many pastors and ministers of Christian education today. People can be challenged only by the information they have about needs and opportunities. Edwards urges:

---

12. Mary Alice Douty Edwards, *Leadership Development and the Workers' Conference* (Nashville: Abingdon Press, 1967), pp. 39-40.

Keep the constituency informed! How else will the congregation know what Christian education means, what it includes,
what it takes, who is doing it, and what is going on? Only when
people are aware can they be ready to respond.[13]

B. Enlisting Leaders

1. *Personnel Committee*

A personnel committee in the church performs two major functions. It has specific responsibility for providing adequate leaders
and for making the most effective use of their abilities. It also
assures coordination in the use of manpower. In a small church, the
pastor and Sunday school superintendent may perform these functions.

The personnel committee should include the leaders of the
major educational agencies of the church. This group establishes
personnel policies in line with denominational guidelines and sees
that they are publicized to the congregation. The policies should include specified terms for appointments, rotation plans, training
opportunities, and descriptions of other privileges and responsibilities.

This personnel group will work constantly with the need surveys and with the talent and interest resource files.

2. *Need for Job Descriptions*

The personnel committee cannot do its work nor can enlisters
adequately challenge candidates until there is a clear understanding
about the obligations and opportunities of each task.

A job description should include not only details of what is
required to be done, but also what materials and facilities are available, what are the lines of authority, what is the length of the
assignment, and other pertinent information.[14]

3. *Plan for Enlistment*

After the personnel committee has given prayerful consideration to matching human abilities to the leadership needs of a job, it is
important that proper procedures be followed for enlisting the worker. The committee should determine who is to present the challenge
to the candidate.

The first essential is a personal approach. The more personal

---

13. *Ibid.,* p. 28.
14. Lee J. Gable, in *Religious Education: A. Comprehensive Survey,* Marvin J. Taylor,
ed. (Nashville: Abingdon Press, 1960), p. 274.

A | 1 2 3 4 5 6 7 8 9 10 11 12 13 14 15 16 17 18 19 20 21 | M | 1 2 3 4 5 6 7 8 9 10 11 12 13

Name...................................... Address.......................... Phone..........................

CHRISTIAN SERVICE SURVEY

As evidence of my love for Christ and my fellowman and my concern that my church

Reach all we can—Teach all we can   Win all we teach—Enlist all we win

Train all we enlist

I indicate below the areas in which I have served, or am willing to prepare to serve as called on:

Write in information or mark the appropriate column with an X	EXPERIENCE		Now doing	Willing to prepare
	Years	When		
ADMINISTRATION				
Church board				
(A) Church school board				
Other committee (Write in.)				
CHRISTIAN EDUCATION:				
(1) Teach class of children				
(2) Teach class of youth				
(3) Teach class of adults				
(4) Associate teacher (What age-group?)				
(5) Home Department worker				
(6) Cradle Roll visitor				
(7) Department supervisor				
(8) Department secretary				
(9) Sunday school class officer				
(10) Work in children's church				
(11) Work in extended session—preschool				

	EXPERIENCE			Willing to prepare
	Years	When	Now doing	
(12) Vacation Bible school				
(13) Librarian				
(14) N.W.M.S. (Write in office held.	)			
(15) Junior Fellowship leader				
(16) N.Y.P.S. (Write in office held.	)			
(17) Youth group sponsor				
(18) Christian Family Life director				
(19) Caravan or Scout leader				
(20) Work with Audio-visual equipment				
(21) Guide craft activity				

MUSIC

Sing in choir

(M) Play piano

Lead group singing

Special music: Vocal _____ Instrumental _____

EVANGELISM *(Check those you will do.)*

- ☐ 1. Visitation evangelism
- ☐ 2. Distribute literature
- ☐ 3. Visit for the Sunday school
- ☐ 4. Survey evangelism
- ☐ 5. Home open for prayer groups

SPECIAL SERVICES *(Check those you will do.)*

- ☐ 6. Secretarial work
- ☐ 7. Make posters
- ☐ 8. Electrician
- ☐ 9. Call on telephone
- ☐ 10. Manual labor
- ☐ 11. Serve in church nursery
- ☐ 12. Use my car to bring people
- ☐ 13. Serve on welcoming committee

In filling out this Service Survey, I realize I am not guaranteed an opportunity to serve in the chosen field, but may be called upon as needed and as God directs.

Signed _____

R-42 Litho in U.S.A.

the contact made, the greater the probability of an affirmative response. An appointment to talk with the candidate at home or in a church office is best.

The interview should begin with an explanation of the work of the personnel committee and the process by which they arrived at their choice of the candidate. Stress the time spent by the committee in seeking the guidance of the Holy Spirit. The job description and other data relating to the work should be presented and discussed. Questions should be encouraged and answered. If the task is not easy, it should not be made to appear so. You may need to stress that Christ's work sometimes calls for self-denial and may appear to include cross-bearing. Jesus said, "Whosoever will come after me, let him deny himself, and take up his cross, and follow me" (Mark 8:34). The greater the spiritual challenge of enlistment, the better the service is likely to be.

Do not ask for an answer at the time of the initial interview. When the candidate is clear about the work and has been given answers to his questions, he should be reminded that the commission is from Christ. Ask him to pray about the opportunity. If he is to say no, let him first say no to God. A time and place for the response from the candidate should be set. If, after prayer, the candidate does not feel this is God's will for his life, you may suggest that he seek guidance from God as to where in the Kingdom he should invest his time and talents.

C. Training Leaders

When sincere Christians have been properly challenged to significant service opportunities, they will usually respond affirmatively. But they often say, "I would be willing, but I don't feel adequate. I would need some training." It is the responsibility of the Christian education leaders of the church to provide such training. This is not easy. Bower writes: "Leadership training, it must be granted, is a difficult and time-consuming task; it nevertheless has always been an important aspect of the church's program and continues to be of great importance in the present."[15]

1. *Pre-service Training*

Adequate training for Christian service begins long before the presentation of a particular leadership responsibility.

---

15. Robert K. Bower: *Administering Christian Education* (Grand Rapids, Mich.: William B. Eerdmans Publishing Co., 1964), p. 108.

Each child and young person in the church should be growing in Christian faith, life, and service in preparation for leadership. The church should encourage persons of every age to accept as much responsibility in learning, worship, service, and fellowship as their stages of development will permit.[16]

Pre-service training should provide development in three areas: self-growth, knowledge of the faith, and skill in leadership. To make this possible, a program for training must be developed. It will not just happen.

Training for effective Christian service must be motivated by a sense of mission. This impulse develops out of the evangelistic spirit of the church and out of the total emphasis upon Christian stewardship. A church membership class is an ideal place to begin such training. New converts and new members should be expected to attend a class particularly designed to prepare them to be witnesses for Christ. Vieth says, "Christian education places a premium on the person who teaches, and is concerned that he be first of all a dynamic, living witness."[17]

A general churchmanship course, insofar as is possible, should involve every member of the church. It may cover the areas of Bible, basic doctrine, church history, missions, stewardship, and evangelism. From this base further classes can be planned to meet organizational and individual needs and interests.

These courses can be taken by individual home study any time during the year. Classes are frequently offered in the local church once or twice annually. Also elective courses are often provided as a part of the Sunday school adult curriculum offering. Outside of the local church, training courses are available in city-wide training schools, zone or district events, conferences, retreats, and workshops at denominational laboratory schools. Summer family camps may also offer training classes. Students attending church colleges are offered or required to take courses that will prepare them for service in the local church.

Informal general training for Christian service is also received by those who assume responsibilities as class officers or as volunteer workers in other departments of the church. These experiences expand one's personal relationships and give opportunities for Christian ministry.

---

16. Gable, in Taylor, *Religious Education,* p. 271.
17. Vieth, *The Church School,* p. 193.

2. In-service Training

The terms "in-service training" and "continuing education" are familiarly used in business, industrial, and professional circles. As Edwards comments, "The constant development of new knowledge and techniques demands that workers in any field continue their learning."[18] With the minimum preparation that most workers have in Christian education, the need for improvement makes in-service training all the more imperative.

Informal training takes place through experience gained when serving as associate teachers, by visiting other schools, and by watching demonstrations. On-the-job training occurs through supervision, evaluation, reporting, and guided practice. The training value of regular workers' meetings should not be overlooked.

Indirect training also takes place in the influence of one life on another. Many Christian workers receive inspiration and guidance in Christian service from the examples of other Christians whom they admire and desire to pattern their lives after. Henrietta Mears was affectionately called "teacher" because of the dynamic effect of her life on college students. "In the course of her career in Hollywood over four hundred collegians heard God's call and turned their energies to pulpits in America or to missionary stations scattered around the world."[19]

We have discussed the role of formal training through leadership development classes for new teachers. Many such courses are also planned to meet the needs of workers in service. A personal training record maintained for each worker makes possible a systematic and continuing growth toward maximum effectiveness.

III. Supervision and Motivation of Leaders

The enlistment and early training of leaders is only the beginning. Their growth and success must be assured through supervision and motivation.

A. Supervision

Supervision is the "process by which a more experienced person shares his knowledge and skills with a less experienced person to the

---

18. Edwards, *Leadership Development*, p. 68.
19. Baldwin and Benson, *Henrietta Mears*, p. 143.

benefit of that individual and of the cause or organization which he serves."[20] The ministry of supervision is probably the most hopeful approach that we have to the training of lay workers. There are three steps in this process: (1) The supervisor planning with the leader and helping him prepare for his responsibility; (2) observation by the supervisor while the leader works with his group; and (3) discussion following the session when the leader and supervisor talk over what happened and what failed to happen. Through this process supervisor and leader work together for improvement.

1. *Preparation for the Task*

The initial step in supervision is for the supervisor to become acquainted with the worker. This may involve some testing and review of records. It certainly includes consideration of the leader's interests and ability to work with those ministered to by him. With this background the supervisor will know the strengths and weaknesses of the leader.

A team approach with cooperative planning provides an ideal setting for the supervisor to give informal and indirect guidance. This arrangement helps build the teacher's security and self-esteem. It also develops a good rapport between the teacher and the supervisor. Many teachers have never had guidance in studying a lesson, preparing a lesson plan, and making other preparations for the class session. A good supervisor will guide teachers in these matters. His reservoir of experience provides an excellent resource from which the beginner can draw. On this solid foundation the supervisor can be sure the worker understands the basic rudiments of preparation for his specific assignment.

2. *Observation of the Work*

Excellent on-the-job training results when a qualified supervisor objectively observes a leader at work. The observer will notice things both good and bad of which the teacher may be unaware. The observer is careful not to interfere in any way with the performance. If notes are necessary, they are made unobtrusively. He is careful to see that the situation is as normal as possible.

It is important for the teacher to know that it is the policy of the school for supervisors to observe workers. If the right relationship exists between the two, the teacher will think of the supervisor as a friend who is eager to help by sharing experiences.

---

20. Edwards, *Leadership Development*, p. 70.

3. *Evaluation and Guidance*

One secret of growth in any human task is evaluative review. Such thinking results from asking honest questions and trying to find honest answers. A good supervisor seeks to stimulate and guide this process.

Relationships are improved and favorable results realized when the supervisor begins by noting the teacher's points of excellence in performance. Before discussing the areas where the teacher's performance needs to be improved, the supervisor may also mention some of his own shortcomings. These approaches generally encourage the teacher to keep an open mind to suggestions from the supervisor. Ideally this evaluation session should not end until some definite plans have been made to improve the teacher's work in the next session.

B. Motivation

Successful businessmen say that the difference between a good organization and a great one is motivation. Of our work in the church, Gable writes: "Sound Christian motivation is essential. If it can be assured, the problems of finding and training staff members will be greatly reduced."[21]

1. *Divine Factors*

The ultimate in motivation for Christian service is expressed by Paul when he testifies, "The love of Christ constraineth us" (2 Cor. 5:14). *The Amplified Bible* reads: "The love of Christ controls and urges and impels us." This is real motivation. *Agape* love puts the "want to" inside.

A sense of mission is a major factor in human motivation. This has been proved by Communism, Hitlerism, and other world-shaking movements. It has certainly been true of Christianity. The redemptive mission of evangelism has moved the Christian Church around the world. It has challenged millions to invest their time and talent in the work of the Church through Christian education, the yoke-mate of evangelism. Bower says, "There is nothing that can inspire a leader to continue his work like the evidence of changed lives within his own class or group."[22]

---

21. Gable, in Taylor, *Religious Education*, p. 271.
22. Bower, *Administering Christian Education*, p. 131.

2. *Internal Human Factors*

Closely related to the divine elements in motivation are the internal human factors. A popular study of motivation is based on Abraham Maslow's "hierarchy of needs."[23]

This ladder of needs has seven steps. They are arranged in an ascending order to suggest that a person's need on a lower level must be met before he can really sense the needs on a higher level and cope with them.

7. Aesthetic—need for order, balance, completeness
6. Knowledge—need to know, and understand
5. Be one's best self—self-actualization, worthy, useful
4. Esteem—need for recognition and status
3. Belongingness—need for love and acceptance
2. Security—safety
1. Physical needs—physiological

The first two levels of physiological needs and the need for safety have little relevance to motivation for Christian service. However, the level of "belongingness" or the need for love and acceptance is directly related to the gospel call to Christian experience. This deep human need also plays an important role in motivation to Christian service. The acceptance demonstrated by being asked to serve on a team of leaders in the church meets a fundamental human need.

Meeting the "esteem" needs (status, prestige, recognition, importance) leads on to being one's best self (self-confidence, adequacy, being of use, and having worth). Certainly growth in these areas motivates people and often affects their vocational choices.

A high level of motivation is found in meeting the needs for knowledge and for human completeness. Also, people motivated at these levels tend to be more altruistic, hence we are coming closer to a genuine Christian motivation. Jesus declared, "I am come that they might have life, and that they might have it more abundantly" (John 10:10). When we offer opportunity for service in the church, we join with Christ in providing maximum opportunities for personal growth and for lives of fulfillment.

---

23. Keith Miller, *The Becomers* (Waco, Tex.: Word Books, 1973), chaps. 12—13, where he attempts to put Maslow's work into a Christian context. Cf. Abraham Maslow, *Motivation and Human Behavior* (rev. ed.; New York: Harper and Row, 1970).

Augustine observed that we are restless until we find our rest in Christ. Because we are created in the image of God, there is woven into the very fabric of our being the need to find real life by losing it in God's redemptive mission.

3. *External Human Factors*

Less powerful but highly significant motivational influences originate outside of the individual. With some persons, these external factors may be the only motivating elements. With other workers, external motivation leads on to the development of high-level motivation within.

a. Appreciation. A first step in showing gratitude to lay workers is a meaningful installation or consecration to the task. Such an expression of appreciation elevates the significance of Christian service for everyone involved. Edwards says: "A service of consecration and public recognition . . . helps underscore the teaching service as an act of worship, putting God at the center."[24]

Words of appreciation for specific activities, letters expressing admiration and love, commendations in church papers and bulletins, and gifts at appropriate times all stimulate motivation.

b. Recognition. Appropriate forms of recognition motivate those who are doing well to do even better. Recognition also tends to prompt less productive workers to improve. Wall charts can be used to display the training courses completed, the reading accomplished, and other professional achievements. The selection of a "teacher of the month" or the "worthy worker of the year" provides recognition and moves people to effort and excellence in Christian service. Another effective incentive is the church offering to pay expenses to conventions, laboratory schools, or other growth opportunities.

*   *   *

The New Testament does not speak much about leadership in today's terms. But the concept and model are clearly reflected there. Jesus says to us, as He said to His early disciples, "I have chosen you and ordained you, that ye should go and bring forth fruit" (John 16:15). The fruit of the gospel is always found somewhere in the transformation of human lives. Whenever we attempt even the smallest task in these roles as Christian leader-servants, He promises us, "Lo, I am with you alway, even unto the end of the world" (Matt. 28:20).

---

24. Edwards, *Leadership Development*, p. 65.

BIBLIOGRAPHY

Edge, Finley B. *The Greening of the Church.* Waco, Tex.: Word Books, 1971.

There are three major emphases: (1) The basic problem in today's church is personal and spiritual; (2) We must recapture a balance between evangelism and social involvement, and (3) Positive, creative proposals are vital if the church is to change from what it is to what it ought to become.

Edwards, Mary Alice Douty. *Leadership Development and the Workers' Conference.* Nashville: Abingdon Press, 1967.

Part I sets forth a philosophy of leadership development. It also offers suggestions for recruitment of new leaders, leadership training classes, individual guidance, supervision, and planning workers' conferences. Part II gives plans and ideas for 10 workers' conferences which may be adapted to the needs of any local church.

Engstrom, Ted W. *The Making of a Christian Leader.* Grand Rapids, Mich.: Zondervan Publishing House, 1976.

The author stresses the elements of leadership that have unique Christian relevance. (1) Christian organizations must place a high value on the personal development and needs of the individual; (2) The local church has few, if any, paid workers. It is one thing to lead a group of people who depend upon the organization for livelihood. It is quite another to motivate a group when 99 percent are volunteers.

Gangel, Kenneth O. *Leadership for Church Education.* Chicago: Moody Press, 1970.

The biblical philosophy of church education is carefully integrated with the organizational aspects of developing an educational program. In Part II, Dr. Gangel explores the nature of leadership, describes the duties of the leader, and deals with the problem of leadership training on the local church level.

Jones, E. Stanley. *The Reconstruction of the Church—on What Pattern?* Nashville: Abingdon Press, 1970.

Dr. Jones builds a strong case for the church of the future to be centered around the laymen as leaders. He shows the importance of small groups and the imperativeness of lay witnessing. He believes that the church which survives must follow this pattern of the Early Church.

Sanders, J. Oswald. *Spiritual Leadership.* Chicago: Moody Press, 1967.

Mr. Sanders believes that "spiritual leadership is a blending of natural and spiritual qualities. Even the natural qualities are not self-produced, but God-given, and therefore reach their highest effectiveness when employed in the service of God and for His glory."

Tead, Ordway. *The Art of Leadership.* New York: McGraw-Hill Book Company, Inc., 1935.

A classic in the field. Everything is included from definition and demand for leaders to the details of training them. Application is made to business, institutions, educational organizations, and the church.

CHAPTER 17

Full-time
Christian Education

The purpose of God is to reconcile the world to himself through Jesus Christ. To accomplish this purpose He has "given to us the ministry of reconciliation" (2 Cor. 5:18).

To carry out this ministry, the Early Church employed four major functions: proclamation *(kerygma)*, fellowship *(koinonia)*, instruction *(didache)*, and service or ministry *(diakonia)*. In the church today these functions are further divided into evangelism, fellowship, social ministry, stewardship, worship, and education.[1]

I. ALL ARE CALLED

For God to realize His purpose and for the church to carry out its function, the time, talent, and commitment of every believer is needed. Paul writes: "God . . . hath committed unto us the word of reconciliation. Now then we are ambassadors for Christ" (2 Cor. 5:19-20). Elsewhere the apostle declares: "His 'gifts unto men' were varied. Some he made his messengers, some prophets, some preachers of the Gospel; to some he gave the power to guide and teach his people. His gifts were made that Christians might be properly equipped for their service" (Eph. 4:11-13, Phillips).

---

1. Ralph D. Heim, *Leading a Church School* (Philadelphia: Fortress Press, 1968), p. 16.

A. Service as Our Motive

Twice as much is written in the New Testament about stewardship and service as about faith and prayer. Jesus ended many of His teachings with the command "Go thou and do likewise" or "This do and thou shalt live." Our love for God is proved by love for our fellowman; worship is never consummated until it is expressed in service. Albert Schweitzer was asked, "Have you found happiness in Africa?" He replied, "I have found service and that is happiness enough for anyone."[2]

Paul declares God's purpose for Christian gifts in these words: "that the whole body might be built up until the time comes when . . . we arrive at real maturity—that measure of development which is meant by 'the fullness of Christ'" (Eph. 4:13, Phillips).

1. *Relation to "fruits"*

Jesus says to His disciples, "I have chosen you and ordained you, that ye should go and bring forth fruit, and that your fruit should remain" (John 15:16). Most commentators agree that the fruit here referred to applies both to the "fruit of the spirit" (Galatians 5) and to reproducing new Christians—the "fruit of the species." Maturity in spiritual experience is characterized by the ability to reproduce our own kind. Just as in the physical realm a mother gives of herself to bring forth new life, so the Christian gives himself in Christian replication.

> Being spiritually adult means getting out into the world as it is and living there as Christians. The kind of witnessing we are expected to do is the hard, unglamorous, untalked of witnessing of simply being Christ's men and women. A witness is one who gives evidence.[3]

2. *Relation to Growth*

Peter admonishes Christians as newborn babes to "desire the sincere milk of the word" that they might grow (1 Pet. 2:12). Paul encourages us to "be no more children . . . but speaking the truth in love . . . grow up into him in all things" (Eph. 4:14-15).

> The evidence of both the Bible and our own lives tells us that as Christians we grow in much the same way that we do on the human level. First babyhood, the simple uncluttered idea that my salvation, my prayers, my happiness are the supreme

2. George L. Smith, "What Is True Happiness?" *Herald of Holinsss*, June 17, 1970 (Kansas City: Nazarene Publishing House), p. 6.

3. Eileen Guder, *To Live in Love* (Grand Rapids, Mich.: Zondervan Publishing House, 1967), p. 163.

concerns of God and His angels. Then, haltingly and with many pauses, comes the process of growth. We begin to turn our attention outward, to see others—really see them—as loving, hating, needing, fearing beings like ourselves. We begin dimly to apprehend something of the grace of God in coming to us, loving us. Our self-absorption is broken by genuine concern for others.[4]

3. *Fulfillment and the Servant Concept*

At the conclusion of His discourse on fruitful living, Jesus says: "These things have I spoken unto you that my joy might remain in you, and that your joy might be full" (John 15:11). Psychologists generally agree that fulfillment in life results from losing oneself in a great cause. Jesus said, "For whosoever will save his life shall lose it; but whosoever shall lose his life for my sake and the gospel's, the same shall save it" (Mark 8:35). He then demonstrated the principle by example. He was the Suffering Servant who became the saving Christ. It is interesting to note that the word *ministry* and the word *serve* come from the same root word. Each Christian is a servant—and a full-time minister of Christian education is a servant of servants. Dr. E. Stanley Jones says:

> Greatness through service is the most constructive drive ever introduced into human nature. It enables those to whom it is directed and it enables the one who serves. Nothing is such an all-around enablement as greatness through service to all.[5]

B. Service and Church Growth

Richard A. Myers concludes that there is a positive correlation between the number of Sunday school classes and the rate of growth in Sunday school attendance and consequently in growth by profession of faith.[6] This means that people are drawn to a church where in small groups they are loved as individuals by others who find joy in Christian service.

1. *Developing the Lay Potential*

Those who have studied the growth of the Christian church are saying that its future depends on how well laymen become involved in its mission. E. Stanley Jones predicts:

> The church of the future must be primarily a lay church, with the laymen as participants playing the game; and with the

---

4. *Ibid.,* p. 160.

5. E. Stanley Jones, *Reconstruction of the Church—on What Pattern?* (Nashville: Abingdon Press, 1970), p. 25.

6. Richard A. Myers, *Program Expansion, The Key to Church Growth* (mimeographed booklet, 1969), p. 1.

clergy on the sidelines as the coaches of a team, as the guides and spiritualizers of an essentially lay movement.[7]

As the early disciples went from place to place proclaiming the good news "He is risen," so the followers of Christ today have a message. We are to be proclaimers of the truth "He lives; I know He lives because He lives within my heart." The many ministries of the modern church make it possible to use the talent and interests of every layman so that we may "by all means save some." This requires that the minister of Christian education give time to planning, organization, and to leadership in order to enlist and train lay people.

2. *Help for the Pastor*

The multi ministries of the modern church make it increasingly difficult for one man to give personal leadership to all of the program. In the smaller church the wise pastor concentrates on training and developing volunteer lay leaders. As the church grows, the demands on the pastor increase until it becomes impossible for him to give the time necessary to personally guide all the lay leadership; some division of responsibility becomes necessary.

This help for the pastor may come from ordained men who are specially equipped for the teaching ministry. But it is not limited to them. Laymen who have not felt called to the preaching ministry can be involved in full-time Christian service: many laymen are now working as associates to pastors in multi-staff ministries.

II. GOD'S CALL TO FULL-TIME MINISTRY

Regarding the vocation of the ministry, G. B. Williamson says,

> The ministry is a calling. As such, the choice is God's; but it is also a profession and, as such requires that all who enter its ranks shall give their best to it. Every man must stir up the gift that is within him.[8]

A. Divine Factors

Finding the will of God for our lives is essential when considering a Christian vocation, but many young people have been confused by misconceptions at this point. One of these mistaken ideas is that the will of God is difficult to find. This is not true. It is God's desire to make His will known to us. That is why Christ came; that is why the

---

7. Jones, *Reconstruction of the Church*, p. 51.
8. G. B. Williamson, *Overseers of the Flock* (Kansas City: Beacon Hill Press, 1952), p. 14.

Bible was given to us; that is why the Holy Spirit is in the world today. If we sincerely want to know God's will for our lives, He will make it known to us. The Bible assures us, "If any man will do his will, he shall know . . ." (John 7:17).

Another misconception is that the will of God is always unpleasant. His way is irksome only when God's will conflicts with ours. When we can honestly pray with genuine meaning, "Not my will, but thine, be done," the will of God becomes a joy. L. J. DuBois testifies: "Of one thing we can be certain, a genuine call will cause one to be happy in doing God's will. God does not expect a person to do something he does not want to do."[9]

Many plans have been suggested for finding God's purpose for our lives. The best beginning point is to be obedient to the will of God as we know it now, and to keep ourselves completely open to His guidance.

Sam Shoemaker recommends Karl Leyasmeyer's three tests for being sure of God's plan for us:

> (1) Test it by the revealed will and plan of God, as we know it in the New Testament. The more we know our Bible, the better will be our contact with Christ and hence our knowledge of His will.
>
> (2) Pray about it, and be ready for an answer. It is possible for us to have halted and wavered so long that we need to give ourselves a push to recognize and accept the guidance God is giving us.
>
> (3) Test it by circumstances. Does God offer you a stumbling block, or an open door? Sometimes God wants us to break through obstructions to find and do His will; but sometimes events positively conspire to make it known to us, and God is in the events.[10]

1. *General Call*

There is a sense in which every believer is called to Christian service. The "Go ye" of the Great Commission applies to all followers of Jesus. The command of Christ "Ye shall be witnesses unto me" is a mandate as well as a privilege for every Christian. Paul admonishes the early followers of Christ, "Walk worthy of the vocation wherewith ye are called" (Eph. 4:1). To the Colossians he writes, "And whatsoever ye do, do it heartily, as to the Lord, and not unto men" (3:23).

---

9. L. J. DuBois, *Careers for Christians* (Kansas City: Beacon Hill Press, 1958), p. 43.

10. Sam Shoemaker, *Extraordinary Living for Ordinary Men* (Grand Rapids, Mich.: Zondervan Publishing House, 1965), p. 42.

So, either every Christian is called to a full-time Christian vocation, or he is called to be a full-time Christian in his vocation—and a volunteer for part-time service in the church.

2. *Specific Call*

There is a difference between choosing a secular vocation which we feel is within the will of God for us, and realizing a specific call to full-time Christian service. In the Upper Room Discourse Jesus said to the Twelve, "Ye have not chosen me, but I have chosen you" (John 15:16).

The realization of a specific call comes to Christians in different ways. This is because people are different and because God is resourceful enough to tailor-make an experience for each individual. But however it comes, we can be sure that it is God's call to us. Nelson puts it this way:

> Thousands of Christians have had a special and unmistakable, sudden call to their vocation. They have found themselves deeply moved at a worship service or a conference, and have gone forward to declare themselves. Or they have seen a vision, or heard a voice, or been suddenly gripped with a conviction which has grown in their lives. Yet, the great majority of effective ministers and church workers today cannot point to that sort of definite and dramatic experience. There has been a calling which has come upon them gradually, with deepening conviction. It has been a quiet, nurtured growth which eventually has flowered into a decision which is definite and without any shadow of doubt.[11]

3. *Guidance of the Holy Spirit*

God is present in the world today in the person of the Holy Spirit. Jesus promised, "When he, the Spirit of truth, is come, he will guide you into all truth" (John 16:13).

The qualification for this guidance is committing ourselves to God for sacrificial service and for His renewing of our mind. Paul writes: "Offer yourselves as a living sacrifice to God, dedicated to His service and pleasing to Him . . . let God transform you inwardly by a complete change of your mind. Then you will be able to know the will of God" (Rom. 12:1-2, TEV).

In this surrendered relationship the Christian lives secure in the confidence that the choices and decisions he makes are divinely guided. Tozer says, "The man or woman who is wholly and joyously

---

11. John Oliver Nelson, *Protestant Religious Vocations* (New York: Vocational Guidance Manuals, 1952), p. 29.

surrendered to Christ can't make a wrong choice—any choice will be the right one."[12] The measure of commitment is the key.

B. Human Factors

From early childhood people begin to think and talk about adult vocations. These ideas are influenced by persons they admire, by occupations they know, and by interests they develop. By the late teens, young people begin making vocational plans on the basis of all of these experiences. At this time, if they have had Christian teaching, they also become aware of God's claim on their time and talents. Often a conflict of interests develops. Our plans lead in one direction while God's priorities seem to point out a different course. However, the realization that God has a plan for every life should make it easier to listen to Him. His call becomes convincing when we begin to understand how our talents, interests, and abilities fit into His plans to minister to the needs of men and women.

1. *Natural Abilities and Interests*

The ability to lead other persons is essential to the administrative and organizational aspects of Christian education. Crossland defines a leader as "a Christlike personality whose wisdom, self-sacrifice, and labor co-operate with others in finding and doing the will of God."[13] Titus lists the six important characteristics of leaders as: "Intellectual capacity, self-significance, vitality, training, experience, and reputation."[14]

Interest in and ability to teach carries a high priority for success in Christian education leadership. Planning teaching ministries and training others to teach will absorb major blocks of time in the schedule of the minister of Christian education.

Spiritual and emotional stability are also essential in the lives of those who would lead others in Christian pursuits. People will overlook some limitations in talents or even technical knowledge if they are confident that their leader is a man of God.

Lowell Saunders expresses well the relation between God's guidance and our abilities:

---

12. A. W. Tozer, "Four Ways to Find God's Will," *Moody Monthly,* vol. 70, no. 10 (June, 1970), p. 79.
13. Weldon Crossland, *Better Leaders for Your Church* (Nashville: Abingdon Press, 1955), p. 12.
14. Charles Hickman Titus, *The Processes of Leadership* (Dubuque, Ia.: Wm. C. Brown Co., 1950), p. 55.

God generally calls a person into a vocational field which he likes and has the ability to perform well. He wants you in the occupation that will make you the happiest and the most productive. So as you check your interests, evaluate your aptitude and intelligence, you can expect God to lead you into the specific job that's best for you.[15]

2. *A Recognized Need*

The cry of need is the call of God. When Paul wrote to the Romans, "I am debtor," he was emphasizing his responsibility to meet their need. Consequently he declared, "I am ready to preach the gospel" (Rom. 1:14-15).

Interest and success are directly related to an awareness of need and to a realization of ability to meet that need.

3. *A Growing Realization*

There must be a third element in God's call and that is a personal commitment to God's plan for one's life as one understands it. Sometimes that understanding develops gradually. . . . Through training and background as a child and adolescent a decision may be reached in the normal course of growing up.[16]

God usually works thus through the law and order that He has written into His creation. He moves upon men through the natural laws of human thought, emotion, and choices. In a Father-and-child relationship He makes His will known. Though this kind of a call is not as dramatic or instantaneous as a sudden supernatural manifestation, it can be just as real and just as satisfying.

III. TO FULL-TIME MINISTRY FROM VOLUNTEER SERVICE

Most full-time workers receive their introduction to Christian education through volunteer service in a local church. They begin exercising their spiritual muscles as assistants to persons with more experience; they advance as they prove their increasing interest and ability.

A. Awareness of Needs

Through volunteer service in the local church one comes into contact

---

15. Lowell Saunders, "What in the World Am I Going to Do?" *Moody Monthly,* vol. 71, no. 10 (June, 1971), p. 36.

16. Erma Paul Ferrari, *Careers for You* (New York: Abingdon-Cokesbury Press, 1953), p. 127.

with people and discovers the deep needs of their lives. This deepening awareness of human need becomes a part of God's call.

B. Knowledge and Experience

The school of life provides knowledge in two ways. By trial and error we learn what is the right way and what is the wrong. One experience builds on another and we increase our knowledge through these personal involvements.

On the other hand, we can learn by studying the work of others. Through these vicarious experiences we learn many important truths that we need not investigate by personal trial and error. Thus, much important learning takes place through association with others involved in service. We learn what to do and what not to do. Both experiences enlarge our knowledge of Christian education and increase our ability to serve efficiently.

IV. PROFESSIONAL PREPARATION

The privilege and responsibility of professional leadership in the church demand the best preparation. The call and enabling of God provide us with vision and motivation. The intellectual preparation and gaining practical experience are our assignments. When we have done our best, God will add enough of His blessing to make us successful. He never calls a person to fail in His work.

A. College

Most church colleges now offer courses in Christian education. Ministerial students are usually required to complete one or two of these basic studies before they are eligible for ordination. Also a growing number of lay students are electing these courses to enrich their service for Christ. Pastors appreciate the college that sends its graduates back to the local church with some training in Christian education regardless of their vocation. It makes their volunteer service much more effective.

Many of the colleges offer a major for students who wish to enter Christian education professionally. An A.B. degree with a major in this field is generally considered the minimum requirement for professional Christian education leaders. College training is almost mandatory today because churches that are large enough to afford a multi-staff ministry generally have a significant group of educated people who expect qualified leadership. An adequate academic background is essential for the assurance of the worker as well as for the confidence of the people. If one cannot get a professional religious education major, a major in religion with a minor in the field of education is good, or a major in education with a minor in religion. Those who plan to specialize in music, in children's work, or in youth work must pursue courses in these fields and even major in them where such specialized majors are available.

B. Graduate School

A minimum requirement for ministers of education in some denominations, and an ideal in all, is two or three years of training, beyond college, specializing in Christian education. Nelson says a director of religious education needs approximately the same education as the pastor. Sometimes four years of college is enough, but he goes on to say,

> Far more usual and advisable is the program of taking one, two, or three years at a theological seminary or a similar school, securing a master's degree (M.A. in religious education), or M.R.E. (Master of Religious Education), or a B.D. (Bachelor of Divinity), the ministerial degree.[17]

C. Course of Study

For those who cannot take formal training for Christian education in college and seminary, one church gives opportunity to pursue a course of study at home. Such training is administered by the Department of Education and the Ministry.

The course includes texts that are to be studied, and the student's understanding is evaluated by examination; other books are required only to be read. They cover professional studies in Christian education, history and missions, theology and evangelism, the ministry of the church, and church administration. This is a three-year course. When completed, it fulfills the academic requirements for a commission which may be awarded by the District Assembly.

D. Titles

Titles for the minister of education have a relationship to his preparation and education. Shelton says:

> The title "Director of Christian Education" should be reserved for persons with adequate training. This includes a bachelor's degree and a master's degree from an accredited educational

---

17. Nelson, *Religious Vocations,* p. 67.

institution, or a bachelor of divinity degree from an accredited seminary wherein the work includes a concentration or major in Christian Education.[18]

The term *minister of Christian education* is generally reserved for those who are ordained or who have met commensurate requirements. The full-time staff member who has only a bachelor's degree, and those without college degrees, are usually called educational associates or assistants.

On theological grounds, some would name all persons engaged in this work as ministers of Christian education. One writes: "The more proper title for any associate in Christian education is 'Minister of Christian Education.' The term 'assistant' should never be used. If all born-again Christians are 'ministers,' then the minister who works with the educational program should be called that."

Regardless of one's formal preparation, the essential quality of a good Christian education leader is a hungering and thirsting for more knowledge and experience. He must be growing. This keeps him alive and creates a spirit of growth among the church workers with whom he serves.

V. Specialized Ministry with Multiple Staff

A. Pastor and Christian Education

Richard McKann writes:

> In a one-clergyman parish, the minister appears to be a kind of "general manager," but is actually required by subtle demands, to be his own committee of specialists. Shortcomings in any of the six central roles—administrator, organizer, pastor, preacher, priest, teacher—can undermine his overall effectiveness.[19]

Certainly the educational ministry of the church requires major attention. Bower says that more than 50 percent of a pastor's time is involved in Christian education.[20] The pastor simply cannot give this amount of time to the teaching ministry and be fair to his other pastoral functions. In small congregations, the best he can do is to develop volunteer laymen who have public school experience or a similar background to lead in the educational activities. However,

---

18. Gentry A. Shelton, in *Introduction to Christian Education*, Marvin Taylor, ed. (Nashville: Abingdon Press, 1966), p. 121.

19. Richard V. McKann, *The Churches and Mental Health* (New York: Basic Books, 1961), p. 41.

20. Robert K. Bower, *Administering Christian Education* (Grand Rapids, Mich.: William B. Eerdmans Publishing Co., 1964), p. 15.

when the church moves beyond 250 to 300 members, it becomes possible to employ a full-time educational director with adequate specialized training. As the work grows, added staff persons may be employed.

Even with a multiple staff, the pastor still plays a key role in the success of the Christian education work. Any effective sermon teaches eternal truth that brings changes in the lives of people. The midweek Bible studies are basically educational. All of the pastor's pulpit ministry provides essential support for the educational program and its activities. His staff guidance and coordination help to develop a harmonious spirit. His vision for the total church ministry gives direction and motivation to the team effort.

B. The Team Concept

Two basic approaches are possible in the administration of a multiple staff. One is authoritarian, with the pastor as the basic planner. He outlines the program and assigns responsibility to subordinates who implement the plans. Staff members report to the pastor who in turn takes the credit or blame for success or failure. He alone is responsible to the church board with each member of the staff responsible to him. This approach limits staff initiative and increases the burden of responsibility for the pastor.

A second approach divides the areas of ministry with carefully designed job descriptions. Each staff member works with and reports to the appropriate boards or committees. The pastor is still the head of the church, but he delegates areas of the work to his specialists. Frequent staff meetings are held to coordinate programs and to build the team spirit. Each staff member initiates the ideas and the plans for his areas of ministry; after clearance in the staff meeting, he carries them through to completion. He usually attends official church board meetings to report on his area of responsibility.

This team concept encourages individual initiative and provides a natural staff motivation. It utilizes the skills of specialists and, with adequate staff meetings, develops a winning team.

C. Concentration Through Specialization

In pioneer days the pastor was often the best educated person in the community. In some cases he was one of the few persons who could read. Consequently, he became the authority on many subjects. He was expected to do everything around the church and perform many ministries in the homes.

But being a jack-of-all-trades and master of none is not adequate in a day when specialization is the rule. Just as industry and business have capitalized on the specific interests and skills of individuals, so the church advances with specialized leadership. The volunteer song leader is being replaced by a minister of music, and the one-finger typist by a trained secretary. God is calling young people to work full time as ministers of youth, as directors of Christian education, and as directors of children's work. This has made it possible for the pastor to concentrate on preaching, general planning, and personal counselling. Lindecker says, "All indications point to the fact that the future of the ministry of Christian education is excellent. 'The church is coming to a new age. Like it or no, the age of the specialist is here.'"[21]

These specialists comprise the church staff. Judy defines the multiple staff as "a group of professional persons, presumably competent in their respective fields, who blend their services together to perform a ministry as a whole to the congregation."[22]

D. Problems

Because people, their work, and their relationships are involved in a multiple staff, there will be problems to solve. But problems become possibilities when approached with Christian faith and determination.

Sweet suggests the nature of these problems in his prescription for the church preparing to enter a multiple-staff ministry:

- The church as a whole must clearly understand why it wants a multiple staff and what it expects from one.
- The pastor must come to terms with the kind of administrator he really is.
- There must be some clear structure within which the staff operates.
- The pastor must review his own ministry.
- The church must spend a year of study and preparation.
- Attention must be paid to staff family relationships.
- The jobs of all staff members must have job descriptions.
- Distinct efforts to keep communications open must continually be made.[23]

---

21. Wayne M. Lindecker, Jr., in Taylor, *Introduction to Christian Education,* p. 128.

22. Marvin T. Judy, *The Multiple Staff Ministry* (Nashville: Abingdon Press, 1969), p. 33.

23. Herman J. Sweet, *The Multiple Staff in the Local Church* (Philadelphia: The Westminster Press, 1963), pp. 116-22.

Kenneth R. Mitchell interviewed more than 350 people involved in multiple-staff ministries; he found the problems related to four areas:

1. The principal need is for a job analysis.
2. Each man on the staff should be recognized as a responsible minister.
3. Authority should be kept in the hands of the pastor.
4. The assistant should have more freedom.[24]

Judy would find solutions to multiple-staff problems by answering these basic theological and administrative questions:

What is the church?
What is the role of the laity of the church?
What is the difference between the laity and clergy?
What is the role of the unordained person on a church staff?
What is the relationship between unordained and ordained members of a church staff?
What is ministry? Lay and clerical?
What is the relationship between the paid church staff and the laity?
What are the purposes, goals and objectives of the employed staff in a local church?[25]

Most of the problems peculiar to multiple-staff situations are in the area of personal relationships. The interpersonal relations are multiplied by the addition of people. Most of these problems can be overcome by an openness in communication that makes understanding possible. Clear-cut job descriptions for everyone and regular staff meetings that are spiritually oriented can solve many of the tensions.

VI. AREAS OF SERVICE

Many churches have started their multi-staff ministry with part-time specialists. A public school music teacher may be employed to direct the choir. An efficient secretary who left the field of business to have a family can often be employed a few days a week to publish the weekly newsletter, type up the bulletin, and handle the pastor's correspondence.

Some of these part-time workers strengthen the ministries of the church so much that the wisdom of full-time employees is soon realized. Also, part-time workers often find such fulfillment in

---

24. Kenneth R. Mitchell, *Psychological and Theological Relationships in the Multiple Staff Ministry* (Philadelphia: The Westminster Press, 1966), pp. 15-21.
25. Judy, *The Multiple Staff*, p. 18.

church work that they are willing to give up better paying positions to go into full-time ministry. There is a place for both part-time and full-time staff members in the growing church.

In the early days of multiple staffs most of the Christian education associates were women. Men lacked interest in educational ministries; also women found it easier to work for wages the church could pay. As the importance of this ministry has been realized, more and more men have entered the field. Today most of the full-time directors and ministers of Christian education in evangelical churches are men. Many women, however, are employed in other staff positions.

The field is open to both. Churches tend to call women for children's ministries, while men are generally preferred as youth and adult workers. Some churches prefer men as staff leaders in order to help challenge other men into service. Individual capabilities and interests of staff persons are the really determining factors.

Most persons in the field of Christian education are well paid. A recent survey shows that associates in local churches receive salaries equal to about four-fifths that of their senior pastor. Since it is the larger churches with higher pastoral salaries that employ educational associates, this ratio provides a very livable wage. Associate salaries are particularly good when compared with pastoral salaries in smaller churches served by men with similar education and experience.

A. Minister of Christian Education

The minister or director of Christian education generally carries responsibility for the structured educational work of the church. This includes church schools, missionary education, and youth work. The church schools include the Sunday school and such weekday education as vacation Bible schools, day-care centers, day schools, clubs, and camps. Additional responsibilities may be assigned in visitation, administration, and other areas depending on the needs of the church and the abilities of other staff members.

The major function of a director is to help lay leaders succeed in the various church educational agencies. Seldom should a paid staff person replace a volunteer worker. The purpose of the staff man is to enlist, train, and supervise laymen so that they mature and succeed in Christian service. Much of the training may be by example as director and layman work together to carry out some ministry of the church. But the aim is always to develop the layman and not to replace him.

Much Christian education leadership is accomplished behind the scenes. The best work is not done from the platform but in the home, the office, the training class, or in team visitation. This close association with lay leaders and with students brings many opportunities to get involved in loving and counselling people as they grow up in Christ.

Three major qualifications are required to succeed in Christian education work: (1) love God; (2) love people, and (3) love to bring these two together. In addition, a thirst for knowledge, abundant energy, and educational know-how will help. Perhaps 90 percent of one's success comes from being able to work successfully with people and especially with the pastor. Finding satisfaction and fulfillment in a secondary position is essential. Loyalty to and appreciation of other members of the staff make good working relationships.

At the heart of all evangelical church work is soul winning. Education and evangelism go hand in hand. Every minister of Christian education should be actively engaged in personal soul winning. This will keep his values straight and his heart full of compassion.

B. Age-group Specialists

1. Children's Directors

Normally a church employs a youth director and sometimes a director of adult work before they consider a paid staff person for children. However, a growing realization of the importance of the early years of human development is increasing the interest of local churches in professional directors of children's ministries.

Also the development of day-care centers and weekday nursery and kindergarten schools has brought about a change. Staff persons employed to operate the day school program are often used to direct the children's program of the church.

The proliferation of programs and materials for children's work has made it almost impossible for a general minister of Christian education to keep current along with his other areas of responsibility. An up-to-date local church program requires someone who can specialize in the children's work.

A good children's worker must be able to work with children, with their parents, and with the volunteer children's workers in the church. Many of the children's weekday activities require the assistance of parents. Also, the younger the child, the fewer one leader can guide in meaningful experiences. Consequently, the larger number of lay workers necessary in the children's program increases the responsibilities of the director of children's ministries.

The genuine affection of children and the sincere appreciation of parents are some of the compensations in this work. There is also a real sense of accomplishment as one sees developing skills, enlarged interests, better attitudes, and more Christlike behavior. The child's openness to Christ provides many opportunities for meaningful spiritual experiences involving the child and the leader.

2. *Youth Ministers*

The demand for full-time youth workers in the church has grown rapidly in recent years. The development of youth movements, the loss of teens to the church, and the pastor's lack of time necessary for youth work have been major contributing causes. Also, success in reaching outside young people through ministers of youth has proved the value of this staff investment.

The significance of adolescence in human development makes youth work particularly important. This is the period of readjustment and reinterpretation. Many of the major decisions of life are being made. Because of the generation gap there is often a breakdown in relationships with parents and with older church leaders. A youth specialist who understands and has rapport with young people can provide a valuable service to the church and its families.

The ability to identify with young people, to get them involved in significant Christian service, and to teach them to take responsibility are major qualifications for this work. The demand on time and energy is great because youth workers must be committed to spending many hours in the evening with young people. An interest in music and athletics is also helpful.

An effective youth worker, however, will be well repaid for these efforts beyond the normal call of duty as he sees young people investing their lives for Christ.

3. *Adult Leaders*

Many churches have employed retired ministers to visit the older adults of the church. Some have expanded this ministry to include planning and directing activities for the senior citizens. A few churches have employed full-time directors responsible for the total adult ministries of the church. Others have assigned the adult education ministries to the director of Christian education or to another minister on the staff.

The myriad responsibilities of pastors is making it impossible for them to give as much attention to this group as they have in the past. Also the need is growing because the adult population is expanding. More and more is being discovered about the learning and production abilities of adults of all ages. Someone is needed on the church staff to spend time understanding the problems of these adults, to help them adjust as they move from one adult age to another, and to make plans to involve them in Christian service.

Adult leadership requires a mature person with the ability to adjust to a variety of personalities. He must be able to empathize with the sorrowing, rejoice with the glad, and always spread a spirit of holy optimism.

The compensations in adult work are both direct and indirect. No age-group is more appreciative of attention and concern than the senior adults. Their continued usefulness is valuable both to themselves and to the church. Also, younger adults are most appreciative of the church's provision for their aged parents.

C. Music

The music of the church is so important that employing a choir leader is often the first staff assignment. Many pastors like to combine this position with youth or Christian education work so that they can employ a full-time associate. Often the church secures a qualified part-time music director who is employed in public school music or in some related vocation.

However, with the development of graded choirs, church orchestras, and other musical activities more and more churches are hiring full-time ministers of music. Sometimes these persons give private voice or instrument lessons as a part of their assignment or for supplementary income.

In addition to professional skill, a major qualification for success in this work is a clear understanding of the purpose of music in the church. Equally important is the ability to work with people. This combination of music expertise and leadership ability is an admirable combination. Those who have it can find important places of service in God's work.

D. Visitation

The evangelical church follows the biblical command to "Go." One leading denomination affirms: "A church is no stronger than its fellowship and no bigger than its visitation." Consequently, leaders for visitation are essential. Such leadership sometimes begins on a volunteer basis and may be enlarged to a full-time ministry. The assignment may also be combined with other staff responsibilities. The term *minister of outreach* is often used. This concept combines directing the visitation program with such activities as the evangelistic bus ministry, extension classes, branch schools, home Bible study, and Cradle Roll work. Training laymen and leading them in personal soul winning is a vital part of the work. This personal evangelism is particularly effective when a bus ministry opens doors to a growing number of unchurched homes.

A genuine love for people, experience in door-to-door contacts, and willingness to work are probably the most important qualifications for the minister of visitation.

E. Combinations

Many churches begin their multi-staff ministry by employing a person to carry several related responsibilities. The assignment for the associate is usually determined by the talents and limitations of the pastor and his family. Music and Christian education are essentials in every church program; these two make an ideal combination if one has the necessary skills.

Often someone in the pastor's family or a layman in the church can handle the music on a part-time basis. In this case the secretarial work and Christian education may be combined. Also, children's work may be successfully combined with secretarial responsibilities in some churches. One of these combinations may be the first job opening for a young woman entering full-time ministry. Christian education and youth work is another of the beginning combinations. Also a job assignment of youth ministry and music is developing rapidly, particularly in churches that already have a minister of Christian education. Still other combinations are possible.

Two elements are essential if combination assignments are planned: (1) There must be a carefully drawn job description that makes responsibility and authority clear to all; (2) Both associate and pastor must be concerned with getting God's work done, and not greatly concerned about who gets the credit.

F. Day Schools

1. *Day-care Centers*

In recent years many churches have found a practical service to the community and an evangelistic opportunity in operating a day-care center. In families where both parents work, they need and are willing to pay for child care. Also the church can usually provide better facilities than can most private homes. For this ministry some- one must give a major block of his time. A love for children and a vision of what can be done at this early age are essential. Christian teachers with special training in early child development make ideal leaders.

Many of the children are starved for love. All of them need training and education. They are open and receptive to spiritual guidance. These formative years provide a challenge to the person who is serious about making his life count for Christ and the church.

City and state laws vary in the qualifications required for this work. However, a college degree with a major in elementary educa- tion is a minimum preparation for the greatest contribution.

2. *Weekday Nursery and Kindergarten*

In weekday nurseries and kindergartens a more structured educational program is followed than in the day-care center. Also, the hours spent each day with the same children are shorter. Usual- ly there is a morning session and an afternoon session with different children in each.

Standard public education teaching qualifications are necessary because this work normally falls under the supervision of the board of education of the city. Some untrained local church persons with- out a teaching certificate may work as helpers, but a well-trained staff elevates the school in the minds of the community and increases its effectiveness.

Parents who are willing to pay tuition for preschool education tend to take a serious interest in their children's development. Con- sequently, there are greater opportunities for the church to work with the home to provide a Christian environment.

3. *Parochial Schools*

As the public schools become more and more secular, parochial schools increase. Also, in some communities the shortage of public school facilities has encouraged churches to use their buildings for weekday schools. There are evangelical educators who question these trends. They doubt the wisdom of taking Christian pupils out of the public schools because they feel that young people grow stronger spiritually when they take their Christian stand in a secular environ- ment.

On the other side of the debate, many feel that when children in the formative years are nurtured in a Christian environment, they are more likely to become strong Christians. These persons are willing to pay the bill to provide parochial schools. Consequently, teachers, principals, coaches, librarians, secretaries, bookkeepers, janitors, and other educational employees are needed.

Personnel and educational requirements for a parochial school are the same as for the public school. The plus factor is in the area of specific Christian education. All subjects can be taught from the Christian point of view and for a Christian response. Religion is not segregated from other subjects as it is in released-time religious education.

Salaries and benefits may not equal those in the public school, but there are compensations that make this form of Christian education appealing to committed teachers.

B. District or State Opportunities

1. *Christian Education*

At the district or state level of church work nearly all denominations have trained leadership in Christian education. Some are responsible for general promotion and administration; others are assigned to specialized ministries carried on by the church. Some are employed; others are elected but serve without salary.

As the significance of Christian education in a denomination is realized, employment opportunities at this level increase. The work requires the skill of a specialist who assists elected leaders in planning and conducting district, state, or area programs. He also works with local churches to improve their Christian education ministries.

2. *Youth*

The work of a youth leader at the district or state level is similar to that of the general director of Christian education except that the youth man serves a more specialized field. Usually he will be directly involved in the camping and other teen activities for the district. Qualification for district leadership is successful educational experience in the local church.

3. *Administration*

District or state offices are maintained by nearly all denominations. Employment opportunities for trained Christian educators include secretarial work, financing, building, and outreach leadership.

C. Denominational Opportunities

Every national and international denominational headquarters offers opportunities in all of the regular administrative, secretarial, and service roles necessary to carry out the mission of the church.

1. *Program Directors*

Working with the department executives are directors of various ministries. The division of Christian education employs full-time directors for children's work, youth ministries, and adult programs. There are also directors for weekday programs and for summertime activities. These experienced Christian educators are responsible for developing and promoting the programs, and for writing or editing material.

2. *Writers and Editors*

Curriculum materials, also promotional and program guides are essential to the mission of a denomination. Writers and editors make them possible. Some serve on the denominational staff at the headquarters location; others work free lance or on assignment in their home communities. Qualification for this ministry requires the ability to put ideas into words that communicate to others. Preparation calls for some training and experience in journalism as well as the foundation experiences in Christian education.

3. *Convention and Fieldwork*

Denominational objectives, goals, plans, and programs must be conveyed and interpreted to those working at district and local church levels. In addition to written media, personal contact in conventions, workshops, assemblies, tours, and rallies is essential. Much of this promotional work is done by headquarters personnel who carry executive or program responsibilities, but there is always need for persons who can spend a major part of their time in fieldwork. This ministry requires a thorough understanding of program and materials as well as the ability to interpret them to others. A love for travel and for promotional work can make this an enjoyable assignment.

F. Mission Fields

Missionaries with special training in Christian education are particularly valuable in our times. In some areas of the world today the only opportunity to spread the gospel of Christ is through education. Also, even where preaching is an open avenue for ministry, some of the greatest results have been realized through Christian teaching in day schools, Sunday schools, and Bible schools.

1. *Church Schools Leaders*

Missionaries in charge of Sunday schools, vacation Bible schools, boys' and girls' clubs, and other Christian activities have been able to change a tribe and, in the long run, to influence nations. Many of the national leaders on mission fields today were first influenced toward Christ through a barrio Sunday school or a vacation Bible school started and directed by a missionary.

2. *Bible School Teachers*

The future leaders of the church on mission fields are developed in the Bible schools. Teachers are needed—teachers of Bible, theology, philosophy, church history, evangelism, pastoral work, and Christian education. Much of such learning takes place in planned fieldwork supervised by the teachers. Also opportunities for guidance and counselling are abundant in the intimate relations of living together at the Bible schools.

3. *Youth Leaders*

As the overseas work advances, specialization in Christian education becomes necessary. A first area of need is youth work. National young people need guidance and encouragement to become involved in the redemptive mission of the church. Also they have many of the same social and personal needs as our young people in the home church. A missionary with special ability and interest in this age-group can advance God's work substantially.

E. Christian Colleges

1. *Teaching*

Church-related colleges need teachers of all the subjects necessary to provide a liberal arts education. As in the parochial school, subjects can be approached from the Christian point of view. In many of these colleges, classes are small enough that teachers can know pupils personally and thus they also teach through influence and example.

2. *Administration*

From the president's office to the janitor's room there is an array of executive, administrative, business, secretarial, and maintenance responsibilities necessary to keep a college in operation. Counselling and guidance is needed in the dormitories as well as in the dean's office. The salaries may not equal those of the state colleges and universities, but there are compensations. Christian teachers often touch students who, without that influence, would be lost to Christ.

F. Interdenominational Ministries

In recent years, opportunities for Christian service on a full- and part-time basis have developed in many interdenominational and nondenominational groups.

1. *Children*

The YMCA, YWCA, and Child Evangelism Fellowship offer the major opportunities for Christian education of children outside of the denominational programs. Though the YMCA and YWCA began as youth movements, their programs today include the younger years.

2. *Youth*

With the YMCA and YWCA leading the way, many youth movements provide opportunity for Christian education service on an interdenominational level. Youth for Christ has been a leader in evangelical Christianity. Other groups include Inter-Varsity Christian Fellowship, Campus Crusade for Christ, Navigators, Young Life, International Students, Inc., and the Fellowship of Christian Athletes.[26] Opportunities for ministry are available in most of these organizations on both the local and national levels. Some even provide international ministries.

Young people with a desire or a call to serve God in Christian education will find ample opportunity. The field is broad and the need is great. The qualified laborers are still few.

BIBLIOGRAPHY

DuBois, Lauriston J. *Careers for Christians.* Kansas City: Beacon Hill Press, 1958.

A concise discussion of Christian vocations geared particularly to high-school-age young people. The four chapters are: Our Vocations as Christians; Discovering Our Abilities; The Choice of a Vocation; and The Call of God to Special Service.

---

26. See chap. 18 for a more detailed description of some of these agencies that offer opportunity for ministry.

Ferrari, Erma Paul. *Careers for You.* Nashville: Abingdon-Cokesbury Press, 1953.

> Although an older book, it contains good guidance for high-school- and college-age young people on how to choose a career through a sense of Christian vocation. It deals with such basic questions as: What do I want to be? Will my personality fit the job? How can I make a success of it? Where can I get information about different careers?

Judy, Marvin T. *The Multiple Staff Ministry.* Nashville: Abingdon Press, 1969.

> Dr. Judy presents a thorough discussion of the essentials of a successful multiple-staff ministry. He then devotes a chapter to each of six staff positions. The appendix includes many actual job descriptions of those working on church staffs. A very complete topical bibliography is included.

Nelson, John Oliver. *Protestant Religious Vocations.* New York: Vocational Guidance Manuals, Inc., 1952.

> An older book but a classic in its field. Dr. Nelson covers vocational opportunities in the local church, mission fields, chaplaincies, campuses, Christian social agencies such as YMCA, and interchurch movements. He also deals with preparation in high school and college and how to choose a seminary.

CHAPTER 18

Wider Perspectives in Christian Education

This chapter seeks to provide important resources for Christian teaching and Christian nurture which are not discussed elsewhere in the text. Placing it under "Structures of Christian Education" is appropriate because we are exploring organizations, not theoretical foundations or principles.

I. Areas of Cooperative Enterprise

A. Outside the Local Church

Most of the work of Christian education takes place in a local congregation. Here teachers, supervisors, superintendents, and pastors seek to share the Christian gospel with other persons. But in this chapter as in the final one, we go outside of the local congregation.

B. Outside the Denomination

Today most of the teaching materials and most of the guidelines for organizing Christian education in the local church originate from denominational planners. These common plans for all the congregations of a denomination contribute to the cohesion and growth of the churches. The teacher who moves from one community to another finds the same curriculum materials. The pastor who moves to a new congregation finds a similar organization and comparable ways of carrying on the work of Christian education. The similarities help him to fit into his new assignment quickly and easily because the programs are familiar to him.

These programs are likely to be effective because they are planned by one's own denominational leaders. Such leaders are chosen for their experience and for their prior achievements in Christian education. Also they plan their materials in harmony with denominational doctrine and practices. They thus offer to the local church the very best that the denomination knows how to give. But in this chapter we shall explore resources beyond those provided by the denominations.

C. Wider Perspectives

The structures discussed in this chapter are in "wider perspectives" because (1) they exist outside of the local church, and (2) they cross denominational lines.

1. *Interdenominational*

Some of the organizations here explored have grown up as cooperative agencies between denominations. For example, there are several groups of editors and writers from different denominations who get together once a year to compare plans and to discuss how best to prepare curriculum materials. Such organizations are self-improvement associations comparable to annual professional meetings of doctors or lawyers.

Other interdenominational organizations, like the Commission of Sunday School Secretaries of the National Sunday School Association, meet annually to plan common enrollment and attendance programs to be used by all the denominations that participate in the planning.

Organizations of this kind have developed because denominational leaders find them helpful in planning the Christian education ministries for which they are responsible. The leader normally chooses to join the organizations where he gets the most ideas to help him in his assignments.

These interdenominational organizations require budget support from the participating denominations. The amount usually depends upon the size of the denomination, the number of representatives who attend meetings, and the cost of the common programs involved.

2. *Nondenominational*

A number of organizations interested in Christian education have no denominational ties. Some, like the American Sunday School Union, started before the Christian education departments of most Protestant churches were established. Others, like the independent publishers, sought to meet a need for curriculum materials in independent churches and in congregations dissatisfied with the literature supplied by their own denominational publishers.

Most of the nondenominational organizations offer services and seek to sell merchandise to leaders of local churches—pastors, directors of Christian education, Sunday school superintendents, teachers, and department supervisors. Some interdenominational organizations also offer services to local churches, but in a much more limited way.

Interdenominational agencies tend to represent denominations working together. *Nondenominational agencies* more often compete with the denominations.

This chapter is planned to: (1) acquaint the reader with these agencies and their functions; (2) point out what services are available, and how local leaders may secure the services desired; (3) help the reader to understand why his denominational leaders may or may not be identified with the interdenominational organizations.

II. ALDERSGATE CHRISTIAN EDUCATION AND PUBLICATIONS ASSOCIATION

Today the term *Aldersgate* means to many people interdenominational projects in Christian education that are based on Arminian-Wesleyan theology. These projects originate from The Commission on Christian Education and Aldersgate Publications Association (CEAPA)—one of five commissions of the Christian Holiness Association (formerly National Holiness Association).

A. Purpose

The Commission was organized (1) to "provide a means by which interested denominations may be brought together to work out cooperative projects and ministries at home and abroad," and (2) "to provide for mutual exchange of ideas and the discussion of ways for improving their Christian education ministries and denominational publications."[1]

B. Membership

The Commission is designed for interdenominational cooperation of Arminian-Wesleyan groups. Any member of the Christian Holiness Association or any denomination doctrinally eligible for such membership may elect Christian education representatives to the Commission. Eight denominations are currently members.[2]

C. Service

This cooperation, organized in 1958, currently offers the following services.

1. *Aldersgate Biblical Series* for adults—40 sets of paperback volumes (one for teachers and one for pupils) covering the entire Bible in book-by-book inductive studies

2. *Aldersgate Doctrinal Series* for adults—elective doctrinal studies arranged in 13-week units

3. *Aldersgate Dialog Series* for adults—courses with a Christian perspective on contemporary issues

4. *Aldersgate Graded Series*—a complete graded Sunday school curriculum, nursery through senior high

5. *Aldersgate Vacation Bible School Curriculum*—a full vacation Bible school course, nursery through junior high

6. *Aldersgate Service Training*—a comprehensive leadership training course for Christian education workers in the local church

7. *Enduring Word Series*—an adult cycle of Bible studies with a Wesleyan theological interpretation

D. Availability

1. Denominations interested in Arminian-Wesleyan Christian education materials are invited to apply for membership and thus share in the planning and use of these teaching tools.

2. Local churches interested in using materials with this doctrinal foundation are invited to write for further information and for

---

1. Constitution, The Commission on Christian Education and Aldersgate Publications Association, Article IV.

2. Churches of Christ in Christian Union, Church of the Nazarene, Evangelical Friends Alliance, Evangelical Methodists, Free Methodist Church, The Missionary Church, The Wesleyan Church, The Evangelical Church of North America.

sample materials. Write to Christian Holiness Association, 21 Beachway Dr., Suite 1, Indianapolis, Ind. 46224.

E. Program and Promotion

The Commission's committees on Sunday Schools, Youth Ministries, and Service Training recommend structures for organizing these functions in the local church. Promotional programs are also planned for guiding congregations in outreach and growth through their Sunday schools and other agencies for Christian education.

F. Meetings

The annual meeting of the Commission is held the first week in December. Standing committees and special task forces often meet in connection with the convention of the Christian Holiness Association the week following Easter.

III. The National Sunday School Association (NSSA)

A. Origin

The National Sunday School Association was born in 1945 as an evangelical protest against biblical and theological liberalism in Christian education. Its parent organization, the National Association of Evangelicals, seeks to provide cooperation among theologically conservative denominations, independent organizations, and local churches; also among individual conservative Christians from liberal churches.

In 1945 the NAE's Church School Commission issued a call for persons interested in a system of uniform Sunday school lessons that would be acceptable to evangelicals. The meeting drew about 100 publishing representatives and Christian educators from evangelical ranks.

In 1946 a new lesson system was adopted but it has never gained wide popularity. One reason was that the lesson committee proposed a uniform plan at a time when most Christian educators were convinced that graded lessons were preferable—at least for children and teens. Also many evangelical publishers considered the historic International Sunday School Lesson Outlines well adapted to sound evangelical treatment.

B. Ministries

NSSA's greatest contribution to Christian education has come from its commitment to "revitalizing the Sunday schools of America."

1. *National Conventions*

Since its organization, NSSA has sponsored Sunday school conventions for local leaders in Christian education. Until 1954 these were annual national conventions. From 1955 to 1968 twin conventions were held—one in the eastern section of the United States and one in the west. In 1969 NSSA began to rely more heavily on local and state associations for the large popular conventions. The parent organization has directed its energies into a National Leadership Seminar in order to strengthen and support evangelical Christian education.

Both seminars and conventions are open to interested Christian educators. They offer annual enrichment and inspiration to all who seek to serve Christ through Christian teaching.

2. *Commissions*

NSSA has organized seven commissions to stimulate improvement of evangelical Christian education.

a. The *Youth Commission* sponsors a National Youth Week. It also seeks to keep abreast of current developments in the youth culture and to relate the gospel appeal to today's teen. Findings and programs are published in NSSA's journal, *Concept,* and through special releases.

b. The *Commission of Denominational Sunday School Secretaries* is an association of persons with executive responsibility for the Christian education programs of their denominations. The Commission develops plans and materials for such programs as National Family Week, National Sunday School Week, and March to ·Sunday School in March. Local churches may secure these plans from the office of NSSA, 370 Main Pl., Wheaton, Ill. 60187.

c. The *Research Commission* conducts studies in areas judged most important for the advancement of evangelical Christian education.

d. The *Camping Commission* studies opportunities and recommends procedures for achieving the goals of Christian education in outdoor settings.

e. The *Publishers Commission* includes both denominational and independent publishers of evangelical literature.

f. The *Curriculum Commission* meets annually to prepare the Bible study outlines upon which NSSA's uniform Sunday school lessons are based.

g. The *Commission of Sunday School Association Chairmen* is composed of the leaders of area Sunday school associations. Its purpose is to provide a forum for exchange of ideas in effective Sunday school promotion.

3. *Regional Associations and Conventions*

NSSA has actively encouraged state and local Sunday school associations. Most of these associations sponsor annual conventions. The conventions make available an evangelical atmosphere and educational guidance to persons living within easy driving distance.

4. *"Concept"* is the official publication of NSSA. Published monthly, it offers a reservoir of promotional and educational plans to encourage better Christian education in evangelical churches. Through *Concept* the subscriber can keep in touch with the various programs and reports originating from NSSA Commissions and from special project groups.

IV. EVANGELICAL TEACHER TRAINING ASSOCIATION (ETTA)

Like NSSA, the Evangelical Teacher Training Association was formed out of concern for a stronger evangelical emphasis. Its special concern is the training of workers for Christian education. The Association began in 1930 under Clarence H. Benson and James M. Gray of Moody Bible Institute.

ETTA has two courses of study. The first is offered through Bible schools and colleges where students are given professional preparation for Christian education. About 100 institutions currently follow the program.

The local pastor or minister of Christian education will be more directly interested in the second program, ETTA's *Preliminary Teacher's Certificate*. The courses leading to the certificate are offered for study in the local church. The certificate requires 72 hours of class study, including Bible and educational methods.

ETTA thus offers a training ministry to the independent evangelical congregation. Also several smaller denominations cooperate and officially endorse ETTA's program as their own denominational structure for leadership training. Other evangelical groups provide their own denominational programs for Christian service training.

V. CAMPUS CRUSADE

It was the personal religious experience of Mr. and Mrs. William (Bill) Bright in the Hollywood Presbyterian Church that led them to share Christ with college and university students. This led to the organization in 1955 of Campus Crusade for Christ. Their purpose is to reach every college student for Christ. An evangelistic zeal has characterized those connected with the group. They have developed a number of pieces of literature to be used in witnessing. The best known is *The Four Spiritual Laws,* designed to help lead a person to accept Christ as Saviour and Lord.

Where a congregation is located near a college or university campus, local church young people can become active in a campus witness through contacts with athletes, musical groups, foreign students, and faculty members.

High school ministries are probably the most accessible contact for the average local church. Teens from the church—especially the small church—can find in these campus groups stimulation for witnessing; they also find supporting evangelical Christian fellowship with young people from neighboring churches.

Like other independent groups, Campus Crusade offers most to the independent local church or to the small congregation isolated from close denominational stimulus and evangelical fellowship.

Headquarters are in Arrowhead Springs, San Bernardino, Calif. 92404.

VI. YOUTH FOR CHRIST

Like Campus Crusade, Youth for Christ is a nondenominational group with a deep concern to communicate the Christian faith. Its ministry appeals chiefly to young people in high school. The *Youth Guidance* division, however, is directed specifically to nonschool-oriented young people—the school dropouts.

Organized in 1944, YFC now has nearly 1,300 Campus Life Clubs operating out of 200 chartered YFC chapters. These clubs are organized for INSIGHT and for IMPACT.

The INSIGHT groups are planned for young Christians who want to practice walking in the Spirit of God. The YFC adult leader teaches the authority and power of the Word of God for all aspects of a teenager's life. In their relationships with each other, teens find new meanings in their faith and effective ways of sharing it naturally with their friends.

IMPACT activities are arranged so that Christian teens can invite their non-Christian friends to join them. It may be a rally, a co-op, a Campus Life meeting. All of these capitalize on the social instinct common to teens. These groups form a backdrop for the message of the gospel through the persuasive influence of one teen life on another.

YFC thus offers Christian fellowship and witnessing activity to the teen. Because it crosses denominational lines, it offers much to the isolated evangelical teen from a small congregation. It also helps young people discover how the Spirit of God is at work beyond the boundaries of their own local church and denomination.

Further information is available from Youth for Christ International, Box 419, Wheaton, Ill. 60187.

VII. INDEPENDENT PUBLISHERS

David C. Cook Publishing Company has, since 1875, published Sunday school curriculum materials. In 1933 Scripture Press was founded in the Chicago area; in the same year Gospel Light Publications began in Hollywood, Calif. These producers, along with Standard Publishing Company of Cincinnati, Ohio, and several smaller organizations are identified with the evangelical movement.

Most of these independent publishing houses were established to meet a concern for Bible-centered curriculum materials. They originated in a period when the emphasis on psychological and sociological factors in religious education tended, in many denominational curricula, to subordinate the teaching of scripture. These nondenominational materials also appeal to the independent congregation because they carry no denominational name or program. However, among the denominations—both liberal and conservative—the independent publisher becomes an out-and-out competitor of the denominational publisher for the loyalty and business of the local congregation.

The same factors that appeal so naturally to the independent congregation become liabilities for congregations that are part of a denomination.

In literature from its own denomination, the local church is assured of commonly accepted theological positions. The local church also has official channels through which it can register its wishes for change. Moreover, through denominational materials the user is kept in touch with the ongoing life and programs of his own church.

Neither of these important advantages is open to those who use independent materials.

VIII. THE DIVISION OF CHRISTIAN EDUCATION, NCC

A. Origin

The Division of Christian Education is one of four program agencies of the National Council of Churches. It currently represents 22 Protestant denominations and 11 Greek Orthodox groups. The present name and structure were adopted in 1950. At that time the International Council of Religious Education, formed in 1922, merged with six other interdenominational agencies to become the National Council of Churches.

The International Council of Religious Education had been preceded by the International Sunday School Association, formed in 1905 as an outgrowth of the great Sunday school conventions begun in 1832. The Division of Christian Education is thus the descendant of the longest line of cooperative Christian education in America.

B. Program Services

The Division offers interdenominational services for persons concerned with Christian colleges. These concerns are administered under the *Department of Higher Education.* Also specialized help for missionary education is provided through the *Department of Education for Missions.*

The *Department of Educational Development* (DED) is of most direct interest to persons concerned with Christian education in the local church. Like other divisions of the National Council of Churches, DED is an interdenominational agency. As Taylor writes, the "goal is to provide a structural framework whereby the denominations can do together those things which they cannot do separately."[3]

Through research and coordinated programming with the member denominations, DED seeks to pioneer and support the work of the churches in selected areas. DED does not have established commissions as appear under NSSA; however, a staff member carries responsibility for each of the following seven areas. On specific programs other staff members may be assigned for consultation and assistance. Denominational representatives are also named to serve

---

3. Marvin J. Taylor, *An Introduction to Christian Education* (New York: Abingdon Press, 1966), p. 309.

on all projects in which a member denomination wishes to participate.

1. *Religion and Public Education* is concerned with how religion may be taught in public schools; also how Through-the-Week curriculum may relate Christian faith to what is learned in public schools.

2. *Urban Education* seeks to help the churches understand how better to serve metropolitan areas. The Department carries on research and experimentation to develop new designs for Christian education—new groupings and new curriculum resources relevant to the urban environment.

3. *Special Education for Exceptional Persons* acquaints the churches with ministries helpful to such people. The staff plans educational resources to meet the needs of the mentally retarded, the emotionally disturbed, and the deaf.

Christian education materials for the blind are provided on an interdenominational basis by the John Milton Society, 475 Riverside Dr., New York, N.Y. 10027.

Braille Bibles and Talking Bible Records are available to the blind from the American Bible Society. A blind person can obtain them for whatever he is able to pay. The address is 1865 Broadway, New York, N.Y. 10023.

4. The section on *Sex, Marriage, and Family* develops programs to train leaders to guide all aspects of the churches' family ministries. They seek to help the churches deal effectively with issues of sexuality, intergeneration conflict, and values in family life.

5. *Church Education* concerns itself with structures for Christian teaching such as ungraded groups, family groups, camps, and conferences. Programs are developed for using new media and technologies in Christian education. Here, too, are lodged responsibilities for recruitment and training programs for local church leaders in Christian education.

6. *Education for Special Groups* is concerned about persons whose needs are unique because of cultural or ethnic backgrounds; unusually low income, social injustices, educational disadvantage, language barriers, and low literacy.

7. *National and International Affairs Education* seeks to stimulate concern for and participation in national policies and practices to help make those policies consistent with Christian values.

Interested persons may secure information in these areas by writing to the Department of Educational Development, 475 Riverside Dr., New York, N.Y. 10027.

C. International Sunday School Lessons

The Committee on the Uniform Series is an interdenominational group appointed by about 30 cooperating denominations. This group of about 50 persons meets annually to plan the lesson outlines for the International Bible Lessons for Christian Teaching, more commonly known as the Uniform Series. The committee itself has full responsibility for what goes into the outlines. The group, however, is administratively related to the Department of Educational Development. The curriculum division of DED handles details of duplicating, copyrighting, and distributing the outlines.

Denominations that serve on the committee and share in the expense of planning the outlines use them free of charge. All others are charged royalty fees based on the circulation of the periodicals in which the outlines are followed.

The Committee on the Uniform Series provides outlines only. All lesson treatments and interpretation of the selected scriptures is the responsibility of the publisher from whom the local church secures its lesson quarterlies.

The Uniform Series of Bible studies was begun as a cooperative interdenominational effort in 1872; it has persisted for more than 100 years. Probably no one factor, except the Bible itself, has served so well to unify the thinking of Protestant lay Christians in America and around the world.

IX. WORLD COUNCIL OF CHRISTIAN EDUCATION

International cooperation in Christian education dates back at least to 1889 when the first World Sunday School Convention was held in London. At Rome in 1907 the World Sunday School Association was formed. From 1950 until 1971 it was known as the World Council of Christian Education and Sunday School Association. In 1971 WCCESSA became the educational division of the World Council of Churches.

The objective of the Council has been to support the growth of Christian education throughout the world. Its quarterly journal, *World Christian Education,* helps to share ideas and experiences with Christian teachers in many lands.

Membership and support comes from national councils of churches, denominational boards of Christian education, and other similar bodies. Support for WCCE makes possible Christian education programs in underdeveloped countries. At times most denominational and independent mission programs derive direct or indirect benefits from the services of this worldwide organization.

X. RELIGIOUS EDUCATION ASSOCIATION

The Religious Education Association carries on scholarly research in theology and education. It was organized in 1903 out of a concern to bring more scientific emphasis into the Christian education programs of the churches. Its journal, *Religious Education,* begun in 1906, is published bimonthly. The Association maintains standing committees on higher education and research. Membership is on an individual basis and the association is a multi-faith group including Protestants, Catholics, Jews, and others.

Religious Education and the periodic national conventions are most likely to appeal to professors of Christian education in Bible schools, colleges, and seminaries. The work of REA will also be of interest to the pastor and local director of Christian education who try to keep current on research projects in this field. For further information write The Religious Education Association, 409 Prospect St., New Haven, Conn. 06510.

*   *   *

Our wider perspectives in Christian education should occasion gratitude on the part of every Christian. Considering these perspectives, we are reminded that the Spirit of God works through many channels beyond those with which we are most familiar. The work of the Holy Spirit is not limited to us and to our organizations. We are grateful for every person who seeks to cooperate with the Spirit of God. We are glad for every Christian who wants to spread the good news of God's revelation in Jesus Christ—because that is the business of Christian education.

BIBLIOGRAPHY

Hakes, J. Edward. "Evangelical Christian Education and the Protestant Day-School Movement," in *An Introduction to Christian Education* (Marvin J. Taylor, ed.). Nashville: Abingdon Press, 1966.

The author describes the work of the National Sunday School Association, the Evangelical Teacher Training Association, Christian Service Brigade, Pioneer Girls, and the independent publishers.

Taylor, Marvin J. "Inter- and Nondenominational Agencies and Christian Education," in *An Introduction to Christian Education* (Marvin J. Taylor, ed.). Nashville: Abingdon Press, 1966.

Wolf, Earl C. *Teaching Adults Today*. Kansas City: Beacon Hill Press of Kansas City, 1974.

In chapter three Dr. Wolf surveys the origin and basic principles of the widely used Uniform Series of Bible studies.

CHAPTER 19

Christian
Higher Education

I. THE IMPORTANCE

In a discussion of Christian higher education we are interested in the concerns of the church in education beyond the high school level. One might question the inclusion of such a chapter in a book that focuses on Christian education in the local church. However, in the light of the church's objective to develop Christians as integrated, whole persons, Christian higher education is a logical extension of the local church program. It would be unreasonable to abandon our exploration of Christian nurture just at the point where young people attain a more complete independence and sense the challenge of their newly developed intellectual powers. Furthermore, the local church depends on Christian higher education to provide the academic preparation for its lay volunteers as well as for its full-time ministers.

A. Preparing Church Leaders

There are at least three contributions of Christian higher education to local church leadership.

First is the obvious role of preparing persons for Christian service. This role, however, is not limited to the professional religious training of ministers and missionaries. The church is interested in the training of workers for all kinds of Christian institutions. For instance, it is important to recognize that a call to service in full-time Christian work can include Christian higher education itself, as well as the more traditional areas of the pastoral ministry and the mission field. This wider perspective of Christian service is also in harmony with the broader types of service now open through the multiple-staff ministries in the local church and through the varied needs on mission fields. Thus, Christian higher education contributes to the preparation of full-time ministers for local churches and to the preparation of those college and university teachers who help prepare such ministers.

Another role of Christian higher education is its instruction in educational theory and practice. The Christian college prepares candidates for full-time service, including the ministry of Christian education. If such persons majored only in religion without devoting some attention to the specialized Christian education tasks, they would be deficient in their training.

There is a final role in relation to the local church. It is to provide academic training for laymen who will serve voluntarily in the local Christian education program while gainfully employed elsewhere. These laymen profit from college-level religion study, especially Christian education courses, and thus provide capable leadership in the local church.

Another dimension goes beyond the function of academic preparation. Many Christian institutions of higher education are involved in cooperative efforts with local churches. It is conceivable that the colleges will become even more involved with Christian education internships and other forms of practical field experiences for their students and for local church workers. This concept of the local church as a training ground for the practical integration of faith and learning should meet the frequent student complaint of lack of involvement and relevance.

Cooperation could extend even to a kind of research partnership where a Christian college would provide consultant services to local churches much as universities do for local public schools and other agencies. Furthermore, Christian higher education might well undertake field research studies using modern techniques. Such studies would help the church identify, isolate, and solve problems, thereby performing its function more effectively in today's world.

B. Preparing Christian Citizens

Beyond the role of preparing local church leaders, Christian higher education can be viewed as an advanced part of the church's program of Christian education. Its goal of developing educated, integrated, whole Christians is designed to produce a more effective Christian witness in all areas and at all levels in the world. This aim fits with the individual Christian's dual obligation of continued self-development of his God-given potential throughout life and of reaching out in witness to others in a world of need.

Sometimes it is easy to overlook the fact that personal development contributes to greater effectiveness in outreach to others. But it does. And the Christian's motivation in Christ should drive him to a level of personal development that exceeds what he would have achieved if he had not been a Christian. Paul writes, "Let everyone be sure that he is doing his very best, for then he will have the personal satisfaction of work well done, and won't need to compare himself with someone else" (Gal. 6:4, TLB). The comparison is always with oneself, not others; it does not mean that Christians always excel others. But to the degree that all Christians are faithful in developing their full and varied potential, the Kingdom can permeate every facet of society.

In God's economy, diversity of talent places Christians in every walk of life, thus making it possible to get the Christian witness to all persons. Every Christian is obligated to prepare himself as fully as possible so that he may effectively enter the doors that God opens to him. Thus the leavening effect of Christian witness can touch every part of man's world through life and word.

C. Preparing Christian Policy Makers

A related dimension of Christian citizenship is in contributing a Christian influence to vital decision-making in society. In addition to the commission to carry the witness to all the world, Christians have a responsibility to participate in the world for two practical reasons. One is that we should be interested in helping the world to operate on as high an ethical level as possible. The second is that if we fail to give this Christian emphasis, the world may increasingly limit our options to witness freely.

With our pluralistic world accepting the Christian concept of marriage less and less, we must articulate the biblical view as a viable position. We may not be able to make Christian marriage universally accepted, but certainly in the midst of trial marriages, and multiple marriages, Christian marriage articulated on biblical principles ought to be retained in public thinking as a viable choice. This will happen only as Christians make their view prominent. In doing so, others will be influenced for good. The world may be persuaded to leave room for Christians to be part of the mainstream of life rather than a forgotten remnant.

A different illustration suggests a more futuristic element of Christian participation in decision-making. We live among trends toward a shorter work week, more leisure time, and guaranteed affluence. What will be the Christian response to a world where the necessity to work at a job to earn a living may become a thing of the past? Will we have thought ahead in creative anticipation to contribute a challenging Christian perspective? Or will we only react reluctantly after such a world is already upon us?

In all areas alert Christians must be futurists in thinking and planning, or the world will be the worse for not having had our contribution. Moreover, the church may be crippled by a lack of true Christian perspective in society. Through both qualified faculty and graduates, Christian higher education has a significant contribution to make in developing a variety of well-prepared individuals to think Christianly and thus to contribute to vital dialogue and decision-making in all facets of life.

II. The Institutions of Higher Education

Variety characterizes the institutions that have provided Christian higher education. Liberal arts colleges have educated by far the largest number of Christian young people in the widest number of fields. There are also theological seminaries, Bible institutes, and Bible colleges. In addition, the Christian opportunities in secular institutions should be recognized. We will examine briefly this range of institutional settings in which Christian higher education takes place.

A. The Christian Liberal Arts College

The Christian liberal arts college aims both at the specific professional purposes and at the broader educational aspects outlined earlier in this chapter. Its history is interwoven with the history of North American education as a whole.

1. *History*

The earliest and strongest motivation for higher education in America was religious. In New England prior to the Revolutionary War, higher education was specifically related to the preparation of ministers. Harvard, Yale, Princeton, and others were all founded primarily for religious purposes. Subsequently the colleges added training for other professions, but the religious concern continued strong.

Most of the institutions founded as the pioneers moved westward were also church related. Dirks writes:

> Some of them, having had no direct denominational ties, became privately endowed and affirmed a status similar to such institutions as Harvard and Yale. Still others became the foundations of state-supported universities. A large number, however, have continued an identification with the denomination which founded them.[1]

Thus American liberal arts education has its roots in the traditional Christian concern for higher education. While many of these early institutions gradually drifted from their religious foundations, there have always been new ones developing out of comparable Christian concern and along similar patterns.

There has been difficulty articulating a coherent philosophy of Christian higher education that could gain consensus, but we should at least explore some of the philosophical underpinnings commonly espoused or tacitly understood. A significant element in the rationale for the liberal arts colleges has been the preparation of individuals for various avenues of full-time Christian service in the church. How would the church vocations be filled if there were no special institutions where individuals could be called and trained?

Also among evangelicals in the 20th century the general philosophy of a Christian liberal arts education has been to counteract the secular influence of other colleges and universities, especially for young people away from home and the home church for the first time. This philosophy is often misunderstood or misrepresented. Therefore, it deserves some careful consideration.

The Christian liberal arts college endeavors to avoid both a sterile religious neutrality and a rigid indoctrination. In avoiding one it may sometimes appear to be guilty of the other. A strong feeling is held by supporting churchmen that the Christian college should be supportive of the faith in its total environment, including its residence life. Academically, this usually means that, along with a fair presentation of conflicting religious and philosophical views, the Christian point of view is investigated and encouraged. This is in

---

1. J. Edward Dirks, in *Religious Education*, Marvin J. Taylor, ed. (Nashville: Abingdon Press, 1960), p. 295.

contrast to the avowed neutrality and often open hostility of the secular institution. It also means that faculty members are expected to exemplify the Christian faith not only in their lives but also, as much as possible, through integration of their academic disciplines with the faith.

It should be pointed out that the oft-called-for detached objectivity in higher education is essentially an impossibility for subjective man. Therefore, the Christian college makes no apology for its Christian bias but, rather, is forthright in making it known. Bias becomes an academic hazard only when it is enforced on students or when it is not acknowledged. If the Christian college needs to guard against a rigid indoctrination, the secular institution needs to be equally on guard against the subtle influences of proclaiming a false objectivity.

2. Program

Christian liberal arts colleges bear primary responsibility for preparing churchmen and Christian civic leaders. In the area of full-time service it is imperative that these institutions make a strong contribution by preparing ministers, directors of Christian education, and missionaries for the church. Without strong religion majors cultivating a climate of interaction, the liberal arts programs can readily dominate and divert the institution from its course.

However, the arts program itself plays the major role in preparing teachers for Christian educational institutions. The arts program also fills a key role in training laymen for their secular vocational fields. Finally, a Christian liberal arts education especially features preparation for Christian citizenship. The program seeks to nurture well-integrated and educated Christians who will participate in and carry the witness to all phases of life.

To serve such a diversity of persons the curriculum in Christian colleges has been equally varied. Buttressing all the programs is a core of studies embracing the humanities, religion, fine arts, social sciences, and natural sciences. Possibly half the total core program of undergraduate requirements is designed to ensure a breadth of conversance with the foregoing disciplines. Beyond this core are opportunities to major in many subject areas. Also beyond the core are professional fields such as preaching, teaching, and nursing. These programs can be terminal or they may lead to graduate study. Frequently there are shorter associate degree programs as well as programs leading to the A.B., B.S., and Th.B. degrees.

3. *Issues and Concerns*

Two concerns confront all Christian institutions of higher education, and Christian liberal arts colleges in particular.

a. Loss of spiritual dynamic. Christian institutions today face the dangers of a loss of spiritual life and an accommodation of moral standards. With the greater permissiveness of our times and the increasing secularism of our pluralistic society, there are new pressures in both of these areas.

b. Accreditation requirements. Matching the educational standards of secular institutions through accreditation has been a driving force in the development of the Christian college. Such pressure, however, has often been blamed for the drift away from evangelical moorings. This must be admitted as a problem, perhaps even the greatest hazard of an evangelical liberal arts college.

Where faculties have failed, it has probably been unintentional. Striving for scholastic excellence has simply overshadowed the need for integration of academic disciplines with the Christian faith. The danger of drifting is real, but it is not an insurmountable hazard. The many sound evangelical colleges with full accreditation and with special accreditation in fields such as teacher education attest to this reality.

c. The junior college movement. A further challenge to the Christian liberal arts college has been to adapt to the junior or community college development. This has meant accommodating an increasing number of transfer students midway toward a baccalaureate degree. More importantly it has meant some modification of philosophy and practice.

When young people and their parents fail to see the need for a full four years at a Christian college, adjustments have to be made for those students who spend the first two years at a secular institution. But this is not necessarily bad in terms of the underlying philosophy for Christian higher education. With special effort, home and local church may be able to extend an effective ministry to these young people for another two years beyond high school. New programs of local ministry to this group are demonstrating effectiveness in substituting for what was previously seen as a primary responsibility of the Christian college.

d. Graduate programs. This postponement of the college's ministry until a student's junior year could add to the clamor for more graduate education in Christian colleges. With rising educational levels graduate study is becoming commonplace. Christian higher education faces crucial decisions at this point. Contemplation of moves to graduate courses requires close scrutiny in relation to basic philosophy and objectives as well as a careful assessment of cost.

Without prejudicing the consideration of such graduate programs, there are, nevertheless, several factors that should be noted relative to basic philosophy. The concept of an educational environment supportive of Christian faith has validity, but conceivably there is a point where it is less necessary than the value of refining one's faith in the midst of the world at large. This refining of Christian faith may fit best into a program of graduate education in a pluralistic setting. Furthermore, before beginning graduate programs it would seem wise for Christian colleges to be sure that their undergraduate courses reflect the best caliber possible.

Finally, perhaps distinction is appropriate between graduate programs in religion, which are best served by the Christian institution, and graduate programs in other fields common to the secular school. One deviation from this pattern could be graduate work in selected professional fields such as teacher education where government regulations require it for certification. But even here the issue needs careful thought. One significant factor is the need for supportive graduate programs in arts areas in addition to the professional education courses. Just because teachers may need graduate study to attain permanent certification is not of itself sufficient justification for Christian colleges to provide it in addition to preservice teacher education.

e. Financial pressure. The need for continuing financial support is common to all Christian higher education. Financial pressures are not new, but today they have taken new forms. The needs of a multi-media, computer age may pose the greatest threat yet to the Christian liberal arts college. There are ominous notes sounding in many quarters and, indeed, numerous small colleges are being forced to close their doors. But it is too soon to write this chapter of history.

One thing is clear. If Christians recognize the full significance of higher education to the growth of the Kingdom, they will know the importance of meeting the financial challenge. We can ill afford to rely too heavily on the changeable availability of government money. And we must always keep in mind the government control that accompanies government support. Christians must be prepared to pay the price for what we value.

A major study undertaken by the Danforth Foundation reported that "a religious orientation should add a dimension to higher education that broadens and deepens the outlook of faculty and students alike, but we can not say that this does in fact occur in most of the 817 institutions we have been studying."[2] Rather than be discouraged by such a report, the evangelical liberal arts college should be challenged by the fact that such a high purpose is being achieved by some institutions.

The report deals with a wide range of elements contributing to the success of the Christian college, including cooperation among institutions as a means of easing financial pressures. The establishment in 1971 of the Christian College Consortium, involving 10 prominent colleges, and an organizational arrangement among the colleges of the Church of the Nazarene illustrate efforts at coordination. These efforts could extend beyond the sharing of personnel and the promotion of different curriculum specializations on different campuses. Such specialization might approximate a university system of Christian colleges—an avowed purpose of the Christian College Consortium—thus opening up additional academic and professional fields to Christian young people. The report makes special note of the unique arrangement in Canada of a cluster of small colleges around a university.

f. Liberal arts vs. vocational objectives. The Danforth Foundation report acknowledges that the church-related institution, in the British tradition of a broad liberal education, has had its strength sapped. This has been caused by the Enlightenment philosophies of the 18th century, by the influence of the German university concept with its emphasis on technical scholarship, by the rapid growth of public higher education, and by a diminution in the influence of the church and religion.

The authors assert, however, that Christian colleges should play an important leavening role in society. They make recommendations on 15 points.

The first is for experimentation and innovation—a theme reflected in all the others. The final recommendation describes four types of church-affiliated colleges. It calls for each institution to "devise for itself a coherent pattern which relates purposes, clientele, staff, program, and church relationship in some such manner as these models."[3] Their four models are the "defender of the faith

2. Manning M. Pattillo, Jr., and Donald M. MacKenzie, *Church Sponsored Higher Education in the United States: Report of the Danforth Commission* (Washington, D.C.: American Council on Education, 1966), pp. 100-101.

3. *Ibid.,* p. 214.

college," the "non-affirming college," the "free Christian college," and the "church-related university." The authors of the report favor the third model but they recognize that each has its assets and liabilities.

Most evangelicals would tend to favor the first model, though they would prefer an alternative title of their own choosing such as the "affirming college." In such an institution the overriding concern is integrating faith and academic excellence. In the scholarly literature on Christian higher education this theme is found again and again in both periodicals and books. Here is the heart of a Christian liberal arts education. Perhaps more courses and retreats for students and faculty devoted to the subject of Christian higher education would enhance such integration and excellence.

Along with the integration of academic disciplines and Christian faith, we should note two structural elements that indicate an awareness of the importance of spiritual life in a Christian college community. When regular chapel services and consistent attendance are maintained, spiritual life is nourished. When required undergraduate courses turn students' minds to explore their Christian faith, we are laying foundations for lifelong spiritual growth and ministries.

In addition to maintaining a distinctive Christian dimension, the church college is concerned with the concept of liberal arts education itself. Such an education is a concept with a long history of ups and downs. Currently it is undergoing reassessment. Without going into a full-scale documentation, let us at least examine the main currents of the present crisis.

Many young people today are turning their backs on university education. Although some of this may be a reaction to the "establishment," another factor is certainly the practical reality of the employment situation. Young people are recognizing that a college degree no longer ensures a job; they are consequently turning toward vocational institutions.

This could be viewed as a serious setback to liberal arts education. But before we make this judgment, we should realize that in recent decades liberal education itself has become a kind of vocational training. Liberal education and an A.B. degree have become important as a route to better jobs and higher pay. Professional programs linked with liberal education have accentuated the same trend. Therefore the shift from the liberal arts in favor of the vocational is not a surprising phenomenon at a time when the job market is glutted with degree graduates.

However, all of this is not necessarily bad. It may offer a real opportunity to emphasize the elements of a true liberal education. As Christians we must understand clearly our central purpose in building worthy human lives, and not fall prey to sheer vocationalism. The Christian liberal arts college has always emphasized more than the vocational. Quality of life has been its higher concern even throughout the era of materialistic perversion. Now anew the development of the whole person must be the clarion call of the Christian liberal arts institution. Young people must see far more than a mere vocational pursuit in their higher education. Effective service requires a fully developed Christian personality.

The golden mean of a balanced program is probably the right emphasis for the Christian college in today's world. Students and their parents are understandably unwilling to pay for an exclusively "liberal" education. In a world that calls for Christian persons in vocation, the church is thinking straight and planning wisely when its colleges are truly Christian, genuinely character building, and effective vocational trainers.

B. The Graduate Level Institution

The primary specialized Christian institution serving the graduate level is the theological seminary, but the graduate programs found in many Christian liberal arts colleges belong in this category also. Because the essential distinctives of undergraduate Christian higher education relate also to the graduate level, it is not necessary to dwell on these programs at length. Both of these programs of graduate theological education are only now developing among evangelicals in Canada. There is a graduate academic program in Vancouver and several graduate seminaries in other Canadian cities.

1. Theological Seminaries

Seminaries have developed to meet the need of specialized Christian education for persons who have already completed a college education. Because the students' educational backgrounds are frequently diverse, seminaries have faced their greatest educational challenge in serving the needs of these individuals. The usual background of an A.B. degree with a major in some field other than religion has meant that seminary entrance requirements in religion have been rather minimal. The Association of Theological Schools

(ATS), the accrediting agency for seminaries, suggests as a minimum background in religion, only eight semester credits. In addition to this minimum suggested, a thorough knowledge of the content of the Bible is important, together with an introduction to the major Christian traditions.

Seminary programs have included a concentration on practical aspects appropriate to the minister's function. Consequently, such programs have tended to be relatively lengthy—a three-year course leading to the Bachelor of Divinity (B.D.) degree. However, in recognition of this long period of study, and more in harmony with other graduate programs, the name of this degree has shifted in recent years to Master of Divinity (M.Div.).

Likewise, academic programs in seminaries have tended to diversify beyond preparation for the pastoral ministry, thus serving the interests of specialized ministries as well. In addition to the usual biblical, historical, theological, and practical areas, there are special courses such as missions education, embracing anthropology and linguistics. The importance of youth, church schools, and music ministries has meant the development of programs to serve the needs of persons preparing for ministry on a multiple staff in the local church. The two-year Master of Religious Education degree (M.R.E.) is commonly tailored to serve these needs.

2. Graduate training in liberal arts colleges

Christian liberal arts colleges have also been alert to the developing need for graduate level education in theology. The early pattern was the Bachelor of Theology (Th.B.) degree, a one-year religion program beyond an A.B. Such a program gave an extra year and opportunity for professional courses that could provide greater competence in the pastorate. However, as the preferred pattern for ministerial education became an A.B. plus seminary, the Th.B. in the liberal arts colleges has given way to a master's degree program in religion. In this way the one-year graduate program in the liberal arts college has sometimes served as a terminal course. For others it has been a stepping-stone, either to the more professionally oriented seminary programs or to further academic graduate study.

The urgent need for continuing ministerial education in our rapidly changing world has also brought about a whole new range of specialized programs for pastors leading to the Doctor of Ministry (D.Min.) degree.

C. The Bible College

Serving a specialized function in Christian higher education are both the Bible institutes and Bible colleges. S. A. Witmer's book[4] offers a thorough treatment of the Bible college movement and will serve as our primary source of information. Prior to his work no complete volume on the subject was available—only articles or sections of books. Bible institutes, like Bible colleges, usually require a high school diploma for admission, but this requirement is not universal. The Bible institute commonly offers a three-year diploma course, while the Bible college requires an additional year of general education for a degree program.

1. *History*

The Bible college movement grew out of essentially the same concerns of the church that kept spawning new Christian liberal arts colleges. Witmer identifies three developments of the past century that altered the pattern of higher education: "Tax-supported education which must be separate from the church . . . great expansion of Catholic higher education . . . and increasing secularization of higher education."[5]

Bible colleges and Bible institutes have had their origin and development in North America in the past three-quarters of a century. The two earliest Bible colleges are now known as Nyack Missionary College, founded in 1882 by A. B. Simpson, and Moody Bible Institute, founded in 1886 by Dwight L. Moody and his associates.

Growth of the Bible college movement has continued with a peak number of new institutions established during the 1940s. Frequently such institutions have been located in the more populous urban areas where opportunities for student ministry abound. However, space needs have forced a trend to suburban relocation. Geographical distribution of the several hundred institutions tends to be fairly even except for the relatively few in New England and in the deep South.

In Canada there has been a disproportionate number in the three prairie provinces because of the influx of devout immigrants and the greater evangelical dynamic in the Canadian West. Some consolidation has now stabilized Bible college growth in Canada.

---

4. S. A. Witmer, *The Bible College Story: Education with Dimension* (Manhasset, N.Y.: Channel Press, Inc., 1962).
5. *Ibid.*, pp. 28-29.

Both denominational and nondenominational Bible colleges are common, although the largest ones are usually nondenominational. But as Witmer points out, "In several denominations that follow the regular college and seminary pattern for ministerial preparation, the Bible Institute has been 'discovered' as a type of school that provides educational services not available in conventional institutions. . . . [in contrast] Canada's educational policies are not conducive to the building and maintaining of liberal arts colleges by religious denominations."[6]

The American Association of Bible Colleges (AABC) was formed in 1947 and soon became recognized as the one accrediting agency in the field of undergraduate theological education.

2. *Program*

In the early days with essentially only religious and practical subjects, these institutions were appropriately called Bible training schools. There has, however, been a steady academic upgrading influenced by a general rise in the educational background of students. Concurrently the curricula have been expanded. In the twenties and thirties the two-year course was extended to three years, and specialized programs were introduced.

Basically four programs are offered: theology, Christian education, missions, and church music. With an expanded curriculum came the resulting shift in name to Bible Institute. The further expansion to degree programs resulted in the name Bible College. This pattern is seen repeatedly even outside of North America. Many schools, especially those in urban settings, offer evening and extension programs. Correspondence courses are available as well; a few schools have massive correspondence programs in various languages and in Braille.

Bible colleges combine two contrasting educational movements with roots in the medieval period—formal education known as scholasticism and practical education known as trade guild apprenticing. Thus practical service plays a key role. Service skills require practice in order to learn them, yet there is more than mere acquisition of skills. The student profits from confronting reality; he grows through personal development and self-expression. For many years this practical dimension was not highly organized nor integrated with the academic program. In recent years, however, it has received

---

6. *Ibid.*, p. 58.

much more attention even to the inclusion of formal internship programs.

While representing diverse groups in faith and practice, Bible colleges belong to one general theological family—conservative and evangelical, with little deviation from orthodox Christianity. They have defended the faith against liberalism "not so much by apologetics as by propagation."[7] They have put deliberate emphasis on the Bible itself as a primary source rather than placing undue reliance on secondary sources, i.e., books *about* the Bible.

3. *Issues and Concerns*

Witmer concludes his book by summarizing some forces and issues in Bible College education:

a. Overcoming the forces of declension through loss of spiritual dynamic.

b. The trend toward cultural accommodation in relation to moral standards.

c. Maintaining the distinctive function of Bible colleges in the face of pressures to broaden their services, thus drifting into liberal arts colleges without deliberate purpose in doing so.

d. The rising educational level making Bible colleges unnecessary.

e. Opportunities and desire of students for graduate studies.

f. Getting qualified personnel who have the ability to integrate an academic field with Christian faith.

g. Obtaining adequate support in the face of intensified current trends in education.

Most of these concerns are common to Christian higher education as a whole. However, those unique to the Bible college deserve some special attention here. These urgent matters grow out of the college's distinctive function in relation to the church, to other institutions of higher education, and to society at large. Witmer calls for greater articulation of the Bible college movement for its own benefit.

> Does development, beginning with a non-graded Bible training school, lead inevitably to a liberal arts college? Is there a significant difference between the Christian liberal arts college and the Bible college? Do Bible schools have to broaden their

---

7. *Ibid.*, p. 58.

services to survive? Is the answer to these questions to be found in the principles of the Christian faith and its unique mission, or is direction to be determined by pragmatic considerations?[8]

The answer to these questions seems to lie in recognition of the valid function of each institution. "There is no question about the need for evangelical liberal arts colleges. They occupy an honored and highly useful place in the pattern of Christian education."[9] Witmer expresses optimism concerning the maintenance of the desired balance when he concludes: "It is unlikely that the addition of liberal arts majors will become a trend, for the great majority of Bible college educators share the conviction that liberal arts majors belong to liberal arts colleges and are outside the purpose of the Bible colleges."[10] If Christian educators as a whole take this balanced view of the distinctive functions of each institution, there can be no threat to either except the threats common to all Christian higher education.

D. The Secular Institution

Evangelicals have been sufficiently concerned to provide Christian institutions for some of their young people. Certainly that same concern should motivate their interest in the larger number of church-related youth who attend secular institutions. Furthermore, evangelistic concern should direct their attention to the large group of uncommitted students in secular education today. The searching openness of this group is evidenced in the recent development and rapid growth of departments of religion at secular institutions. These courses, however, seldom meet the students' need for personal Christian faith. They are most often studies in comparative religion in which teachers endeavor to maintain a detached academic objectivity and neutral pluralism.

1. *Christian Education*

The issue then is: How can Christian education become a part of secular education? This subject has not yet been articulated better than by Sir Walter Moberly in 1949. He criticizes university education for its concentration on means rather than ends, on the handling of tools as opposed to purposes for which the tools are used. He also contends that behind a presumed objective neutrality are uncriticized

---

8. *Ibid.*, p. 17.
9. *Ibid.*, p. 181.
10. *Ibid.*, p. 120.

presuppositions about which he says, "The most pernicious kind of bias consists in falsely supposing yourself to have none."[11] He suggests that "what is essential to honest thinking is not that all presuppositions should be discarded, but that they should be uncovered, clearly expressed and thoroughly scrutinized [because] an open mind need not, and should not be an empty mind."[12] It is in this context that he calls for Christians to be educators in the secular institutions.

Moberly asks for an open forum encouraging discussion of basic issues as a means of having positive rather than negative neutrality. Such opening of communications should occur not only among students but also among faculty. He calls for acceptance of common academic postulates which include an intellectual passion, intellectual thoroughness, and meticulous accuracy in dealing with empirical evidence. Moberly also wants an approach to controversial questions as a judge rather than an advocate, freedom of thought and publication, and conviction that the university's social responsibility is primarily that of focusing the community's intellectual conscience. He also favors constant probing for common basic values.

Finally, on this basis, Moberly claims that teachers and administrators must be more concerned about the crisis in the university, and that "every group within the university which has a positive faith must feel a challenge to play the part of [Toynbee's] 'creative minority.'"[13]

It is in this academic climate of liberal arts education that he particularly challenges Christians to respond. If evangelicals as faculty members and students in secular institutions interact in this open atmosphere, Christian education could conceivably take place in such institutions of higher education. There is greater openness and opportunity for such interaction today than when Moberly wrote.

There is, therefore, a genuine need for Christian faculty members in the secular university, just as in the Christian college. In Moberly's words:

> Certainly it is no part of the duty of a university to inculcate any particular philosophy of life. But it is its duty to assist its students to form their own philosophies of life, so that they may

---

11. Sir Walter Moberly, *The Crisis in the University* (London: SCM Press, Ltd., 1949), p. 67.

12. *Ibid.*, pp. 64-65.

13. *Ibid.*, p. 126.

not go out into the world maimed and useless. . . . The university cannot itself be the sower of the seed, though it can give [the student] his opportunity. . . . It can, and should provide a soil which will be favorable to growth and not so arid that the seed withers nor so full of thorns that it is choked.[14]

2. *Campus Evangelism*

The renewed emphasis on campus ministries is most appropriate in the setting just described. Such ministries have long been a part of the secular campus, but newer dimensions are being pursued through denominational as well as interdenominational groups.[15] Coupled with the academic effort outlined by Moberly, the challenge of campus evangelism is truly great for ministering to Christian young people as well as to the uncommitted students in the secular institution.

a. Inter-Varsity Christian Fellowship. Originating in Great Britain as Inter-Varsity Fellowship, this organization was introduced into the United States in 1941. Its aim is cultivation of spiritual life among college and university students. Activities have increased in Bible study, prayer, spiritual growth, evangelism, and missions. In recent years outstanding missions conferences have been held following Christmas vacation on the university campus at Urbana, Ill. They have attracted university and college students by the thousands. Inter-Varsity Press at Downers Grove, Ill., has published significant titles dealing with some of the problems faced by the Christian student in the intellectual world.

b. Fellowship of Christian Athletes. This organization has endeavored to unite and minister to athletes since 1954. It sponsors conferences for evangelism and growth in the Christian life. Outstanding athletes are encouraged to give their testimony for Christ at rallies and banquets sponsored by the FCA. Besides emphasizing physical fitness, it encourages Christian attitudes on and off the playing field, while stressing the priority of making Jesus Christ Lord of one's life.

c. Church-sponsored student groups. For many years the church has served student groups on secular campuses. The *Newman Club* has involved Roman Catholic students. The Methodist church has honored her founder in the *Wesley Foundation.* The *Baptist Student Union* is the name chosen to serve Southern Baptist young people. The Church of the Nazarene has the *Bresee Fellowship.*

---

14. *Ibid.,* p. 303.
15. See chapter 18 for details of other campus programs.

The activities of these groups may take the students into fellowship with local churches. Some groups are able to erect or buy buildings for the purpose of serving the students. Meeting spiritual, social, and recreational needs are the primary purposes of these student groups.

III. The Personnel of Christian Higher Education

People make any human institution. This is certainly true of Christian institutions of higher education. It has been said that the history of an institution is but the lengthened shadow of a man. As we view Christian higher education, we see the long shadows of dedicated men and women who have sacrificially breathed life into our Christian schools.

A. The Faculty, Staff, and Administration

1. *Needs*

The requirements of persons serving in Christian higher education are demanding. Special qualifications are needed to meet the challenge. Whether one is an administrator, teacher, or staff member, he influences the lives of students through his personal contacts and in the way he conducts his own life. There is a sense in which each one is a counsellor. Therefore, all persons in Christian higher education must possess a spiritual dimension as part of the necessary job qualifications.

Because of the educational nature of the institution, however, the greatest responsibility rests with the faculty. Ramm writes:

> The first requirement of a faculty member is that he be Christian throughout in his daily life, that he maintain a quiet Christian stance in his classroom, in his academic community, and in his local community. The second requirement is that he know how to correlate his specialty with the Christian faith.[16]

This is a large order, in addition to the need for excellent graduate-level academic achievement. The integrating of one's specialty with Christian faith is what makes the faculty member's task unique in Christian higher education. It is at this point of integration and correlation that students frequently need the greatest help. Without faculty members who have already thought their way through the

---

16. Bernard Ramm, *The Christian College in the Twentieth Century* (Grand Rapids, Mich.: William B. Eerdmans Publishing Co., 1963), pp. 116-17. See also D. Elton Trueblood, *The Idea of a College* (New York: Harper and Brothers Publishers, 1959).

issues, a student may face his greatest spiritual hazard during college years. To be prepared to meet such needs underscores the necessity for faculty members who respond to the call of God to this specialized full-time service. When the needs and challenge are faithfully made known, men and women will sense and respond to God's call.

2. *Contributions*

If the needs for Christian higher education personnel are great, their contributions have been even greater. The influence of individuals and of personnel collectively on the lives of multiplied thousands of students is immeasurable. To single out individuals would be hazardous because they are many. A tribute to the group in general seems more fitting. The Kingdom has been increased by the impact of secretarial, maintenance, residence, and food service personnel as well as by administrators and teachers. All of these persons have given more than generously of their time and talent. They have been exemplary stewards—on a par with any of God's full-time servants.

Their stewardship of time and talent is often too easily taken for granted; moreover, their stewardship in terms of money deserves special mention here. Constituents have done well in their support, but as a group the personnel of Christian higher education have been the greatest financial contributors. The reduced salaries that prevail amount to a contribution that sets the pace for giving from any other source. Virtually every person involved in Christian higher education receives a salary considerably less than he would receive in a comparable position elsewhere—sometimes even less than many others in full-time Christian service. Thus the institution benefits by a direct financial gift from each employee. Other supporters of Christian higher education should remind themselves of this fact and be challenged in their own giving.

More detail could be given on the contribution of persons in Christian higher education. Enough has been said, however, to offset the mistaken notion that the institution somehow exists for the sake of the people employed by it. The institution exists to serve its students, constituents, and sponsoring body. Staff, faculty, and administration are a privileged group chosen of God as special servants of His in this institutional setting.

3. *Concerns*

There are serious problems that threaten Christian higher education. Not the least of these is the financial pressure, but let us first examine matters that involve personnel more directly. The context for this discussion must be excellence for both the institution and the individuals involved.

Much of the current emphasis on love and caring, especially among young people, appears to be an effort to recover a degree of humaneness. Christian young people are particularly responsive to this need for a personal dimension in life. Therefore, today's students, more sensitive to the impersonal, can be a challenge to Christian college personnel practices as well as to the academic curriculum. In his chapter "The Truth Beyond the Classroom,"[17] Gaebelein recognizes the importance of the institution as a whole. Thus, as the teacher's life must demonstrate integration of faith and learning, so also must the institution itself embody such an integration. We may take for granted the teacher's personal concern for the student, but the institution's responsibility to deal Christianly with its students, teachers, and constituency, may be less obvious.

Persons make the institution. Concentration on enhancing personal effectiveness in Christian higher education should be central to any material concerns. Faculty effectiveness is the most important factor in promoting student development. Such priority of persons has its parallel in other areas of Christian education as well. Persons and their growth toward Christ are the chief concerns of all who are in full-time service. Governing boards, constituency, and alumni deserve much credit for supporting administrative measures that enhance staff effectiveness in Christian higher education.

B. The Students

It is only appropriate that we conclude this chapter by devoting a separate section to the students—those for whom Christian higher education exists. Unfortunately people sometimes seem to think that a Christian college serves only a particular church organization or the college employees. But the true purpose of the college is to serve young people in their development toward becoming whole Christians and fulfilling God's will.

The diversity of institutions described in this chapter illustrates the various interests of individuals whom Christian higher education serves. Their needs and objectives are legion. Therefore, flexibility and variety must characterize our efforts to meet them.

Educational diversity to serve free individuals inevitably in-

---

17. Frank E. Gaebelein, *The Pattern of God's Truth* (Chicago: Moody Press, 1968).

volves a risk. Not every person will become what we might wish, but there is really no alternative to such freedom if we hold to the high purposes set forth in this book. If, as suggested in an earlier chapter, maturity may be measured by the degree of freedom from both hereditary and environmental forces, then we must be prepared to accept the individual's ultimate responsibility for himself. The Danforth Report reminds us that "it is the mark of a good teacher that he can guide the student's judgment and still leave him free to reach his own conclusions."[18]

The narrow view of rigid indoctrination as a form of environmental determinism just does not fit. More than ever before in our kind of wide-open communications such indoctrination eventually falls short as the individual subsequently encounters the world and its ideas. At such a point the superficially indoctrinated person may feel betrayed by his past or at least bewildered and ill-equipped to retain a viable Christian faith. Consequently, there will be less ultimate risk in an education that provides a sound Christian environment in which to examine a wide range of views and which supports the emergence of a tested faith.

Students must be challenged to pursue the best preparation of which they are capable, especially if they are called to full-time Christian service. Stott underscored this in his 1972 presidential address to the Inter-Varsity Christian Fellowship:

> I pray earnestly that God will raise up today a new genera-
> tion of Christian apologists or Christian communicators, who will
> combine an absolute loyalty to the biblical gospel and an unwav-
> ering confidence in the power of the Spirit with a deep and sensi-
> tive understanding of the contemporary alternatives to the gospel;
> who will relate the one to the other with freshness, pungency,
> authority and relevance; and who will use *their* minds to reach
> *other* minds for Christ.[19]

Gaebelein concludes his book with the exhortation: "Our task is not only to outlive and outserve those who do not stand for God's truth; it is also by God's grace to outthink them."[20]

It is this context which calls for some assessment of an ideal theological training offered by the institutions discussed earlier in this chapter. Probably the most desirable pattern for those entering

---

18. Pattillo and MacKenzie, *Church-sponsored Higher Education*, p. 75.
19. John R. W. Stott, *Your Mind Matters: The Place of the Mind in the Christian Life* (Downers Grove, Ill.: Inter-Varsity Press, 1972), p. 52.
20. Gaebelein, *The Pattern of God's Truth*, p. 107.

the ministry is the Christian liberal arts college followed by seminary. For others who lack the academic background, or who because of more mature age, do not have seven years for training, the Bible college offers solid biblical and theological specialization. The two patterns do not compete, because each serves a distinct and worthy purpose. In either case, lifelong education must be maintained through a continuing pursuit of learning.

IV. CONCLUSION

The record of Christian higher education is good—especially in light of the manifold handicaps it has faced. Only eternity will show the full effectiveness of the large numbers of college-prepared full-time workers and laymen who have served or are serving around the world. But we must continue to strive for greater excellence.

There needs to be greater documentation of the values of Christian higher education through carefully conducted research. The computer opens up immense opportunity for such studies. It is encouraging to see new evangelical organizations being formed to undertake significant research studies in missions and Sunday schools. There is comparable need for research into the impact of education on student values. Evangelical higher education might discover further justification for itself in such research and gain direction for more effective work with student values. Articulation of research and philosophy must be intensified in order that both the constituency and society at large may understand Christian higher education.

Today's students are tomorrow's personnel of Christian higher education—the alumni, constituency, faculty, and board members. Much appreciation is due for the faithful support—prayer, finances, students—given by the alumni, constituencies, and boards. Tomorrow's support depends on the college's effectiveness with today's students. We must face the challenge of Christian higher education on every front—the Christian liberal arts college, the graduate Christian institution, the Bible college, and the secular institution through its Christian personnel. Only thus can the church serve the diversity of students and programs in today's world.

BIBLIOGRAPHY

Blamires, Harry. *The Christian Mind*. London: S.P.C.K., 1963.

The author condemns the lack of a Christian mind and today's surrender to secularism. He then considers the marks of a mind that would think Christianly.

Dyrness, Enock C. "The Christian Liberal Arts College," in *An Introduction to Evangelical Christian Education* (J. Edward Hakes, ed.). Chicago: Moody Press, 1964.

Dyrness examines the concept of a Christian liberal arts college, the role such colleges play in our world today, and some basic factors to guide one's evaluation of these institutions of Christian education.

Gaebelein, Frank E. *The Pattern of God's Truth: the Integration of Faith and Learning*. Chicago: Moody Press, 1968.

The author analyzes Christian education in terms of integrating truth as it relates to the teacher, the subject, and beyond the classroom.

Holmes, Arthur F. *The Idea of a Christian College*. Grand Rapids, Mich.: William B. Eerdmans Publishing Co., 1975.

This book deals with the rationale for a Christian liberal arts education and its central task of integrating faith and learning since all truth is God's truth. It is the most current book amplifying the theme of this chapter.

Moberly, Sir Walter. *The Crisis in the University*. London: SCM Press, Ltd., 1949.

Moberly proposes a philosophy of higher Christian education relevant to the British university setting, but transposable to other situations.

Ramm, Bernard. *The Christian College in the Twentieth Century*. Grand Rapids, Mich.: William B. Eerdmans Publishing Co., 1963.

The views of Augustine, Melanchthon, Newman, Kuyper, and Moberly and their meaning for the Christian college today.

Stott, John R. W. *Your Mind Matters: the Place of the Mind in the Christian Life*. Downers Grove, Ill.: Inter-Varsity Press, 1973.

In this his 1972 IVF presidential address the author underscores the importance of thinking Christianly and its implications.

Trueblood, Elton. *The Idea of a College*. New York: Harper & Brothers Publishers, 1959.

The author's idea of a Christian college as it applies to the various facets of higher education.

Witmer, S. A. *The Bible College Story: Education with Dimension*. New York: Channel Press, 1962.

Here we find the history, philosophy, and patterns of Bible colleges and Bible institutes in the United States and Canada.

Appendix I

Buildings, Equipment, and Materials

The broad concept of curriculum includes buildings, equipment, and materials. But even if we do not accept this inclusive definition, we know that facilities are an important part of the total atmosphere that helps bring about changes in the lives of pupils.

I. GENERAL PRINCIPLES

A. Buildings

Educational buildings should be designed to provide the proper space for learning activities planned by the church for all of the age-groups and for all of the programs to be carried on. The ideal building is all on ground level. However, if several levels are needed, a second floor is preferable to a basement. The floor plan should be developed by those who know what the programs are and understand how they are to be carried out. After this an architect should be engaged to design a building that can most efficiently and beautifully house the floor plan needed.

As far as possible plans should be made for the eventual complete building necessary to carry out the Christian education responsibilities in that location. Then the first unit can be constructed to fit into the master plan. This will eliminate needless remodeling when the other units are constructed.

Even with the best of planning, it is impossible to anticipate changes in educational trends and to foresee all the future needs. Consequently, ceilings and floor coverings should be installed before partitions are constructed. This makes the movement of walls possible without leaving patched ceilings and floors.

Educational buildings should be zoned so that areas not used during the week or for a specific program can be locked off from the rest of the building to save utility and maintenance costs. Kitchens, rest rooms, and nurseries should be located with this zoning plan in mind.

Provision should be made for maximum versatility and adaptability. Planned circulation of people by proper location of halls and doors increases the use of rooms. Stairs limit the use of space by young children and older adults. Space should therefore be allotted to age-groups with these needs in mind. Rooms should vary in size. Sound-proofing is essential for efficient multiple use of space. Adequate storage for various programs and personnel will help eliminate conflicts. Ten percent of the total space should be planned for storage.

Large, open rooms are more versatile than assembly areas with small classrooms adjacent to them. Rooms should be planned for future growth as well as for present department needs. The frequency with which kitchens are used should be considered in allotting space. However, properly designed kitchens can also be used for classrooms.

Windows in educational rooms should be of clear, unobstructed glass; they should be equal in area to not less than 18 to 25 percent of the floor space of the room. Windows are best located at the side and rear of the room. Floor covering should be selected for beauty, durability, and ease in maintenance. Carpeting is being used more and more in educational buildings. Hat and coat racks should be located inside department areas below junior age; they may be recessed along corridors for older ages.

Heim* lists the following standards for Christian education buildings: beauty, utility, comfort, economy, and adaptability.

B. Equipment

Equipment should be selected and used to meet the physical needs and assist the methodology used with each age-group. All equipment should be placed in the room to take advantage of lighting and ventilation. Seating should be arranged so that late arrivals do not attract attention. Rectangular tables make better use of space than those that are round or horseshoe shaped. The trapezoidal table with a 45 percent angle on both ends provides opportunity for varied table arrangements. Folding chairs create hazards for young children.

Heim (p. 241) suggests two basic standards for equipment. The first is utility. Each piece of equipment must adequately perform the function for which it is intended; it should help reach the objective of Christian learning. The second standard is economy. Equipment should be durable and efficient without unnecessary cost. Portable and multi-purpose equipment contributes to economy.

C. Materials

Materials include the printed curriculum and supplies necessary to complete the learning experiences initiated by the curriculum materials and by creative teachers. Curriculum materials should be selected to help reach the objectives of Christian teaching. It is important that schools of a particular denomination use the denominational materials. These have been written and designed in harmony with the theology, goals, and practices of that denomination.

---

*Ralph D. Heim, *Leading a Church School* (Philadelphia: Fortress Press, 1968), pp. 237-38.

II. Room Arrangements

A. Class

Youth and adult classes, too large to gather around a table, are best seated in a semicircle. The door of the room should be at the back. The semicircle provides more open space and encourages participation by allowing class members to face each other.

B. Department

There are five arrangements of department rooms that provide for an assembly or large-group experiences, and also for class or small-group experiences.

1. *Preschool Room with Activity Centers*

The Nursery and Kindergarten Department rooms should be of a 3 x 4 or 4 x 5 rectangular shape; warm and well lighted (Diagram A, below). Corners, low windows, raised areas, and other irregularities can be used to advantage in creating interest or activity centers. Pastel colors that provide needed temperature or lighting effects are best. Light can be increased in a dark room and a feeling of warmth in a cold room by the right selection of colors.

In the same large room, areas should be arranged (1) for large-group experiences in come-together time, and (2) for small-group learning experiences at interest centers and around tables.

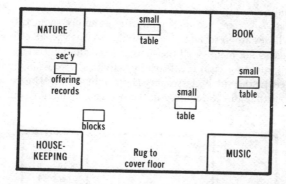

DIAGRAM A

2. *Open Department Room*

The Primary, Middler, and Junior Departments may also be housed in one large open room (Diagram B, p. 478). Presession, class, and department groupings all take place in this room. Tables are usually placed in the corners or at the back of the room leaving the center or front open for assembly. Presession activities may take place at tables by classes; or as a department activity at tack boards, chalkboards, or other locations in the room.

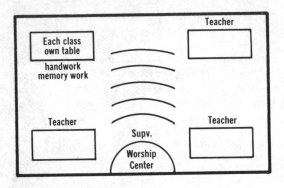

DIAGRAM B

3. *Assembly and Individual Classrooms*

Junior and Junior High Departments usually use the assembly and individual classroom arrangement (Diagram C, below) more than other age-groups. However, in large churches High School and Adult Departments may also be housed in this way. The walls of classrooms afford class privacy and provide a place to mount chalkboards, tack boards, pictures, and other teaching aids. The individual classrooms tend to increase the teacher's sense of responsibility.

The classrooms are not used while the assembly room is being used; and when classes are in session, the assembly room is vacant. Consequently, maximum use is not made of all the space. By scheduling the larger space in the assembly room for class use, learning activities are possible that cannot be conducted in the small classroom. The combined area in this arrangement is about the same as required in the open department room.

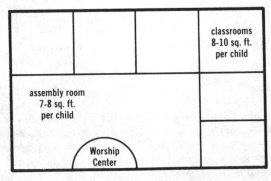

DIAGRAM C

4. *Combined Department and Classrooms*

A Youth or Adult Department may meet in a large rectangular room, have their devotional service together, and then pull folding doors to divide the area into classrooms (Diagram D, below). This makes maximum use of the space. If the acoustics are right, the folding doors will provide an adequate sight and sound barrier for teaching. Wall space for teaching aids and floor space for seating arrangements are limited.

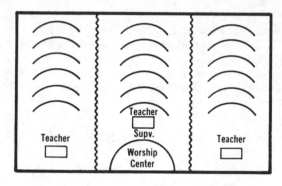

Teacher

Teacher
Supv.
Worship
Center

Teacher

DIAGRAM D

5. *Multi-purpose Rooms*

Fellowship halls, libraries, lounges, and other areas can be used for Christian education teaching activities with youth and adults by providing moving or removable walls; also by using team teaching. Folding walls are expensive and provide an adequate sound barrier only when rugs, drapes, acoustical ceiling, and other provisions have also been made to deaden sound. Removable walls can be made soundproof but they take time to move. In team teaching the lecturing is done with the entire group together. The small-group activity is primarily discussion that causes little distraction, so walls or curtains are unnecessary. Church auditoriums can also be used in this way.

III. ROOM LOCATIONS

A. Preschool

Preschool rooms should be located on the foyer level, near young adults, away from drafts, and near rest rooms. A rest room between two rooms is ideal. Nursery rooms should not be mothers' rooms with a window into the auditorium. Dutch doors help control traffic and encourage sanitation.

B. Children

Children's rooms can be located up or downstairs and do not need to be near any particular facilities since elementary children are old enough to find their way around by themselves. Rest room facilities near the departments help.

C. Youth

Youth should have some of the nicest rooms available. They will not invite their friends to facilities they are ashamed of. Fellowship halls, lounges, and other areas designed for informal activities make good housing for them.

D. Adults

Young adults should be located near the preschool area. Senior adults like to be located in or near the sanctuary. Overflow space from the sanctuary makes good adult classrooms. The auditorium can be used for an opening devotional service. The sanctuary may also be used in a team teaching arrangement with a number of discussion groups meeting in different areas of it.

IV. SPECIFICATIONS

Space and Sizes

Nursery:

Floor space: 25-35 sq. ft.
    per person
Chairs: 10" high
Tables: 20" high, 24" x 36"
Tack boards and picture
    railings: 24" from floor

Equipment and Material

Ball
Beds 27" x 48"
    hardwood: name and
    feeding schedule attached
Beds, 18" x 36"
Bible
Books
Bottle warmer
Chests or utility cabinets
Dolls
Floor toys
Graded literature
Housekeeping toys
Large blocks
Large crayons, paper, 12" x 18"
Linen storage
Open shelves for toys
Pictures
Picture rail and/or tack board
Playpen
Record player:
    "Listen and Sing!" records
    1, 2, 3, 4
Rocking boat

Rocking chair
Rug
Small, low table for Bible
Storage for teacher supplies
Storage for wraps (teachers' and
pupils')
Stuffed animals
Wooden puzzles
Worker uniforms

Kindergarten:

Floor space: 25-30 sq.
ft. per person
Chairs: 10"-12" high
Tables: 20"-22"
high, 30" x 48"
Tack boards and picture
railings: 27" from floor

Bible for department
Bible for each class
Building blocks
Clean, warm floor
or plain floor covering
Dolls
Finger plays
Floor toys
Graded literature
Housekeeping toys
Rhythm instruments
Secretary's table
Small table for Bible
Low, open shelves for children's
materials
Paper, crayons, scissors, paste
Piano
Picture books
Picture file
Picture rail
Pictures
Plants
Resting mats
Songbooks
Storage for wraps
Tack board
Teacher supply cabinet

Primary:

Floor space:
Assembly: 8-10 sq. ft.
per person
Classroom: 12-15 sq. ft.
per person

Bible for each class
Bulletin board
Cabinet for supplies
Chalkboard
Graded literature

Open room: 20-30 sq. ft.
    per person
Chairs: 12"-14" high
Tables: 22"-24" high,
    30" x 54" or 30" x 60"
Tack and chalk boards:
    30" from floor

Large Bible for department
Paper, pencils, crayons
Paste, scissors
Piano
Picture books
Picture rail or easel
Pictures
Place for wraps
Small table for Bible
Songbooks for leaders
Song charts for children
Storage
World globe

Middler:

Floor space:
Assembly: 8-10 sq. ft.
    per person
Classroom: 10-12 sq. ft.
    per person
Open room: 20-30 sq. ft.
    per person
Chairs: 13"-15" high
Tables: 23"-25" high,
    30" x 60"
Tack and chalk boards:
    33" from floor

Bible for each class
Bible for each pupil
Bible picture books
Bible storybooks
Bulletin board
Cabinet for supplies
Graded literature
Large Bible for department
Maps, globe
Paper, pencils, crayons
Paste, scissors
Picture file
Picture rail or easel
Pictures
Small table for Bible
Songbooks for pupils
Storage for wraps

Junior:

Floor space:
Assembly: 8-10 sq. ft.
    per person
Classroom: 9-10 sq. ft.
    per person
Open room: 20-30 sq. ft.
    per person
Chairs: 14"-16" high
Tables: 24"-26" high,
    30" x 72"

Bible for each class
Bible for each pupil
Bible dictionary
Bible picture books
Bible storybooks
Bulletin board
Cabinet for supplies
Chalkboard and/or tack board
Concordance
Graded literature
Large Bible for department

Tack and chalk boards:
33" from floor

Maps, globe
Paper, pencils, crayons
Paste, scissors
Picture file
Picture rail or easel
Pictures
Small table for Bible
Songbooks for pupils
Storage for wraps

Junior High:

Floor space:
Assembly: 7-8 sq. ft.
per person
Classroom: 8-10 sq. ft.
per person
Chairs: 16"-18" high
Tables: 26"-28" high
30" x 72"
Tack and chalk boards:
36" from floor

Bible for each class
Bibles, pupils' own
Bulletin board
Cabinet for supplies
Chalkboard
Graded literature
Large Bible for department
Paper, pencils, maps
Picture file
Picture rail
Pictures
Songbooks
Storage for wraps
Tack board

Senior High, Adults:

Floor space:
Assembly: 7-8 sq. ft.
per person
Classroom: 8-10 sq. ft.
per person
Chairs: 17"-18" high
Tack and chalk boards:
36"-42" from floor

Bibles for each pupil
Bulletin board
Cabinet for supplies
Curriculum materials
Curtains
Easel
Large Bible for department
Maps
Piano
Pictures
Plants
Small table for Bible
Songbooks
Storage for wraps

Appendix II

Teacher's Self-improvement Guide

Our Lord has called us to teach (Matt. 28:19). He expects us to be the best teachers it is possible for us to be, and there are some basic qualifications that we can and should possess. With diligent effort and by God's help, any sincere follower of Christ can qualify within God's will.

This *Teacher's Self-Improvement Guide* is provided to help you grow as a teacher. It is designed for your personal use—to help you evaluate yourself and your teaching practices. The score you receive is confidential. By using this evaluative tool more than once, you can measure your own improvement.

Read each statement carefully. Ask yourself, Am I successful at this point? If you feel you are, place the figure 4 in the blank. If you are really working to improve, but not fully successful at this point, give yourself a 3. If you are not making as much effort as you could, give yourself a 2. If you are aware of a need but not doing anything to improve, give yourself a 1.

Should Others Follow My Example?

Desiring my personal life to be an example for my pupils, I seek by God's help to:

_____ 1. Maintain a sincere, positive, personal Christian experience.

_____ 2. Live in harmony with the doctrines and practices of my church.

_____ 3. Maintain a Christian consecration that leads me to make all personal decisions in the light of the teachings of Jesus.

_____ 4. Have daily fellowship with God through prayer, meditation, and Bible study.

_____ 5. Be faithful in attendance at regular Sunday and midweek services, and at revival services.

_____ 6. Support the work of my church through systematic giving of tithes and offerings.

_____ 7. Set an example of reverence in God's house.

_____ 8. Maintain a friendly, cooperative relationship with all persons, especially other workers in my Sunday school.

_____ 9. Cooperate in the spirit of Christ with the decisions and plans of the church school board, the superintendent, and others who have administrative responsibilities in the school.

____ 10. Notify my supervisor, or superintendent, as far in advance as possible when I must be absent.

____ 11. Have a neat and attractive personal appearance.

Do My Pupils Feel I Am Sincerely Interested and Personally Concerned About Them?

Knowing that rapport with my pupils is essential to effective teaching, I:

____ 12. Strive to build genuine relationships with my pupils and know their individual differences in order to help each one with his specific needs.

____ 13. Counsel personally with pupils concerning their conversion, entire sanctification, and spiritual growth.

____ 14. Follow the suggestions in my teachers' materials for dealing with the age-group with which I work.

____ 15. Pray regularly for my pupils by name.

____ 16. Encourage my pupils to attend and participate in church services regularly.

____ 17. Include in my class plans activities which give pupils opportunity to participate in the total program of the church through service projects and special offerings.

____ 18. Encourage the spiritual growth of pupils by involving them in visitation of prospects and absentees, and in personal witnessing

____ 19. Strive to give my pupils an understanding of church membership and encourage pupils who testify to a definite experience of conversion to join the church.

____ 20. Show a fair, impartial attitude toward each pupil in order to help the class feel confidence in my personal concern for each of them.

____ 21. Keep an up-to-date information record of each pupil.

____ 22. Visit, telephone, or send a card or letter whenever a pupil is absent.

____ 23. Visit, telephone, or send a card whenever a pupil or some member of his family is ill.

____ 24. Send a card or remembrance to pupils on birthdays and other special occasions.

____ 25. Secure the name, address, and telephone number of every new person who attends my class.

____ 26. Make every visitor feel welcome and help him to become acquainted with class members.

____ 27. Keep a prospect list for my class and follow a planned program to get these prospects enrolled in the Sunday school.

____ 28. Visit pupils at home, at school, and other places—and invite them into my home occasionally.

____ 29. Plan weekday activities for my class suitable to the age-group with which I work.

Am I Improving in My Effectiveness as a Teacher?

Convinced of the importance of my teaching task and the need to become a better teacher, I:

____ 30. Use literature recommended by my church for the age-group I teach, and try to follow the suggestions in the teachers' material.

____ 31. Begin my lesson preparation in the early part of the week, spending at least two hours preparing the lesson.

____ 32. Go over the entire unit or quarter, keeping in mind the purpose of the unit, before making plans for the first session.

____ 33. Keep my pupils in mind as I prepare, and plan the lesson to fit their needs.

____ 34. Evaluate each Sunday morning session in the light of the lesson purpose and results.

____ 35. Attend workers' conferences and teachers' meetings planned by my local church.

____ 36. Attend district conventions, zone rallies, and workshops in an effort to improve my teaching.

____ 37. Participate in a planned reading program for self-improvement.

____ 38. Earn at least one credit each year in the teacher training program.

____ 39. Seek to improve my teaching by observing other teachers and by counseling with my supervisor, superintendent, minister of education, or pastor.

Do I Motivate My Pupils to Learn and Grow in the Christian Life?

Knowing that the pupil himself must be inspired and guided to learn and grow in the Christian life, I:

____ 40. Arrive at Sunday school early enough (at least 10 minutes early) to get the room and materials ready and to welcome pupils as they come.

____ 41. Keep the room neat and attractive, and try to create an atmosphere of beauty, worship, work, and friendliness.

____ 42. Plan presession activities as suggested in my teaching materials, so that my pupils have full advantage of the longest and best learning session possible.

____ 43. Complete records with a minimum of interference with the class session and so that they make a maximum contribution to the class growth.

____ 44. Encourage each pupil to express his ideas freely and to take active part in the work of the group, so that he may develop a sense of belonging.

____ 45. Maintain an orderly, but relaxed, atmosphere in the classroom.

___ 46. Use a variety of methods, projects, and activities to involve pupils in the class session.

___ 47. Use audiovisuals as recommended in the Sunday school material and provided in the resource packets.

___ 48. Plan ways for pupils to use their own Bibles meaningfully during the class session.

___ 49. Encourage pupils to do home study as recommended for them.

___ 50. Follow plans for organizing my class as suggested in teaching materials, and encourage class officers to carry out their responsibilities.

*   *   *

Finding and Interpreting Your Score

Make sure you have checked each item in the scale with either a 4, 3, 2, or 1 rating. If any item does not apply to your age-group, give yourself a 4 rating on that item.

Add all of the numbers and write your total score here. _____
Rate yourself on the following basis:

180 to 200—excellent. You show a good understanding of the teaching task and the function of the teacher. Keep up the good work, "till we all come in the unity of the faith, and of the knowledge of the Son of God, unto a perfect man, unto the measure of the stature of the fulness of Christ" (Eph. 4:13).

160 to 174—good. Your score is above average, but your teaching will be even more effective if you work out a program to improve your weak points as revealed by the *Guide*.

140 to 159—fair. You have possibilities for becoming a truly effective teacher, but your score indicates that you need to make a real effort to improve. Study carefully the items that you checked 1 or 2 and make specific plans to strengthen your life and teaching at these points.

Below 140—Your score is low, but this does not mean that you cannot become a truly effective Christian teacher and render useful service to Christ and the church. It will take some hard work, but you can do it with God's help and by diligent effort. Now that you have located your weaknesses, set a goal to eliminate them and begin today.

"I press toward the mark for the prize of the high calling of God in Christ Jesus" (Phil. 3:14).

Appendix III

Guide to Sunday School Success

To bring each pupil into a personal relationship with Jesus Christ as Saviour and Sanctifier and get him involved in the redemptive mission of Christ! This is the ultimate goal of all our work through the Sunday school. In administering the school, we must remember that the real success of a Sunday school is in the number of pupils who are won to Christ and brought into the fellowship and work of the church, not into Sunday school attendance alone.

Yet it is true that to win souls through the Sunday school we must concern ourselves with leaders, materials, organization, finances, records, and equipment. The Sunday school which rates high in these things usually wins its pupils.

To help you in the task of building the Sunday school your Division of Christian Life has prepared this *Guide*. It is not intended to be a measurement for comparing one Sunday school with another. Rather it seeks to help the local church determine the true condition of its own Sunday school by rating it against a recognized standard.

This *Guide* considers 10 areas to which the local school must give attention if it is to be successful. Exploration of all 10 areas will help you to find those places in your program where special attention is needed.

Justifiable differences exist between the programs of large and small Sunday schools. These have been kept in mind, so that this *Guide to Sunday School Success* is applicable to schools of all sizes.

Interpretation of Scoring

Since the primary purpose of the *Guide* is to help you discover areas in your Sunday school program that need improvement, it obviously is better to be hard than lenient when checking an item. When using the *Guide*, use the following interpretation:

"Yes" means you are doing this.
"No" means you are not doing this.
"Partially" means you have started but need improvement.

USING THE *Guide*

The *Guide* can be used successfully in a number of ways . . .

1. At the beginning of the year. Plan your first workers' conference for a study of the *Guide*. Secure a copy for each teacher and officer of the Sunday

school and go over all 10 sections. Each item needs to be understood and carefully applied to the school. Compare the "No" and "Partially" lists and determine priorities. On a yearly calendar, list by months the items you are going to begin or improve that month. Review progress at your workers' meeting each month. One year later complete another *Guide* to see the success you have attained.

2. A monthly study. The *Guide* can be considered section by section as a part of the program in 10 monthly workers' meetings. Reports can be given each month on specific items improved during the past 30 days.

3. Conduct a training class. The Christian Service Training text *How to Improve Your Sunday School* was written to give a detailed explanation of each item in this *Guide* and to offer suggestions on how each item can best be used. This text can be studied in a class made up of your Sunday school teachers and officers and those interested in becoming Sunday school workers.

THE GUIDE

A. Leadership (Chapter 1)‡ (21-36)†   *Yes   No   Partially*

1. Officers and teachers professing Christians, exemplary in life, and in full harmony with the doctrine and polity of the church   ____ ____ ____

2. Officers and teachers attend church services— Sunday morning and evening, prayer meeting, and revivals   ____ ____ ____

3. Teachers and officers present in Sunday school at least 10 minutes ahead of the opening time   ____ ____ ____

4. In case of necessary absence, teachers and officers report to supervisor or age-group director as soon as possible   ____ ____ ____

5. Teachers spend at least two hours per week in lesson preparation   ____ ____ ____

6. In order to become better acquainted with each pupil, teachers should spend at least one hour weekly in home visits or in other weekday contacts (75, 108-10, 135-37, 150-54)   ____ ____ ____

B. Outreach and Evangelism (Chapter 2)

1. Planned effort to lead pupils to definite Christian experience—especially middlers and older pupils (106-8, 133-36, 154-55, 176-78, 193-94)   ____ ____ ____

‡Reference is to *How to Improve Your Sunday School,* Beacon Hill Press of Kansas City.

†Numbers in parentheses refer to pages in *The Nazarene Sunday School in the 70's,* Beacon Hill Press of Kansas City.

	Yes	No	Partially

2. Survey the community regularly to secure prospects ___ ___ ___

3. Each class or department maintains responsibility list and visits prospects ___ ___ ___

4. Planned welcome and follow-up of visitors ___ ___ ___

5. Planned visitation of absentees ___ ___ ___

6. Increase enrollment over the previous year ___ ___ ___

7. Increase average attendance over the previous year ___ ___ ___

8. Conduct a vacation Bible school ___ ___ ___

9. Provide weekday activities—Caravan and/or teen activities ___ ___ ___

C. Church Loyalty (Chapter 3) (105-6, 124-25)

1. Work to secure regular pupil attendance at church—Sunday morning and evening, prayer meeting, and revivals ___ ___ ___

2. Effort to lead converts into church membership—especially juniors and older pupils (145, 185-86, 229-33) ___ ___ ___

3. Encourage pupils to improve in churchmanship through study and/or service ___ ___ ___

4. Participate in district and general projects ___ ___ ___

5. Report to district board of Christian life as requested ___ ___ ___

6. Send representatives to district conventions, zone rallies, and workshops ___ ___ ___

D. Administration (Chapter 3)

1. The board of Christian life meets monthly or at least once a quarter (23-27) ___ ___ ___

2. Sunday school cabinet or workers' conference meeting weekly or at least once a month (35) ___ ___ ___

3. Public services of installation for officers and teachers conducted by the pastor at the beginning of the assembly year (204-5, 250) ___ ___ ___

4. Begin and close Sunday school on time ___ ___ ___

5. Close count of attendance not later than midpoint of the Sunday school hour ___ ___ ___

6. Opening devotional service in school, department, or classes should be well planned and continue not more than 15 minutes (52-53) ___ ___ ___

7. Maintain class periods of at least 40 minutes ___ ___ ___

	Yes	No	Partially

8. Plan presession activities for children and youth who arrive early ___ ___ ___

9. Provide and use *Teacher's Self-Improvement Guide* (see Appendix II) ___ ___ ___

E. Organization (Chapter 4)

1. Provide adequate departmentalization. A minimum should be separate meeting places for at least children (first through sixth grades) and youth-adult (seventh grade and older), and a separate room for preschool classes (2- through 4-year-olds) (48-49) ___ ___ ___

2. Assign pupils to classes and/or departments in accordance with the recommended age-group or public-school-grade divisions (38-48) ___ ___ ___

3. Organize all junior and older classes with appropriate officers and committees (142-43, 168-70) ___ ___ ___

4. Promote all pupils according to age-group recommendations ___ ___ ___

5. Maintain a Cradle Roll of babies from non-church homes with a supervisor and visitors who provide help for parents, and visit homes at least once a quarter (55-63) ___ ___ ___

6. Maintain a Nursery Roll of babies under two years of age enrolled in the church nursery with teacher providing help for parents, and visiting homes at least twice a year ___ ___ ___

7. Maintain a Home Department with a supervisor and visitors who provide for home study and who visit in each home at least once a quarter (171-82) ___ ___ ___

8. A director of Christian Family Life elected and guiding a program ___ ___ ___

9. Secure or renew annually family pledges to maintain family altars and win new families to Christ ___ ___ ___

10. A director for Christian Service Training elected and working ___ ___ ___

F. Training (Chapter 4)

1. Using a planned program for enlisting new workers (197-216) ___ ___ ___

2. Provide training for prospective teachers ___ ___ ___

3. All teachers taking some teacher training ___ ___ ___

Yes No Partially

4. Each worker receiving at least one credit per year in the teacher training program

5. A plan for age-group assistants or prepared substitute teachers

6. Hold age-group teachers' meetings to preview lesson materials for next unit or quarter

7. All officers and teachers reading books recommended for the church schools library (212-14)

G. Lesson Helps (Chapter 5) (67-75, 82-93, 97-108, 110-15, 119-33, 144-50, 188-93)

1. Use literature recommended by the church in all departments

2. Provide each teacher with proper age-group teacher quarterlies

3. Use recommended pupil materials in line with age-group designations

4. Maintain adequate supply of pupil literature—lesson leaflets, Bible story books or quarterlies, and story papers

5. Use the recommended Teaching Resources packets and other audiovisual aids

H. Records and Reports (Chapter 5) (30-33)

1. Use the record system recommended

2. Maintain a permanent file of enrollment information centrally located

3. Maintain weekly pupil records reported to Sunday school secretary by class or department

4. Teachers and officers make a monthly study of records to plan for progress

5. Encourage teachers to maintain a personal information record of each pupil and give such information to the pupil's next teacher

I. Housing and Equipment (Chapter 6) (63-66, 81-83, 97-99, 118-120)

1. Provide clean, well-lighted, and ventilated rooms adaptable for guiding pupils through various learning experiences

2. Provide chairs and tables of recommended height (see Appendix I)

Yes No Partially

3. Provide open-room space for nursery through primary. Either open-room space or assembly room with individual classrooms are approved for middler and older pupils. ___ ___ ___

4. Maintain workers' library with at least three new books added each year (33-34) ___ ___ ___

5. Provide storage space for pictures, maps, and other teaching materials ___ ___ ___

6. Add supplementary materials such as chalkboards, tack boards, and easels ___ ___ ___

J. Financial Program (Chapter 6) (31-32)

1. Encourage regular offerings equal to 20c per pupil per week ___ ___ ___

2. Establish a budget for the operation of the Sunday school ___ ___ ___

3. Set aside for missions 10 percent of the total Sunday school offering or take a monthly offering for missions ___ ___ ___

4. Contribute to expense of district board of Christian life as requested ___ ___ ___

5. Contribute to expense of workers attending conventions, rallies, and workshops ___ ___ ___

Follow Through

This *Guide* is designed not only to help the local Sunday school analyze its strengths and weaknesses, but its growth potential as well. Remember that the first step to Sunday school growth is found in your willingness to take a frank look at your Sunday school.

However, the ultimate value of using the *Guide* rests in your determination to follow through on eliminating areas of weakness. Begin now to develop a time priority list and follow through until every item checked "Partially" can be marked "Yes."

Appendix IV

A Philosophy of Christian Education

(Drafted by the Advisory Curriculum Study Committee, Church of the Nazarene)

Introduction

The following is an attempt to present the philosophical foundations on which to structure a curriculum for Christian education in the Church of the Nazarene.

A philosophy of education provides guidance for:

1. Planning curriculum
2. Writing curriculum
3. Using curriculum
4. Evaluating curriculum

A. The Nature of Reality

This foundational statement answers the metaphysical question: "What is real?" By "real" we mean the essential nature, the permanent or unchanging essence of an object, person, or concept.

1. *God-centered*

   To the Christian, God is the center and ultimate of reality. The existence of God and His incarnation in human flesh are immediate and primary expressions of ultimate reality. Christian education must begin, proceed, and end with the reality of the Triune God.

2. *Creation-oriented*

   Christian education also accepts the reality of God's creation. Though secondary to the primary reality of God, the objective expressions of reality are seen in the realm of things—observable data, nature, and human experience. Despite the limitations of time and space and the physical world, reality resides in creation and is inextricably bound to God.

B. The Nature of Knowledge

This foundational statement answers the epistemological question: "What is truth and how do we know?"

1. *Special Revelation*

   For the Christian there is ultimate truth, even though finite man cannot fully understand infinite truth.

   a. Jesus Christ is the focal point of ultimate truth. As ultimate truth, He is divine, eternal, and personal (John 1:1 ff.).

b. The Bible is the written expression of divine revelation in history.

c. The work of the Holy Spirit is to bear witness of the truth (Christ) especially to the believer in the community (the church).

2. *General Revelation*

Secondary sources of knowledge also serve to reveal truth.

a. Nature bears overwhelming evidence to God and His greatness. Though it does not contradict the truth of the Bible, it neither reveals His love nor imparts knowledge of personal redemption and eternal life.

b. Reason is highly respected but not ultimately authoritative. It offers supportive or partial truth but cannot alone lead to ultimate truth.

c. Intuition is able to aid man in perceiving and linking himself to truth.

3. *Human Experience*

Human experience contributes to one's knowledge of God and man. Both the individual experiences of man-in-society and the collective experiences of tradition, history, and the church attest to truth. Human experience and conduct, however, must submit to biblical approval.

C. The Nature of Value

This foundational statement answers the axiological question: "What is of value?"

1. God is Absolute Good and true happiness consists in becoming godlike and therefore doing the will of God. He is the everlasting Reference Person and the ultimate Source of a Christian scale of values.

2. Ethical value equals doing the will of God, or reflecting attitudes and actions in harmony with God's being and nature. Whatever is ethical is determined by the will of God; and to know His will, one must study His Word. Ethics is the "oughtness" of the *divine revelation to man.*

3. Aesthetical value equals harmony with the being and nature of God. Whatever is out of harmony with the nature and purposes of God for man in the world lacks aesthetical value. That which reflects the nature and purposes of God in this natural world is beautiful, enjoyable, and good.

D. The Place of Logic

Logic deals with the various relationships of ideas and correct reasoning. There is the belief that subject matter has a built-in, logical order of presentation. In Christian education, one must remember that some Christian content cannot be dealt with logically. "Sin" is not a logical act or condition. It cannot be solved through logical processes. "Faith" is not primarily a logical matter. It is better described in a nonlogical fashion. The nature of the content of Christian education should determine the method of its presentation. The primary application of the modern tool of "language analysis" would be an intense scrutiny of terminology in Christian education.

E. The Nature of Human Nature

Basic to the application of any philosophy of Christian education is an understanding of the nature of the learner. The following presents a view of the moral nature of man in relation to his education and designed to harmonize with a biblical perspective.

1. The fall of Adam makes man inherently evil—a total depravity—known as original sin—that affects every part of him without necessarily manifesting itself in every act.
2. God's prevenient grace provides a potential for good in man intended to lead him to salvation.
3. Education can cooperate with prevenient grace to build on this potential for good, and Christian education specifically will aim to see the intended salvation accomplished.
4. Christian education can be used by the Holy Spirit as one of the means by which a nonbeliever's mind and spiritual response are opened to the truth of Jesus Christ and thus brought into a state of personal salvation.
5. Entire sanctification is a means of dealing with the educational hindrance (intellectual handicap) of original sin, thus further enhancing the process of education.
6. Growth in grace continues throughout life, making it easier for Spirit-directed education to cultivate goodness and to develop full human potential.

F. Practical Implications

The overarching task of Christian education is to present Christ as Savior so that the Holy Spirit may effect and maintain a saving relationship between the student and God. There are three biblically based and cooperative aspects to this task.

1. Reaching students for Christ, leading to a positive response by the student, namely evangelical conversion.
2. Teaching students about Christ for the development of Christian character and behavior.
3. Maturing of students in the Christian faith and helping them to live out that faith.

    "The Son of man is come to seek and to save that which was lost" (Luke 19:10).

    "Go ye therefore, and teach all nations, baptizing them in the name of the Father, and of the Son, and of the Holy Ghost" (Matt. 28:19) "that the man of God may be perfect, throughly furnished unto all good works" (2 Tim. 3:17).

    The role of the teacher is primarily to be an acceptable model of concerned, loving, Christian living. He must initiate a climate for the teaching/learning process. He must be skilled in transmitting knowledge vital to living the Christian life and in guiding students through the experiences in the educational process. In addition the teacher must: love each child, no matter what; recognize his responsibility before God; depend completely upon the Holy Spirit to achieve the desired results.

The role of the pupil is to be an interactor in the teaching/learning process. He is an imitator, a discoverer, and an assimilator of the knowledge, feelings, and behaviors that are taught and experienced.

The curriculum of Christian education is the medium, whether content material or life-experience, selected for use in the teaching/learning process to achieve the goals of Christian education. Christian curriculum is centered in Christ and based on the authoritative teachings of the Bible. It recognizes the authority of Christ in all aspects of life. It uses the realization of His authority in our lives as the criterion by which all educational activity is judged.

Our philosophy allows for a variety of methodological practices with limitations in accordance with our philosophical views.

G. Conclusion

The philosophy we must seek is a Christian philosophy. As such, it is Christ-centered, Bible-based, and need-related. Our philosophy calls for the incorporation of sound educational theory and the utilization of all effective educational methodology not contrary to a Christian value system and philosophy of education. A Christian philosophy recognizes both the reality of God's sovereign love and of man's dignity and worth.

—ADVISORY CURRICULUM STUDY COMMITTEE

Richard Spindle, Chr.	Udell Moss
James Cummins	John Nielson
Ronald Gray	J. Ottis Sayes
Ruth Henck	Wesley Tracy
William McCumber	

Appendix V

Age-Level Structuring

(Division of Christian Life, Church of the Nazarene)

The 1976 General Assembly of the Church of the Nazarene authorized a major restructuring of its organizations for Christian education. The plan altered the framework for Christian teaching at all levels—local, district, and general. Its goal was "to eliminate overlap and duplication of age-group programming, promotion, and materials, and to provide a unified program service to help carry out the mission of the church."*

The plan coordinates all local church ministries for Christian nurture under three age-level divisions—

      Children (birth to 11 years)

      Youth (12-23 years, including college and singles)

      Adult (24 years and older, or married)

The children's, youth, and adult ministries in the local church are served by the programs, materials, and promotion developed by the corresponding departments at the general and district levels.

The name *Division of Christian Life* replaced the older terminology of Church Schools and Young People's Society, and organizationally merged the functions of these two predecessor departments. The name was designed to suggest that Christian education is something more than the mere teaching and learning of religious facts. Christian education as it is understood today involves the whole of the Christian life—preparation for it, entrance into it, growth in it, and sharing that life with others.

BOARD OF CHRISTIAN LIFE

In the local church the Board of Christian Life is responsible for the total Christian education program. It picks up most of the functions of the former church school board (or committee for Christian education). This Board of Christian Life is also ultimately responsible for the youth ministry in the local church. Direct leadership of the youth program, however, is still in the hands of the executive council of the youth organization (NYI). The formula reads, "The local Board of Christian Life plans, promotes, and coordinates youth ministries in the local church *in conjunction with the local Nazarene Youth International* (NYI), the local church youth organization" (italics added).

---

*Quotations, unless otherwise indicated, are taken from the *Handbook, Division of Christian Life*, 1977.

The chairman of the Board of Christian Life is elected by the congregation, just as the Sunday school superintendent was formerly elected. In addition the congregation elects from three to nine members to the Board of Christian Life. Ex officio members include the pastor, president of the missionary society, president of the young people's society, and director of outreach. This board then nominates to the church board persons to be elected as directors of children's, youth, and adult ministries. Upon election by the church board these three directors become ex officio members of the Board of Christian Life.

If desired, the Board of Christian Life may be elected at the annual church meeting as an integral part of the church board, thus functioning as an educational committee of the church board.

In small churches (50 members or less) the church board may function as the Board of Christian Life.

LOCAL DIRECTORS

Primary responsibility for planning and promotion of Christian education rests with the directors of ministries for children, for youth, and for adults. "These directors will provide meaningful ministries and will serve as superintendents of the Sunday school for their age-groups."

A composite statement of the duties of directors is as follows (with minor differences at the three age levels):

1. To plan, administer, supervise, and coordinate an active ministry by and for (children, youth, or adults).

2. To serve as the superintendent of the (children's, youth, or adult) division of the Sunday school.

3. To be responsible for other Sunday and weekday educational, worship, evangelistic, and social programs for (children, youth, or adults).

4. To recommend to the Board of Christian Life the curriculum and other resources to be used.

5. To nominate to the Board of Christian Life, in consultation with the pastor and the chairman of the Board of Christian Life, the leaders for the various ministries (children's, youth, or adult), including Sunday school teachers and officers.

6. To provide leadership training for (children's, youth, or adult) workers in cooperation with the director of Christian Service Training.

The age-group director carries responsibility somewhere between that of a department supervisor and a Sunday school superintendent. He functions in relation to *an entire age-group* (children, youth, or adult) in a capacity roughly paralleled by the duties of a department supervisor within a single department of the Sunday school. However, the duties of a children's director, for example, include not only supervision of all the children's departments of the Sunday school but also all the children's ministries beyond the Sunday school (children's church, Caravan, etc.). The local director is an age-group superintendent responsible for the church's total educational ministry to persons within that age-group.

AGE-LEVEL COUNCILS

Under the age-level directors, provision is made for age-level councils. A children's council, for example, would be composed of the age-level director, the Sunday school supervisors of each of the children's departments in the Sunday school, the Caravan director, children's church director, and heads of all other organizations ministering to children of the congregation. The councils are the effective planning groups and clearing houses for all age-level activities in the church.

ORGANIZATION CHART

The organizational lines of responsibility are as follows:

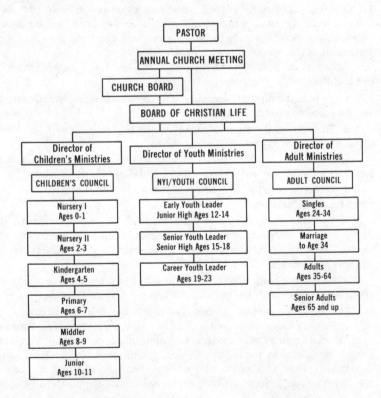

IMPACT ON EXISTING ORGANIZATIONS

1. *The Sunday School*

Under this structure the organizational dynamic for the Sunday school will come chiefly from the age-level directors. There is no provision for a single organizational leader comparable to the stature of the former Sunday school superintendent. The chairman of the Board of Christian Life is the nearest counterpart. The *Handbook* says, "In effect, he (the Board chairman) becomes the senior superintendent of the Sunday school." There is, however, no provision for direct and strong personal leadership of the Sunday school except in his role as chairman of the Board of Christian Life.

The Sunday school bylaws provide for "a cabinet in which the administrative and promotional work of the school is vested. This cabinet shall be composed of the division superintendents and the department supervisors, if any. . . . The cabinet is the goal-setting, program-planning, and problem-solving organization of the Sunday school" (*Manual, Church of the Nazarene,* 1976; Par. 812, Art. VI, Sec. 2).

In smaller churches (up to 50 members) the chairman of the Board of Christian Life serves as the overall Sunday school superintendent (the church board serving as the Board of Christian Life). In churches from 50 to 100 members he serves both as chairman of the Board of Christian Life and as Sunday school superintendent. In larger churches he functions, as indicated above, as "the senior Sunday school superintendent" with direct leadership coming from the age-level directors.

2. *Nazarene Youth International*

This organization functions much as did its predecessor, the Nazarene Young People's Society, except that the age span to be served includes only ages 12 through 23. (Elected officers, however, may be up to 40 years of age, and the president must be at least 15 years of age.)

Responsibility for the youth of the Sunday school (classes for junior high, senior high, and singles under age 24) belongs to the youth division It is suggested that the president of NYI may become the director of youth ministries. Such a dual role would tend to coordinate the total youth ministry. However, if such a person were quite young it could be unwise to assign larger responsibilities to him (or her).

3. *Missionary Education*

Age-level missionary education and activities likewise fall under the jurisdiction of the various age-group councils and directors, along with any special programs such as stewardship education.

Index

502